THE MUSIC IN THE DATA

Putting forward an extensive new argument for a humanities-based approach to big-data analysis, *The Music in the Data* shows how large datasets of music, or music corpora, can be productively integrated with the qualitative questions at the heart of music research. The author argues that as well as providing objective evidence, music corpora can themselves be treated as texts to be subjectively read and creatively interpreted, allowing new levels of understanding and insight into music traditions.

Each chapter in this book asks how we define a core music-theory topic, such as style, harmony, meter, function, and musical key, and then approaches the topic through considering trends within large musical datasets, applying a combination of quantitative analysis and qualitative interpretation. Throughout, several basic techniques of data analysis are introduced and explained, with supporting materials available online. Connecting the empirical information from corpus analysis with theories of musical and textual meaning, and showing how each approach can enrich the other, this book provides a vital perspective for scholars and students in music theory, musicology, and all areas of music research.

Christopher White is Assistant Professor of Music Theory at the University of Massachusetts Amherst.

THE MUSIC IN THE DATA

Corpus Analysis, Music Analysis, and Tonal Traditions

Christopher White

NEW YORK AND LONDON

Designed cover image: amiak/Shutterstock

First published 2023
by Routledge
605 Third Avenue, New York, NY 10158

and by Routledge
4 Park Square, Milton Park, Abingdon, Oxon, OX14 4RN

Routledge is an imprint of the Taylor & Francis Group, an informa business

© 2023 Christopher White

The right of Christopher White to be identified as author of this work
has been asserted in accordance with sections 77 and 78 of the Copyright,
Designs and Patents Act 1988.

All rights reserved. No part of this book may be reprinted or reproduced
or utilised in any form or by any electronic, mechanical, or other means,
now known or hereafter invented, including photocopying and recording,
or in any information storage or retrieval system, without permission in
writing from the publishers.

Trademark notice: Product or corporate names may be trademarks or
registered trademarks, and are used only for identification and explanation
without intent to infringe.

Library of Congress Cataloging-in-Publication Data
Names: White, Christopher (Christopher Wm.) author.
Title: The music in the data : corpus analysis, music analysis, and
    tonal traditions / Christopher White.
Description: [1.] | New York : Routledge, 2022. | Includes bibliographical
    references and index.
Identifiers: LCCN 2022030364 (print) | LCCN 2022030365 (ebook) |
    ISBN 9781032259222 (paperback) | ISBN 9781032259239 (hardback) |
    ISBN 9781003285663 (ebook)
Subjects: LCSH: Musical analysis. | Music—Mathematics. | Musicology—
    Data processing.
Classification: LCC MT90 .W52 2022 (print) | LCC MT90 (ebook) |
    DDC 781.1—dc23/eng/20220808
LC record available at https://lccn.loc.gov/2022030364
LC ebook record available at https://lccn.loc.gov/2022030365

ISBN: 978-1-032-25923-9 (hbk)
ISBN: 978-1-032-25922-2 (pbk)
ISBN: 978-1-003-28566-3 (ebk)

DOI: 10.4324/9781003285663

Typeset in Bembo
by Apex CoVantage, LLC

Access the Support Material: www.routledge.com/9781032259222

To Rob.
I wouldn't want to be doing this with anyone but you.
I love you, and I'm so proud of you.

CONTENTS

Acknowledgments		*viii*
1	Introduction and Methodology: Corpus Analyses and Music Theory	1
2	What Is Style? An Essay	54
3	What Is Harmony? A Narrative	96
4	What Is Function? An Epistolary	137
5	What Is Meter? A Dialogue	189
6	What Is Key? A Diatribe	245
Index		*310*

ACKNOWLEDGMENTS

Many thanks to the music-theory graduate students of Yale University and Florida State University, Ian Quinn, Nick Shea, Megan O'Harra, Kathleen Coker, Samantha Franciosa, Iliana Fuentes Ordaz, Jess Racco, Eric Elder, Tanushree Agrawal, David Temperley, Jason Yust, and the Lab Group (you know who you are!) for feedback and support on this project.

1
INTRODUCTION AND METHODOLOGY

Corpus Analyses and Music Theory

Let's begin with a hypothetical tale of potential plagiarism. The story features an underground electronic dance music (EDM) producer who specializes in composing original tracks for house parties, small festivals, clubs, and the like. One day, the Producer listens to a new song that a famous and established Emcee just dropped. With surprise, they recognize one of the melodies. After listening to the track a few times, their suspicions are confirmed: the melody is identical to one the Producer had written several years ago. Furious with this apparent and blatant musical theft, the Producer contacts an intellectual property lawyer, who in turn files a plagiarism lawsuit against the Emcee. After assembling their own legal team, the Emcee retorts that the supposedly stolen melody is too simple to be covered under copyright – the melody is so generic that anyone writing in the EDM style could stumble upon this sequence of pitches. Of course, the Producer vehemently disagrees. Both teams then attempt to quantify their claims in order to prove their arguments. Each seeks to show how likely the melody was to spontaneously arise in the EDM repertoire – was it likely or unlikely that both musicians would have independently produced the same melody?

To answer this question, the litigators might use a *corpus* – a large dataset – of EDM melodies. As our story stipulates that the Emcee's track was released several years after the producer wrote their melody, a relevant corpus might include EDM hits that span those years. Such a dataset would quantify some baseline norms within that style: melodic characteristics common to this dataset could be imagined as prevalent in mainstream EDM music in that time period.

We can play out this hypothetical courtroom drama using a corpus of EDM instrumental melodies I compiled along with one of my graduate students, Poe Allphin. The dataset – what we call the Top-EDM corpus – consists

DOI: 10.4324/9781003285663-1

2 Introduction and Methodology

of transcriptions of the digital/instrumental melodies from some of the most popular songs on the *Billboard* EDM charts between 2014 and 2019. At present, the corpus consists of 43 melodies (although we are in the process of expanding the dataset) and can be found at chriswmwhite.com/edm_corpus. With this corpus in hand – and with the help of computational and statistical techniques – an investigator could provide quantitative values for *how* idiomatic some melody is within EDM music during this time period and could use those calculations to approximate the probability that a melody would have been written in this style.

But returning to our tale of alleged melodic piracy, we should be skeptical that a series of probabilistic calculations would proverbially crack this case, at least in and of themselves. Instead, we would imagine that – upon reading some array of quantifiable observations and corpus analyses – each side would interpret those numbers very differently, spinning the data to fit their different arguments. On the one hand, these kinds of disagreements are to be expected – par for the course in an adversarial legal system. But on the other, we might also be surprised that the cold, hard numbers of a quantitative corpus analysis can be debated at all. If an analysis simply reports how frequently or infrequently certain events occur within a musical corpus, what is there to disagree with? Are the actual numerical claims arguable, or is it simply the interpretation of those numbers? For that matter, how can we connect quantifiable analyses to larger and more subjective claims and interpretations in rigorous and believable ways? In this specific case, we might wonder to what extent musical statistics can actually provide evidence about how, where, and why a melody was written. Putting this question more broadly, we might ask: How can corpus data support investigations into compositional procedures, aid in musical interpretation, and shed light on the listening processes?[1]

This book demonstrates ways that corpus studies can contribute to music analysis. In my formulation, corpus analysis involves analyzing large datasets using statistics and computation, and this book shows ways that those analyses can be connected to larger concepts and can inform musical interpretations. I will outline methods for investigating these large datasets, including statistical tests, probabilistic formulations, and computational models, and I will demonstrate how such quantitative techniques can inform musical interpretation, speculative theory building, and musicological exploration. In the course of this book, I discuss musical norms and trends that can be observed in corpora, and I situate the methods, insights, values, and weaknesses of corpus analysis within broader musicological and music-cognition discourse. Each subsequent chapter will demonstrate how these observations can specifically contribute to our understanding of music-theoretical concepts like harmonic function, musical syntax, meter, and even the constitutive nature of "a chord." As I build my methodology, I will suggest that musical corpora can be treated as texts to be read, digested, and interpreted in much the same way as individual pieces. Even though the quantitative and computational instruments of corpus analysis might differ from those used in the analysis of individual pieces, I will argue that we often use the same broader techniques when making sense of both domains. That is, although we might use different tools to mine data from corpora than from individual pieces, the processes of interpreting those data often overlap more than they differ. Throughout, my primary goal will be to demonstrate the value of corpus analysis to music theorists and musicologists. To that end, the quantitative tools I present are generally restricted to straightforward computational implementations and basic statistical methods, the likes of which are approachable to a readership whose native discourse is musical rather than data-scientific. The book also provides appendices that walk the reader through each method, along with online supplements that provide prefabricated calculations and computer code that demonstrate the engineering behind some of the techniques used in each chapter.

In the current chapter, I outline my approach to corpus analysis as a music theorist, demonstrating the ways that corpus data can add insights specifically into musical analysis and interpretation. I also discuss some strengths and weaknesses of corpus analysis, outline what kinds of claims corpus analysis can make, and address the sorts of corpus-based claims that might be worthy of skepticism. To this end, I first turn my attention back to the case of the Producer versus the Emcee to investigate how musical statistics can be collected, constructed, and wielded in the service of a larger argument. In what follows, I outline the corpora, mathematical engineering, statistical approaches, and argumentative logic behind my theory of how one might investigate a potentially plagiarized melody.

The Producer Versus the Emcee

Figure 1.1 shows two versions of a melody I've constructed for our hypothetical courtroom procedural.[2] I've labeled the first the *Producer's version* and the second the *Emcee's version,* and I will analyze their relationship as if the latter is potentially a plagiarism of the former. Such a claim of plagiarism would seem reasonable: both melodies contain identical pitch sequences and differ only in their

FIGURE 1.1 Reconstructions of the Producer's and Emcee's melodies

4 Introduction and Methodology

rhythmic dispositions. However, putting the rhythmic differences to the side for a moment, it certainly seems conceivable that this pitch sequence is so simple – and so idiomatic – that two musicians steeped in this style could have both written these identical pitch sequences: the melodies are very repetitive, and both heavily rely on scale degrees from the tonic triad.

We can begin our analysis of the melody by considering the structure of these melodic repetitions. As shown by the brackets in Figure 1.1, both melodies repeat the same three-note motive at the one-measure level. The first and third measures also explicitly repeat, indicating a repetition at the two-measure level. Fully 26% of the Top-EDM corpus's melodies follow this structure. This percentage is calculated by dividing the number of the specific case – here, the number of phrases that follow this particular repetition structure – by the general case – here, the number of all phrases in the corpus regardless of repetition structure. If 11 tracks out of the 43 total tracks in the Top-EDM corpus feature a melody that follows this structure, then 26% of the pieces have this structure (11 divided by 43 is 0.256, which rounds to 26%). We can easily reimagine these percentages as *probabilities*: given that 26% of the melodies within the corpus featured this manner of internal repetition, we can expect that given their track record, there's a 26% chance (a 26% probability) that any new melody in this style will be composed along these lines. Put another way, we can extrapolate from our data that if we were to listen to 100 popular EDM melodies from this time period, we should expect around 26 of them to have this phrase structure. (For more on the exact calculation of probabilities, see the chapter's appendix for a step-by-step explanation.)

Having analyzed the melody's phrase structure, we might turn our attention to its actual notes. To quantify how expected this sequence of scale degrees is, we can use a simple way of imagining how often a series of events occurs, an approach called *conditional n-gram probabilities*. This approach calculates how often particular events follow other particular events; or, put another way, how often some event appears *conditioned on* prior events. This approach can be used to quantify how often each scale degree follows any other scale degree. Again, the chapter's appendix provides a more detailed explanation of the underlying calculations; but briefly, these probabilities divide how often some specific event occurs in a corpus by how often a more general form of that event occurs. If *n*-gram probabilities calculate how often some event succeeds some other series of events in a corpus, then they divide how often that succession occurs (the specific event) by how often all events succeed the series of events in question (the general case). To illustrate: if I were interested in how often $\hat{1}$ follows the sequence $\hat{5}$-$\hat{4}$-$\hat{3}$-$\hat{2}$ within tonal melodies, I would be considering the conditional probability of the 5-gram $<\hat{5}, \hat{4}, \hat{3}, \hat{2}, \hat{1}>$, or $\hat{1}$ conditioned on $<\hat{5}$-$\hat{4}$-$\hat{3}$-$\hat{2}>$. This probability would be calculated by finding how often $<\hat{1}>$ follows $<\hat{5}, \hat{4}, \hat{3}, \hat{2}>$ in the corpus (the specific case) and dividing that number by how often $<\hat{5}, \hat{4}, \hat{3}, \hat{2}>$ is followed by any scale degree at all (the general case).

Conceptually, we can understand conditional *n*-gram probabilities as describing how surprising (or expected) an event is considering the prior events: a 2-gram accounts for the presence of some event by considering the single event that immediately precedes it, because something (event #1) determines the probability of what follows it (event #2). Chaining *n*-grams together can also allow a researcher to assess the conditional probability of a longer sequence: the 2-gram conditional probability of the first four notes in Figure 1.1's melodies <$\hat{1}, \hat{2}, \hat{3}, \hat{5}$> would be the combined probability that $\hat{2}$ follows $\hat{1}$, the probability $\hat{3}$ follows $\hat{2}$, and the probability $\hat{5}$ follows $\hat{3}$.

Figure 1.2 shows the calculations for the 2-gram conditional probabilities of <$\hat{1}, \hat{2}, \hat{3}, \hat{5}$>. Figure 1.2a shows how often each scale-degree sequence occurs in the Top-EDM corpus: 23% of tonic scale degrees rise to the supertonic, 20% of supertonic degrees rise to the mediant and 14% of mediant degrees leap upwards to $\hat{5}$. Figure 1.2b shows how these probabilities chain together to assess the 2-gram probability of this sequence, divided into four discrete steps. Step 1 considers all possible transitions from $\hat{1}$ and imagines that the entire pie represents these probabilities. Step 2 finds that 23% of those transitions move to $\hat{2}$ in this corpus: the first portion of the pie (the dotted outline) therefore slices a 23% portion of the larger pie. Step 3 then recalls that the probability of the 2-gram <$\hat{2}$–$\hat{3}$> is 20%. The process therefore deduces that 20% of those sequences

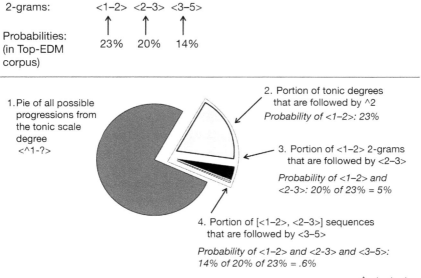

FIGURE 1.2 (a) The conditional 2-gram probabilities of the sequence <$\hat{1}, \hat{2}, \hat{3}, \hat{5}$>, and (b) the combination of those probabilities

6 Introduction and Methodology

that progressed from the tonic scale degree to the supertonic will then subsequently progress to the mediant: 20% of 23% is 4.6%. Finally, 14% of mediants continue to the dominant scale degree; 14% of 4.6% is roughly 0.6%. In total, therefore, we should expect that 0.6% – or about 6 in 1,000 – of all melodies in an EDM corpus that begin on $\hat{1}$ will feature the scale-degree sequence <$\hat{1}$, 2, 3, 5>. (These calculations, along with the source transition probabilities, are included in the online supplement.)

This final number is quite small, and the longer a sequence becomes, the smaller these slices (that is, these slices of slices) will become. However, this small number does not necessarily mean this melodic fragment is *not idiomatic*. There are simply a great many possible four-note sequences, and dividing a probability pie amongst each of them will produce very small slices. To determine how idiomatic this melody is, we need to compare the size of this slice to other comparable four-note slices. To do this, I can program a computer to generate thousands and thousands of random four-note melodies based on the 2-grams of the Top-EDM corpus and then observe whether their resulting probabilities are similar to that of this four-note sequence. This comparison illustrates whether the melody is more or less probable to occur within an EDM corpus than some random melody. To do this, I can computationally generate sequences of scale degrees with the corpus's 2-grams, using the amount that scale degrees follow one another in the Top-EDM corpus to produce note-to-note successions. For instance, recall that the probability of the supertonic following the tonic scale degree is 23% within this corpus; if the computer's melody begins on $\hat{1}$, there would be a 23% chance its next note would be $\hat{2}$. After computationally generating 100,000 melodies along these lines and subjecting each to the same probability assessments as in Figure 1.2, their average probability was roughly 1.8%, a number notably higher than the first melodic fragment's 2-gram probability. (Importantly, the most likely progression in this corpus is for a note to be repeated a number of times, and the melody in question does no such thing.) In other words, the sequence <$\hat{1}$, $\hat{2}$, $\hat{3}$, $\hat{5}$> is about 3 times less probable than the average four-note sequence in the Top-EDM corpus, mostly due to its lack of immediate pitch repetitions.

Figure 1.3 and Table 1.1 extend this logic to the full pitch sequence of Figure 1.1.[3] The Figure's first two rows show the Producer's melody and replicate Figure 1.1's phrase-structure annotations with solid and dotted boxes. In what follows, I show all the component scale-degree 2-grams within the sequence and the probabilities associated with each. (The figure and table illustrate an alternate way of representing probability, using decimal proportions instead of percentages; the first 2-gram's probability is shown as the proportion 0.21 rather than the percentage 21%.) While one approach might simply combine all 2-gram probabilities together to assess the probability of the entire pitch sequence, such an approach would disregard the phrase structure. The C that begins measure 2 is not there *because* of the preceding G but *because* of the melody's repetition

Introduction and Methodology 7

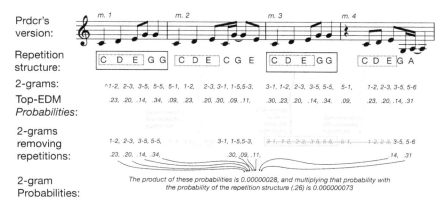

FIGURE 1.3 The combined conditional probabilities and repetition-structure probability of the Producer's melodic sequence

TABLE 1.1 probabilities associated with the hypothetical melody

How Probable Is the Note Sequence to Occur?	
Melody Tested	Probability (%)
2-grams of the melody, removing 2-grams involved in structural repeats	0.000028%
Random melody of same length with same structural repeats	0.0009745%
The complete melody combined with probability of repetition structure (see Figure 1.1)	0.0000073%
Random melody of same length and same repetition combined with probability of that repetition	0.0002534%

structure. Accounting for its probability using a 2-gram therefore seems less warranted than accounting for it by the phrase structure. To this end, the final two rows in Figure 1.3 remove all 2-grams whose pitches can be accounted for by the repetition structure. The remaining 2-grams capture the probability of the pitches that are *not* determined by motivic repetition. We then must account for the repetition structure itself. Recall from earlier that 26% of melodies in our corpus feature this type of phrase repetition. The proportional probability of a melody in this corpus having a melody with such a repetition structure is .26. The combined probabilities of all the remaining proportions – a step that can be done simply by multiplying each 2-gram probability proportion together – produces the very small number 0.00000028, shown as the percentage 0.000028% in Table 1.1.[4] Finally, I use the Top-EDM corpus to determine the average probability of a random note sequence that features the same phrase/motivic repetition as the original melody.

The resulting probabilities are quite small. But again, this number is best compared to average random melodies of the same length. The differences between the probabilities of the first four-note fragment and the average four-note fragment have now magnified into larger differences between the full melody

8 Introduction and Methodology

and an average melody of the same length and structure. The actual melody is now approximately 34 times less probable than an average random melody in the Top-EDM corpus.

We could go further down this probabilistic path, assessing the choice of scale and scale degrees, the tunes' rhythmic differences, their metric placements, etc. But it is worth pausing for a moment to consider the meanings of our calculations. At this point, we might ask ourselves: Do these assessments go any distance in proving or disproving the Emcee's alleged copyright infringement? Taken on their own: not necessarily. Just showing that the melody is less probable than average is no obvious indictment. After all, composers are themselves unlikely to strive to write "average" melodies, and while it is unlikely that two musicians experimenting within the EDM style would arrive at the same note sequence *and* the same phrase structure, it's not *impossible*. And so: what kind of evidence do these numbers provide? How are we to imagine the relationship between these probabilities and relevant non-musical information? Would we read these numbers differently if our story included evidence that the Emcee had repeatedly heard the Producer's melody? Or if we knew for certain that the Emcee had never heard the Producer's melody before? And would we be inclined to interpret extramusical events differently were the data different? If this melody was, for instance, a thousand times less likely to occur than the average melody would we be certain the melody had been plagiarized? How should we interpret our musical probabilities, how would we relate them to other non-musical events, and how do we ascribe *meaning* to a corpus analysis's raw quantities and statistics?

Before addressing these larger topics, I will briefly situate corpus analysis within the history of music-theory discourse. While a full history of corpus analysis in the humanities is outside the boundaries of this book, the following section sketches how statistics and large datasets have become important tools for music analysis and research over the last several decades. Knowing where the subfield comes from will help us better understand the tools and assumptions underpinning the discourse. To that end, I will now turn to the historical context surrounding some of the first forays of humanities research into corpus analysis.

The Noisy Channel, Corpus Analysis, and Their History in Music Theory

The role of Alan Turing's protocomputer in World War II code breaking has become an increasingly well-known facet of popular culture in recent years. But Turing's work also showed the power of corpus analysis. One crucial aspect of the code-breaking process was to associate certain symbols present within the encoded Nazi ciphers with statistical properties of the German language.

Turing's early computers were designed to test various solutions until they returned an ideal alignment of German words and the cipher's symbols. The Nazis' cipher machine encoded a message with some statistically consistent properties, and the premise of this code-breaking work was that another deciphering machine could use these same statistical consistencies to decode the message. A corpus of German text could be used to provide the statistical consistencies for this deciphering.

Fresh off his own wartime research into code breaking, Claude Shannon (1948) proposed his *noisy channel model* (see Figure 1.4). Working at Bell Labs, Shannon designed this model to generalize the code-breaking work of the previous decade to telephonic engineering. In Shannon's model, a message is sent from a source through a transmitter that translates it into a signal. In this formulation, the *message* is some concrete idea while the *signal* is the medium in which that message is embedded. The signal may encounter noise along its journey, after which a receiver translates the message at its final destination. As in code breaking, the transmitter and receiver must share the same mechanisms for translating messages and signals, respectively.

A crucial epistemological move occurred the following year, in 1949, when Warren Weaver theorized the universality of this model. Weaver suggested that the noisy channel describes any situation in which a message moves from one party to another: "For instance, when I talk to you, my brain is the information source, yours the destination; my vocal system is the transmitter, and your ear . . . is the receiver" (Shannon and Weaver, 1949, 3).[5] A truck outside the window, a physical distance, or any number of other factors can introduce noise into this conversational system. In the words of John Sinclair, the "message" concept involves "two basic assumptions . . . that the message can be separated from the medium, and that it can be transferred from one individual (or machine) to another" (2004, 156).

The work of Shannon and Weaver sparked broad interest in mathematical models of communication throughout mid-century academic humanities departments, and the rise of information theory brought with it the "first wave" of music informatics (Margulis and Beatty, 2008).[6] In 1957, Leonard Meyer summarized for the readership of the *Journal of Aesthetics and Art Criticism* what he

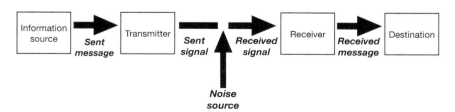

FIGURE 1.4 The noisy channel model from Shannon (1948)

10 Introduction and Methodology

believed to be the benefits of information theory to the larger humanities, and in the same journal, five years later, Joel Cohen's "Information Theory and Music" reviewed the discipline's foundational assumptions and boundaries as regards music studies.[7] In articles for the 1958 volumes of the *Journal of Music Theory*, Joseph E. Youngblood, Edgar Coons, and David Kraehenbuehl argued for informatics' utility in their studies of musical style and structure, with theorists like Gift Siromoney and K. R. Rajagopalan expanding the focus beyond the Western European common practice to the Carnatic music of southern India in 1964.

Readers ensconced in the field of music theory will be struck by how relatively unknown this first wave of research is. Leonard Meyer – whose writings remain a staple of bibliographies and comprehensive exams – provides the exception that proves the rule. However, unlike most other first-wave authors, Meyer generally did not rely on actual computation or mathematics in his writings but rather scrutinized how information theory's concepts and methodologies could benefit the study of music.[8] This first wave of informatics work in music studies, particularly work focusing on computational and mathematical applications, appears not to have gained wider traction, becoming something of an epistemological dead end in the history of music theory.[9]

Statistical Learning and the Increased Sophistication of Computers

A second wave of computation and statistics entered music studies in the late 1990s, at least partially in response to two trends: (1) the rise of the statistical learning hypothesis in psychology and (2) the increased availability of datasets, computational power, and data-crunching tools.[10] The statistical learning hypothesis claims that humans can learn linguistic structures and expectations simply through exposure to a language. This ability, sometimes also called the *connectionist* approach to learning, involves gaining facility with a language system not by being explicitly taught the system's rules but by passively hearing and processing examples of the language and then gleaning its rules and tendencies from this exposure (see Bharucha, 1987, 1991). Of course, this theory was not born out of whole cloth in the late 20th century; theories of exposure-based learning can be traced at least as far back as the psychologist John Dewey (1884), if not earlier. (For instance, one can find passages from Eduard Hanslick's 1854 *Vom Musikalisch-Schönen* that appear to take a proto-statistical-learning stance!) The 1990s, however, saw studies that specifically connected statistical properties of a corpus to the expectations of listeners, a trend that began in music with work of Carol Krumhansl (1990) and in language with Jenny Saffran and her colleagues (1999, 2000) and which has grown to include applications to musical grammar (Creel et al., 2004; Louie, 2012) and even to more abstract concepts like timbre (Louie, 2022). A crucial addition to the approach involved

Introduction and Methodology **11**

incorporating the "mere exposure effect" into models of musical learning. In the 1960s, Robert Zajonc (1968) demonstrated that humans tend to develop a preference for things with which they are more familiar, and by the end of the century, music researchers were connecting this effect to notions of musical stability and hierarchy. This research suggests that we learn to associate feelings of resolution, primacy, and stability with those scale degrees, chords, and chord progressions common in the music to which we've been most exposed and are most familiar (Krumhansl, 1990; Aarden, 2003; Huron, 2006).[11]

Crucially, this approach treats the aggregate events of a corpus not only as a tool to encode and decode messages but also as the venue by which humans can learn musical/linguistic systems. If we learn things like musical grammar, stability, and expectation from being exposed to the events of a corpus, we can equate the statistical properties of that corpus – what does and does not happen in that set of music – with how we come to represent a musical system in our minds. A corpus, in this formulation, represents the cognitive substance of a language, showing both what learners learn and how communicators communicate. It follows, therefore, that we can observe how a composer is cognitively representing a musical system by observing a corpus of their compositions. For instance, if corpus statistics represent the cognitive substance of a language, then in cases in which the mental state of a speaker of that language deteriorates in some way, the corpus statistics should analogically reflect that deterioration (Le et al., 2011 has studied this effect in authors known to have been afflicted by stroke or dementia, while Coutanche and Paulus, 2018, show changes in word usage of Presidents Ronald Regan and Donald Trump over time).

The second trend to arise in the late 1990s – the increasing availability of datasets, computational power, and data-crunching tools – developed from the ubiquity of computers and computation in 21st-century life and culture. Computers have become ever more powerful and available, and musical production, consumption, and storage is increasingly digitized. Whereas a music informatics researcher in the 1950s would have had to encode their data on punch cards fed into their university's (likely only) computer, in contemporary society, computers are not only in every office but in almost every pocket, with music stored in formats readable by those computers. For instance, several corpus analyses in this book rely on the Yale-Classical Archives Corpus (YCAC): if this corpus were stored on punch cards, it would comprise approximately 19 million cards, a stack of cards three miles high. And, depending on the parameters used, the calculations underpinning Table 1.1 would have taken approximately six months to complete. As things currently stand, my laptop is about a half-inch thick, and the calculations for Figure 1.2 take less than five minutes.

In sum, we can heuristically divide the historical use of corpus analyses into two epistemological waves. The *information theory* wave used large datasets to formalize some message transfer between two entities, while the *psychological* wave used corpora to investigate statistical models' roles in learning and

12 Introduction and Methodology

cognition. The continuation of these trends has been supported by the increase in computing power and the availability of computer-readable music datasets. Naturally, this narrative is a simplification of the various swirling forces within different modes of academic and industrial research. I haven't, for instance, mentioned the considerable use of corpus analysis in language-processing research, in streaming music services, or in automated music production (Huang et al., 2020). Regardless, my two-pronged informatics/psychology heuristic approximates the central forces and influences at play within corpus-based music analysis, especially in the discipline of music theory. In the next section, I examine this very topic: how corpus analysis can inform music-theory research.

Music Theory's Draw to Corpus Analysis

In the noisy channel model, a source encodes an idea into a message, and a receiver decodes that idea using the same model. Because of this reciprocity, a corpus produced by this relationship will exhibit properties of both the language's encoding and decoding processes. In the statistical learning hypothesis, a series of phenomena with some regular set of statistical properties can be internalized by a listener as they learn about the language underpinning that corpus. Here, the learner masters the act of decoding by using a corpus's statistical properties; with that expertise, they can now produce examples of that corpus that feature the same statistical properties. Analyzing a corpus, then, yields insights into both how learners learn a language from that corpus and how creators produce examples of that corpus. It is not surprising that humanities scholars – and particularly music-theory researchers – would be drawn to corpus analysis. Some of music theory's fundamental research topics concern the musical systems used by various composers and traditions, the ways in which those systems can express expectations and ideas, and how individual pieces manifest those systems and expressions. (See, for example, Lewin, 1969; Kerman, 1980; Tomlinson, 1992; McCreless, 2000; Agawu, 2004; Kramer, 2011.) Indeed, there are several research trends in contemporary music theory that rely on how expected, unexpected, innovative, or deviant certain compositional choices are, and in so doing, they informally engage with musical corpora. These include studies of the normative disposition of classical sonata form (Hepokoski and Darcy, 2006), stylistic trends that hallmark a national style (Long, 2020), and composers' novel harmonic experiments (Harrison, 2016). In this type of research, authors make claims about what is musically expected, normative, or unique by studying and comparing a large number of musical pieces. Furthermore, theorists often informally connect expressive potential to statistical events, showing how a particular deformation of formal expectations might create surprise within a listener or how a particular kind of harmony might invoke a certain national or social identity. All such claims rely on the logic that the statistical properties of a corpus are central to how musical expectations and norms are communicated by composers and performers and how they are learned and interpreted by listeners.

Figure 1.5 shows what I call the Meaningful Corpus Model, or MCM, a concept I also introduce in White (forthcoming). The MCM outlines how corpora are used to make meaningful claims and arguments and ultimately illustrates what I see as the overlapping logic between humanities research (and specifically music theory), the noisy channel conception of communication, the statistical learning hypothesis, and corpus studies.

The MCM can be broken down into three component parts, represented by the figure's three rectangular panes. The leftward *expression pane* corresponds to the meaning that is either embedded in or derived from the middle *events pane*. The events pane, then, is some way of representing or making sense of musical events, while the *corpus pane* is the raw data being produced by a composer or interpreted by a listener. In the MCM's top formulation, following the arrows left to right, the composer makes a series of choices that lead to observable events being present within a corpus of music.[12] The listening/learning process – the right-to-left process at the bottom of the figure – reverse engineers the same series of steps, observing a corpus to understand its embedded meaning or expression. The MCM's relationships evoke the dynamics of the noisy channel, insomuch as the composer encodes the "message" of the expression pane as observable events in a corpus that can be decoded by a listener. The logic of statistical learning is also present within the MCM, as a learner can gain knowledge and interpretive ability from being exposed to and making sense of a corpus of data.

As an example, consider how Western European classical composers create moments of surprise via deceptive cadences. In this style, composers conclude musical sections most often by using authentic cadences (i.e., dominant-to-tonic progressions ending in a tonic triad) but sometimes surprise their listeners by replacing the expected tonic with a submediant triad. (Chapters 3 and 4 take an in-depth look at chord progressions.) The motivation to create this surprisal

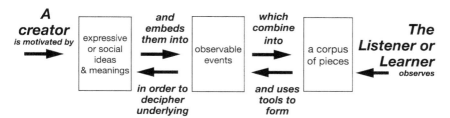

FIGURE 1.5 The Meaningful Corpus Model (MCM), showing relationships between meaning, observations, and corpus data first from the producer's perspective and then from the listener's perspective

14 Introduction and Methodology

would populate the leftward expression pane, while their resulting musical choices would be embedded features in the rightward corpus pane. The middle observation pane connects these two with representations that add interpretation to musical events, such as the notions of authentic and deceptive cadences. A listener can then learn to experience this surprise by being exposed to the corpus. As they notice, categorize, and compare events that end phrases, they compile the particulars of the events pane. Finally, the resulting effect of these observations – a moment of surprise at a deceptive cadence – is the realm of the expression pane.

When a music theorist analyzes a piece of music, they are following the right-to-left logic to unearth the ways in which the music expresses a set of ideas. Conversely, when a music theorist interprets a compositional choice using a biographical, expressive, or social explanation, they are trying to establish some manner of causality between the production and interpretation of musical texts, and so they would follow the left-to-right logic.

I return to the MCM and the issues, insights, and problems it holds later. However, it's important to note that its mechanics show similarities between music theorists' interest in musical corpora and the interests of psychologists and information theorists. A corpus potentially illustrates how some style of music communicates ideas and meanings and yields insights into how we learn to interpret those meanings. More specifically, music theory is interested in the ways in which expressive ideas are embedded within musical pieces and how broader musical systems and styles are built, both of which can be informed by how a corpus connects to musical learning or communication.[13]

With all this in mind, let's return to our ongoing courtroom drama and reevaluate the claims being made in terms of the MCM. With the probabilities of Table 1.1 in hand, the case's complainant could construct an argument as follows: (1) While the melody's phrase structure and its individual pitch elements are somewhat idiomatic within the Top-EDM corpus, (2) the sheer length of the tune makes it highly improbable to arise within the corpus, and (3) the melody is considerably less probable than the average melody within this style. Therefore (4) it is reasonable to assume that the Emcee's melody was implicitly influenced by – or explicitly copied from – the Producer's melody. In terms of the MCM, this argument takes the Top-EDM as the rightward pane, and the observable-events pane is composed of the conditional probabilities between 2-grams of scale degrees and the comparisons between those probabilities. The leftward interpretation pane then stresses how improbable it would be for two melodies with the same properties to arise within this corpus by chance, ultimately explaining the observations of the middle pane by the influence of the Producer on the Emcee, or by the Emcee's outright plagiarism.

The defense could argue with several aspects of this logic, and these arguments can all be pinpointed within the MCM. For instance, the defense could construct the following logic: (1) the melody's phrase structure and pitch contents are relatively idiomatic, and while (2) the combination of these building blocks creates a melody that is more unique than average in this style, (3) the melody is certainly not an impossibility within the broader EDM style, and therefore (4) it is very possible that two EDM producers trying to create unique melodies with idiomatic elements would arrive at the same solution. Here, the corpus and observation panes remain the same, but the interpretation pane now stresses that the co-occurrence of these two melodies is by no means impossible. Furthermore, the defense could argue with the corpora's constituents – with the makeup of the corpus pane. They could claim that the Emcee was not constructing melodies under the influence of contemporary EDM but was inspired by some other source. They could similarly argue that the way of representing these melodies is insufficient. The corpus does not contain harmonic annotations, nor does it include microtimed events, both of which could be potentially important when quantifying the norms of the style. They could also take issue with the choice to use 2-grams to model the data. On the one hand, they could claim that the note-to-note progressions captured by n-grams do not adequately represent the compositional process. On the other hand, they could also claim that 2-grams do not contain sufficient context for melodic construction. Each of these contentions concerns how the observations of the middle pane are constructed. One strength of the MCM, then, is its ability to segregate the data, the analyses, and the interpretation into separate components, allowing for the logic to connect a corpus to broader claims to be better understood.

When examining how this type of logic maps onto the MCM, one is struck by the number of choices and leaps that a corpus analyst must make in order to connect the properties of some statistical analysis to an extra-musical interpretation. Such connections are certainly not wrong or even necessarily suspect. However, these connections require many more caveats than we might have initially imagined. Before I dive further into this methodological morass, I will first take a detour to consider several initial methodological aspects of musical corpus analysis and then undertake an analysis that connects the properties of a corpus to musical expression and meaning using the MCM.

An Aside: Interdisciplinarity, Musical Corpus Analysis, and the Tactics of the MCM

When writing about a "neurohumanities approach to language, music, and emotion," Hartley and Poeppel (2020) outline three paradigms that can arise from mixing the quantitative methods of the hard sciences with the qualitative approaches of the humanities. The least desirable outcome is for the resulting research question to become so watered down – to act as a proverbial least-common denominator between the disciplines – that the findings are uninteresting to either research community. A second option describes a collaboration that produces insights that are of interest to only one of the contributing

16 Introduction and Methodology

disciplines. Here, the mixed disciplinary methods yield some new perspective on the research discourse from one of the disciplines while contributing minimally to debates and priorities in the remaining disciplines. Finally, an optimal collaboration enriches both disciplines, with the resulting work contributing to both disciplines' academic discourses.

The MCM can be used to imagine such interdisciplinary research programs, and their potential value to the constitutive disciplines. For instance, Hartley and Poeppel challenge their readers to imagine ways that neurobiological observations can contribute to how humans interpret texts or react to music and – conversely – ways that human interpretation of texts can inform research into neurobiology. In such a formulation, we can imagine the quantitative exploration of brain activity providing the MCM's rightward pane, a reader's/listener's interpretation comprising the leftward pane, and the modeling of their interactions filling the middle window. If the more humanities-oriented leftward pane assisted in the understanding of the more neuro-scientifically oriented rightward pane, the interdisciplinary collaboration would mostly benefit neurobiologists. If the hard-science-oriented rightward pane unlocked insights into reader's interpretations, the collaboration would primarily benefit humanities researchers. Additionally, both disciplines could benefit from a two-way flow of the MCM. Finally, the interactions could be so simple that neither party would benefit.

Importantly, this book does not strive for an idealized two-way street: I will not aim to produce analyses that mutually benefit the humanities and computational informatics. Rather, my work will focus on the benefits that corpus analysis can afford music-theory research. My goal is to learn more about musical concepts like key, meter, style, and interpretation by framing these topics through a corpus-based computational lens. My goal is *not* to advance state-of-the-art computational technologies by producing, say, more efficient computational systems for key finding or to innovate the field of music cognition by developing a more convincing model for, say, the perception of musical meter.

The fallouts of this stance are twofold. Most basically, because I am not interested in developing the *best* algorithms, I will use validations and efficacy tests more as a "sanity check" than as a means to strive toward some gold standard. My methods will be framed to ask questions like: "If we computationally operationalize and formalize a musical concept in such-and-such a way, what can we learn about that concept?" In this formulation, we simply need to know that a computational approach meaningfully interacts with some musical concept, not that it is the *best* way of engineering some task. For instance, a model of musical meter does not need to be the fastest and most accurate method in order to usefully yield insights into how downbeats manifest in a corpus of music.

Second, my stance will be to prioritize relatively simple computational approaches in this book. Since my methods will use the engineering and outputs of computational models to investigate music-theory concepts, it will behoove me to use optimally approachable engineering with accessible outputs. Again, these will often demonstrably *not* be the state-of-the-art approaches used in fields like music information retrieval or music cognition research. However, in almost all cases, the more-accessible approaches I adopt will be simplified versions of (or at least relatable to) the state of the art and will therefore provide a useful introduction to the kinds of approaches used by more results-driven research programs.

I must admit that I have chosen this tactical approach because of my own background: I am a music theorist who uses computation to investigate topics important to my discipline, my colleagues, and my students. It is possible (and I hope likely!) that the research program outlined in this book may be of use to scholars outside of music theory – that the MCM networks underpinning my logic could potentially activate Hartley and Poeppel's ideal interdisciplinary two-way paradigm.

Having outlined the MCM and having situated my own research priorities, I now turn my attention to a well-known essay of musical analysis in order to illustrate some specific ways that corpus analysis might interact with traditional music-theoretical concerns.

A Statistical Intermezzo: An Example From Music Theory

In Edward T. Cone's seminal 1982 article on musical interpretation, the author meticulously analyzes the musical events of the first section of Franz Schubert's *Moment Musical* in A-flat, Op. 94, no. 6, focusing particularly on surprising harmonic resolutions. He also connects the piece's lavish, almost incoherent harmonic syntax to Schubert's worries about his syphilitic condition.

Figure 1.6 quantifies one aspect of Cone's analysis: the unexpected resolution of the C major triad in measure 12, which is excerpted in Example 1.1a. The figure shows the frequency of chord types and root motions following major triads in 19th-century pieces in the Yale-Classical Archives Corpus. I describe this corpus in far more detail in Chapter 2, but in short: the dataset is comprised of user-uploaded MIDI files available at classicalarchives.com, and each of the YCAC files is divided into points at which individual notes are added to or subtracted from the musical texture (White and Quinn, 2016). The figure's horizontal axis shows each chord/root-motion pair that follows a major triad, ordered from left to right by decreasing frequency. I track "chord type" simply by using transpositionally equivalent but inversionally nonequivalent set classes (such that all major triads are the same set class, but the inversionally related minor triad would be a different set class), and measure the distance between these set classes by calculating the interval between the roots of each corresponding set of pitch classes. (A D-major triad moving to a G minor triad would be s.c. [047] moving to s.c. [037] at an interval of 5 semitones.)[14]

18 Introduction and Methodology

The vertical axis of the figure shows the frequency of these progressions as a percentage-of-occurrence within the YCAC. Note the cliff-like distribution.[15] A few progressions happen most frequently, followed by a dramatic dip into a "long tail" of events that occur very infrequently.[16] For instance, the two most frequent progressions are to a major triad a fifth away, lower or higher.[17] If we consider only progressions to dominant seventh chords – as in the Schubert passage – the highest-ranked option is to move a fifth higher (i.e., a C major triad moving to G^7). This progression is ranked as the 14th-most frequent resolution overall. The next most common progression involving a dominant seventh is to one a whole step higher (a C major triad moving to D^7), which is ranked 24th overall. Lower in the distribution, one finds more extravagant resolutions, including to the dominant sevenths a major third lower (C major to A^7; ranked 159th) and a half step higher (C to D-flat^7; ranked 189th). The actual event with which Cone is concerned occurs at rank 76. In other words, the chord progression Schubert uses is a surprising event but not *as surprising* as it might be.

Of course, there are many dynamics at play in Schubert's harmonic choices in addition to simply what chord type and root interval follow a major triad. The progression from a C major triad to an E-flat dominant seventh points back to the home key of A-flat, which – given that this moment is placed near the end of a well-defined phrase – is a very expected move indeed. However, these statistics do show one aspect of the surprise associated with this moment. By leading the music toward this C major triad, Schubert has taken us to a harmonic point that invites an unusual harmonic juncture. Cone's analysis (and the takeaway from Figure 1.6) suggests that the move between the C major triad and an E-flat dominant seventh is unusual enough to raise the attention of the listener and to invite an explanation by the analyst. Our analysis shows that this progression of chords is used very infrequently, but it still provides a resolution within the broad realm of reasonable possibilities.

Figure 1.7 quantifies another moment highlighted by Cone, the modulation in measures 27 through 29. As seen in Example 1.1b, the key shifts from A-flat major down a major third to E major. The figure's vertical axis again shows how often these events occur, and the horizontal axis shows the distance of modulations, organized by ascending and descending fifths. So organized, the disposition follows something like a bell-curve distribution (albeit a sharply curved bell!). Again, Schubert's choice is improbable but not *as improbable* as it might be. While modulations to keys one fifth away are most frequent, and modulations by two fifths (by whole step) are next-most frequent, Schubert modulates by four fifths (by major third), again choosing a less-frequent (but not most-infrequent!) option. In both of these contexts, Schubert has chosen a deviant solution that is relatively more probable within the panoply of possible but improbable harmonies.

Introduction and Methodology 19

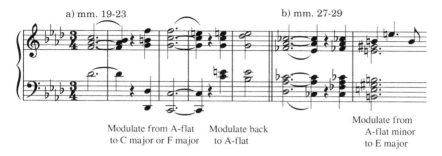

EXAMPLE 1.1 Franz Schubert, *Moment Musical*, Op. 94, no. 6, mm. 9–13 and 27–29

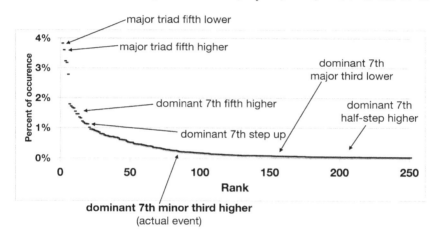

FIGURE 1.6 The frequency distribution of set classes that follow major triads in 19th-century YCAC pieces

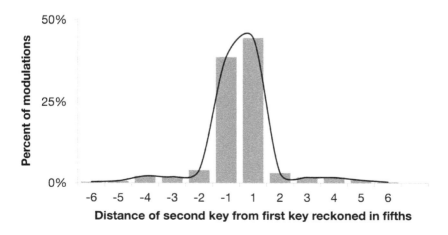

FIGURE 1.7 Proportion of modulations in 19th-century YCAC pieces

20 Introduction and Methodology

In terms of the MCM, these corpus analyses produce the observations of the middle pane, organizing the text into specific, observable phenomena that can be described and quantified. The pieces of the YCAC constitute the rightward corpus pane. With these events in hand, we can now follow Cone down his interpretive path and draw connections to the MCM's leftward expression pane, arguing that his consistently improbable-but-not-too-improbable choices reflect Schubert's worries about his syphilitic condition.

To be sure, there are plenty of reasons to be skeptical of these analyses. Note, for instance, that we cannot be sure that Schubert was, indeed, in a state of agitation and worry about his health while writing this piece. And while my analysis focuses on events with low frequencies and probabilities, I did not provide any evidence that using infrequent events (rather than, say, using very predictable events) is salient to understanding a composer's mental condition. Finally, we could argue that the YCAC – perhaps because of the music used within the dataset or because of its method of chord representation – is not an appropriate corpus to use for this analysis. As before, each of these concerns can be pinpointed within the MCM, as applied to the interpretations, the observations, or the corpus used in the larger argument.

I want to again table these concerns for a moment to consider the potential values afforded by this corpus-centered approach to musical interpretation. In the sections that follow, I describe the strengths associated with a corpus-based toolkit, pinpointing several benefits that corpus data affords to arguments like Cone's. I then outline some of the ways in which corpus analysis in music – and in the historical humanities in general – is different from corpus methods in informatics and psychology and how these differences pose unique challenges to music analysts employing these tools.

Some Benefits of Using Corpus Analysis Within Music Theory

The use of corpus statistics affords music theorists six particular strengths: (1) subjective observations can be reframed as independently verifiable claims; (2) musical events can be contextualized using comparisons to averages, norms, and baselines; (3) computation and statistical analyses encourage clear and thorough argumentation as they require one to operationalize and lay bare the assumptions being made; (4) statistical models allow for connections between music analysis and music cognition; (5) using large datasets allows theorists to observe and analyze aspects of a musical tradition that they would be hard-pressed to identify without the use of computation and statistical analysis; and (6) corpus statistics allows theorists to alienate themselves from at least some of their musical preconceptions and biases. Taken together, these strengths add up to a model that operates somewhat externally from the analyst or reader, creating what I call the Martian effect.

Let's consider each of these benefits in turn. First, statistical properties of corpora simply exist, regardless of whether and how they are used. From this perspective, a complaint from a curmudgeonly reader that they "just don't hear it that way" would be beside the point within the frame of a corpus analysis. In terms of corpus-derived statistics, one can take issue with the corpus used, the ways it is measured, or the interpretation of the data, but *the observed properties of a corpus are not up for debate*. When using corpus data in music analysis, analytical claims are based on independently verifiable phenomena. If the curmudgeon ran the same statistical modeling on the same corpus, they would find the same result.

Second, corpus analysis can provide a baseline against which to compare the events of a particular piece. Since corpus analysis deals with large datasets, it can rely on the average properties of these datasets to establish norms and to contextualize observations. The chord change in measures 12 to 13 of the Schubert example, for instance, is situated within an array of more and less probable resolutions. Construed with corpus data, a theorist can say something is more surprising than other possible events and even say *how surprising* that event is relative to other events that could have happened.

Third and relatedly, computational models make the researcher specifically operationalize all aspects of their claims. Computers do nothing except what they are told, and they know nothing except what they are taught: the results of a computational model are not influenced by unseen biases or *a priori* intuitions.[18] When I program a computer to analyze how keys manifest throughout tonal corpora or to tally the use of specific chords within some dataset, I must engineer exactly what the computer does and how it undertakes these tasks, defining such simple constructs as pitch, chord, harmonic progressions, function, etc. And because these aspects are all clearly defined, any other theorist can trace how I've come to my conclusions by following the painstaking steps required to implement a computational model – the entirety of a claim's logic is laid bare.

Fourth, because of the parallels with psychological research, using corpus statistics in music analysis allows for potentially compelling connections to the listening experience. Recall that, according to the statistical learning hypothesis, listeners can learn the properties of a musical corpus through mere exposure to that corpus. Analytical claims can therefore often be framed in terms of a listener's experience. For example, one might argue that a listener whose musical exposure is approximated by the YCAC would be surprised by Schubert's chord progressions and modulations in a manner commensurate with the distributions of Figures 1.6 and 1.7.

Fifth, the computational collation of large amounts of corpus data allows us to observe trends and tendencies that would take a prohibitive amount of time for a human to decipher or that may even be impossible for an individual analyst to observe. Consider, for instance, how long it would take an individual human

22 Introduction and Methodology

to compile the statistics used in the earlier analyses.[19] Figure 1.6 tallied 616,979 individual chord-progression instances. If each of these represents, say, 10 seconds of human analytical work, it would take 192 nine-hour days to complete those analyses. In addition to completing analyses faster, the speed of computational analysis allows researchers to observe larger trends and ask broader questions. The prohibitive amount of human effort that would be required to produce Figure 1.6 alone essentially means that this sort of birds-eye view of 19th-century music would not be available to analysts without the help of computational technologies. In these terms, corpus analysis allows researchers to observe trends and tendencies that previously would have been relegated to hunches and intuitions at best and, at worst, would have been simply unavailable.[20]

This broader analytical focus afforded by corpus analysis has been variously described by humanities scholars, aligning with what Franco Moretti (2005) has identified as *distant reading* and what Matthew Jockers (2013) calls *macroanalysis*. Contrasted with the "close reading" strategy that thoroughly digests the properties of some individual work, these tactics endeavor to identify trends and larger contours within a corpus of texts, treating statistical tendencies as the object of measurement and observation rather than analyzing individual pieces or texts.[21] From this perspective, a strength of corpus analysis is that it allows historical contours and statistical trends – phenomena otherwise obscure to the naked eye/ear – to become the object to be read and analyzed.

Finally, by shifting the act of producing observations to a computer or other automated process, corpus analysis mitigates confirmation biases. When a theorist sets up an experimental question in a rigorous and data-driven (really, any empirical) format, they are at the mercy of the process they have set in motion. If a computational researcher engineers a model that they believe will produce a particular result and their preconceived expectations do not pan out, they must confront the possibility that they are wrong. For instance, I often find myself thinking that a particular event in a piece is unique, but when I model the aggregate properties of some larger corpus to which that piece belongs, I find that the event is more common than I initially intuited. My bias, in other words, was checked: what I believed to be true was stymied by the actual observed data.[22]

In aggregate, these strengths combine to create what I call the Martian effect. Programming a computer to use corpus data to model music-theoretical concepts is tantamount to a Martian learning about the concept by observing only corpus data. In both situations, the only tools available are the statistical properties of the dataset and the ways one arranges and makes sense of those properties. Also, in both situations, anyone can reconstruct and interrogate the resulting model, and the inner workings of that model approximate how an observer learns about and cognizes the concept. The Martian effect forcibly alienates researchers from their assumptions and intuitions about complicated music-theoretical constructions while explicitly laying out all the constituent components that underpin

Introduction and Methodology **23**

not only the concept at hand but also the potential connections to human cognition and ways to make sense of individual pieces in that corpus. The Martian effect will be particularly important in later chapters as I investigate such complicated musical concepts as chords, keys, and function.

Another Statistical Intermezzo: Musical Complexity and the German Tradition

Figure 1.8 shows two graphs that measure the average diversity and complexity of chords used in each year between 1650 and 1900. The first uses all pieces in the YCAC that were written by composers active in Germany, and the second uses those pieces in the corpus by composers active in all other regions. These graphs use *entropy* to approximate complexity. In contrast to *probability*, in which a set of expectations predicts some series of observations, entropy uses the probabilities of a series to determine how easily the events of that series can be predicted. A situation with one or two possible outcomes is easier to predict and less diverse and complex than a situation with many different equally likely outcomes: the former will have a lower entropy than the latter. The specific mathematics behind entropy can be found in this chapter's appendix, but in short: entropy converts a series of probabilities into a single value by more or less averaging them and then inverting them, with lower average probabilities becoming higher values of complexity and *vice versa*. This process means that a system with mostly low-probability events will produce a high entropy, while a series with mostly high-probability events will produce a low entropy. The results of flipping a two-sided coin, for instance, are all 50% probable, while the results rolling a six-sided die are all 16.67%: the former is less complex, more easily predicted, and has a lower entropy than the latter. However, if a six-sided die were unfairly weighted such that one of the outcomes occurred 99% of the time, it would be more predictable and have a simpler series of outcomes than either the coin or the equally weighted die and would have the lowest entropy of all. (The online spreadsheet supplement includes examples of converting probabilities to entropies. Note that all entropies are reported using a base-2 logarithm, as described in the appendix.)

In Figure 1.8, I calculate the entropy of the chords used in both German and not-German pieces in the YCAC, and I average the entropies within each year. For these calculations, I examine the chord types used within the YCAC. As in the Cone/Schubert analysis, I use the transpositionally equivalent (but inversionally inequivalent) set classes within the YCAC. (Recall that the YCAC represents each moment within its constituent pieces where pitches are added or subtracted from the texture, including not only harmonically stable moments but every fleeting dissonance and ornament as well: it is from these simultaneities I derive the set classes.) I select the 100 most-frequent sets for each year, and count how often each set appears as vertical simultaneities in this corpus. Using these counts, I can then calculate the probability of each of these occurring in that year. These probability values serve as the input for the entropy calculations. If, for instance, composers primarily used major and minor triads with very few other chord types within a given year, there would be very high probabilities for those chords, and – like our weighted die – the entropy would be low. If they use many different chord types more equally within a given year, the entropy would be high.

In both divisions of the YCAC, a positive trend holds: chronologically later pieces use a greater diversity of chords – they use increasingly more complex harmonic vocabularies. However, this trend is more stark when isolating German composers. Both sets of data are fit with a *regression line*, a slope that tracks the overall relationship between the data points. This regression features both a slope ("How much does entropy generally increase each year?") and a measurement of fit ("How much of the variation in entropy is explained by the year?"). Note that the German data not only produces a more steeply increasing slope, but German pieces also have a better fit to the trend line. (Again, more on regression lines can be found in the chapter's appendix.)

Provocatively, this finding tracks with what Carl Dahlhaus (1983) has identified as the rise of "autonomous music," a Western-European (and particularly German) phenomenon in which the inner workings of a piece of music are considered its expressive message, independent of any lyrical, programmatic, or even biographical meaning, a goal that encourages musical innovation and novelty. It additionally tracks with several Marxist accounts of Western European musical development, which describe the increasing intellectualism in musical aesthetics as a symptom of the rise of the bourgeoisie in German-speaking countries, reflecting music's role as both a social commodity and an expression of the utopian ideals of an imperfect society (Adorno, 1973; Greenberg, 1939).

Using these ideas as a backdrop, we could argue that the corpus shows an increase in harmonic complexity that is symptomatic of social and aesthetic

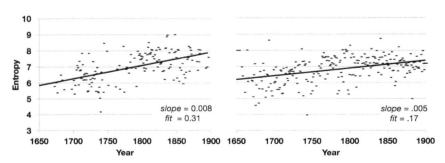

FIGURE 1.8 Average entropy for chord usage for each piece in each year for composers active in Germany (left) and not active in German (right)

changes throughout Western Europe, an increase that was particularly acute in German-speaking countries. In terms of the MCM, this argument uses pieces within the YCAC as the corpus pane. The events pane then organizes that data by set class, country of origin, and date, as well as by how often each set occurs. The events pane would also include the entropy measurements and the regressions that result from correlating nationally segregated entropy with chronology. The increased valuation of complexity within Western European society as the 19th century progresses – either for aesthetic reasons, sociopolitical reasons, or both – represents the motivation behind this trend and would therefore be placed in the expression pane.

These corpus statistics show the potential to connect quantifiable aspects of a corpus to qualitative social analysis. An examination of chord-based entropy shows that harmonic events on the musical surface grow in complexity more dramatically in the YCAC's selection of German music than in non-German music, and this fact parallels many qualitative and social analyses of German musical values and aesthetics. And in addition to claims about compositional motivations, the use of corpus statistics allows us to broach aspects of the listener's experience as well. On the one hand, composers write more complicated music to capture the values of their listeners and patrons, while on the other, social values and the corpora to which listeners have been exposed lead them to value and expect a certain complexity in the music that they consume.

Again, several stations within this logical flow should give us pause. For one, the conflation of listener expectations and the motivations of composers is anything but foregone in music analysis. And – more contentiously – we might argue whether the Marxist or the expressive explanation better explains these data. In the following section, I tease out one of these issues: the frequent conflation of the ways that listeners and composers engage with music, marking it as a recurrent issue in musical corpus analysis. I then return to the dicey connections between corpus statistics and qualitative, interpretive, and social analyses.

Some Issues With Importing the Noisy Channel and Statistical Learning Into Historical Corpus Analysis

Because of its historical connections to these fields, many of the tools used in musical corpus analysis have been drawn from information theory and cognitive psychology. These tools were, however, developed for formats in which both the producer and the reader of a text use the same engineering to produce and read that text. Deciphering Nazi cables works best when the decoding mechanism is the same as the encoding mechanism, and telephonics works well when both the sender and receiver use the same complementary processes. More mundanely, we generally assume our conversational interlocutors to possess basically the same linguistic comprehension as we do: listeners who are equipped to fluently

26 Introduction and Methodology

interpret the English language are most frequently equipped to expertly produce English-language utterances.

However, this equation does not exist in music. Only a very small proportion of an audience could reproduce the musical utterances they hear. Music has a unique relationship between the encoder (the composer, performer, improviser, etc.) and the decoder (the listener, learner, or analyst). I'll refer to this relationship as the magician's paradox after a provocative discussion of this topic by Dmitri Tymoczko (2011, 22), in which he draws a comparison between composers and magicians. Tymoczko argues that one needs to know neither the mechanics of the magician's illusions nor the details of their methods in order to enjoy magic acts and that this same logic holds for musical performances. In fact, both musical and magical audiences potentially garner more delight and entertainment when they are at a loss to explain what they are observing or hearing. (This dichotomy is also present in Lerdahl's (1992) distinction between what he calls "compositional" versus "listening" grammars, and in Nicholas Cook's (1992) "modes of listening.") The paradox, then, is that the two sides of a musical noisy channel relationship may not be equal, and yet communication still occurs.

Figure 1.9 shows several potential explanations of this paradox. In Figure 1.9a, the corpus sits at the center of the scheme, created by a composer and interpreted by a listener. The composer's process and listener's approach are represented as two models, m_c and m_l, respectively. (I use the word *model* here to mean a formal explanation of some data or procedure: a compositional model would trace the processes that produce musical pieces, while a listening model would be the process through which those works are interpreted.) At the left of Figure 1.9a, we find a composer producing some outputs by using the leftward model, m_c, which creates the corpus. On the right side of the figure, a listener interprets the corpus using model m_l, which must adequately describe aspects of the corpus.

While both m_c and m_l account for or interpret some aspect of the corpus, within the magician's paradox, the two models are not necessarily equal. The Venn diagrams comprising the remainder of Figure 1.9 show the various relationships that could account for the differences between compositional and listening models. One explanation is that the listening model is a simpler version of – a subset of – the compositional model, a scheme illustrated in Figure 1.9b. While many properties of the corpus can be explained by both the generative and interpretive models, several properties of the corpus are not available to the listener. It might also be the case that a compositional system is entirely different from a listener's model, a scheme related by the non-overlapping circles of Figure 1.9c. In this scheme, m_l has no overlap with m_c. Here, the corpus's data and statistics are overdetermined, insomuch as both models explain the same corpus using completely different models. Finally, the process might involve some hybrid, as in Figure 1.9d.[23] While there exist compositional and listening practices that

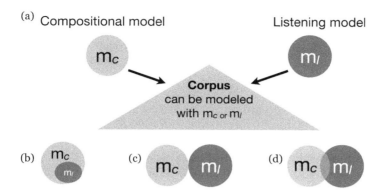

FIGURE 1.9 Several potential relationships between compositional and listening models

are not salient to each other, there are statistical properties of the corpus that are important to both how music is written and how it is interpreted.

All of these possible relationships are anathema to a strict noisy channel of musical communication: each diagram shows that the generating and receiving models are different in some way. Similarly, a model of musical learning based on statistical exposure is complicated by the magician's paradox as well, as it blurs the relationship between the information listeners use when interpreting music and that used by composers.

This paradox has several other additional implications. For instance, it can extend to the differences between score-based and aural information. The information gleaned from hearing a tritone can be very different from the tonal information derived by visually identifying a diminished fifth. While composers and performers have access to both of these domains, listeners generally only have access to the former. Furthermore, "listeners" are by no means a monolithic community, and therefore, no single model will apply to all listeners or interpreters in all situations. Figures 1.9b, c, and d could all describe different listeners in the same concert hall, or they could capture the experiences of one listener at different times or in different situations.

In my corpus analysis comparing chord usage in German and non-German repertoires, I suggested that the increase in entropy might reflect a rise in the social value of complex music. Such a premium on complexity would mean that composers would be encouraged to write more complex music and consumers would learn and appreciate this new complexity. However, demonstrating the magician's paradox, just because composers used a more complex harmonic palette does not mean that all listeners became increasingly musically savvy in quite the same way. It is possible, for instance, that many listeners appreciated some of the harmonic innovations but did not notice the more sophisticated

28 Introduction and Methodology

harmonic experimentation. This account tracks with Figure 1.9b, in which the listener and composer use the same model but with a different granularity or specificity. We could imagine other listeners simply appreciating the greater variation in texture and color that could accompany an increasingly complex harmonic vocabulary, letting the thicker textures wash over them, oblivious to any specific harmonic event. This follows the interpretation of Figure 1.9c, in which the two parties use separate models. Finally, some listeners could undertake a combination of these, appreciating the presence of some newly extravagant harmonies while also enjoying the resulting colors and textures. Figure 1.9d's separate but interacting models capture this situation.

One further aspect of the noisy channel must also be accounted for in this discussion: noise itself. Especially because the sender's and receiver's models in a musical noisy channel are not necessarily identical, "noise" can manifest in many diverse ways. In practice, the concept has been extended to include any way in which a signal might be different from the intended ideal. Most straightforwardly, "noise" could manifest as mistakes within a score or as a corrupted computer file: here, noise acts as a degrading of the initial intended signal in a way that changes the final received product. But there are many additional ways that the intended signal could lose its initial content on its way to a musical consumer. For example, Leonard Meyer's (1957) "cultural noise" – a phenomenon that inhibits an analyst's ability to decode the information embedded in an artwork from another culture or time period – might contribute to "noise" in this context.[24] Or noise might be generated if we treat non-chord tones as "misspellings" of some underlying consonant/triadic signal, as I do in subsequent chapters. In this book, I'll treat the concept of "noise" in a nimble and variable manner, applying it as appropriate to the situation.

Throughout this discussion, I have simply assumed that the increase in harmonic complexity in Germany could be attributed to the social factors described by the commentators cited earlier. I did not lay out any specific evidence definitely connecting the rise in German entropy with the rise in bourgeois consumer culture or the rise of the autonomous music aesthetic. Similarly, in my description of the legal case of the Producer versus the Emcee, I simply assumed that there was some causal connection between musical probability and human behavior without explicitly making that argument. The following section discusses the difficulty of testing these kinds of conclusions, arguing for caution when connecting corpus statistics to social and biographical forces and suggesting some strategies to make such connections as robust as possible.

The Difficulty of Testing Historical and Correlational Data

Some years ago, David Huron (1999) identified several limits associated with *historical* and *correlational* studies of music. In his estimation, such studies are "historical" when a researcher cannot directly observe the text's creation.

Historical studies are often also "correlational," meaning that the researcher cannot manipulate the conditions and variables surrounding the production of the text. In such studies, the researcher cannot determine whether a given outcome was caused by a particular variable (say, the rise of bourgeois consumer culture), or was, in fact, caused by some other circumstance and the observed correlations were coincidental.

All my analyses so far have been historical and correlational. We will never be able to directly observe Schubert's mental state, nor can we look over the shoulders of German composers as they created increasingly complex harmonic vocabularies. We cannot run a controlled experiment using a second timeline in which Schubert did not contract syphilis and then observe whether or not he wrote the same chord progressions, nor can we test an alternate reality in which Western European aesthetics did not value autonomous music and observe whether the resulting chord choices featured different levels of entropy. Without direct observation and experimentation, it is almost impossible to know beyond a reasonable doubt what causes the phenomena we observe in our corpora. Perhaps the unusual musical events of the *Moment Musical* came in response to a syphilis diagnosis, or perhaps Schubert's friend bet him that he couldn't embed a particular modulation into his music. Without direct observation and experimentation, we can never know.[25]

Even analyses of contemporary composition can be historical and correlational. Consider the case between the Producer and Emcee. Just as in the earlier example, an ideal experimental design would construct multiple timelines, some in which the Emcee was not exposed to the Producer's melody and some in which they were; if previous exposure to the Producer's melody resulted in the Emcee composing the melody in question and non-exposure did not, we could be sure that hearing the Producer's melody had caused the Emcee to write this pitch sequence. Additionally, if someone had directly observed the Emcee using the Producer's melody in their compositional process, we could also be sure of a causal connection between these two melodies. But without direct observation – or access to a science–fiction–style time machine that produces multiple timelines – our analyses must do their best with the available historical and correlational data.

The MCM's Utility in Outlining Analytical Logistics

This discussion, as well as the previous issues raised about the choice of corpora and modeling techniques, suggests that there are two different kinds of claims at play in corpus analyses: there are observable facts and measurements, and then there are claims and interpretations concerning these facts. It is one thing to say that the entropy of chord usage increases more in the music of German-speaking composers in the YCAC than in other composers' music. This fact is observable and testable. It is quite another to argue that this difference was due

30 Introduction and Methodology

to particular social trends at play in German-speaking countries. Similarly, it is one thing to argue that an EDM melody is less probable than average within a particular time and place. It is quite another to argue that this evidences plagiarism. Heuristically, we can call the former *quantitative* claims and the latter *connective* claims; these two types of claims correspond to the MCM's boxes and arrows, respectively.[26]

Quantitative claims – the contents of the MCM's boxes – are simply the properties of some object or process and are essentially inarguable. Any resulting quantitative claims are the fallout of how a dataset or group of observations is constituted. It is within this domain, however, that *noise* finds its home. The only reason that a quantitative claim can be incorrect is the result of incorrect data, a mistake in computation, or an error in encoding: all of these examples are degradations or alterations of the original data, and, as such, all these errors instantiate noise.

On the other hand, connective claims, the arrows between the boxes, arise from how these quantitative constructs are constituted. Because this act of constructing quantitative claims involves choices and interpretations, these connective claims are open to argument and are subject to the pitfalls of correlational, historical, and subjective logic. For instance, the following statements are verifiably true: the YCAC contains particular musical events represented in certain ways; applying entropy measurements to these events results in certain values; the values associated with German-speaking composers in this dataset are higher than entropies associated with music from other regions; and contemporary German society demonstrably valued absolute music increasingly as the 19th century progressed. These are all quantitative claims, and their data creates the three boxed panes within the MCM that underpinned the analysis of Figure 1.8. The only argument one can mount about these values is that some manner of noise has been introduced into the process, be it degraded or incorrect data within the corpus, a malfunctioning computer, or an error within a mathematical model. On the other hand, the construction of and connections between each of these panes are eminently arguable. Questions about the pieces contained in the YCAC, its data representation, the choice of entropy, or the equation of complexity with absolute music are all arguable – these are the connective arrows that engineer the flow between the MCM's quantitative panes.

Of course, corpus analysis isn't uniquely beholden to such larger issues of evidence, testability, argument, and speculation. These kinds of methodological questions and challenges haunt any intellectual endeavor on some level. However, because of its interdisciplinary nature, these questions are foregrounded in musical corpus analysis. Analyses like those mentioned jump between highly technical assessments of empirical facts and speculative or correlational interpretations of those facts. Flipping between these kinds of approaches means that the evidentiary ground rules shift underneath an analyst's feet as they move between different kinds of logics.[27]

In particular, music theory and musicology have struggled with this methodological blending for decades, if not centuries. After all, connecting the musical events within a score to some biographical occurrence, social trend, or other extramusical meaning – one of music analysis's frequent endeavors – involves traversing exactly the same kinds of historical/correlational pitfalls as those we find in corpus analysis. The next section argues not only that corpus analysis might benefit from the foundational work done in music analytical scholarship but that corpus analysis often tracks the same argumentative structures found in this scholarship.

How Music Analysis Can Benefit Corpus Research

To find an example of a music analyst roping together musical events and interpretive meaning, we can simply return to Cone's Schubert analysis. In the article, Cone spends several paragraphs diving meticulously into the piece's unusual musical events. Upon resurfacing, he specifically cites the concept of *hermeneutics*, a strategy widely invoked in the humanities that seeks to understand authorial intention and bridge the gap between a text's creator and its reader (Gadamer, 1989; Jauss, 1982; Iser, 2000).[28]

Hermeneutics is, however, not the only methodological foundation for interpretation valued by musicologists: Vladimir Jankélévitch (1961) and Carolyn Abbate (2004) have emphasized the subconscious and sensual nature of musical meaning; Janna Saslaw (1996), Nicholas Cook (2001), and Lawrence Zbikowski (2002) have theorized the role of bodily, spatial, and other non-musical experiences in forming musical meanings; and musical semioticians have outlined ways that we associate musical gestures with ideas, events, and concepts (Agawu, 1991; Chung, 2019; Cheng and Fosler-Lussier, forthcoming; Hatten, 1994), to name just a few broad approaches. And the theorizing of musical meaning extends to the tools of music analysis: David Lewin (1987) argues that the analytical language with which one discusses music will determine the kind of analysis that results.[29] Steve Rings (2011) illustrates how different types of analytic representations highlight different aspects of a piece of music, while Brown and Dempster (1989) show that scientific rhetoric conditions the kinds of analyses produced. These instances each show researchers worrying about the baggage and constraints inherent in analytical tools. Echoing my earlier dichotomy between observable and connective claims, Lawrence Kramer (2011) writes that "no degree of analytical details can establish an interpretation as true" and that the purpose of analysis is to do the "best it can" to construct a well-informed, meaningful interpretation of some piece of music. Each in their own way, these thinkers are concerned with the ways we form observations about musical events and how we connect those observations to broader ideas.

Corpus analyses may add more data to the act of music analysis and interpretation – it may widen and solidify the boxes in the MCM – but the tools

32 Introduction and Methodology

and results of corpus analysis add little insight into the figure's arrows – into its connective claims. But if corpus analysis can add precision to musicological observations, musicology can add precision to the interpretation.[30] Historical corpus analysis may indeed interact with concepts from informatics and psychology, but because of its particular difficulties and confounds, if it is to contribute to research into human culture, social interaction, and expressive meaning, it must rely on the foundations laid by musicology. As Jesper Andersen (2017) points out in his dissertation *How to Think Music With Data*, data will tell a researcher the "what," but musicology provides the "how" and "why."

To that end, a corpus analysis should essentially follow the logical flow of any study that relies on music analysis, diving deeply into a sea of observable musical data but resurfacing into the unobservable and untestable logic of interpretation. Regardless of its information-theoretical, linguistic, and psychological tools, corpus analysis is still subject to the methodological strictures of traditional musicology and music theory. I would argue, therefore, that corpus analysis does not, in fact, constitute a departure from traditional music studies. Rather, it functions as an expansion of music theory's research tools.

Corpus Analyses and Music Analysis

In his 2015 essay "Statistical Analysis at the Birth of Close Reading," Yohei Igarashi demonstrates the ways that close readings in the early 20th century relied on "word books" of the English language's most frequent words to distill and translate the complexities and metaphors embedded within a poem into its constituent meanings and ideas. In this way, these precomputational compendia of statistical data supported human analyses, with quantitative word books bolstering the search for a meaningful interpretation of an obscure text. This strategy again features the mixture of quantitative and interpretive logic outlined within the MCM and is replicated countless times within various analyses throughout the humanities that endeavor to better understand some text using empirical methods. Here, and in most arguments that can be represented by the MCM, the role of empirical and corpus data is not necessarily to prove some final conclusion to be definitively true but to assist in making a convincing and meaningful interpretation of some text.

But then, how are we to interpret these situations when we are confronted with them? Indeed, there are numerous consequential cases within the real-world court system reminiscent of my hypothetical Producer-versus-Emcee tale, and they deal in the kind of probabilistic reasoning I've outlined in this chapter. Is data analysis so fundamentally subjective – so interpretive – that every explanation is equally valid? Are the probabilities outlined in the pages of this chapter simply another random card to play in what is ultimately a series of arbitrary connections and conclusions?

Introduction and Methodology **33**

Absolutely not. One of the primary lessons humanities-based analytical theory teaches us is that we move through the world, form beliefs, and make consequential decisions based on incomplete information. When we communicate with one another or read a work by some author, there is always the possibility that we and our interlocutor are using fundamentally different methods to encode and decode our positions within the noisy channel; but, for the sake of necessity and facility, we often assume this not to be the case (Barthes, 1977; Hirsch, 1967; Sinclair, 2004). When we negotiate a text with more than one potential meaning, in the moment, we generally pick a single interpretation for the sake of a comprehendible cognitive experience (Agawu, 1994; Poudrier and Repp, 2013). And famously in law, a prosecutor's goal is to prove their case beyond a reasonable doubt (in a criminal case in U.S. law) or with a preponderance of the evidence (in a civil case). Corpus analysis can be comparably imagined: it should be thought of as one among a suite of tools used to offer compelling arguments and interpretations that are optimally convincing among the alternatives (Kramer, 2011; Rothstein, 1995). In the words of David Huron (2013, 8), because "any set of observations is open to more than one interpretation . . . scholars [must] simply endeavor to show that, on balance, one interpretation is more parsimonious, or more coherent, or better dovetails with other theories, or is parallel in structure to similar phenomena in other domains, or better fits with commentary fragments made by major figures, and so on." In sum: while corpus analysis may bring precision to the components of some analysis, it still relies on the same processes as other interpretive and convincing acts.

Finally, if musical corpus analysis is to adhere to the argumentative designs of other music analyses, it must be *accessible*. Any black-boxing of the data used within an MCM will preclude a convincing logical flow between a corpus, the corresponding observations, and their interpretation. If one's readers do not understand *how* observations are being made, one forfeits the opportunity for those observations to be convincing representations of the corpus. In short, corpus modeling must be understandable to one's audience if it is to be convincing to one's audience. For sure, there are specialized venues in and audiences for which the technical components of state-of-the-art corpus tools and models are appropriate. However, music analysis is not necessarily that venue! While this pressure toward accessibility is, admittedly, a notable challenge for an approach that relies on technical methods whose engineering may be less known to non-specialists, accessibility is still crucial to argument-driven music analysis.

Tonality as Text

The linguist Jonathan Sinclair (2004) distinguishes a "corpus analysis" from a traditional analysis by the very fact that the former uses observations that simply could not be produced by an individual human. To Sinclair, a corpus analysis

34 Introduction and Methodology

"entails a change of methodology; a corpus in its characteristic mode lies almost by definition outside . . . of close reading and control" (pp. 188–189). Such a definition of corpus analysis focuses on the change of relationship between the human analyst and the object of their analysis, and this stance is adopted by many musical corpus analysts in some implicit or explicit form (Huron, 2013; London, 2013). From this perspective, when conducting a close reading of an individual text (or small group of texts), an analyst directly observes the properties of the object they are studying, yielding an immediacy to their insights. In contrast, the magnitude of a corpus requires the mediation of a computer, with observations being the result of a slower and more deliberate process of computational programming and statistical testing.

I would add a significant caveat to this assessment. Earlier, and along similar lines to Sinclair's ideas, I suggested that corpus techniques allow a researcher to quickly ascertain certain properties and characteristics of corpora that would, without the aid of a computer, have otherwise taken months or years to analyze. I would argue that this immediacy allows the act of computational analysis to move closer to the act of observation and away from that of a calculated test. Indeed, such a shift in perspective allows us to *read* corpus data in much the same way we read an individual piece of music. Earlier, when describing the Martian effect, I outlined ways that computational methods alienate a researcher from their preconceptions, guiding their methods towards the hypothesis testing and objective results of empirical and experimental paradigms. However, the immediacy inherent in contemporary computational technologies *also allows for the opposite to be true*: the act of quickly manipulating a few lines of code to explore a corpus is potentially as similar to flipping through a score as it is to designing an empirical experiment. From this perspective, even if the object of study might differ between a corpus analysis and a close reading, the two analyses may not have markedly different relationships to their objects of study. Furthermore, earlier, I also suggested that every meaningful interpretation of corpus data involves some degree of not-directly-provable argumentation. I showed that the logic underpinning claims made within traditional music theory potentially differ very little from that underpinning corpus analyses. If the immediacy of computational analysis allows a corpus to be read in much the same way as an individual piece of music, the differences between the approaches shrinks even further.

Certainly, I am by no means arguing against wielding corpora in the service of empirical and experimental investigations – indeed, many aspects of my ensuing chapters will rely on such methods. However, I am arguing that this immediacy yields new opportunities for using corpus analysis within the realm of music theory. The ability *to read* corpora is liberating – it opens a potential space for more creative, intuitive, playful, and subjective applications of corpus analysis. If the humanistic side of music analysis seeks to investigate the human musical experience through acts of interpretation, close reading, and

Introduction and Methodology **35**

introspection, then corpus studies have the opportunity to enact the same kinds of interpretation on large swaths of data.

Steven Rings (2008) writes that "analysis, at its best . . . [is] the process of making us more alive to [music] as a material, sonic phenomenon" (180). If one of music analysis's main goals is to enrich our musical experiences – to tell compelling and meaningful stories about music (Maus, 1991) – then musical corpora offer new and interesting campfires around which we can tell those stories.[31] As I argued earlier, large datasets and powerful computational tools are relatively recent inventions; as such, they offer new and fertile ground from which captivating and insightful analyses can be cultivated. However, to do so, an analyst must balance the technical aspects of corpus research with the artistry and rhetoric of musical interpretation.[32]

Throughout the course of this book, I will ask familiar music-theoretical questions, and it will mostly ask them of 17th- to 20th-century Western European and American musical corpora. I will, in other words, treat tonal traditions as texts to be read, darting between immediate observation, empirical testing, historical reflection, and other cross-disciplinary tactics to reinvestigate how style, meter, harmonic function, chord syntax, and other phenomena are manifested in the tonal tradition. My stance will adopt much of the methodology that Franco Moretti's (2005) *distant reading* and Matthew Jockers's (2013) *macroanalysis* have applied to literary analysis, focusing on what trends, contours, and corpus-based computer models can tell us about the music comprising the corpus being studied. However, I will also adopt an aggressively humanities-oriented stance to my studies, connecting empirical observations to larger theoretical notions and arguments. Just as this chapter reframed music-theoretical discussions by using corpus analysis, this book will investigate and debate some of music theory's fundamental concepts using the contours and trends of tonal traditions themselves.

To this end, Chapter 2 asks "What is a style?" and shows how statistics drawn from musical corpora can demonstrate ways in which the compositional practices of individual composers can be grouped into larger styles and how these stylistically defined groups evolve and interact. I use techniques like linear regression and cluster analysis to quantify the similarities between the music of different time periods and composers and even to measure the success of musical forgeries and stylistic emulations, all the while comparing my models to historically and socially driven approaches to style. Chapter 3 discusses what corpus analysis can show us about the nature and meaning of a "chord" in the tonal tradition. Here, I build a model that observes a musical corpus, balances the scale-degree and contextual similarities of its constituent events, and produces a harmonic vocabulary of that corpus, again comparing the results to theoretical notions of chord and function. Responding to the results of Chapter 3, Chapter 4 considers the concept of harmonic function from broad and contrasting perspectives, outlining several models that group chords by their corpus characteristics, with each model

36 Introduction and Methodology

adhering to different definitions of "function." I then conclude the chapter by outlining some overlaps between corpus models of harmonic function and linguistic theories of word and concept categorization. In Chapter 5, I use corpus analysis to investigate how different kinds of musical events (e.g., accents, chords, set classes) recur at consistent time intervals and how these periodic recurrences align with notated musical meter. I compare how these correspondences manifest in various corpora, including datasets of classical, pop/rock, drum-set, and Malian jembe music, arguing that the ways that strong and weak pulses are expressed can dramatically change between musical cultures. Finally, Chapter 6 investigates how key and tonal orientation can be expressed and communicated through corpus statistics. This chapter will link issues raised in previous chapters by arguing that pitch parameters within corpora whose music expresses tonal centers generally follow certain types of distributions in order to communicate coherent key orientations.

Throughout this chapter, I have argued that corpus analysis relies on persuasion and argumentation in much the same way as other interpretive and historical music analyses and suggested that the methods of a corpus analysis must be accessible to its audience in order to be persuasive. To that end, this book is committed to making its methods accessible to a wide readership of music researchers. First, I design my discussions so that a reader with no experience in this subfield may gain a basic understanding of and comfort with the standard statistical and computational techniques used in musical corpus analysis. My approaches themselves are also chosen to support this accessibility; when the choice is available, this book often employs simpler methods for their illustrative capacity over more complicated state-of-the-art modeling. As mentioned throughout this chapter, the book's appendixes will aid readers interested in more in-depth explanations of the methods employed, and open-access spreadsheets will provide examples of many of the computational approaches used. To highlight the creative, playful, and interpretive stance I take, each chapter is also written in a different literary form. Chapter 2 shall be a traditional essay, Chapter 3 is written as a narrative, Chapter 4 is an epistolary, Chapter 5 is a dialogue, and Chapter 6 is a diatribe.

Finally, a broader methodological point: treating tonal traditions as texts to be read shifts the analytical focus away from individual "masterpieces" that supposedly represent their respective musical traditions and toward broader trends and larger groups of music and musicians within those traditions. This shift is accomplished both by including a much greater number of pieces in those traditions and by focusing on the relationships between these pieces rather than the pieces themselves in isolation. Sociopolitically, this is not trivial. Deemphasizing individual pieces removes the need for a "canon" of masterpieces. For instance, if a corpus is indeed representative of the early-19th-century tonal tradition, it will not only have the most famous pieces by Ludwig Beethoven, Johannes Brahms, Robert Schumann, and Franz Schubert but will also include a panoply of those composers' lesser-known pieces and pieces by lesser-known composers. Beethoven's *Ninth Symphony* can potentially be just another statistical data point treated equally to, say, the symphonies of Otto Nicolai (1810–1849). (See London, 2022, for a broader argument along these lines.)

Recapitulation

Corpus analysis first entered music theory via informatics research in the mid-20th century. This discourse imagines a message being sent between two parties, with the sender encoding content into a message and the receiver decoding the message using the same system. The statistical analysis of large datasets helps reverse engineer the properties of this encoding/decoding relationship by studying the properties of the intervening messages.

In a later but parallel trend, corpus analysis was used to describe one's ability to learn a language simply by being exposed to it. The statistical learning hypothesis describes how humans extract the statistical regularities, correspondences, and recurrences within a language through prolonged exposure, with those aggregated statistics constituting the learner's knowledge of that language. From this perspective, musical corpus statistics show ways in which someone can learn expectations or become familiar with a musical style through repeated exposure to a particular repertoire.

I argued that importing corpus analysis into music theory has six particular benefits: (1) independent verifiability, (2) the availability of averages, norms, and baselines to which one can compare observations, (3) the rigor with which one must operationalize computational and statistical analyses, (4) the connections these models allow between music analysis and cognition, (5) the ability to observe and analyze larger and broader aspects of a musical tradition than human analysis supports, and (6) the potential removal of some human biases and preconceptions when undertaking an analysis. I then suggested that these benefits add up to what I call the Martian effect, which arises from a model being somewhat alienated from the researcher and reader. I also suggested that these benefits highlight the fact that linguistic and engineering research does not map perfectly onto musical analysis, invoking the magician's paradox, in which composers and listeners do not share the same cognitive templates. I further argued that music analysis also has a complicated relationship to evidence. Because the objects of our analyses are historical (they come from the past, and their creation cannot be directly observed), many of our claims are correlational (we cannot manipulate the variables within our research questions to establish causality). These characteristics create a fraught relationship to a corpus's observable properties. We can directly observe musical events, and we can find verifications of historical and biographical facts, but the connections between these events and facts can be neither directly observed nor tested.

38 Introduction and Methodology

I isolated many of these issues within the Meaningful Corpus Model that delineates the three primary components of a musical corpus analysis: the text (or corpus), the observations (the analysis of the corpus), and the interpretation. I argued that each of these components share the property of being *quantitative*, or are simply the characteristics of some object (as is the case of a corpus or a documented biographical fact) or the logical result of some process (as is the case in the statistical analysis of some corpus data). In contrast, corralling the components of an MCM into a logical flow that involves making choices about which corpora to use, how to model and measure that corpus, and how to connect an analysis to some larger interpretation – these choices will inevitably be arguable, be open for debate, and show the values of the analyst constructing the MCM.

With the characteristics of the MCM in mind, I argued that just as corpus analysis may afford benefits to music studies, music studies can afford benefits to corpus analysis. Musicology and music theory have struggled with connecting musical observations to expressive, social, and biographical meaning for some time. Rather than being strictly a part of informatics or psychological research, corpus analyses of historical datasets are best situated within the intellectual framework of existing research into human culture and expression. Indeed, I argued for the humanistic potential of corpus analysis, specifically in treating corpora as texts to be read and digested in much the same way as music theorists read individual musical pieces.

In the ensuing chapters, I investigate such topics as the statistical properties of strong pulses in corpora, how a computer model might learn to identify harmonic function, and what a formal model of musical style might look like. To be sure, the models, tools, and arguments underpinning these investigations will be beholden to informatics and psychology. My larger agenda, however, is solidly based in music theory. Shifting the focus from individual pieces to tonal corpora, I will investigate how music-theoretical concepts like style, meter, harmonic function, and chord syntax are manifested in tonal traditions.

Notes

1. These connections are what the digital humanities scholar Alan Liu (2013) has called the "meaning problem" for quantitative analyses.
2. The melodies I use are based on the 2021 song "Pink Lemonade" by Edmund Bagnell and are used with his explicit permission.
3. For this heuristic demonstration, I do not quantify how probable each beginning note is to be selected. Standard practice is to employ an empty "start token," such that the first 2-gram in this melody would be <__, $\hat{1}$>. Such a procedure quantifies how probable the first event is to be $\hat{1}$ as opposed to other degrees. For simplicity's sake, I dispensed with this step in the current demonstration. However, to make sure I was comparing this melody – which begins on the very-often-used tonic scale degree – with similar random melodies, I stipulated that my random melodies could begin only on the most probable scale degrees in this corpus: $\hat{1}$, $\hat{2}$, $\hat{3}$, $\hat{5}$, and 6. Chapter 6

uses empty start tokens in its analyses. I must stress that none of this analysis was used in a real court filing.

4. As a sanity check on moving between ratios and percentages: Percentages represent events out of 100, such that 10 out of 100 is 10%, and 0.02% means 0.02 units out of 100 units. Decimal ratios represent events as a fraction of 1. 10 out of a 100 would now be 0.1 (because 10 divided by 100 is 0.1), and 0.02 divided by 100 is 0.0002. Moving between these two representations of probability is simply a matter of shifting the decimal two places. Moving from a percentage to a decimal ratio entails moving the decimal point left two positions (10.0% becomes 0.1), while moving from a ratio to a percentage moves the decimal in the opposite direction (0.0002 becomes 0.02%).

5. This epistemological move was echoed by interest in the practical aspects of computational analysis in the humanities. Famously, Fr. Roberto Buso began his *Index Thomisticus* in 1946, a project that converted the complete writings of St. Thomas Aquinas to a computationally searchable format. Scholars often point to this initiative as the beginning of the digital humanities (Jockers, 2013). However, Yohei Igarashi (2015) has argued that this kind of quantitative approach to textual analysis can be traced to the incorporation of "word books" – compendia of English's most-frequent words – in literary analyses in the early 20th century, which Lydia Liu (2011) argues belies "a conception of English as a statistical system." This view of language as a machine-like process that can be understood with quantitative methods then feeds back into the Shannon-Weaver noisy channel, in which the encoding and decoding of meaning is done in such a way that can be described using mathematics and statistics.

6. "Informatics" does not always imply "information theory" in contemporary research, although the two are almost certainly connected within music research. For instance, the Music Informatics Group of the Society for Music Theory was founded by scholars who were engaged in information theory, while the purview of that group is certainly wider at present. Huron (2013) provides another description of (and perspective on) these early developments in corpus studies.

7. These authors amply explore the noisy channel model. For instance, regarding the structure of the noisy channel model, both discuss several assumptions concerning the information's sender. Cohen argues that the model assumes the information producer to be a "random source emitting signs according to probabilities. The statistical structure of the source is [therefore] its mathematical definition" (1962, 140). In other words, a message's source can be defined as a series of probabilities, or a "stochastic machine." From a more musical perspective, Meyer connects this to musical production, writing, "musical styles are internalized probability systems [and this is] demonstrated by the rules of musical grammar and syntax found in textbooks on harmony, counterpoint, and theory in general." Meyer imagines composing within a particular musical style, then, as essentially emanating from Cohen's "statistical structure," with the decision of what chord follows another being based on the syntax's probabilities. Connecting this idea to musical style, Meyer writes that "Styles in music are basically complex systems of probability relationships in which the meaning of any term or series of terms depends upon its relationships with all other terms possible within the style system" (1957, 414). Cohen takes this idea one step further when he articulates another basic assumption of information theory, that of "ergodicity." In order to assume that the statistical properties of a score or group of scores represent the stochastic compositional system that created them, one must accept "that a sufficiently large sample from an infinite sequence has the same statistical structure as the infinite sequence" (Cohen, 1962, 155).

40 Introduction and Methodology

8. See Byros (2012). It's worth noting that schema theory – a current trend in music theory epistemologically beholden to Meyer's work – is generally not approached from a strictly computational or statistical perspective but rather by the collection and curation of large numbers of musical examples that are then analyzed by a human (*not* a computer).

9. The cause of this failure is likely multifaceted, ranging from the restrictions of mid-century computing power (Huron, 2013, describes this era's ambitions as have having "outpaced reality when it came to computers" [p. 4]) to the mass exodus of its primary practitioners out of music theory and into nascent computational/empirical fields. For example, Joel Cohen now teaches in a geography department, Gift Siromoney works in computer science, and Edgar Coons is a professor of psychology.

10. Margulis and Beatty (2008), in fact, read three waves of publication and research in musical informatics, first from the 1950–60s, then the 1980s, and finally in the 2000s. Their analysis, however, specifically addresses entropy as a tool and the relative difficulties (and misunderstandings) that arise when applying this tool. In my narrative, the researchers that Margulis and Beatty associate with the middle wave would be something of a postlude to the first wave and prelude to the second, as they appear to be motivated by the availability of greater computing power but do not appear to be motivated by something like a statistical-learning argument (see Knopoff and Hutchinson, 1981, 1983). My reading is indebted to John Sinclair (2004), who identifies similar trends in English and Linguistics departments, and the research trends outlined in David Temperley's *Music and Probability* (2007).

11. The reader familiar with the statistical learning hypothesis may be surprised that the story I'm telling begins in music research rather than linguistics or psychology: Krumhansl's initial contribution to this concept occurred almost a decade prior to that of Saffran! Regardless of the narrative often told within exposure/statistical-learning theory, there is an argument to be made that Krumhansl – and *not* Saffran – pioneered the modern idea that a corpus's statistics could determine human expectations. And of course, connecting musical expectations to a listener's musical diet is not foreign to music theory. The idea that some event is unexpected within some repertoire but expected in another also underpins schema theory (Gjerdingen, 2007), studies of form (Hepokoski and Darcy, 2006), and early music analysis (Long, 2020). Vasili Byros (2009) has even suggested that studies of musical expectation using historically situated datasets can shed light on *historically situated cognition*, revealing the kinds of musical expectations that audiences or composers of a given corpus would have had.

12. At this point, I should admit that by relying on the engineering of the noisy channel, I am implicitly assuming that interpreting a text involves some sort of recovery of authorial messaging. These pages are not the venue to litigate such topics in depth. However, I would argue that even if we admit that the authorial intention behind a text is impossible for a reader to truly access, we still opt into *some* notion of communication when we engage a text, even if – ultimately – the meaning comes from the subjective experience of the reader themselves, and even if the idea of an "author" is merely a polite heuristic fiction. At least insomuch as the fundamental act of interpretation involves mining meaning from an object not explicitly made by the reader, engaging with a text involves searching for and applying tools that seem to be adequate to understanding that text. Similar arguments are made by such diverse thinkers as Barthes (1977), Hisch (1967), and Agawu (2004). In terms of the noisy channel and the MCM, I would connect the act of "deciphering" and "parsing" to this act of reading and analyzing a text, and I would argue that the tools that corpus analysis

affords us are among the tools a reader might grasp onto when recovering meaning from a text.

13. One notable parallel with this discussion is David Lewin's (1986) often-cited approach to musical phenomenology, an approach that also situates musical observations in terms of their context and the concepts and assumptions used to produce those observations. Lewin's work was, however, influenced not only by philosophical phenomenology but by contemporary work in computing (Kane, 2011).

14. Computationally, I track the interval between the pitch class associated with the zeroth member of the set class, which is not always the root. A C major triad moving to a G dominant seventh would be s.c. [047] progression to [0368] down by one semitone (or adding 11 semitones, mod 12), because the zeros associated with each set class correspond to pitch class C and B, respectively. For the figures and discussion, I translate these relationships into root motion for ease of reading.

15. This distribution is a hallmark of natural language usage and has been pointed to as an example of the overlap between music and language (Manaris et al., 2005; Zanette, 2006). I return to the significance of this ubiquitous property of corpus distributions in my fourth and last chapters.

16. Again, the YCAC shows every moment a note is added to or subtracted from a texture. This means that every passing or neighboring tone – or even every motion in a written-out trill – is registered as an event. Therefore, in the raw data, the most frequent "chord progressions" involve some chord sandwiching a passing or neighboring dissonance. The highest-ranked successions from a major triad, then, are the addition of a chordal eleventh or ninth. However, these moments are generally the result of dissonant counterpoint between chord tones. This kind of surface action will be important in subsequent chapters, but I've excluded these initial most probable/ non-triadic transitions from this chapter's Schubert analysis for simplicity's sake. Also, the reader will be struck by the extreme initial plunge in this distribution: a handful of progressions dominate the mass of the distribution, and the rank is roughly exponentially proportional to its frequency.

17. These events occur 3.8% and 3.6% of the time, respectively, while the last several progressions on the chart occur a very improbable 0.007% of the time. The last progression in the chart, for instance, is a major triad moving to an open fifth one half step higher, a very unlikely but possible event.

18. One should note, however, that a human's programming of a model can reflect these biases!

19. Indeed, isolated studies of musical probabilities have been intermittently produced non-computationally in musicology (Jeppesen, 1927; McHose, 1947), but prior to computational corpus analysis, such studies were exceptional novelties.

20. In White and Quinn (2018), we divide a computer's superhuman capacities into two categories with analogies to the backhoe and the microscope. Backhoes complete some tasks that a human *could* do but take a shorter time to do them, while microscopes do things that are outside of a human's capacity. Computational methods can generally be categorized into one of these two analogies. This approach is similar to Andersen's (2017) contention that a primary utility of data analysis is that it helps musicology "pose new questions" (64).

21. The notion of close reading is generally traced to the work of I.A. Richards (1929). Recently, Yohei Igarashi (2015) has argued that early practitioners of close reading were, in fact, reliant on statistical analyses (like word counts) when mining meaning from dense and obscure texts, with later theorists of close reading (e.g., Brooks, 1947) moving away from this strategy.

42 Introduction and Methodology

22. There is, in fact, a cottage industry of corpus analyses that identify some generally accepted theoretical premise and disprove it through corpus statistics. See, for example, von Hippel and Huron (2000), Aarden and von Hippel (2004), and White (2021).
23. There is a fourth, logically exhaustive possibility: m_c could be a superset of m_l. If a music teacher is coaching a neophyte student in composition or improvisation, the relationship between the musical production and the interpretation would be opposite of Figure 1.9b, insomuch as the composer's model is a less-sophisticated version of the listener's model. This relationship, however, is a bit of a pedagogical novelty, does not account for the magician's paradox, and does not seem to be generally useful for describing how historical corpora are created and interpreted. However, I thank the graduate students of Florida State University for challenging me to account for this possibility.
24. Importantly, there is a lot of history behind Meyer's concept and my use of "noise." In a play on Proust, Carl Dahlhaus (1983) called the language of bygone eras "*à temps perdu*" to highlight the fundamental difference in past and present expressive languages. In a similar vein, Hans Robert Jauss (1982) crafted the notion of a "horizon of expectation" to describe the expectations that both an author and reader bring to a composition/reception relationship. Different horizons of expectations would result in Meyer's cultural noise, or evidence of a language *à temps perdu*.
25. There is an overlap between what I'm describing and the concept of *non-falsifiable* claims, or claims for which there could not exist evidence that renders them false. One of the main personalities surrounding this concept is Karl Popper (1934). He argued that intellectual programs like Marxism and Freudian psychology cannot be proven *wrong*, and therefore, it's hard to verify whether they are *right*. If a patient is introverted, socially middling, or extroverted, each could be explained by an overbearing mother; there is no instance in which the theory cannot explain the observed evidence. The diagnosis is non-falsifiable. Similarly, my corpus data does not exactly prove anything. The contours of the Schubert graphs do not *prove* that the composer projected struggles with his deteriorating health onto his music. As such, the connections between Schubert's musical choice and his mental state are, in a certain sense, non-falsifiable.
26 *Many* disciplines discuss these different types of data. Historians in particular make a distinction between internal and external evidence to distinguish between extratextual historical facts and speculations about a text's expressive motivating potentials (Kerman, 1985). External evidence is direct, clear-cut, and generally falsifiable. For example, external biographical and medical evidence can be cited to point to Schubert having contracted syphilis. The unique nature of some of his harmonic choices constitutes internal evidence, evidence that is harder to causally connect to Schubert's mental state.
27. Specifically, it is tempting to assume that when we introduce the rigor of formal computation and statistics to an investigation, this rigor infuses all aspects of that argument. Instead, it is important to remember that while these methods bring testability to our observations, how we decide upon methods of measurement and testing is as culturally situated as any intuitive, interpretive, or speculative claim. Shalizi (2011) discusses this very concept in relation to the "distant reading" of Moretti (2005). Additionally, the idea that ideology can affect an outcome tracks many philosophy-of-science writers focused on the presuppositions inherent in an author's identity. See, for example, Gould, 1981; Hubbard, 1990; Schiebinger, 1993.
28. "Hermeneutics" is a term with broad usage in music analysis. Many analysts use it as an umbrella term for the pursuit of meaning in music. However, it originated in

Introduction and Methodology **43**

religious studies with attempts to understand the original intentions of the authors of the scriptures. From there, analysts used these concepts to investigate authorial intention in general. It is in this more constrained sense that I use the term.

29. In the words of John Rahn: "In analyzing a piece, the choice of a theory, and then of a description among those possible in the theory, should be made according to not logical or dogmatic but aesthetic criteria; the description that results should be the most musically satisfying description among the alternatives" (1980, 68).

30. Gjerdingen (2013), for instance, argues that computational corpus analyses must be sensitive to the kinds of theoretical structures that the composers and listeners of a historical repertoire would have originally used to produce and make sense of that music. From his perspective, a corpus analysis using, for instance, Roman numerals would have limited historical validity if that repertoire's listeners and producers did not employ that theoretical apparatus. The choices of how to represent musical events – and the justifications of these choices – are precisely those captured by the arrows connecting the corpus/corpus pane and the observations pane.

31. In fact, Rings (2008) argues that a good analysis should increase the *pleasure* of interacting with music – that music analysis is an essentially hedonistic act. I would suggest that corpus analysis can function in the same way by making us more sensitive to interesting and compelling properties of a musical tradition. By creatively and playfully reading a corpus, we deepen our experience with that dataset and enrich our experience with the constituent musical pieces and the connections and relationships between them.

32. In one sense, this approach is foundationally different from that advocated by David Huron (2013). Huron discourages exploratory analyses for two reasons. First, he worries that fishing within a large dataset for connections and correlations without predetermined hypotheses will inevitably produce *some* kind of significant results. Huron's logic runs like this: if we define "significant" results as those that are 95% probable to have not arisen by chance, then every time we run an exploratory test, we are taking the chance that a result will fall into the 5% window of appearing by pure chance. Running hundreds or thousands of tests to find a handful of these "significant" relationships increases the likelihood that a researcher stumbles on one of these relationships that falls into this window. I am less worried about such spurious results given that statistical tests frame the probability of a this pure-chance appearance as: "given that the following observable relationship exists, how probable is that relationship to have arisen by chance" rather than "given that I looked for this relationship and ran this test, how probable is this relationship to have arisen by chance?" In other words, running prior exploratory tests shouldn't diminish the actual probability that results are believable. Huron's second point, however, outlines a more fundamental difference between his experimental approach and my concept of treating corpora as texts to be read: he argues that exploratory analyses will often confuse a study's justification/ hypothesis with its initial motivation. He writes that if "you make an observation, you cannot pretend that you predicted that observation." In my reading-/decoding-based approach, I am often letting observations rather than hypothesis testing sit in the driver's seat. However, such are the mechanics of reading! We do not predict and test hypotheses as we move through a text (or listen to a piece or analyze a passage of music) but rather digest and interpret the information available to us. I would argue that there is a place for both of these approaches to corpus analysis – for rigorous hypothesis-driven investigations and those that embrace intuition, exploration, and fascination – and that the kinds of insights yielded by both approaches are not mutually exclusive.

44 Introduction and Methodology

References

Aarden, B. J. 2003. *Dynamic Melodic Expectancy*. Ph.D. Dissertation, The Ohio State University, Columbus, OH.

Aarden, B. J. and P. T. von Hippel. 2004. "Rules for Chord Doubling (and Spacing): Which Ones Do We Need?" *Music Theory Online*, 10/2. www.mtosmt.org/classic/mto.04.10.2/mto.04.10.2.aarden_hippel.html

Abbate, C. 2004. "Music: Drastic or Gnostic?" *Critical Inquiry*, 30, 505–536.

Adorno, T. 1973. *Philosophy of Modern Music*. Translated by Anne G. Mitchell and Wesley V. Blomster. New York: The Seabury Press.

Agawu, V. K. 1991. *Playing with Signs: A Semiotic Interpretation of Classic Music*. Princeton: Princeton University Press.

Agawu, V. K. 1994. "Ambiguity in Tonal Music: A Preliminary Study." *Theory, Analysis and Meaning in Music*. Anthony Pople, ed. Cambridge: Cambridge University Press, 86–107.

Agawu, V. K. 2004. "How We Got Out of Analysis, and How to Get Back in Again." *Music Analysis*, 23/2&3, 267–286.

Andersen, J. S. 2017. *How to Think Music with Data: Translating from Audio Content to Analysis to Music Analysis*. Ph.D. Dissertation, University of Copenhagen, København, Denmark.

Barthes, R. 1977. "The Death of the Author." *Image, Music, Text*. Translated by Stephen Heath. New York: Hill and Wang.

Bharucha, J. J. 1987. "Music Cognition and Perceptual Facilitation: A Connectionist Frame-Work." *Music Perception*, 5, 1–30.

Bharucha, J. J. 1991. "Pitch, Harmony and Neural Nets: A Psychological Perspective." *Music and Connectionism*. P. M. Todd and D. G. Loy, eds. Cambridge, MA: MIT Press.

Brooks, C. 1947. *The Well Wrought Urn: Studies in the Structure of Poetry*. New York: Harcourt.

Brown, M., and D. Dempster. 1989. "The Scientific Image of Music Theory." *Journal of Music Theory*, 33/1, 65–106.

Byros, V. 2009. *Foundations of Tonality as Situated Cognition, 1730–1830*. Dissertation, Yale University, New Haven, CT.

Byros, V. 2012. "Meyer's Anvil: Revisiting the Schema Concept." *Music Analysis*, 31/3, 273–346.

Cheng, W., and D. Fosler-Lussier (eds.). forthcoming. *A Cultural History of Western Music in the Modern Age*. New York: Bloomsbury Academic.

Chung, A. 2019. *Music as Performative Utterance: Towards a Unified Theory of Musical Meaning with Applications in 21st-Century Works and Social Life*. Dissertation, Yale University, New Haven, CT.

Cohen, J. E. 1962. "Information Theory and Music." *Behavioral Science*, 7/2, 137–163.

Cook, N. 1992. *Music, Imagination, and Culture*. New York: Oxford University Press.

Cook, N. 2001. "Theorizing Musical Meaning." *Music Theory Spectrum*, 23/2, 170–195.

Coutanche, M. N., and J.P. Paulus. 2018. "An Empirical Analysis of Popular Press Claims Regarding Linguistic Change in President Donald J. Trump." *Frontiers in Psychology*, 9, 2311. https://doi.org/10.3389/fpsyg.2018.02311

Creel, S. C., E. L. Newport, and R. N. Aslin. 2004. "Distant melodies: Statistical learning of nonadjacent dependencies in tone sequences." *Journal of Experimental Psychology: Learning, Memory, and Cognition*, 30, 1119–1130.

Dahlhaus, C. 1983. *Foundations of Music History*. Translated by J. B. Robinson. Cambridge: Cambridge University Press.

Dewey, John. 1884. "The New Psychology." *Andover Review*, 2, 278–289.

Gadamer, H. G. 1989. *Truth and Method*, (orig. *Wahrheit und Methode* 1960; Translated by Joel Weinsheimer and Donald G. Marshal). New York: Crossroads.

Gjerdingen, R. 2007. *Music in the Galant Style*. Oxford: Oxford University Press.

Gjerdingen, R. 2013. "'Historically Informed' Corpus Studies." *Music Perception*, 31/3, 192–204.

Gould, S. J. 1981. *The Mismeasure of Man*. New York: W.W. Norton.

Greenberg, C. 1939. "Avant-Guard and Kitsch." *Art and Culture: Critical Essays*. Boston: Beacon Press.

Hanslick, E. 1854. *Vom Musikalisch-Schönen*. Translated as *The Beautiful in Music* by Gustav Cohen, edited with an introduction by Morris Weitz. New York: The Liberal Arts Press, 1957.

Harrison, D. 2016. *Pieces of Tradition: An Analysis of Contemporary Tonality*. New York: Oxford University Press.

Hartley, A. H. and D. Poeppel. 2020. "Beyond the Stimulus: A Neurohumanities Approach to Language, Music, and Emotion." *Neuron*, 108, 597–599.

Hatten, R. 1994. *Musical Meaning in Beethoven: Markedness, Correlation, and Interpretation*. Bloomington: Indiana University Press.

Hepokoski, J. and W. Darcy. 2006. *Elements of Sonata Theory: Norms, Types, and Deformations in the Late-Eighteenth-Century Sonata*. New York: Oxford University Press.

Hippel, P. T. V., and D. Huron. 2000. "Why Do Skips Precede Reversals? The Effect of Tessitura on Melodic Structure." *Music Perception*, 18/1, 59–85.

Hirsch, E. D. 1967. *Validity in Interpretation*. New Haven: Yale University Press.

Huang, A., H. V. Koops, E. Newton-Rex, M. Dinculescu, and C. J. Cai. 2020. "AI Song Contest: Human-AI Co-Creation in Songwriting." *Proceedings of the 20th International Society for Music Information Retrieval Conference (ISMIR)*, virtual, Montreal, Canada.

Hubbard, R. 1990. *The Politics of Women's Biology*. New Brunswick: Rutgers University Press.

Huron, D. 1999. "The New Empiricism: Systematic Musicology in a Postmodern Age." *The 1999 Ernest Bloch Lectures: Lecture 3, Methodology*. http://csml.som.ohio-state.edu/Music220/Bloch.lectures/3.Methodology.html

Huron, D. 2006. *Sweet Anticipation: Music and the Psychology of Expectation*. Cambridge: The MIT Press.

Huron, D. 2013. "On the Virtuous and the Vexatious in an Age of Big Data." *Music Perception*, 31/1, 4–9.

Igarashi, Yohei. 2015. "Statistical Analysis at the Birth of Close Reading." *New Literary History*, 46, 486–504.

Iser, W. 2000. *The Range of Interpretation*. New York: Columbia University Press.

Jankélévitch, V. 1961. *La Musique et l'Ineffable*. Paris: Seuil. (tr. Into English by Carolyn Abbate, 2003. Princeton: Princeton University Press).

Jauss, H. R. 1982. *Toward an Aesthetic of Reception*. Translated by Timothy Bahti. Minneapolis: University of Minnesota Press.

Jeppesen, K. 1927. *The Style of Palestrina and the Dissonance*. New York: Dover.

Jockers, M. L. 2013. *Macroanalysis: Digital Methods and Literary History*. Champaign, IL: University of Illinois Press.

Kane, B. 2011. "Excavating Lewin's 'Phenomenology'." *Music Theory Spectrum*, 33/1, 27–36.

Kerman, J. 1980. "How We Got into Analysis, and How to Get out." *Critical Inquiry*, 7/2, 311–331.

Kerman, J. 1985. *Contemplating Music: Challenges to Musicology*. Cambridge: Harvard University Press.

46 Introduction and Methodology

Knopoff, L., and W. Hutchinson. 1981. "Information Theory for Musical Continua." *Journal of Music Theory*, 25/1, 17–44.

Knopoff, L., and W. Hutchinson. 1983. "Entropy as a Measure of Style: The Influence of Sample Length." *Journal of Music Theory*, 27/1, 75–97.

Kramer, Lawrence. 2011. *Interpreting Music*. Berkeley: University of California Press.

Krumhansl, C. 1990. *The Cognitive Foundations of Musical Pitch*. Oxford: Oxford University Press.

Le, X., I. Lancashire, G. Hirst, and R. Jokel. 2011. "Longitudinal Detection of Dementia through Lexical and Syntactic Changes in Writing: A Case Study of Three British Novelists." *Literary and Linguistic Computing*, 26/4, 435–461.

Lerdahl, F. 1992. "Cognitive Constraints on Compositional Systems." *Contemporary Music Review*, 6/2, 97–121.

Lewin, D. 1969. "Behind the Beyond: A Response to Edward T. Cone." *Perspectives of New Music*, 7, 59–69.

Lewin, D. 1986. "Music Theory, Phenomenology, and Modes of Perception." *Music Perception*, 3/4, 327–392.

Lewin, D. 1987. *Generalized Musical Intervals and Transformations*. New Haven: Yale University Press.

Liu, A. 2013. "The Meaning of the Digital Humanities." *PMLA*, 128/2, 415.

Liu, L. H. 2011. *The Freudian Robot: Digital Media and the Future of the Unconscious*. Chicago: University of Chicago Press.

London, J. 2013. "Building a Representative Corpus of Classical Music." *Music Perception*, 31/1, 68–90.

London, J. 2022. "A Bevy of Biases: How Music Theory's Methodological Problems Hinder Diversity, Equity, and Inclusion." *Music Theory Online*, 28/1: DOI: 10.30535/mto.28.1.4

Long, M. K. 2020. *Hearing Homophony: Tonal Expectation at the Turn of the Seventeenth Century*. New York: Oxford University Press.

Louie, P. 2012. "Learning and Liking of Melody and Harmony: Further Studies in Artificial Grammar Learning." *Topics in Cognitive Science*, 4, 1–14.

Louie, P. 2022. "New Music System Reveals Spectral Contribution to Statistical Learning." *Cognition*, 224, 105071.

Manaris, W., J. Romero, P. Machado, D. Krehbiel, T. Hirzel, W. Pharr, and R. Davis. 2005. "Zipf's Law, Music Classification, and Aesthetics." *Computer Music Journal*, 29/1, 55–69.

Margulis, E. H., and A. P. Beatty. 2008. "Musical Style, Psychoaesthetics, and Prospects for Entropy as an Analytic Tool." *Computer Music Journal*, 32/4, 64–78.

Maus, F. 1991. "Music as Narrative." *Indiana Theory Review*, 12, 1–34.

McCreless, P. 2000. "Music Theory and Historical Awareness." *Music Theory Online*, 6/3. www.mtosmt.org/issues/mto.00.6.3/mto.00.6.3.mccreless.html

McHose, A. I. 1947. *The Contrapuntal Harmonic Technique of the 18th Century*. New York: F.S. Crofts & Co.

Meyer, L. 1957. "Meaning in Music and Information Theory." *The Journal of Aesthetics and Art Criticism*, 15/4, 412–424.

Moretti, F. 2005. *Graphs, Maps, Trees: Abstract Models for a Literary History*. New York: Verso.

Popper, K. 1934. *Logik der Forschung. Zur Erkenntnistheorie der modernen Naturwissenschaft.* (Trans. into English as "The Logic of Scientific Discovery, 1959). Heidelberg: Mohr Siebeck.

Poudrier, È., and B. H. Repp. 2013. "Can Musicians Track Two Different Beats Simultaneously?" *Music Perception*, 30/4, 369–390.

Quinn, I., and P. Mavromatis. 2011. "Voice Leading and Harmonic Function in Two Chorale Corpora." *Mathematics and Computation in Music*. Carlos Agon, ed. Heidelberg: Springer, 230–240.

Rahn, J. 1980. "On Some Computational Models of Music Theory." *Computer Music Journal*, 4/2, 66–72.

Richards, I. A. 1929. *Practical Criticism: A Study of Literary Judgment*. New York: Harcourt, Brace & Co.

Rings, S. 2008. "*Mystères limpides*: Time and Transformation in Debussy's *Des pas sur la neige*." *19th-Century Music*, 32/2, 178–202.

Rings, S. 2011. *Tonality and Transformation*. New York: Oxford University Press.

Rothstein, W. N. 1995. "Analysis and the Act of Performance". *The Practice of Performance: Studies in Musical Interpretation*. John Rink, ed. Cambridge: Cambridge University Press.

Saffran, J. R., E. K. Johnson, R. N. Aslin, and E. L. Newport. 1999. "Statistical Learning of Tone Sequences by Human Infants and Adults." *Cognition*, 70, 27–52.

Saffran, J. R., M. M. Loman, and R. R. W. Robertson. 2000. "Infant Memory for Musical Experiences." *Cognition*, 77/1, 1–9.

Saslaw, J. 1996. "Forces, Containers, and Paths: The Role of Body-Derived Image Schemas in the Conceptualization of Music." *Journal of Music Theory*, 40/2, 217–243.

Schiebinger, L. 1993. *Nature's Body: Gender in the Making of Modern Science*. Boston: Beacon Press.

Shalizi, C. 2011. "Graphs, Trees, Materialism, Fishing." *Reading Graphs, Maps, Trees: Responses to Franco Moretti*. J. Goodwin and J. Holbo, eds. Anderson: Parlor Press.

Shannon, C. E. 1948. "A Mathematical Theory of Communication." *Bell System Technical Journal*, 27, 379–423 and 623–656.

Shannon, C. E., and Warren Weaver. 1949. *A Mathematical Model of Communication*. Urbana: University of Illinois Press.

Sinclair, J. 2004. *Trust the Text: Language, Corpus and Discourse*. London: Routledge.

Siromoney, G., and K. R. Rajagopalan. 1964. "Style as Information in Karnatic Music." *Journal of Music Theory*, 8/2, 267–272.

Temperley, D. 2007. *Music and Probability*. Cambridge: The MIT Press.

Tomlinson, G. 1992. "Musical Pasts and Postmodern Musicologies: A Response to Lawrence Kramer." *Current Musicology*, 53, 18–24.

Tymoczko, D. 2011. *A Geometry of Music: Harmony and Counterpoint in the Extended Common Practice*. New York: Oxford University Press.

White, C. W. forthcoming. "The Meaningful Corpus Model: Connecting Musical Corpora, Analysis, and Interpretation." *The Oxford Handbook of Musical Corpus Analysis*. Burgoyne, Quinn, and Shanahan, eds. New York: Oxford University Press.

White, C. W. 2021. "Some Aspects of Pedagogical Corpora." *Empirical Musicology Review*, 16/1. https://emusicology.org/article/view/7785/6281

White, C.W., and I. Quinn. 2016. "The Yale-Classical Archives Corpus." *Empirical Musicology Review*, 50–58.

White, C. W., and I. Quinn. 2018. "Chord Content and Harmonic Function in Tonal Music." *Music Theory Spectrum*, 314–350.

Zajonc, R. B. 1968. "Attitudinal Effects of Mere Exposure." *Journal of Personality and Social Psychology*, 9/2, 1–27.

Zanette, D. H. 2006. "Zipf's Law and the Creation of Musical Context." *Musicae Scientiae*, 10, 3–18.

Zbikowski, L. 2002. *Conceptualizing Music: Cognitive Structure, Theory, and Analysis*. New York: Oxford University Press.

APPENDIX TO CHAPTER 1

Probabilities Used in This Chapter

Equation A shows the notion of probability at its most basic. The probability of a specific event can be calculated by dividing the number of times that this specific event occurs by the number of times that all possible events occur. Consider a coin flip: the probability of heads is 0.5 because roughly half of all outcomes are heads. If you flipped a coin 2 million times, roughly 1 million would be heads; 1 million (the count of the specific event) divided by 2 million (the count of all events) is 0.5. The spreadsheets posted in this chapter's supplementary material demonstrate this basic calculation.

$$\text{Probability} = \frac{\text{Number of times a specific event occurs}}{\text{Number of times all types of events occur}}$$

EQUATION A1.1 Basic probability calculations

In the analyses of the Producer's melody within this chapter, I relied on n-gram conditional probabilities, the calculations for which are shown in Equation A1.2. These particular probabilities are calculated as the number of times some event occurs in some context divided by the number of times any event occurs in that context. This formula is operationalized by defining "context" as a certain number of previous events. Here, n refers to the length of the whole sequence under consideration. If you were interested in how often an event occurs given only the previous event (i.e., how often chord x follows chord y), n would equal 2, as the length of your whole sequence would be two. And $n = 4$ would indicate that the current event is conditioned on the three previous events

Introduction and Methodology **49**

(i.e., how chord d follows chords a, b, and, c). Recalling that probability calculations divide the count of some specific event by all possible events, to calculate an n-gram probability using a corpus, we divide the count that a specific event completes some sequence (or that a particular event appears in that context) by the number of times that any event appears in that context. As seen in Equation A1.2, this creates the probability of how often an event occurs given a series of previous events. In the Producer-versus-Emcee analysis, the probability of notes following each other note were calculated by converting a corpus of melodies to series of scale degrees, treating each pair of notes as a 2-gram, and using those 2-grams to represent the probability that each degree progresses to each other scale degree. The conditional probability of the 2-gram $<\hat{1}, \hat{2}>$ is the probability that $\hat{2}$ occurs given $\hat{1}$, and is calculated by dividing the count that the specific sequence $<\hat{1}-\hat{2}>$ occurs in a corpus divided by the count of all two-note sequences beginning with $\hat{1}$. The probabilities for each transition are shown in a table within this chapter's supplementary spreadsheet.

$$n\text{-gram probability} = \frac{\text{Number of times an event occurs in some context}}{\text{Number of times that context occurs}} = \frac{\text{Number of times that a sequence of length n occurs ending with event}}{\text{Number of times that series occurs ending with any event}} = \frac{\text{Number of times the events at time points } [a, a\text{-}1 \ldots a\text{-}n] \text{ occur}}{\text{Number of times the events at time points } [a\text{-}1 \ldots a\text{-}n] \text{ occur}} = \frac{\text{How often does this this event occur...}}{\text{given the events that came before it?}}$$

EQUATION A1.2 n-gram probability

Representing Chords

From a computational perspective, there are many ways you might ask a computer to represent "chords." Are you asking the computer to imagine chords as groups of pitches? As groups of pitch classes? As set classes? As ordered scale-degree sets? As unordered scale-degree sets?

I will explore many of these options throughout this book, but this chapter's computational analyses represent harmonic events as inversionally non-equivalent prime forms. This method distinguishes, for instance, between major chords and minor chords (represented as [047] and [037] sets, respectively) but conflates all transpositions of those structures. The probabilities for my German/not-German analysis are based on the probability that one of these chords appears in a piece during a particular year. This method simply counts how often each inversionally non-equivalent prime form was used in an individual year within the YCAC and divides each of these values by the total count of all chords that occur in each year. That is: the probability of a chord a in year z is the number of times chord a appears in compositions in year z (the specific case) divided by the number of all chords that appear in that year (the general case). The Schubert analysis, on the other hand, does rely on transitions between chords. Progressions between sets are represented by calculating the intervals separating the sets' members and tallying the frequencies with which these progressions

50 Introduction and Methodology

occur. This method creates two-chord progressions like: "a major triad followed by a dominant seventh chord, with the latter chord's root transposed +7 semitones (mod 12) from the root of the former." C-G^7 or F-C^7 would both be represented as this two-chord progression. For the sake of computational ease, and following Quinn and Mavromatis (2011), I remove all events that occur fewer than four times in these distributions.

Entropy

Entropy averages how well an observed series predicts itself and, in so doing, represents the complexity of that series. As shown in Equation A1.3, entropy relies on a probabilistic model derived from the observations themselves. The probability of some observation $P(o)$ is reckoned by how often that particular o appears in the series of observations, O. In other words, by using expectations based on the same series it is assessing, entropy captures how much O surprises itself. More random sequences will be less self-predictable, will have higher entropies, and can be considered more complex. More ordered and predictable sequences will have lower entropies and can be considered less complex.

This process effectively averages a series of probabilities: the equation combines the probabilities of a sequence ($P(o_1, o_2 \ldots on)$) and then divides by the number of probabilities contained in the sequence being assessed ($1/n$). However, the equation features a logarithm and a negative sign as well. Each of my entropy calculations uses a *binary logarithm*. A binary logarithm ($\log_2 n$) is the power to which the number 2 must be raised to obtain the value n. Raising a number to an exponent denotes how often you multiply that value together; $2^2 = 4$ because $(2 \times 2) = 4$. Raising a number to a negative exponent indicates a reciprocal value, or the result of the positive version of the exponent becoming a fraction over 1. 2^{-2} is the reciprocal of 2^2, or $(1/2^2)$. If 2^2 is 4, then 2^{-2} is $1/4$, or 0.25. Because of this reciprocal relationship, binary logarithms of fractions will always be negative numbers.

The use of a binary logarithm within this calculation has a practical foundation in computation and telephonics, as it has the potential to quantify exactly how much storage or memory is needed to represent some event or system. The resulting value of a binary logarithm captures the number of binary choices that can represent a given probability distribution. In other words, using a binary logarithm for entropy answers the question: "How many zeros and ones do we need to encode this signal?" which, in turn, corresponds to the amount of storage needed in a computer's binary memory. A coin flip, for instance, represents a single binary choice – there are two outcomes (heads or tails), each having an equal probability of 0.5. The value of ($\log_2(.5)$) is -1; that is, $2^{-1} = 0.5$. The negative sign of the equation then converts this result to a positive number, showing that one binary choice can represent the two outcomes of a coin flip. Two coin flips – two binary choices – produce four possible outcomes, each with a probability of 0.25 (heads/heads, heads/tails, tails/heads, tails/tails). The (positive) value of ($\log_2(.25)$) is 2, the number of bits one would need to encode two binary choices. The former is a less complex system and therefore needs fewer bits to be represented or stored in memory; the latter is more complex and requires more space. Invoking this sense of entropy, I will use base-2 logarithms throughout this book. (It should also be acknowledged that – on a practical and heuristic level – a logarithm scales tiny numbers into more usable values!)

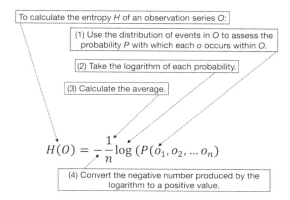

EQUATION A1.3 Entropy

Other Equation Formats for Entropy

When comparing my approach to other corpus analyses that use entropy, it should be noted that entropy is often represented using an alternate equation format. These different versions will generally look something like Equation A1.4.

$$H(O) = -\sum_{x \in X} p(o_x) \log(p(o_x))$$

EQUATION A1.4 The entropy equation, reformatted

Again, the average log probabilities are rendered by calculating how often each event occurs using the probability distribution of the sequence itself. And as before, this value is converted to a logarithm. However, instead of assessing the probabilities of each individual o within a sequence of observations, the equations are assessing all instances of each event type o_x within the universe of all event types. Let's say, for instance, that a hypothetical corpus shows a major chord resolving 20% of the time to major triad a whole step higher (as in a IV-V progression). Taking the logarithm of the probability would calculate the base 2 logarithm of 0.2. However, in this approach, the log probability is

52 Introduction and Methodology

not assessing a particular instance of this chord progression within the sequence but is rather assessing the probability of *all* instances of that chord progression. Because this value represents many individual instances, this format weights that logarithm by how often those instances occur, or the probability of the event type $p(o_x)$. In our hypothetical example, let's imagine that 1% of all two-chord progressions in this corpus are two major triads separated by an ascending whole step: we would therefore multiply the logarithm of 0.2 by 0.01. This weighting takes the place of the averaging that occurs within the earlier entropy formulas. The weighted log probabilities are summed together for the final entropy/cross-entropy value. These different formats produce the same results, and are useful in different contexts. For instance, while I find the first representation to be more intuitive, some calculations in the online spreadsheet use the latter process, as it is better suited to situations in which one only has access to the probabilities of a system rather than the original series of observations.

Regression and Statistical Significance

This chapter's comparison between German and non-German entropies relies on a linear regression analysis. These kinds of analyses test the relationship between two variables: by "linear" we mean that when one variable changes, the other changes at some constant multiplicative rate – these two values increase or decrease in tandem. In order to quantify this correspondence, we can treat the two variables as points on two axes – what we conventionally call x and y – and we plot these points on horizontal and vertical axes, respectively. In Figure 1.8, for instance, the horizontal x axis plots dates of composition, and the vertical y axis plots the entropy. Each two-dimensional coordinate $[x, y]$ then represents these two pieces of data within the plot. If a later date (the x value) means an increased entropy (the y value), then plotting many $[x, y]$ coordinates should create an upward trend.

Linear regression fits a single line to this data, predicting the rate by which the two values move in tandem. The process (the engineering of which one can find in any standard statistics textbook or relevant Wikipedia entry) finds the line that explains the most variance of the trend – that is, it maximizes how close the points are to the line and minimizes the deviance. The line will be captured by the equation $y = mx + b$, where b is the value of y when x is zero (for instance, what the expected entropy would be at the beginning of the chronological epoch being considered) and m is the *slope*, or the factor by which y and x change together (for instance, if every year the entropy increased by 1 unit, m would be 1). In Figure 1.8, the "slope" is the value of m associated with the regression line.

Linear regression also produces a *correlation* value r between -1 and 1 that quantifies how similar the trends of two data series are to one another, with 1

Introduction and Methodology **53**

indicating that they track each other perfectly, -1 indicating a perfectly opposite relationship (when one dimension increases by some amount, the other always decreases by the same amount), and zero resulting from a random relationship.

Squaring this value produces r^2, which represents how much variance is captured by the regression line. Higher r^2 values mean that the points are closer to the line, while lower values indicate more random and variable data. While connected, correlation and linear regression are not identical: correlation is agnostic as to which series of values constitute x and y, while the trend line will be different depending on which values occupy those roles. (See the spreadsheet for this chapter for an example of linear regression with r values that can be manipulated and studied further.) What I show as "fit" in Figure 1.8 is the r^2 associated with the correlation.

Additionally, I noted that the differences in the reported regression lines in Figure 1.8a and 1.8b were *significantly different*, a concept important in statistical analysis and corpus analysis. Again, the underlying mathematics can be found in any statistics textbook (or online resource), but in short: the analysis uses the number of data points (i.e., the population size) and the variation around each of the lines in order to determine whether there is truly a difference between the two slopes. These tests ensure that the reported results are consistent enough and use a sufficient number of datapoints to be reliable and believable. If the test determines that there is less than a 5% chance that the difference between the two lines arises by pure chance (rather than as a result of an actual difference between the two trends) then the two trends are "significantly different" with a probability of less than 5%, reported as $p < 0.05$. In the German/not-German comparison, the differences were significant, $p < 0.05$. I add a bit more discussion of statistical significance in the appendix to Chapter 2.

Importantly, these two values have notable relationships within corpus analysis. While many empirical and behavioral studies use these approaches to test the relationships between tens or hundreds of datapoints, corpus analyses often operate in the realm of tens or hundreds of thousands (if not more!) datapoints. These larger sample sizes can, in a sense, overwhelm the statistical test, with miniscule trends rising to the level of significance due to an incredibly large dataset – if statistical significance relies on a balance of sample size and variability to establish whether two values are believably different, a huge sample size can exert so much pressure into the process that small differences with a lot of variation can achieve significance. For this reason, the size of the effect is an important facet to corpus studies. That is, the difference between two slopes (m) and the goodness of fit (r^2) within a regression are as important to a corpus analysis as the significance of those regressions. To this end, this book will emphasize trends and effects as much as the significance of these trends. (See Huron, 2013, for a further discussion of this issue.)

2

WHAT IS STYLE?

An Essay

Working my way through a Johann Sebastian Bach organ prelude, I came across a progression that I had played probably a thousand times before but that, in the moment, struck me as unusual: at the point of an expected (minor-mode) cadence, Bach inserted a minor dominant in place of a major V chord and used that chord to evade the cadence. This moment drew my attention because that very week, I had warned a class of part-writing students away from the minor dominant, with the explanation that dominant triads and sevenths always include the raised leading tone, regardless of mode. I texted a friend of mine who specializes in Baroque keyboard music and asked about the minor dominant: does this chord happen with some degree of frequency in that repertoire? His intuition was that yes, this chord tended to happen more in that repertoire than other repertoires, especially more than in 18th- and early 19th-century classical music – the repertoire from which we tend to derive the edicts of our theory classrooms.

Figure 2.1 shows the relative frequency of the minor v chord in minor-mode music in quarter-century segments of the Yale-Classical Archives Corpus. In other words, the figure tracks all major and minor triads rooted on $\hat{5}$, and shows the proportion of those triads that are minor.[1] While more dominant triads are major in every historical epoch, a greater share of dominant triads are minor in the bookending chronological eras, with a precipitous drop in the 18th and early 19th centuries. The lowest nadirs appear in the 1750–1824 range, a range that roughly corresponds to Viennese Classicism. According to this modeling, my friend's intuition was correct: v occurs proportionally less in so-called classical composition than in other historical repertoires, including the Baroque.

DOI: 10.4324/9781003285663-2

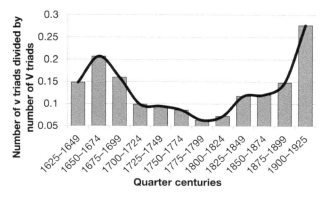

FIGURE 2.1 Ratio of major and minor dominant triads in quarter-century periods in the YCAC

These are the sorts of corpus-derived observations that will serve as the basis for this chapter's investigation of *style*. This chapter will describe ways to represent similarities and differences between the types of musical materials used within groups of pieces. Relying on observations like those of Figure 2.1, I will suggest ways that these quantitative similarities might be related to broader historical or social forces and will use these insights to interrogate the definition of "style" itself.

Musical style is, however, a malleable and slippery concept. Most simply, "style" might be defined historically, with music being composed at the same time and place operating within the same style. Music written, for instance, in the court of Louis XVI could be considered to be in the same style because the music shares a historical context. It follows that similarities between pieces written in the same context are a symptom of their historical proximity. Such culturally situated approaches to musical style often find their home in musicological studies that foreground historical narratives, a viewpoint native to historical overviews and textbook formats (e.g., Burkholder et al., 2018; Taruskin, 2005). Relatedly, a style can be imagined as a manifestation of social identities, such as race, class, and gender. Richard Middleton (1990), for instance, argues that genres of popular music are best understood as expressing the identities of the consumers who listen to and purchase some array of music. Similarly, Rachel Lumsden (2020) describes the role of gender in musical style by inspecting the kinds of music-theory and compositional pedagogies specifically geared toward 19th-century Western European bourgeois women. While historical contexts and cultural pressures obviously inform and constrain the kind of musical choices a composer makes, many data-driven approaches to style primarily rely on pieces' musical characteristics at the expense of extramusical information. Such perspectives base a style's identity solely on the shared characteristics of a group of pieces. This approach has been adopted by many cognitively oriented music researchers who view these common characteristics as crucial to establishing shared norms and expectations between composers and listeners (c.f. Byros, 2012; Crerar, 1985; Meyer, 1957). This stance is similarly useful for computational music-production and music-recommendation software: generating something in the "style" of some composer, for instance, can be computationally undertaken by replicating the overall practice of that composer (Cambouropoulos, 2001; Conklin, 2010; Cope, 1987; Huang et al., 2020; Miller, 2020; Yust, 2019). Following the same logic, interfaces like Spotify and Pandora identify a listener's preferred "style" of music by extracting recurrent musical characteristics from the tracks that a enjoys. Of course, these categories are by no means mutually exclusive: Komaniecki (2021), Walsch (2021), and Shea (2022) show, for instance, that certain styles of rap are defined by a confluence of the music's characteristics, the performers' and producers' identities, and the identities of the music's consumers and fans.

The notion of *genre* also heavily intersects and overlaps with style. Genre, however, is less concerned with the broad norms that inform a composer's compositional choices and more with the expectations associated with a very specific type or category of music. As Carl Dahlhaus writes, "an example of a genre . . . [is] formed not so much an isolated, closed whole, an individuality enduring in itself, as, rather, it exemplifie[s] a type" (1982, 15). A Viennese waltz has certain generic expectations that contrast with a Sarabande or with a march or even with a folk waltz or power ballad – these are differences of genre. Generic expectations are clearly a mixture of cultural exposure and explicit learning (the result of taking a class in ballroom dancing that covers the Viennese waltz, for instance), and as such, the discourse surrounding the notion of genre is often focused on its cultural situation and the economic and racial associations that accompany such situations (Drott, 2013; McLeod, 2001). However, there exist stable musical characteristics native to different genres (Tlacael et al., 2015; Johnson, 2018), and these characteristics are evoked in listeners – in the words of Jeffry Kallberg (1988), genre is a "contract" that develops between composers and listeners in which "the composer agrees to use some of the conventions, patterns, and gestures of a genre, and the listener consents to interpret some aspects of the piece in a way conditioned by this genre" (243). As a confluence of social pressures that circumscribe a set of concrete musical tropes, tropes that both produce a group of pieces with similar musical characteristics and also inform a listener's expectations, genre functions in much the same way as does style but with somewhat different purviews – types of pieces rather than chronological and geographic eras of music production. From this vantage point, most of this chapter's conclusions will be applicable to the notion of genre, although more work would need to be done to describe these applications.

This chapter will present a series of computational analyses that illustrate various ways to group pieces within a corpus by their internal as well as extramusical similarities. These analyses will concentrate on the surface harmonies and textures within music written in Western Europe between 1650 and 1900, using the Yale-Classical Archives Corpus. I experiment with various ways to group pieces by date (an extramusical characteristic) as well as by their internal musical characteristics. I introduce metrics to assess how similar (or how different) pieces within groupings are, along with how distinct (or overlapping) these groups are when compared to one another. I use these metrics to investigate the properties of the various groupings I create, and I link my observations to notions of social, historical, and geographic proximity. I also show how this approach can be used to identify attributes of pieces with unknown origins and to identify spurious and fraudulent pieces in a corpus. After these computational analyses, I circle back to the very notion of style itself and show ways that a computational and corpus-based approach can aid in negotiating this thorny and multifaceted concept.

But before I undertake these analyses, I detail the corpus I will rely upon throughout this chapter: the Yale-Classical Archives Corpus. This detailing will not only provide an understanding of the data being used in my stylistic analyses but will also provide some insights into the kinds of choices made within computational studies of musical texts in general.

The Corpus and the Representations

This chapter will primarily rely on the Yale-Classical Archives Corpus, a corpus I designed in collaboration with Ian Quinn (White and Quinn, 2016). This corpus collects MIDI files from classicalarchives.com (a website of user-sourced MIDI files), each associated with metadata that specifies the file's opening key, meter, composer, date of composition, instrumentation, composer's nationality, genre, and so on. The corpus has also been tonally analyzed using an automated key-finding algorithm, indicating the likely key and mode for each passage in the corpus.[2] In total, the corpus contains 13,769 MIDI files by 571 composers. (The hosting website, ycac.yale.edu, contains detailed information about the corpus's constituent composers, styles, dates, etc.; for a summary of issues and challenges within this corpus, see de Clercq, 2016.[3])

The YCAC divides each MIDI file into *salami slices* (Quinn, 2010); the corpus as a whole contains more than 14 million of these slices. As shown in the top-left pane of Figure 2.2, this approach divides a musical surface into each moment where the pitch content changes. The resulting slices include both new note attacks and pitches held over from previous attacks. These slices are then represented in the corpus in a number of ways, again shown in Figure 2.2. First, the slices are represented as pitch sets, showing both the pitch height and doublings of each slice. In the figure's example, the first simultaneity sounds the pitches

58 What Is Style?

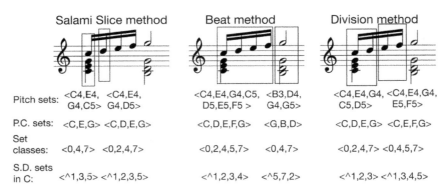

FIGURE 2.2 The three methods for grouping YCAC surface events

<C4, E4, G4, C5>; then, while the lower three pitches are sustained, the top voice releases C5 and strikes D5, creating a new salami slice. Second, these lists are reduced to pitch-class sets with doublings removed. In the figure, the two consecutive salami slices comprise the p.c. sets <C, E, G> and <C, D, E, G>. Next, the transpositionally equivalent (but not inversionally equivalent) set classes are shown. The C major triad of Figure 2.2 becomes set class [0,4,7], and the latter p.c. set translates into s.c. [0,2,4,7]. (NB: while a major triad would be s.c. [0,4,7], a minor triad would be the set [0, 3, 7] in this representation. Additionally, note that I will generally be using square brackets for transpositionally equivalent sets, and triangular brackets for transpositionally inequivalent sets, like groups of pitch classes or scale degrees.) Finally, the local key area is used to convert the pitch-classes into scale degrees. Figure 2.2 shows the corresponding scale-degree sets in the key of C, with the pitch-class set <C, E, G> becoming scale-degree set <$\hat{1}$, $\hat{3}$, $\hat{5}$>. (In what follows, I will use Roman numerals when scale-degree sets correspond to a recognizable triad or seventh chord.)

Within this corpus's 571 composers, a small handful account for a disproportionally large part of the corpus – Johann S. Bach, Ludwig Beethoven, Johannes Brahms, William Byrd, Frederick Chopin, Claude Debussy, George Handel, Joseph Haydn, Franz Liszt, Felix Mendelssohn, Wolfgang Mozart, Camille Saint-Saens, Domenico Scarlatti, Franz Schubert, Robert Schumann, Peter Tchaikovsky, Georg Telemann, Antonio Vivaldi, and Richard Wagner. While they represent only 3% of the overall pool of composers, their pieces constitute 37% of the corpus's files and 54% of the corpus's slices. (These personalities will become important as I design tests to identify differences and similarities between composers.)

For the ensuing stylistic analyses, I assembled the corpus's salami slices into two groupings using the YCAC's metric data. This data is derived from the source files' MIDI time signature information, which specifies the signature's numerator and denominator. As shown in the middle pane of Figure 2.2, the "beat" method bundles together the pitch contents within the denominator's durations, essentially collecting the contents of each beat into one envelope. The "division" method – the rightward pane of Figure 2.2 – analogously gathers the contents of durations that are half the denominator's value. In this chapter's analyses, I pool the data from all three methods when collecting information about a style's practice.

There are three issues to keep in mind about this approach. First, there will certainly be some redundancy between the salami slice, beat, and division methods. For instance, consecutive salami slices will sometimes also constitute consecutive beats. In this case, that progression will be counted twice, both by the salami slice method and by the beat method. However, this redundancy is a feature and not a bug. If progressions are favored in a compositional style such that they appear at multiple durational levels, this approach will magnify those kinds of progressions. Second, MIDI time-signature data in the YCAC is error prone (or, in terms of the previous chapter, its encoding includes quite a bit of *noise*). MIDI files contain two important metric defaults: without explicit intervention, the time signature defaults to 4/4, and the first event – again by default – falls on the first downbeat. A file's creator must intentionally change these defaults – adding rests to the beginning of the file if the first event is an upbeat or manually changing the time signature metadata if the piece is not in 4/4 – and in some cases, these changes are neglected.[4] Even in these cases, the beat and division methods still capture *something* about broader durations, even if these durations do not align with the piece's meter.

Third, and perhaps most importantly: we should not think of this data as analogous to a harmonic or chordal analysis but rather as a representation of what types of events occur on the musical surface. Indeed, surface-oriented events capture as much about the music's texture as about its harmony. While many of the simultaneities that result from my methods will be familiar chords (like diatonic triads and sevenths), many common sets will be the result of figuration. For instance, one of the most common salami slices in this corpus is the scale-degree set $<\hat{1}, \hat{2}, \hat{3}, \hat{5}>$, or a I^9 chord. This "chord's" frequency evidences the textural nature of the salami slice method: every turn of a trill over a I triad and every melodic passing tone between $\hat{1}$ and ^3 that expands a sustained tonic chord would produce this scale-degree set. Looking at the sets within this corpus, it will be important to remember that they are based on these sorts of surface textures and ornaments and are not meant to approximate harmonic syntax. (My next chapter takes up the question of "what is a harmony?")

To capture how these surface events connect with one another, my analyses will organize these slices and metric groupings as three-chord progressions, or *3-grams*.[5] While in Chapter 1, I used *n*-grams to determine the probability of chords following other chords, here I am using these *n*-grams to track how often the entire progression of *n* chords occurs. The relative frequency with which these 3-grams occur in each sub-corpus (or a division of a larger corpus) will provide the basis for comparisons between potential "styles" within the YCAC.

60 What Is Style?

Chord Progressions and Chronology

Intuitively, it seems that composers who lived during similar time periods should favor similar chord progressions – or at least engage in more similarities than do composers who lived in vastly different time periods. To quantify this, I tracked progressions of scale-degree sets for each composer in the YCAC. Table 2.1 shows the top 10 scale-degree 3-grams (again, progressions of three chords) in the music of three composers from very different time periods: Byrd, Handel, and Brahms. (The table translates scale-degree sets into their corresponding Roman numerals when possible, such that the set $<\hat{5}, \hat{7}, \hat{2}>$ is represented as a V triad.) The most frequent 3-gram in the Handel and Brahms sub-corpora is I-V-I, while Byrd's most frequent 3-gram is I-I⁹-I, a passing supertonic tone connecting two tonic triads. Notably, this contrapuntal event occurs in Handel and Brahms's distribution as well, but less frequently; similarly, the Handel/Brahms top-rated I-V-I 3-gram occurs in Byrd's corpus but with less relative frequency. Furthermore, notice that the I-I⁹-I progression's decline manifests relatively linearly: while it is the most frequent 3-gram in Byrd's distribution, the progression is Handel's second-most-frequent 3-gram and Brahms's fourth-highest ranked.

It seems possible, then, that chronological distance might predict the amount of difference in the 3-gram distribution of different composers. Figure 2.3 tests this intuition by comparing Beethoven's 3-gram usage with that of other composers in the YCAC. This analysis isolates the 25 most frequent 3-grams in the YCAC and tallies how often each composer uses those 3-grams.[6] I then convert each value to a percentage and measure the difference between these strings of percentages: those composers who use the same 3-grams about as often as Beethoven will be less different than those who have completely different 3-gram usages. To quantify these differences, I treat the series of percentages as points – as coordinates – between which I can measure distances: the greater the difference

TABLE 2.1 The most frequent 3-grams in the Byrd, Handel, and Brahms sub-corpora

Byrd		Handel		Brahms	
I-I⁹-I	1099	I-V-I	552	I-V-I	727
I-<$\hat{1},\hat{4},\hat{5}$>-I	760	I-I⁹-I	481	V-I-V	634
I-I^add4-I	759	V-I-V	466	I-V⁷-I	474
I-<$\hat{1},\hat{2},\hat{5}$>-I	734	I-I^{9/add4}-I	292	I-I⁹-I	452
<$\hat{1},\hat{4},\hat{5}$>-I-<$\hat{1},\hat{2},\hat{5}$>	458	I-I^add4-I	266	V⁷-I-V⁷	425
<$\hat{1},\hat{2},\hat{5}$>-I-<$\hat{1},\hat{4},\hat{5}$>	433	I-V⁷-I	252	I⁹-I-I⁹	241
I⁹-I-I^add4	429	I-vii°-I	211	I-<$\hat{2},\hat{4},\hat{5}$>-I	228
I-V-I	409	I-IV-I	210	I-IV-I	222
I⁹-I-I⁹	347	I⁹-I-I⁹	194	I-IV⁹-I	208
V-I-V	308	V⁷-I-V⁷	192	<$\hat{2},\hat{4},\hat{5}$>-I-<$\hat{2},\hat{4},\hat{5}$>	167
3-gram	*Freq.*				

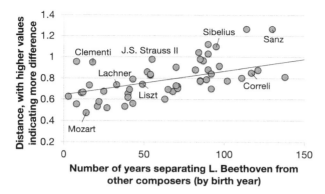

FIGURE 2.3 Plotting the "distance" between Beethoven's 3-gram practice and other composers by chronological difference

between composers' 3-gram usages, the greater the distance. (The appendix entry on clustering further describes this distance calculation.) The figure plots these distances on the vertical axis. To approximate chronological distance, I calculate the years separating Beethoven's birthdate from each other composers' birthdate and show that difference on the horizontal axis. To orient these relationships, Figure 2.3 labels a selection of points with the composers that they represent.

Figure 2.3 shows that greater chronological distances usually mean greater distance (i.e., a greater difference in 3-gram usage). This tendency is reinforced by the figure's trend line. (I discuss these regression lines in Chapter 1's appendix.)[7] This finding is not atypical: repeating this method across all the composers represented here returns comparable results.[8]

These findings support the intuition that greater chronological distance means greater difference in how composers deploy chord progressions. However, there exists reasonable amounts of variation around the trend – composers' points do not strictly hew to the trend line. The sub-corpus of Johann Strauss II, for instance, contains 3-grams that are more different from Beethoven's than one would expect given the 55 years separating their births: Strauss's point sits above the trend line, meaning there is a greater distance than that predicted by the trend. Conversely, Mozart's has more similar 3-gram usage (i.e., his distance is lower) than his 14 years of chronological difference would predict. In other words, while composers who are closer in time have similar surface 3-grams, chronology does not perfectly explain every relationship. The next section, then, investigates ways we might group data other than simple chronology.

Clustering Composers

A *cluster analysis* expands upon the distance metrics used in Figure 2.3, now interrelating many composers at once. Imagine two groups of hypothetical composers. One group uses the dominant seventh chord (V^7) quite a bit, and the other almost never uses that chord. We could think of each composer existing as points or coordinates on a continuum, with one pole representing a practice that uses many V^7 chords and the other pole representing the exclusion of that chord. We would be measuring the distance between these hypothetical composers using one *dimension*: the distance between composers relies on the number/frequency associated with a single variable. We could then add dimensions by adding variables. We could, for instance, count how often each composer uses the mediant (iii) triad; we could use these counts to add a second dimension that represents how often each composer uses that harmony. Composers would then cluster together within this two-dimensional space if they used these two parameters similarly.

We can apply the same logic to our 3-gram distributions. If we measured how often the YCAC's 50 most-frequent 3-grams appeared in each composer's sub-corpus, we would be treating each 3-gram as an individual dimension. A composer's 3-gram frequency can be treated as a coordinate in a 50-dimensional space, and we can then measure distances between each composer within this space.

This principle underpins cluster analysis.[9] Figure 2.4 shows a hierarchical cluster analysis, using the 19 composers with the largest sub-corpora to create a tree diagram that groups together composers with similar 3-gram usage and separates composers with divergent practices.[10] The diagram shows various

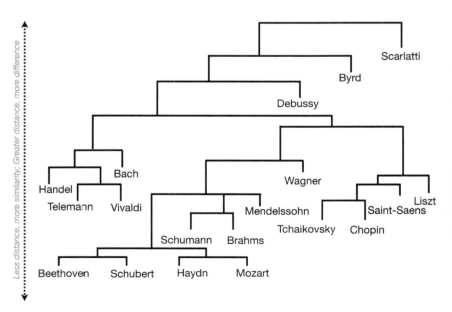

FIGURE 2.4 A hierarchical clustering of composers' 3-gram frequencies

What Is Style?   **63**

hierarchical levels of similarities, translating the distances between each composer's datapoint in 50-dimensional space to a 2-dimensional representation of those relationships. Here, the vertical axis (the height) shows how different the composers' 3-gram usages are, with greater vertical distance indicating greater distance in the space. (The horizontal dimension in these representations is arbitrary: we can imagine such a diagram acting like a hanging mobile in a child's room, with, for instance, the Teleman and Vivaldi nodes being rotatable, with neither being necessarily closer to the Handel node than the other.)

Figure 2.4's clustering mostly conforms to our earlier chronological models, but adds some further intuitive gradations of nuance. Note that, for instance, composers of the First Viennese School occupy the same cluster, as do the colleagues Brahms and Schumann. Looking at the underlying dataset (either at *ycac.yale.edu* or in the material excerpted in the online supplement), the musical factors contributing to the clustering are multifaceted, but one hallmark of the clustering has to do with the composers' use of chordal sevenths and how relatively often they employ consistent non-triadic figurations. For instance, the Bach/Handel/Telemann/Vivaldi cluster uses I-V-I and V-I-V more frequently than I-I^7-I and V^7-I-V^7, while this situation is reversed in the First Viennese cluster. Additionally, in Brahms's and Schumann's sub-corpora, 3-grams representing dissonant figurations (for instance, I-I^{add9}-I or I-$I^{add\ 4}$-I) are more frequent than they are in the First Viennese cluster. Within the Chopin/Tchaikovsky/ Saint-Saens/Liszt cluster, these figurations rise even more in prevalence, becoming these composers' most frequent 3-grams.

The clustering shows Byrd, Debussy, and Scarlatti as outliers. Byrd's most frequent 3-grams are contrapuntal, the most frequent of those being 3-grams that prolong a tonic triad using passing or neighboring tones. Debussy's chordal 3-grams seem to represent a different practice altogether, while Scarlatti's frequent progressions are more dyadic than other corpora due to the prevailing two-voice texture of his keyboard sonatas.

While hierarchical clustering can show nested levels of similarity, other approaches to cluster analysis can quantify the optimal number of groupings for a set of data points. *k-means clustering* cordons a set of points into k number of groups and then returns a measurement of the tightness and distinctness of those k groups. Values of k that organize some dataset into tidy and well-defined groups are then considered the best ways of grouping those points, while values of k with messy, overlapping, and diffuse groupings are considered poor solutions. An analyst can then apply k-means clustering for every possible number of clusters and then observe how tightly or loosely each number of clusters organizes a set of data points. With these assessments in hand, an analyst can argue that a group of points is best divided into, say, three clusters as opposed to two or four. (I've added further explanations of these techniques in this chapter's mathematical appendix, and the online supplement contains the data and sample code underpinning this analysis.)

64 What Is Style?

TABLE 2.2 The groupings resulting from a k-means cluster analysis on composers' 3-gram frequencies

	k- *means Clusters*	
	k = 7	k = 10
Clusters	Bach	Bach
	Byrd	Byrd
	Beethoven, Mozart, Haydn, Schumann, Mendelssohn, Brahms, Schubert, Wagner	Beethoven, Mozart, Haydn, Mendelssohn, Schubert,
	Tchaikovsky, Liszt, Chopin, Saint-Saens	Tchaikovsky, Liszt, Chopin, Saint-Saens
	Telemann, Vivaldi, Handel	Telemann, Vivaldi
	Debussy	Debussy
	Scarlatti	Scarlatti
		Wagner
		Brahms, Schumann
		Handel

I applied k-means clustering to our 50-dimensional space for values of k between 2 and 19. (k = 2 would be the smallest possible number of clusters, as it divides the data points into two groups, while k = 19 would sequester each of the 19 data points into their own clusters.) Table 2.2 shows the two optimal groupings returned by the k-means clustering method: 7 clusters and 10 clusters. Again, the groups conform to many intuitions about chronology and stylistic similarity. What we might call the "Romantic school" clusters together (see the fourth row of the table) as do a group of German speaking composers (see row three). Notably, Schuman, Brahms, Handel, and Wagner cluster with other composers when k = 7 but break off to form their own cluster with the higher value of k, indicating that their 3-gram usages are certainly similar to those of the other composers with whom they are grouped but are relatively more distinct than other composers. Byrd, Debussy, and Scarlatti are once again the outliers.

In sum, this method groups composers' sub-corpora according to their chord-progression practices and results in clusters that seem to align with historical and chronological similarities. Notably, this method does *not* take extramusical factors (like date, country of origin, etc.) into consideration when forming the clusters. There is more to say about how this clustering approach interacts with notions of style, and I will indeed return to these topics at the end of this chapter. But first, the next section uses extramusical classifiers to group these sub-corpora in various ways and tests the performance of these groups. In other words, while this section groups music by its internal musical properties, the next section groups musical data by musicological factors and tests how well those groupings account for the music's internal properties.

"Style" as Unique and Coherent Groupings

When we say that a piece of music participates in a particular compositional style, we are generally imagining that it not only shares similar traits with other music in that style but also that the piece is somehow different from music *not* in that style. This section presents the concepts of *coherence* and *uniqueness*, measurements I developed in White (2017) to model these two connected and complementary factors. Coherence asks how similar the constituent pieces within a group are to one another, while uniqueness asks how distinct those pieces are from other pieces outside that group. With these yardsticks in hand, I can compare different ways to classify pieces, quantifying the coherence and uniqueness of those different groupings.

Figure 2.5 illustrates the concepts of coherence and uniqueness using hypothetical toy sub-corpora, each of which is made up of pieces that use three "chords," shown with three bracketed letters. *Uniqueness* is a property of a sub-corpus if its constituent pieces have internal characteristics that are different from every other sub-corpus. In Figure 2.5's top row, Sub-Corpus A is unique because its pieces feature chords *x*, *y*, and *z*, while no other sub-corpus's pieces feature those chords. In the second row, however, Sub-Corpus A is now not unique, as each other sub-corpus also contains pieces that feature its same chords.

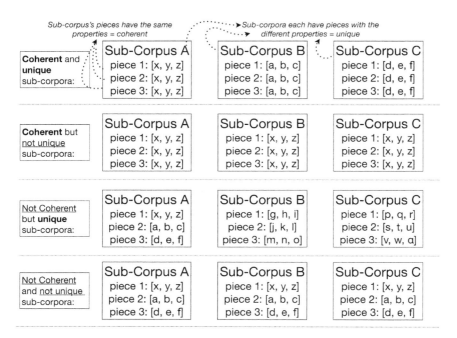

FIGURE 2.5 An illustration of coherence and uniqueness

66 What Is Style?

Coherence, on the other hand, captures how similar pieces within a sub-corpus are to one another. In the first two rows, Sub-Corpus A is coherent, because all of its constituent pieces use the same chords, x, y, and z. In the final two rows, however, Sub-Corpus A is not coherent: each constituent piece uses different chords from one another. These attributes can be combined in various ways. While row 1 illustrates sub-corpora that are both coherent and unique, row 3's sub-corpora are unique from one another (that is: the pieces of each sub-corpus feature different arrays of chords) but, the sub-corpora are not coherent (that is: each sub-corpus's individual pieces use different chords). Row 4's sub-corpora are not unique because each sub-corpus contains the same array of chords (x, y, z, a, b, c, d, e, and f); and, because each piece within each sub-corpus also differs from each other piece within the same sub-corpus, this arrangement is also not coherent.

From the standpoint of stylistic analysis, the concepts of coherence and uniqueness can describe the properties of groups of pieces – potential "styles" – in relation to one another. Given that distinguishability and consistency are crucial to certain definitions of style, an analyst can wield these ideas to describe how distinct or similar, overlapping or independent groups of pieces are from one another; the concepts of coherence and uniqueness can tether these observations to the internal characteristics of the group and demonstrate how those characteristics relate to other musical groupings.

However, from the standpoint of corpus analysis, these concepts can be operationalized to quantify the characteristics of – and relationships between – sub-corpora. To quantify how similar or different pieces and sub-corpora are from one another, I use a technique called *cross entropy*.[11] Recall from Chapter 1 that entropy converts a series of probabilities derived from some dataset into a single value that measures the amount of disorder present in that dataset. I described that value as capturing the complexity of these probabilities: it is easier to predict a series with fewer, very probable (less complex) outcomes than one with many equally likely (more complex) outcomes. That is, a high entropy value means that a dataset is more chaotic, that it contains more equally likely outcomes, and that it is harder for its own events to be predicted given the probabilities that describe that dataset.

Cross entropy, on the other hand, measures how easily some *other* model predicts the events of some dataset. Again, the measurement converts a series of probabilistic assessments into one single value, but now the probabilistic expectations are drawn from a different dataset than the events whose probabilities are being assessed. If entropy describes a dataset's complexity by measuring how easily that dataset predicts its own events, cross entropy describes how easily the probabilities drawn from one dataset predict the events of another dataset. A higher cross-entropy value, then, means that the events of one dataset are predicted poorly by the expectations/probabilities derived from some other dataset. In other words, the events being predicted do not align with the dataset used for the predictions. Conversely, a low cross entropy means that there is much alignment between the events being predicted and the dataset used for the predictions. Because cross entropy involves two separate components – the events being assessed and the dataset from which probabilities are being derived – we can say that we are assessing the probability of some series *given* some dataset or probabilistic model. The specific mathematics for cross entropy are outlined in this chapter's appendix, but in sum: a low cross entropy will result when the assessed series is very similar to the given probabilities, and a high cross entropy will result from comparisons between dissimilar datasets.

Finally, to create a series of probabilities, I use the frequencies with which each 3-gram occurs. Recall that in Chapter 1, I described probabilities as being the count of a specific event divided by the count of all events. To calculate the probability that a 3-gram occurs in some sub-corpus, one simply divides the count that some specific 3-gram occurs in a sub-corpus by the total count of all 3-grams in that sub-corpus. (The probability of <I-V-I> in Sub-Corpus A, for instance, is the number of times that I-V-I appears in Sub-Corpus A divided by the number of all 3-grams in Sub-Corpus A.) Cross entropy, then, uses the 3-gram probabilities derived from one sub-corpus to assess the 3-grams of some other sub-corpus. If, for instance, Sub-Corpus A was being used to predict the 3-grams in, say, Sub-Corpus B, then the probability of each 3-gram in Sub-Corpus B is calculated using the counts of all the 3-grams in Sub-Corpus A. This process results in a series of probabilities that represent how often each 3-gram occurs within Sub-Corpus B's piece given the expectations of Sub-Corpus A. Just as entropy captures the relative complexity of a series of probabilities by converting them into a single value, cross entropy will convert this series of probabilities into a single value to capture how well Sub-Corpus A predicts Sub-Corpus B's 3-grams.

Figure 2.6 shows how I operationalize the concepts of coherence and uniqueness using cross entropy and 3-gram probabilities to compare pieces of different sub-corpora (i.e., inter-sub-corpus comparisons) and pieces within the same corpus (i.e., intra-sub-corpus comparisons). First, I measure uniqueness with inter-sub-corpus comparisons. The 3-grams of each piece within a sub-corpus are assessed given the 3-gram probabilities of some other sub-corpus.[12] For example, in Figure 2.6's representation, probabilities of events in Sub-Corpus A are derived from Sub-Corpus B: 3-grams that happen often in Sub-Corpus B will be considered probable, and events that happen infrequently will be improbable. These probabilities are used to assess – or predict – the 3-grams in Sub-Corpus A's piece 1, then piece 2, piece 3, and so on until all *n* pieces in the sub-corpus are assessed. Each of these predictions returns a single cross-entropy value. The average of these cross entropies describes the overall uniqueness of Sub-Corpus A compared to Sub-Corpus B. This process is repeated, as Sub-Corpus C predicts all of Sub-Corpus A's pieces, then Sub-Corpus D, and so on, each producing an averaged cross entropy. Each of these values, then, tells you how different – i.e., how unique – Sub-Corpus A is from each of these other sub-corpora.

68 What Is Style?

FIGURE 2.6 An outline of coherence and uniqueness, as assessed by inter- and intra-sub-corpus cross entropies

To assess coherence — again as shown in Figure 2.6 — I compare pieces within a single sub-corpus. This intra-sub-corpus analysis isolates each individual piece within a sub-corpus and measures how well that sub-corpus predicts its own piece's own events. This assessment is done by calculating the cross entropy of each piece within a sub-corpus given the events of the sub-corpus's remaining pieces — again, 3-grams that appear frequently in the remaining pieces will be probable, and infrequent 3-grams will be improbable.[13] This process produces a cross-entropy value for each piece within the sub-corpus, and these values are then averaged.[14] This resulting value shows how similar each of the pieces within a sub-corpus are to one another, thus capturing the sub-corpus's coherence.[15] If the pieces within a sub-corpus all have the same sorts of events, then the sub-corpus will predict its own pieces well, and it will be coherent.

In order to more rigorously compare the coherence and uniqueness values, I additionally calculate a confidence interval around each average. These intervals capture a margin of error around these averages, a margin based on the variation in the values that contribute to that average (i.e., are most of the values quite close to average, or does the average simply represent the midpoint of wildly divergent values?) and the number of pieces used (i.e., do very few or very many pieces contribute to that average?). We can say some average cross entropy is "significantly" lower than some other cross entropy if the first value is not only less than the second value, but the confidence intervals (i.e., the margins of error) surrounding those two averages do not overlap. (Again, this chapter's appendix shows the mathematics behind these intervals.)

These average cross entropies can help quantify the coherence and uniqueness of groups of pieces. We can then call a sub-corpus coherent and unique if it predicts its own pieces better than any other sub-corpus does — if its average intra-sub-corpus cross entropy is significantly lower than any of the averaged inter-sub-corpus cross entropies. Conversely, we can call a sub-corpus incoherent and not unique if every other sub-corpus predicts its pieces as well or better than it does itself — if its average intra-sub-corpus cross entropy is the same or higher than the inter-sub-corpus cross entropies.[16]

However, we might imagine that situations often fall into some gradation between these two extremes. To quantify the spectrum, I use what I will call the coherence/uniqueness rate, calculated as the number of inter-sub-corpus cross entropies that are either significantly lower or within the margin of error of a corpus's intra-corpus cross entropy. If, for instance, we were analyzing 11 sub-corpora, and one of those sub-corpora predicted its own pieces better than did 8 of the other sub-corpora (i.e., that sub-corpus had a lower intra-corpus average cross entropy than 8 inter-corpus average cross entropies) but two sub-corpora predicted its pieces comparably (i.e., 2 inter-corpus average cross entropies were within the margin of error surrounding the intra-corpus average), then the coherence/uniqueness rate for that sub-corpus would be 80%: of 10 inter-corpus assessments, 8 were significantly higher than that sub-corpus's

70 What Is Style?

intra-corpus average cross entropy. This value can then capture how coherent and unique each sub-corpus is within the larger array of sub-corpora.

In sum: if a sub-corpus's pieces use surface harmonies and textures similar to most other pieces in that sub-corpus, then each piece's 3-grams will be successfully predicted by the other pieces in that sub-corpus; the intra-sub-corpus cross entropy will be low, indicating coherence. If a sub-corpus's pieces are very different from pieces in other sub-corpora, then each piece will not be successfully predicted by the other sub-corpora; the inter-sub-corpus cross entropy will be high, indicating uniqueness. The coherence/uniqueness rate is then a single value that represents these relationships by showing how many other sub-corpora predict a particular sub-corpus worse than that sub-corpus predicts its own pieces.

With this method in hand, we can now observe the uniqueness and coherence of different potential groupings of the YCAC. I first group pieces using only the composers' identities themselves, after which I group them based on the music's date of composition. Finally, I use the k-means clusters produced earlier in this chapter to create sub-corpora. Experimenting with these different groupings will postulate different basic parameters by which one might group pieces into a "style" using combinations of musical and extramusical characteristics. Throughout, the coherence/uniqueness rate will describe the similarity of pieces within that grouping and illustrate how distinct groupings are from one another.

Dividing by Composer

Dividing the corpus by composer (as before, I use the 19 composers with the largest sub-corpora) returned an overall coherence/uniqueness rate of 74%. Only two composers – Byrd and Handel – registered perfect (100%) individual coherence/uniqueness rates: these trials produced significantly lower cross entropies when comparing these composers' own pieces to their own sub-corpora than when comparing them to any other composer's sub-corpus. Figure 2.7 shows Handel's sub-corpus compared to those of each other composer. The average cross entropy of the composer's pieces when compared to the other composers' sub-corpora (the inter-sub-corpus values) are shown by solid bars, and the self-wise comparison (the intra-sub-corpus value) is shown by the white bar. Note that Figure 2.7a's white bar (and its margin of error) is lower than other bars (and their margins of error). Handel's own pieces are predicted significantly better when they are judged by his own corpus than when they are judged by other corpora: the sub-corpus appears to be coherent and unique.

However, more than a quarter of the time, this process judged other corpora to predict a composer's pieces with either a lower or roughly the same level of cross entropy when compared to the composer's own intra-sub-corpus assessments. Mendelssohn's corpus, for instance, is shown in Figure 2.7b with its 78%

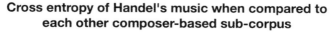
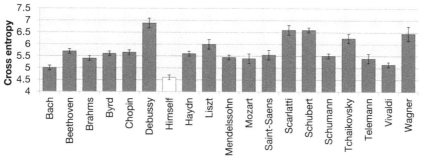
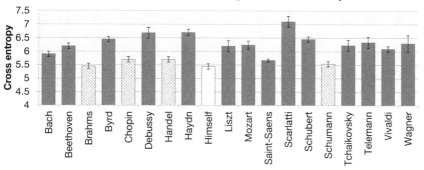

FIGURE 2.7 (a, top) Comparative cross entropies using Handel's sub-corpus and (b, bottom) using Mendelssohn's sub-corpus

coherence/uniqueness rate. The figure shows the four non-unique comparisons as striped bars. The cross entropies of the Brahms, Chopin, Handel, and Schubert sub-corpora were not significantly different from the cross entropy resulting from Mendelssohn's self-comparison – note that their error bars overlap with Mendelssohn's own margin of error and are therefore not statistically distinguishable from the composer's intra-sub-corpus average cross entropy. On the whole, it seems that these results suggest that grouping corpora by composer often creates coherent and unique assessments, although these models are not sufficiently distinguishable from one another around a quarter of the time.

Dividing by Chronological Epochs

To investigate another potential method of compiling sub-corpora, pieces were divided into sub-corpora based on their date of composition, first into 50-year epochs and then into 30-year epochs. The 50-year approach performed worse

72 What Is Style?

than when using composer-defined trials, returning a 68% overall coherence/uniqueness rate. One time period, 1751–1800, did not have a single coherent/unique comparison. Figure 2.8a shows the offending epoch's results. Again, the composer's intra-sub-corpus cross entropy is shown as a white bar; but now, since all inter-sub-corpus cross entropies are either comparatively lower or overlap with the target corpus's margin of error, all other bars are striped. Not only can the late-18th-century sub-corpus not be significantly distinguished from the late-17th-century corpus, but the other three corpora produce *lower* cross entropies, indicating that these corpora predict the 3-grams within the late-18th-century corpus *better* than the 1751–1800 corpus predicts its own pieces. This sub-corpus is therefore not coherent/unique.

Figure 2.8b shows the case of the 1801–1850 corpus, a relatively successful example. This era demonstrates a trend within these data: most of the non-unique comparisons involved time periods adjacent to one another. In fact, if we do not include the late-18th-century results (the particularly unsuccessful epoch of Figure 2.8a), *all* incoherent/non-unique comparisons involve neighboring epochs. Reflecting the connection between chronology and stylistic similarities we have noted throughout this chapter, sub-corpora that predict one another's pieces relatively well tend to be chronologically adjacent within the larger corpus.

Dividing the corpora into 30-year segments produced similar results. The overall coherence/uniqueness rate was 69%. Half of the non-unique comparisons involved adjacent time periods, and 80% were within two time periods (i.e., within 60 years). As with the 50-year segments, the remaining 20% were not evenly distributed throughout the results but rather appeared within two particularly incoherent/non-unique epochs: the 1801–1830 and 1891–1920 divisions. Figure 2.9a shows a typical example, the 1741–1770 corpus, while Figure 2.9b shows the largely incoherent/non-unique 1801–1830 results. Note that the two sub-corpora adjacent to the 1801–1830 sub-corpus (i.e., the 1771–1800

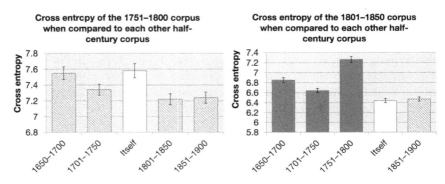

FIGURE 2.8 Comparative cross entropies of (a, left) the 1751–1800 sub-corpus and (b, right) the 1801–1850 sub-corpus

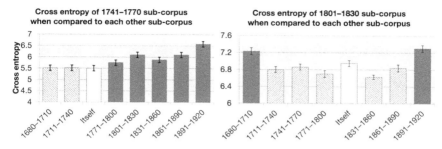

FIGURE 2.9 Comparative cross entropies of (a, left) the 1741–1770 sub-corpus and (b, right) the 1801–1830 sub-corpus

and 1831–1860 sub-corpora) register significantly lower cross entropies, indicating that the sub-corpus seems to be quite incoherent – it is *worse* at predicting its own pieces than the surrounding periods!

These results suggest that dividing a corpus by chronological epochs may be successful in some respects, but it also generates several sub-corpora that are not coherent/unique – they do not predict their own pieces particularly well, and other sub-corpora predict their pieces comparably to (or better than) their own sub-corpora.

This incoherence/non-uniqueness could be explained by the presence of multiple or overlapping 3-gram practices within a single sub-corpus. Consider again the 1751–1800 sub-corpus, the epoch in Figure 2.8a whose constituent pieces are better predicted by the statistics of neighboring time periods than the pieces in its own time period. Looking inside that dataset, one finds groups of composers who would seem to be drawn from divergent compositional practices. It is a time period that saw not only the late works of Telemann and Scarlatti but also the complete works of Mozart and Haydn and ended with the early works of Beethoven. Given that these composers had such different practices that they occupied different groups in the clustering solutions outlined above, it is no surprise that this sub-corpus would be so incoherent/non-unique. This incoherence/non-uniqueness suggests that this time period hosts more styles and stylistic shifts than its surrounding eras, at least as represented within the YCAC. If dividing corpora by composers seemed to create too many divisions, dividing by chronology seems to be too broad, creating incoherent and non-unique sub-corpora with multiple musical practices contained in a single grouping.

Clustered Sub-Corpora

Using the *k*-means clusters derived earlier in this chapter produced markedly more unique and coherent results. The seven clusters provide nearly perfect coherence/uniqueness rates, with only Debussy's sub-corpus providing

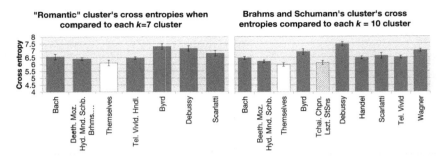

FIGURE 2.10 Comparative cross entropies of (a, left) the "Romantic" Tchaikovsky, Chopin, Liszt, and Saint-Saens sub-corpus and (b, right) the Brahms and Schumann sub-corpus

insignificant/non-unique comparisons. Figure 2.10a shows a typical seven-cluster result, using the Tchaikovsky/Chopin/Liszt/Saint-Saens cluster's sub-corpus (i.e., using Table 2.2's fourth row; for simplicity, I call this the "Romantic" sub-corpus in the Figure.). The 10 clusters performed slightly worse, with an 88% coherence/uniqueness rate. Figure 2.10b shows one of the non-unique comparisons, involving the Brahms/Schumann cluster's comparison to that of Tchaikovsky/Chopin/Liszt/Saint-Saens.[17]

Compared to composer-only and chronologically based sub-corpora, using groupings of composers derived by k-means clustering produces the most coherent and unique divisions of the broader corpus. While there is a certain tautology present in these observations – grouping pieces by their 3-gram usage unsurprisingly creates groups with similar 3-gram usages – I want to point out three observations that arise from this result. First, the success of this approach demonstrates that using internal musical properties *can* group composers together into categories that have similar characteristics while also being distinct from other categories. Earlier, I theorized that stylistic categories based on internal musical characteristics should be both coherent and unique, and these results show something of a proof of concept for this approach to grouping: this method is indeed capable of grouping a corpus into coherent and unique sub-corpora. Second, the relative success of this method shows that chronological distance and even composer identity may be insufficient to create optimal groupings on their own – some composers write similarly to one another, and some time periods host multiple musical practices. Third and relatedly: these tautological categories are not devoid of sociocultural information but rather beg for extramusical interpretation. These groupings do not show that information like date and identity are insufficient to categorize styles but rather that they are insufficient *on their own*. Instead, our larger groupings of coherent and unique music invite explanations involving complex swirls of interrelated factors. The Johannes Brahms and Robert Schumann pairing, for instance, invites a story not only of geography and chronology but of the mentoring and friendship between these two men; the Vivaldi and Telemann cluster suggests an explanation involving not only dates and places but – potentially – of shared influences and the instruments and textures they used in their compositions. In other words, while this computational approach may place music in unique and coherent categories without regard for extramusical associations, these groupings invite explanations for why such a consistent and distinct musical practice would arise.

An Intervening Summary

Before proceeding, it is worth taking stock of this chapter's observations and theorizations thus far. I began by noting that there are several competing, complementary, and overlapping components of musical definitions of "style," including those reliant on internal musical characteristics and on sociocultural information. My subsequent computational investigations have ricocheted between these two approaches, treating surface 3-grams as a proxy for the former and chronology as a synecdoche for the latter. We found that chronology does appear to indicate internal similarities – not only did we see that similarities between composers' use of 3-grams positively correlate to their birthdates, but we also saw that chronologically adjacent sub-corpora often predicted the 3-grams within other sub-corpora's constituent pieces comparable to how well sub-corpora predicted their own pieces.

To investigate groupings with internal similarities, I presented and formalized two theoretical constructs: uniqueness and coherence. If a "style" is meant to be a distinct musical practice, then the pieces in that group should share the same musical characteristics (i.e., the group should be coherent), and that practice should distinguish that group from other musical practices (i.e., the group should be unique). I used measurements of cross entropy to quantify how well pieces in some grouping conformed to that grouping's 3-gram practices and found that the most unique and coherent categories grouped pieces and sub-corpora by their musical similarities. That is, grouping pieces by their internal characteristics produced categories that were more coherent and unique than did chronological groupings and even more than did the sub-corpora of the composers themselves. I then suggested that while these groupings may eschew extramusical information in their creation, they invite extramusical descriptions that explain the forces that might account for such unique and coherent musical practices.

In what follows, I make some larger connections between these observations and broader notions of musical style, arguing that grouping music by its corpus-derived similarities and differences offers certain insights into what it means to be a "style." But first, I engage in a brief aside, analyzing two examples of stylistic emulation to show how my models of musical style engage with authorship, imitation, and forgery.

76 What Is Style?

Stylistic Emulation

As described previously, coherence/uniqueness rates can illustrate how similar and different the pieces within a sub-corpus are from those in other sub-corpora. It stands to reason, then, that we could modify the process to quantify how similar any group of pieces is to each of these sub-corpora. I could, for instance, submit a musical forgery or stylistic reproduction to these measurements in order to discuss the quality of its emulation. These kinds of questions ultimately address an interesting facet of larger definitions of musical style, as musical mimicries like these specifically attempt to produce a piece with internal characteristics that evoke some social, chronological, geographic, or authorial context: these pieces are supposed to "sound like" they were written by particular composers at certain times and places. That is, stylistic emulations and forgeries are examples of pieces explicitly trying to participate in a style while being disconnected or removed from that style's social, historical, or authorial context. Studying these pieces will also demonstrate some provocative ways that computational measurements can act as a springboard for broader interpretive analyses of these pieces and their styles.

This section uses the concepts of coherence and uniqueness to investigate two examples of stylistic mimicry. To do this, I reengineer the approaches of the previous section to now ask, "Into which sub-corpus does this piece best fit"? In other words, I will use cross entropy to see which style a set of pieces best emulates.[18]

Case 1: A Reconstruction of Early Beethoven Sketches

In 2012, the Dutch musicologist Cees Nieuwenhuizen collected a series of "Fantasy Sonata" sketches produced by a 22-year-old Ludwig Beethoven three years before his first published sonata, Op. 2. Nieuwenhuizen used these sketches to create a performable multimovement work. The musicologist imported the more fully completed sections wholesale and filled in the more skeletal sketches with material inspired by Beethoven's early-period sonata forms.[19] The result is a three-movement sonata that incorporates all the material from the sketches, stitched together and elaborated by material emulating Beethoven's early style.

Figure 2.11 shows the average cross entropy of the reconstructed "Beethoven" sonata's 3-grams when compared to each composer's sub-corpus. Here, I modify the process used earlier in order to test which sub-corpora predict this reconstruction *better than average*. The grey bar at the far right of the example will now indicate this average prediction by representing the mean of all assessments by each sub-corpus with the vertical line capping the column indicating the margin of error around that average. The striped bars now show assessments that are significantly worse than average or are within the margin of error. The white bars, then, represent those models that are more likely than average to

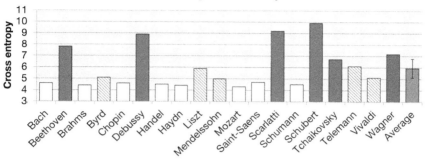

FIGURE 2.11 Average cross entropy of the reconstructed sonata when compared to each composer's corpus

have produced this piece's chord progressions (Bach, Brahms, Chopin, Handel, Haydn, Mozart, Saint-Saens, and Schumann). Note that there are now no error bars in this figure: because there's only one piece being assessed, these bars represent a single cross-entropy value: the reconstruction as judged by each sub-corpus. Because there is only one value being calculated (rather than the average of multiple pieces' cross entropy as used earlier), there is no variation with which to create a margin of error.

The Mozart and Haydn sub-corpora produce the lowest cross entropies. Based on the model, therefore, this piece's 3-gram practice most closely resembles Mozart's and Haydn's sub-corpora. However, the model also judges the piece to be very unlike Beethoven's corpus. This result potentially conforms to our notions that Beethoven's very early style (which this piece emulates) was much like his that of predecessors and that Beethoven's aggregate compositional career represents a departure from this very earlier practice.[20] Additionally, these findings might also suggest that Nieuwenhuizen calibrated his reproduction to be "too conservative," evoking earlier Viennese styles instead of that of Beethoven!

We might also use the tools at our disposal to situate this reproduction within chronological epochs and within our *k*-means clusters. Figure 2.12 shows comparisons between the reproduction and the 30-year divisions of the YCAC. The earliest and latest corpora predict this piece significantly worse than average, and the four corpora stretching between 1741–1800 and 1831–1890 predict it significantly better than average. The remaining two are not significantly distinguishable from the average. 1741–1770 produces the lowest result. (Recall that the 1801–1830 corpus was judged to be incoherent and not unique by the previous experiment, so its poor results are not surprising.) These results suggest that the events of this reconstruction are not predicted particularly well by any one chronological epoch but rather match with the 3-gram practice of several

78 What Is Style?

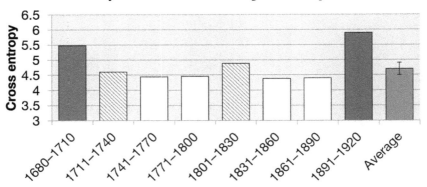

FIGURE 2.12 Average cross entropy of the reconstructed sonata when compared to each chronological corpus

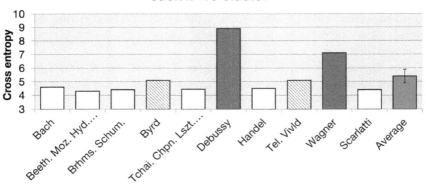

FIGURE 2.13 Average cross entropy of the reconstructed sonata when compared to each of the 10-cluster corpora

epochs between 1741 and 1890. Figure 2.13 undertakes the same test again, now using the 10-cluster corpora (a solution that produced the coherent and unique groupings in the models). The process shows several clusters predicting the sonata's 3-grams better than average, but the Beethoven/Mozart/Haydn/Mendelssohn corpus registers the lowest results. Here, the model indicates that the sonata's surface events are similar to many sub-corpora (perhaps indicating that Nieuwenhuizen deployed relatively generic harmonic and textural choices), yet it is most aligned with the cluster that includes the musicologist's intended stylistic target: Beethoven.

Case 2: The Vivaldi Imposter

Paris: 1737. Over the last 30 years, the city had been in a love affair with Italian music, particularly that of Antonio Vivaldi. But it had been almost a decade since Vivaldi's Opus 12 had appeared in 1729, and when his Opus 13 appeared courtesy of the neophyte-publishing house of Jean-Noël Marchand, the music flew off the shelves. The only problem was that Vivaldi never wrote an Opus 13 and apparently did not even care for the musette, the double-reed French bagpipe which the solo concertos prominently featured. Twelve years later, the French court system would find that Nicolas Chédeville, musette virtuoso, had produced the imitations and reaped their profits.

Figure 2.14a shows Chédeville's Vivaldi imitations and their cross entropies compared to the 7-cluster corpora, and Figure 2.14b then shows the same test using the 10-cluster corpora.[21] In the former, the Handel/Telemann/Vivaldi sub-corpus returns a cross entropy significantly lower than average, and many other sub-corpora fall within the margin of error of the average assessment (as before, these are shown as lined bars). In the latter figure, two sub-corpora perform better than average: the Handel and Telemann-Vivaldi clusters. These results seem to indicate that these forgeries' 3-grams do indeed adequately imitate Vivaldi but do so in a way that they could potentially also be passed off as being written by Handel!

These relative cross entropies seem to be basically successful at placing these pieces into the emulated style's sub-corpus: the method places the Beethoven sketch reconstruction solidly within the German Viennese tradition and the Vivaldi forgeries within the High Baroque. Importantly, this method does not provide anything like a perfect methodology for authorship forensics. That is, while it does show how similar sets of surface chord progressions are to one another, it does not say for certain who specifically wrote those chord progressions. On the one hand, datasets like the Chédeville reconstruction or a single sonata are dwarfed by the size of a composer's entire output, let alone the constituency of a cluster of composers. Similarly, we are only observing these pieces' surface 3-grams – a true forensic approach would surely involve many other parameters, including harmonic melodic, textural, and instrumental information.

But even more fundamentally, much of the work of this chapter has pointed to coherent and unique musical styles transcending authorship and chronology, something that makes "stylistic emulation" all the more slippery. This section demonstrates that identifying a piece's "style" appears to work best when placing it within a constellation of other pieces' practices rather than trying to align it squarely within some year or within the output of a single composer. Indeed, throughout this chapter, my models work best when using groups of composers rather than using individual composers or time periods.

80 What Is Style?

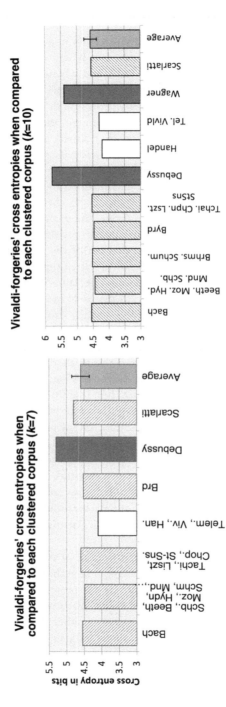

FIGURE 2.14 (a, left) Chédeville's imitations of Vivaldi compared to the 7-cluster sub-corpora and (b, right) his imitations of Vivaldi compared to the 10-cluster sub-corpora

Moving from the computational to the theoretical, I now turn to larger issues of musical style. I will consider how my focus on internally consistent groupings might interact with the notion of "style," and I will reexamine the relationships between the corpus statistics used in my analyses and sociocultural aspects of musical style.

A Corpus-Based Definition of "Style"

And so: what is *style*? In the previous analysis, I showed ways we can group pieces and composers by their similar practices. Earlier, I suggested that we might usefully apply the constructs of coherence and uniqueness to discuss how similar pieces within a group are to one another and how distinct that group is from other groups. I framed these characteristics as potentially crucial for a musically oriented definition of style: after all, if a style is to represent some kind of recognizable practice that is distinguishable from other practices, it should have internal coherence and be unique from other styles. However, I then applied these concepts with a continuous gradient by using the coherence/uniqueness ratio: sub-corpora were situated on a continuum between complete coherence/uniqueness and total incoherence/non-uniqueness. This ratio allowed me to show which corpora seemed to be relatively incoherent (perhaps containing multiple divergent practices, for instance) as well as which sub-corpora seemed to be similar to one another. When these ratios were not 100% – and even when they were low – they still described *something* about the musical groupings being assessed. For instance, in Figure 2.10b, Brahms and Schumann's sub-corpus is unique in all but its comparison to the Tchaikovsky–Liszt–Saint-Saens–Chopin sub-corpus. Even though the comparison shows an aspect of non-uniqueness, it still yields information about these two clusters, potentially pointing to the music of Brahms and Schumann influencing the practice of these later Romantic composers. Analogously, we also noticed that epoch-based sub-corpora were often similar to (i.e., not unique when compared to) chronologically adjacent sub-corpora. Here, the non-unique comparisons can potentially be explained by the chronological developments of historical styles, with sub-corpora that are historically close sharing statistical tendencies.

I would therefore posit a corpus-based definition of style: *a style is a way of grouping pieces that expresses specific relationships between pieces within that group and with pieces not in that group.*

Again, this is not to say that this is the only definition of this concept. As discussed earlier, the concept of "style" is notoriously multifaceted and invokes overlapping aspects of history, identity, social forces, and musical characteristics. However, I would argue that such a framing affords four primary benefits to stylistic analysis: (1) it clarifies the scope of, boundaries of, and assumptions behind some style, (2) it decenters individual creativity in favor of larger creative trends, (3) it encourages connections between corpus data and sociocultural

82 What Is Style?

interpretation, and (4) it links the social and the cognitive aspects of the concept of style. To conclude this chapter, I will discuss, in turn, each of these potential benefits of my corpus-based definition of style.

The Scope and Boundaries of a Style

Colloquially as well as academically, the notion of "style" can be used to refer to various gradations of musical practice, from the very specific to the very broad. A style can be associated with a composer's own identity ("Alma Mahler's style") to a composer's specific period of composition ("Ludwig Beethoven's early style") to a chronological period ("the classical style") to a geographic distinction ("the French style") to a social role ("the popular style").[22]

A corpus-based definition of style removes such ambiguities by operationalizing the act of grouping: it computationally defines a style along particular lines. In such an approach, a piece is either in a specific group or it is not, and that group has observable and reproducible within-group characteristics and intergroup relationships. Furthermore, these methods can also show nested groupings, illustrating smaller practices that group together into larger practices (as was the case in my cluster analyses).

But more fundamentally, a corpus-based approach also adds a flexibility and nimbleness to the concept of style. While such methods create well-defined groups, they do so using relationships to other groups and to the larger corpus under consideration: the size and boundaries of a style rely on the presence of contrasting styles. If a style's constituent pieces are ideally more similar to one another than they are to pieces in other styles, this requires the presence of other styles with which to contrast those pieces. It follows, then, that the same set of pieces might be grouped differently when using different corpora with different constituencies. To use an example from the 20th and 21st centuries: when considering a corpus of only heavy metal music, the music of the band Black Sabbath would likely have internally consistent characteristics that make it markedly different from the music of other bands. Black Sabbath's sub-corpus would have a style that is coherent and unique relative to other heavy metal. But taking a larger corpus – say, all guitar-based music from the 20th century – potentially reframes stylistic boundaries. Now, Black Sabbath's music might best be grouped with other heavy-metal music. Perspectives of different scopes, as well as different-sized corpora, will potentially lead to different relationships between stylistic groupings. "Beethoven's early style" might be a coherent and unique sub-corpus when considered relative to a corpus of Beethoven's overall output, whereas that small distinction might not hold in a larger corpus of 18th- and 19th-century Western European art music.

By tethering ideas of style to corpus properties, we therefore gain both precision and a certain relativism. On the one hand, a "style" becomes defined by explicitly operationalized parameters with clear assumptions and observable groupings and relationships. On the other hand, styles become fluid constructs that shape themselves to the context of the particular corpus being studied.

Emergent Creativity

A corpus-centric reorientation of style also entails a shift in the way we think about musical creativity. At least insofar as creativity can be equated with producing innovative and unique musical materials, the personalities sometimes touted as "creative geniuses" – the Beethovens, Chopins, and Wagners in our historical narratives – may be better understood as points within constellations of creative actors rather than lodestars of innovation. In this thinking, while Ludwig Beethoven himself may have been an innovative and creative composer, the properties of his individual sub-corpus are not what produce a coherent and unique musical style; rather, the amalgamated choices and innovations of a group of composers are what produce that style. While this concept is not new to music historians (see, for instance, Tomlinson, 2015), these analyses computationally support the idea that the most distinct and coherent streams of creativity arise as emergent phenomena within groups of chronologically and geographically proximate composers.[23]

Style and the Meaningful Corpus Model: Interpretation, Constituency, and Learning

While corpus-based methods encourage a quantitative approach to stylistic groupings and even refocus traditional ideas of musical creativity, this approach is less a redefinition than a reorientation – it is a complement to other approaches to style. From any perspective, musical style invokes notions of similarity, whether one is approaching the question statistically, socioculturally, or just intuitively. When foregrounding social forces in stylistic analysis, researchers investigate the kinds of musical similarities that arise from historical affinities. A corpus-based definition flips this dynamic, with an analyst first pinpointing musical similarities and then investigating the kinds of extramusical forces that might account for those observations.

In fact, this two-step process seems fundamental to a corpus-based approach. As I noted, there is a potential problem embedded within a purely data-centric definition of style: using coherence and uniqueness to both group and evaluate a style is tautological. Rather, these groups need some sort of external validation or interpretation to be imbued with some kind of meaning. Throughout this chapter, I have commented upon the intuitiveness of certain groupings or explained some result by referencing related historical information. This impulse toward explanation results from the fact that corpus data *mean nothing in and of themselves*; rather, they gain meaning by being related to extramusical – social, cultural, bibliographic, expressive, etc. – concepts, ideas, and interpretations.[24]

84 What Is Style?

This dynamic shows Chapter 1's Meaningful Corpus Model once again at work. Recall that the MCM outlines that corpus analyses, especially within music-theory studies, generally: (1) select a corpus (the rightward pane), (2) analyze and model that corpus in some way (the middle pane), and then (3) connect that analysis to interpretations or non-musical concepts (leftward pane). Validating or describing the kinds of relationships produced by my various groupings of sub-corpora using historical, biographical, or social information exemplifies the connection between the middle and leftward panes. My corpus-based definition of musical style produces data-driven groupings and relationships using statistical and computational methods, but – again – those analyses (of the middle pane) must be connected to the extramusical ideas (of the leftward pane) to be meaningful. For instance, the similarities and differences observed between Nieuwenhuizen's sonata reconstruction and other corpora have little use as simply cross-entropy values, but they garner meaning when those cross entropies are related to Nieuwenhuizen's goal of mimicking Beethoven's early compositional practice and to the dates and identities associated with the sub-corpora being compared to the reconstruction. The statistics mean very little without such historical and social interpretation.

It is also worth noting that a corpus-based approach to style highlights other components of the MCM as well. As outlined, this approach requires specific musical characteristics to be defined and specific analytical choices to be made when describing a style: these choices are the domain of the MCM's middle pane. In this chapter's analyses, a piece's musical characteristics were captured using surface 3-grams drawn from the salami slice, beat, and division methods. For instance, we could have tracked the usage of some specific chords (like, say, the minor v chord, as done in my opening vignette), melodic characteristics, instrumentation, pitch range, etc.; using any of these parameters would have altered the analytical apparatus (the middle pane) and potentially led to different results. In other words, a corpus-based approach requires a style to be analyzed (i.e., the MCM's middle pane) using specific, precise, and explicitly operationalized terms, and these particular choices lead to the analyses' outcomes.[25]

Similarly, I noted earlier that changing a corpus's constituency could result in different coherence/uniqueness relationships: if you change the corpus, you change the resulting groupings and relationships. These aspects of a stylistic analysis are the domain of the MCM's rightward pane. Again, a corpus-based definition of style encourages these components to be operationalized and made explicit, down to the very basic question of what dataset – what corpus – is being used to generate stylistic groupings and comparisons.

Finally, the MCM also offers a connection between style and musical learning – namely that aspects of listening, learning, and composition can potentially be located within corpus statistics. To echo Robert Hatten's (2004) observation: "structures and meanings [are] wrapped by a symbol system (style) and unwrapped by a series of interpretive acts (presumably guided by the style)" (Hatten, 2004,

279). In this framing, *style* becomes the key with which musical meaning and interpretation can be unlocked by providing a listener with a suite of normative expectations. Using a corpus-based approach to style, then, has the potential to promote the similarities with corpora and sub-corpora from a point of statistical novelty to a critical component of the way that music is learned, composed, and heard.

The logic runs like so.[26] If we imagine "style" as some way of grouping pieces that have similar properties, then a corpus (or sub-corpus) of the same style will share certain statistical characteristics. In other words, the pieces within a style will share some coherent and unique statistical or probabilistic hallmarks. In this chapter, I also showed that there was some connection between chronology and similarity and embraced connections between statistical similarity and biographical, social, and geographic information – similar properties were seen in the sub-corpora of composers that lived in the same time and place and who affiliated or studied with one another. Overall, stylistic groupings (and, therefore, coherent and unique statistical properties) are generally linked to particular times, places, and circumstances.

Continuing along this argumentative thread: in the previous chapter, I argued that in order for people to learn the expectations and norms of some musical system, they need to be exposed to some consistent set of statistical properties. Additionally, in order for a relationship to exist between composers and listeners – a relationship again schematized by the noisy channel and the MCM – this statistical system needs to be shared, at least partially, by both the music's creator and its consumer. If we imagine that a style is defined by a group of consistent musical statistics associated with a particular time and place, then style becomes at once a learnable musical system (insomuch as the consistency of the statistical system provides an access point to learners), the key by which listeners decode musical ideas (insomuch as its consistency provides a system ubiquitously used at some time and place), and the system that composers count on as being accessible by their listeners (insomuch as a composer at a particular time and place can expect listeners and learners to be exposed to that consistent statistical system). A style – by providing statistical consistency and predictability – allows for musical communication to happen. In terms of the noisy channel, "style" could even be considered equivalent to the statistical model that encodes and decodes the musical message. This definition of style transforms the concept into an active participant in music cognition and expression.

Summary

In this chapter, I began by asking whether composers who were born closer in time to one another would write proportionally similar chord progressions, and we found that to be the case. However, upon inspecting the results of several cluster analyses, we found that categorizing composers by their harmonic

86 What Is Style?

practices created groups that corresponded not only to date but to geography and compositional schools as well. I then introduced ways to use cross entropy to quantify how well certain groups, or sub-corpora, divide a larger musical corpus. The concept of *coherence* showed the consistency of the musical practice within a sub-corpus, and *uniqueness* showed how different the music within that sub-corpus was from the music of other sub-corpora. I used these values to argue that certain sub-corpora represented consistent systems, while other sub-corpora appeared to contain moments of innovation and change. I also observed that the most coherent and unique groupings involved clustering composers by similar practice: not surprisingly, dividing a corpus by its harmonic practice creates the most consistent and distinct groupings of that harmonic practice. I then used these groupings to test how well two musical reconstructions – one a completion of Beethoven sketches, the other by a forger trying to capitalize on Vivaldi's fame – conformed to the music they were trying to emulate. I finally argued that a corpus-oriented approach to a musical style might be framed as a strategy of dividing a corpus into various sub-corpora. These sub-corpora – or "styles" – can be described in terms of the similarities and differences between pieces within that grouping as well as in terms of the similarities and differences between that sub-corpus and the other divisions of the larger corpus. I suggested that defining style through the constituent statistical properties of some musical corpus (and its sub-corpora) clarifies the scope of, boundaries of, and assumptions behind some style while decentering the role of individual composers in favor of larger groups of composers and encouraging connections between corpus data and extramusical interpretation. Finally, I suggest that if musical creators, learners, and listeners need to rely on consistent musical expectations to encode and decode meaning, then the statistical consistency of a style is not simply a surface attribute of some set of musical pieces but rather a fundamental facet of musical expression and learning.

Notes

1. These proportions use V and v chords that appear in all YCAC composers, using only stretches that the YCAC's metadata indicates as being in the minor mode. The average number of v and V chords in each quarter-century window was 926.667 and 8,456.833, respectively (SD = 590.029 and 6,176.343). 1700–1724 had the maximum counts (1,938 and 19,618) and 1625–1649 had the lowest (68 and 459).
2. The corpus uses a "key profile" analysis for these tonal designations. I return to the specifics of this type of key-finding model in Chapter 6.
3. De Clercq's main issue with this corpus is its error rate, citing Huron (2013)'s argument that small errors can compound – if 3% of chords are erroneous in a corpus, then 6% of 2-grams become infected with these errors, and so on until these percentages bloom into increasingly large numbers. To my mind, this argument discounts how noise manifests within statistical models. Random errors will be just that: random. Even if a large portion of a dataset's statistics are in error, these errors are very unlikely

to exert any pressure on the trend being studied, as each erroneous datapoint will not participate in some contrasting single trend but rather will have random attributes.

4. Again, de Clercq (2016) provides a thorough summary of the messiness, noise, inconsistencies, and errors within this corpus. As I outlined earlier the size of the dataset outweighs its errors.

5. When I ran pilot studies for these analyses, two-chord progressions didn't capture enough information, and four-chord progressions were too granular for the models.

6. Specifically, I use only composers whose top 3-gram appears more than 100 times. Composers with sparse data tended to populate their vectors with zeros, which confounded the distance metric. Additionally, this choice seemed to optimize visual clarity of the results!

7. I have reported similar findings in White (2017) and (2016).

8. As described in Chapter 1's appendix, the line is the result of a linear regression, a method that outputs a value called R^2 that captures the proportion of the data's variation that is explained by the line, and a p value that indicates how sure a researcher should be that the line actually describes the data trend. The R^2 of Figure 3 is 0.32, and the average R^2 of all regression lines for these composers is 0.26. And 93% of these regressions returned p values that indicated that the statistics are sufficiently robust to be trusted (i.e., the regression was not likely to have arisen by chance; I also address p values in Chapter 1's appendix).

9. I use the R programming language and its library of clustering functions for these analyses. In the analysis I show here, I use *divisive* implementation. This process works from the top down, first dividing the corpus into groups that are the most different and then subsequently dividing those groups into successively smaller groupings based on more finely grained differences. Running the same clustering procedure using an agglomerative approach, or on a table containing intercomposer cross entropies, produces similar results, indicating the robustness of this clustering.

10. Why did I draw the line at 19? Classicalarchives.com devoted individual pages to 19 composers while relegating the remaining composers to alphabetized pages; this organizational structure is retained in the YCAC's constituent files.

11. Temperley (2007) can be credited with introducing the concept of cross entropy to musical corpus analysis.

12. This approach is similar – and indebted – to that developed in Conklin (2010).

13. I use the sub-corpus minus the piece under consideration so that a piece is never predicting its own events.

14. As in Chapter 1, I represent the cross entropy in bits (log 2). Importantly, coherence and uniqueness both have conceptual overlaps with the central idea of "entropy" as outlined in Chapter 1. When applied to a single dataset, entropy rises when each event is more random in terms of the other events, and falls when each event is more predictable. Uniqueness and coherence manipulate these relationships by comparing a dataset's randomness not simply to the dataset itself but to other potential datasets with which the original dataset has some relationship. In other words, these ideas capitalize on the original informatic structure of entropy to draw out additional relationships between datasets.

15. A heuristic smoothing procedure was performed using the assumption that transition probabilities follow a power-law distribution (something I'll return to in subsequent chapters). These distributions tend to be roughly cubic: if a transition from a particular chord had never been observed in a corpus, the frequency was judged to be the

88 What Is Style?

cubed root of the lowest observed transition frequency from that chord. The heuristic was based on observations about the probability distributions present in the data.

16. Importantly, I've operationalized coherence and uniqueness as relative rather than absolute characteristics, resulting in their interdependence. In my formulation, there is no cross-entropy value below which an intra-sub-corpus cross-entropy value designates coherences, nor is there an absolute value above which inter-sub-corpus cross-entropy values must remain to denote uniqueness. Rather, in my implementation, I have tethered these two properties to one another, with uniqueness and coherence both depending on the relationship between inter- and intra-sub-corpus cross entropies. In this formulation, something cannot be coherent while not being unique nor unique and incoherent. If a sub-corpus's coherence value is significantly below all its uniqueness values, it is both coherent and unique. If its coherence value is higher than many or all of its uniqueness values, that is either because its coherence value is high, because its uniqueness values are low, or a combination of the two. Such diagnoses, however, are best undertaken when analyzing specific arrays of coherence and uniqueness values. As outlined in Figure 2.5, these concepts are not theoretically dependent, and another implementation could easily separate them more crisply. However, given that my investigation works on the assumption that a style should be internally consistent *and* distinct from other styles, pairing these parameters seems reasonable in the current situation. This interdependence is then captured by my single coherence/uniqueness ratio.

17. Most of these insignificant/incoherent comparisons involved the two smallest sub-corpora: Debussy's and Wagner's. Excluding comparisons involving these two sub-corpora, the coherent/uniqueness rate rises 97.22%.

18. This sort of question has been asked since the beginnings of music informatics with Mendel (1969) and has continued over the next several decades with work like that of Crerar (1985), Meyer (1989), and Manaris et al. (2005).

19. http://ceesnieuwenhuizen.com/

20. While the corpora of Bach, Chopin, and Saint-Saens predict this piece significantly above average, it should be remembered that this model only takes into account the corpus's chord progressions, ignoring things like instrumentation and form, parameters that would likely serve to distinguish this piece from these composers' outputs.

21. For consistency, I treat these pieces as a single piece in the computational implementation.

22. Some theorists react to this taxonomical imprecision by offering more terminological specificity. Richard Middleton, for instance, focuses on the size and scope of the music's production to distinguish between "style" and "idiolect," with the latter describing the practices of a particular composer or ensemble, while "style" specifically describes the practices of a tradition. For instance, in this approach, the band Black Sabbath has an *idiolect* within the larger heavy-metal *style*. In this solution, theorists rely on an analogy with spoken language: individual speakers have their own peculiarities, groups of individuals may have certain linguistic markers, larger communities may develop their own dialect, and yet larger communities share the same language. Speaking broadly and heuristically, these terms and technologies rely on the identity of the music's producer and how that producer is situated within relation to other composers to explain musical similarities and differences. I say "broadly" because there is naturally a two-way street between these sorts of groupings and musical characteristics: if Black Sabbath put out a bluegrass album, we would probably not classify it as heavy metal – here, the musical characteristics would trump classifying the music

based on the band's identity. However, it stands that this sort of approach orients toward identity and social structures in its definitions of style.

23. Elsewhere, I have called this *emergent creativity* (White, 2017). I have also heard the dichotomy between individual-driven and group-driven innovation described in the business community as the Superman model and Avengers model of progress, respectively.

24. This observation is heavily indebted to Meyer (1957), Hatten (2004), Gjerdingen (2007), and Byros (2012).

25. My corpus-based definition of style is also contingent upon the parameters with which one measures similarities and differences. Indeed, one can easily imagine two composers having affinities in one domain but being very different in other domains. While I used harmonic 3-grams in this chapter's modeling, different groupings might have resulted from tracking melodic patterns, large-scale forms, or instrumentation.

26. This logic is not new. Leonard Meyer (1959) indicated this very conceptualization more than a half century ago. Meyer argued that if the fulfillment and thwarting of expectations underpin musical meaning and communication, then there must be some consistent and predictable set of probabilities shared by a group of pieces. Without this consistency, listeners wouldn't know what kinds of expectations to bring to a piece of music, and composers wouldn't have ways to communicate musical meaning.

27. Even more specifically: this procedure used the R programming language (version 2.13.0) to run a divisive, agglomerative, and *k*-means cluster analysis on a dissimilarity matrix derived from the cosines of these vectors' angles. In principle, though, one can simply use a vector of normalized frequencies, as I used when testing the correlation between date and 3-gram usage.

References

Burkholder, J. P., D. J. Grout, and C. V. Palisca. 2018. *A History of Western Music*, 10th edition. New York: Norton.

Byros, V. 2012. "Meyer's Anvil: Revisiting the Schema Concept." *Music Analysis*, 31/3, 273–346.

Cambouropoulos, E. 2001. "Melodic Cue Abstraction, Similarity, and Category Formation: A Formal Model." *Music Perception*, 18/3, 347–370.

Conklin, D. 2010. "Discovery of Distinctive Patterns in Music." *Intelligent Data Analysis*, 14, 547–554.

Cope, D. 1987. "Experiments in Music Intelligence." *Proceedings of the International Computer Music Conference*, San Francisco: Computer Music Association, 170–173.

Crerar, M. A. 1985. "Elements of a Statistical Approach to the Question of Authorship in Music." *Computers and the Humanities*, 19/3, 175–182.

Dahlhaus, C. 1982. *Esthetics of Music*. Translated by William Austin. Cambridge: Cambridge University Press.

de Clercq, T. 2016. "Big Data, Big Questions: A Closer Look at the Yale: Classical Archives Corpus (c. 2015)." *Empirical Musicology*, 11/1, 59–67.

Drott, E. 2013. "The End(s) of Genre." *Journal of Music Theory*, 57/1, 1–45.

Gjerdingen, R. 2007. *Music in the Galant Style*. Oxford: Oxford University Press.

Hatten, R. 2004. *Interpreting Musical Gestures, Topics, and Tropes: Mozart, Beethoven, Schubert.* Bloomington: Indiana University Press.

Huang, A., H. V. Koops, E. Newton-Rex, M. Dinculescu, and C. J. Cai. 2020. "AI Song Contest: Human-AI Co-Creation in Songwriting." *Proceedings of the 20th International Society for Music Information Retrieval Conference (ISMIR)*, virtual, Montreal, Canada.

Huron, D. 2013. "On the Virtuous and the Vexatious in an Age of Big Data." *Music Perception*, 31/1, 4–9.

Johnson, T. 2018. *Analyzing Genre in Post-Millennial Popular Music.* Ph.D. Dissertation, CUNY Graduate Center, New York, NY.

Kallberg, J. 1988. "The Rhetoric of Genre: Chopin's Nocturne in G Minor." *19th-Century Music*, 11, 238–261.

Komaniecki, R. 2021. "Vocal Pitch in Rap Flow." *Integral*, 34, 25–45.

Lumsden, R. 2020. "Music Theory for the 'Weaker Sex': Oliveria Prescott's Columns for *The Girl's Own Paper*." *Music Theory Online*, 26/3. https://mtosmt.org/issues/mto.20.26.3/mto.20.26.3.lumsden.html

Manaris, W., J. Romero, P. Machado, D. Krehbiel, T. Hirzel, W. Pharr, and R. Davis. 2005. "Zipf's Law, Music Classification, and Aesthetics." *Computer Music Journal*, 29/1, 55–69.

McLeod, K. 2001. "Genres, Subgenres, Sub-Subgenres and More: Musical and Social Differentiation within Electronic/Dance Music Communities." *Journal of Popular Music Studies*, 13, 59–75.

Mendel, A. 1969. "Some Preliminary Attempts at Computer-Assisted Style Analysis in Music." *Computers and the Humanities*, 4/1, 41–52.

Meyer, L. 1957. "Meaning in Music and Information Theory." *The Journal of Aesthetics and Art Criticism*, 15/4, 412–424.

Meyer, L. 1989. *Style and Music: Theory, History, Ideology.* Chicago: The University of Chicago Press.

Middleton, R. 1990. *Studying Popular Music.* Philadelphia: Open University Press.

Miller, B. 2020. "'All of the Rules of Jazz': Stylistic Models and Algorithmic Creativity in Human-Computer Improvisation." *Music Theory Online*, 26/3. https://mtosmt.org/issues/mto.20.26.3/mto.20.26.3.miller.html

Quinn, I. 2010. "What's 'Key for Key': A Theoretically Naive Key: Finding Model for Bach Chorales." *Zeitschrift der Gesellschaft für Musiktheorie*, 7/ii, 151–163.

Shea, N. 2022. "A Demographic Sampling Model and Database for Addressing Racial, Ethnic, and Gender Bias in Popular-Music Empirical Research." *Empirical Musicology Review*, 16/2.

Temperley, D. 2007. *Music and Probability.* Cambridge: The MIT Press.

Tlacael, M. E., J. B. Bello, and E. J. Humphrey. 2015. "From Genre Classification to Rhythm Similarity: Computational and Musicological Insights." *Journal of New Music Research*, 44/1, 39–57. DOI: 10.1080/09298215.2014.929706

Tomlinson, G. 2015. *A Million Years of Music: The Emergence of Human Modernity.* Cambridge: MIT Press.

Walsch, C. 2021. *Popular Music Styles.* Honors Thesis, UMass Amherst, Amherst, MA.

White, C. W. 2014. "Changing Styles, Changing Corpora, Changing Tonal Models." *Music Perception*, 31/2, 244–253.

White, C. W. 2017. "Locating Emergent Creativity with Similarity Metrics." *Journal of Creative Music Systems*, 2/1. http://jcms.org.uk/issues/Vol2Issue1/locating-emergent-creativity/article.html

White, C. W., and Quinn, I. 2016. "The Yale-Classical Archives Corpus." *Empirical Musicology Review*, 50–58.

Yust, J. 2019. "Stylistic Information in Pitch-Class Distributions." *Journal of New Music Research*, 48/3, 217–231.

CHAPTER 2 APPENDIX

Cluster Analysis

Figure A2.1 shows a series of points on a graph with two axes – or what we can call two *dimensions*. If we compared each point to each other point, we could construct a table of distances between each point. This table would quantify which points are closer to one another and which are farther apart. The distance between the point [1,1] and [2,2] is shorter than between [2,2] and [5,6], as indicated in the graph. Cluster analysis takes the table of distances and organizes the points into groups by their relative proximity to one another. Figure A2.1 shows two clusters with points [1,1] and [2,2] in one cluster and the remaining points in the other cluster.

However, it is not always obvious how many groups one should use to cluster a series of points: should there be two, three, or even more clusters in Figure A2.1? For instance, why not place points [4,4] and [4,3] in their own cluster? In agglomerative and divisive clustering, all solutions are shown. Agglomerative analysis first groups the data into many groups, then groups those groups into increasing large clusters; divisive does the opposite, starting with the largest possible clusters and dividing those into sequentially smaller groups. Both processes produce a tree diagram showing these relationships, as in Figure 2.4. (These two approaches don't always produce the same results; however, when they do – as is the case in Figure 2.4 – the clusters are considered more robust.) k-means clustering – the approach behind Table 2.2 – quantifies whether certain cardinalities of clusters provide better solutions than others. This is done using a measurement called *silhouette width*. The silhouette width of any point can be found first by computing the average distance between that point and each other point in its potential cluster (this value tells us how well that point is

92 What Is Style?

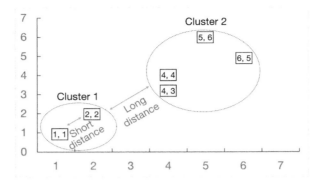

FIGURE A2.1 A 2-dimensional example of cluster analysis

matched with other points in its own cluster) and second by computing the average distance between that point and the points in its closest neighboring cluster (this value tells us how distinct the point is from its closest cluster). The silhouette width then subtracts these two values from one another and divides by the larger of the two. Assuming the point is situated in the best cluster, the number will always be between 0 and 1 (if the point is in the wrong cluster, the number will be less than 0). The closer the value is to 1, the better the fit to its cluster. For an overall measure of an entire clustering solution, the mean silhouette width simply averages the values of all the individual points. When I argued that 7 or 10 clusters provided an ideal grouping of composers in Table 2.2 (i.e., $k = 7$ and $k = 10$), I was relying on peaks in silhouette widths at those values.[27] (The accompanying spreadsheet for this chapter contains 3-gram data derived from the YCAC, along with sample code that can cluster that data using the open-source programming language R.)

Confidence Intervals

One of the most important tools afforded by statistical analysis is the confidence interval. The confidence interval assumes that we are working with incomplete and noisy data and that whenever we take an average within this imperfect data, we should not simply rely on that single value but rather admit the fallibility of the data at hand and imagine the observed average being an approximation of a perfect "true" average. For instance, let's imagine we look at a set of pieces by some composer and find that on average, their dominant chords resolve to tonic chords 80% of the time within a single piece. And let's further imagine that the data available do not include the composer's entire output. And so we want to admit that while we found that 80% of dominant chords go to tonic chords, it is possible the actual value isn't *exactly* 80% but somewhere around 80%.

We calculate this imprecision by balancing two factors: how variable the data is and how much data we're using. For the variability, we use the standard deviation, or the average amount of variation around some mean. If, within each of our hypothetical composer's pieces, around 80% of the dominants resolve to tonics, the standard deviation will be low. But, if in some of these pieces almost all dominants move to tonics while in other pieces the dominants resolve elsewhere, the standard deviation will be high. For the quantity of data, we simply use the number of data points used in calculating the average. In my hypothetical example, we would use the number of pieces.

The mathematical implementation of the confidence interval is best relegated to a statistics textbook (or, for that matter, the Wikipedia material linked in this chapter's online materials); however, the basic process constructs normal distribution – a type of bell curve – around the average and uses connections between this type of distribution, the number of observations, and the standard deviation to figure out the range in which we would expect errors to occur. These margins of error are usually framed in terms of a confidence interval *of some percent*. A 95% confidence interval is the range in which 95% of varia-tion is expected to occur – the confidence interval therefore indicates you are 95% certain that the "true" average is within that margin. (Smaller standard deviations and higher sample sizes create tighter intervals, while the opposite would create wider margins.) Conversely, however, there is still a 5% chance that the true average is outside that margin, and this is what is meant by a "p value." When a researcher reports something like "$p < 0.05$," they are say-ing that there is a less than 5% chance that their data's true average (or whatever statistical value they are presenting) is actually outside of their confidence interval.

Researchers can then use these confidence intervals to compare averages. If two different averages' confidence intervals do not overlap, we can confidently believe them to be significantly different. If our hypothetical composer's 80% average has a confidence interval $+/- 5\%$, and a second composer had an aver-age of 82% with a similar confidence interval, we'd say that even though the second average is higher, these two averages are *not significantly different*. However, if this second composer resolved an average of 70% of dominant chords to tonics, and this average also had a confidence interval $+/- 5\%$, we *would* believe these averages to be significantly different. (Again, the online materials show an example of confidence intervals, along with some open-source links to resources surrounding their calculation.)

Cross Entropy

Cross entropy was initially introduced into mainstream music theory discourse by Temperley (2007) and is fundamentally based on the notion of entropy. As introduced in Chapter 1, entropy quantifies the disorder within a dataset and can be used to quantify the level of complexity in that dataset, with more disorderly datasets being more complex and difficult to predict than orderly and simple datasets. Cross entropy works in much the same way but quantifies how

94 What Is Style?

well a set of expectations predicts the events of a dataset: it captures how easily or hard some external system must work to predict that dataset. The measurement can also be used to discuss how similar a series of expectations are to that dataset, since a model that is poorly calibrated to a series of observations will have to work harder to predict that dataset than a model whose expectations are well aligned to the observations.

In Equation A2.1, I have annotated the cross-entropy process. The equation takes the average log probability of a series of observations $(o_1, o_2, \ldots o_n)$ according to some probabilistic model m. That is: m is a set of expectations, and O is a dataset of events made of individual observations o. $m(o_1)$ would then be the probability of the first event in some series as assessed by those expectations. The "$\ldots o_n$" designation means that the process assesses the probability of every event in the sequence. The "log" converts those probabilities into logarithms (just as in Chapter 1's entropy calculations), and the $1/n$ averages those log probabilities. Finally, recall from Chapter 1 that a logarithm of a fraction will be a negative number; the negative sign makes this negative value a positive number. Chapter 1's appendix discusses the information-theory reasoning behind applying the logarithm; but, in short: this process provides a single usable value that shows how "surprised" model m is by the observations O. Higher values will mean that a model is more surprised by (and assesses lower probabilities to) the series of observations, indicating a potentially greater mismatch between the model and the observed dataset. Lower values, conversely, indicate less surprise and a greater level of match between the model's expectations and the dataset's events.

If the model m is a set of probabilities drawn from one dataset and each o in O is drawn from another dataset, then we can say that the model m is assessing observations O and that the cross entropy shows how well the dataset from which the probabilities of m are drawn predicts the events of dataset O. In this chapter, we used exactly this relationship, using the 3-gram of some sub-corpus to create a probabilistic model m, in which, for instance, the 3-grams that appeared frequently in that sub-corpus would be relatively probable according to the model m, and those that appeared infrequently would be improbable. These probabilities were then used to assess the 3-grams of some other piece or pieces not in the sub-corpus, treating those 3-grams as each observation o in O. Framed this way, the initial sub-corpus's 3-gram usage assesses the probability of the 3-grams in some other piece (or pieces): the sub-corpus's model m is used to assess the probability of each observation o (or 3-gram) in the piece under consideration. If the piece's 3-grams are similar to those in the sub-corpus, the probabilities will be high: the sub-corpus will predict that piece easily, and the cross entropy will be low. However, if the piece's 3-gram usage is quite different from the sub-corpus being used for the model m, then the sub-corpus will not be able to predict that piece easily, the probabilities will be low, and the cross entropy will be high.

What Is Style? **95**

To calculate the cross entropy H of an observation series O given some probabilistic model m:

(1) Use the model m to assess the probability of each individual observation o.

(2) Take the logarithm of each probability.

(3) Calculate the average.

$$H_m(O) = -\frac{1}{n}\log\left(m(o_1, o_2, \ldots o_n)\right)$$

(4) Convert the negative number produced by the logarithm to a positive value.

EQUATION A2.1 Cross entropy

3

WHAT IS HARMONY?

A Narrative

Imagine you are an alien researcher on assignment to study the Western classical music tradition. As a complete newcomer to human musical systems, you decide your first order of business is to peruse several textbooks and treatises to get a general idea of how this music works. You see that since the likes of Zarlino (1558) and Lippius (1612) more than four centuries ago, theorists have understood chords made from stacking thirds on top of one another – what these humans often refer to as *triads* – as something like the building blocks of this repertoire. The vast majority of contemporary textbooks seem to agree with this approach, as they mostly rely on a basic tonal vocabulary of triads and seventh chords, using Roman numerals to signal the rooted triads underpinning this music's harmonic events. You find that even theories that dissent from this traditional Roman numeral usage still rely on some basic conception of the third-based harmonies as foundational to tonality (Riemann, 1893; Harrison, 1994; Quinn, 2005).[1]

As you peruse these sources, your ship's computer purrs in the background, processing the moment-by-moment surface harmonies that occur within thousands of pieces in the Western classical tradition (what some humans call the "common practice"). Imagine your surprise when your ship's computer finds that most pitch sets that occur on these musical surfaces are neither triads nor seventh chords. You look on in disbelief as the computer, using a dataset called the Yale-Classical Archives Corpus, tallies the sets of simultaneously occurring pitches and outputs Figure 3.1. Dividing this corpus into tertian (triads and seventh chords) versus non-tertian sonorities, you see that only 34% of the corpus's events involve a triad or seventh. A shocking 66% do not.

DOI: 10.4324/9781003285663-3

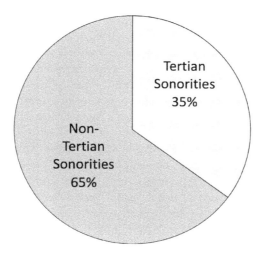

FIGURE 3.1 Tertian versus non-tertian sonorities in the YCAC

After a moment of scratching your (Martian version of a) head, you remember that human learning and communication depends upon discernable and predictable statistical properties. Clearly, humans have believed for centuries that this tertian minority of musical events is somehow fundamental to tonal composition, listening, and learning: the people who produce, listen to, and study this repertoire seem to intuit triads and seventh chords as tonal music's foundational vocabulary and grammar. You reason that if they learn, interpret, and deploy the language of tonality by using third-based harmonies, then such tertian harmonies must have some special characteristics. In other words, if they make sense of the events within Figure 3.1's 65% slice by relating or reducing them to some simpler system of triads and seventh chords, then chords within that simpler system must have distinctive, learnable, and consistent statistical properties.[2]

You program your computer to reexamine the music's surface events. You begin looking for statistical properties that explain how human composers and listeners might map between the complexities of musical surfaces and the simple vocabularies and grammars you found in their textbooks and treatises. You search for ways that audiences might learn these simple vocabularies after being exposed to such variegated surface statistics. You try to figure out why that 35% of chords is so important.

In this chapter, I explore these questions by building a model of tonal harmony from the ground up, step by step, using only observable properties of the musical surface. Beginning with no preconceptions, I assemble a harmonic vocabulary (the universe of possible chords) and grammar (how these chords

98 What Is Harmony?

move from one to another) using the statistical properties of a corpus of tonal music. In Step 1, I make some basic observations, identifying which scale-degree sets, set classes, and progressions happen most frequently in the corpus. This will provide an overview of the kinds of events that occur within the raw data of the musical surface. In Step 2, I identify some recurrent properties of the surface data, and I use these properties to implement a machine-learning algorithm that simplifies the surface data into a "reduced" vocabulary. This model assumes only that more frequent and more contextually predictable events – the underpinnings of learnable statistical systems as outlined in Chapter 1 – are more fundamental to a musical grammar. Following our musical intuitions, this reduced vocabulary involves primarily triads and seventh chords. Step 3 is a "sanity check." I compare my results against textbook models of tonal syntax, finding that they reasonably approximate how music theorists describe tonal harmony. I also provide a brief analysis to show the reduction method in action.

Step 4 outlines how groups of chords within this grammar act in similar ways, evoking the music-theoretical concept of harmonic function. In Step 5, I further reduce the chordal vocabulary by arguing that chords connected through stepwise voice leading are equivalent, touching once again upon harmonic function. I then indulge in a second short analytical exercise to observe this more aggressive reduction process at work. Step 6 shows how statistical properties can be used to construct a hierarchy of chords within a tonal vocabulary, thereby recovering notions of dissonance. Finally, in Step 7, I apply this method to other corpora to illustrate how chord vocabularies and grammars change between different styles and time periods. I then connect this to music psychology and, specifically, to the notion of "heuristic listening." Overall, this chapter approaches harmonic grammar through the *Martian effect* introduced in Chapter 1, alienating the process from preconceptions about triadic harmony to better understand the statistical underpinnings of tonal chord grammars and to show the properties of corpora we emphasize when adopting such grammars.

The Corpus

Because I am interested in surface events, I will again be using the YCAC in this chapter. The reader will recall that the pieces in the corpus date from 1650 to 1949, that the corpus represents each piece as a time-indexed list of pitch simultaneities, and that these simultaneities are registered at every moment a note is added or subtracted from the texture. These "slices" capture very fine-grained surface events, from each note struck in a melody to every pitch of an Alberti bass pattern to each turn of a trill. These slices are represented not only as absolute pitches but also as scale degrees, both reckoned in relation to the piece's beginning key (as determined by experts), but also using local key information (as determined by a windowed key-profile analysis). Local scale degrees are used in the following models; all pieces in the corpus were used.

A note again about the visual representation of scale-degree information: while the YCAC represents scale degrees according to a modulo-12 universe (such that the tonic scale degree is 0, the dominant 7, and the leading tone 11), this chapter will use traditional scale-degree numbers (with tonic referred to as 1, the dominant 5, and the leading tone 7; these are assigned using a combination of the curators' assessments of each piece's key and the results of automated key-finding algorithms.). When sets comprise a triad or seventh chord, I use a Roman numeral to designate that harmony, but when the set does not conform to this nomenclature, I show it as a bracketed set. Therefore, while a major tonic triad would be represented as "I," a tonic triad with the fifth omitted would be "<1̂, 3̂>." I also ignore inversion throughout. While chord inversions doubtlessly contain syntactic information, for this corpus analysis, I take the simplifying step of grouping together all orders and permutations of scale-degree sets as different manifestations of one harmony.

Step 1: Frequency and Predictability in the YCAC

Figures 3.2 through 3.4 exemplify the statistics with which our alien observer would be initially confronted when processing a corpus drawn from musical surfaces. Figures 3.2 and 3.3 show the relative frequencies of all scale-degree simultaneities in the YCAC. Figure 3.4 shows a contextual property of the dataset, the simultaneities which most frequently follow V. Here, the relative thickness of the arrows reflects the frequency of the progressions.[3] Again, sets recognizable as functional tonal harmonies are represented with Roman numerals, while those that are not are represented as scale-degree sets. Throughout this chapter, I adopt a modal agnosticism, grouping the respective chordal data of major and minor music (and of all other possible modes, for that matter!) together into one large dataset.[4] Recall, too, that these pitch-class sets are reckoned not by the global key but by the local key as designated in the YCAC's data. (Also, note that this tactic contrasts with the one to be used in Chapter 6!)[5]

These statistics represent the raw vocabulary of the YCAC: they have immediate proximity to the musical surface, and as such, they are a relatively

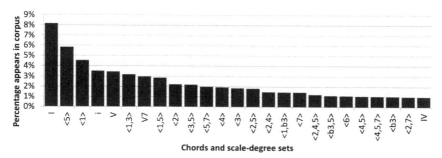

FIGURE 3.2 The 25 most frequent chords in the YCAC raw vocabulary (60% of all chord events)

100 What Is Harmony?

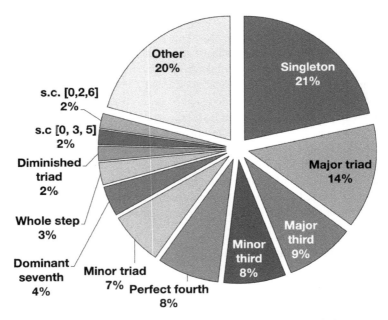

FIGURE 3.3 The distribution of prime forms in YCAC's raw vocabulary

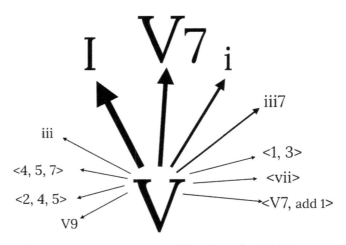

FIGURE 3.4 The most common transitions from V in the YCAC

theory-agnostic and minimally organized representation of the corpus's scale-degree sets.[6] The chords and chord progressions involved constitute the vocabulary and grammar of a basic and rudimentary system of musical expectations. Figure 3.4 could be read, for instance, as capturing the normative behavior of a V chord, revealing which progressions are expected and which are surprising.

Step 2a: Some Recurrent Properties That Can Be Used to Create a "Reduced" Vocabulary

These statistics have taught our Martian something about tonal musical surfaces, but the alien scholar is no closer to understanding how these data connect to some simpler, textbook model. For one thing, the raw vocabulary is disorderly and unintuitive. The distribution also involves both traditional and non-traditional scale-degree sets, and it is highly divided: no individual chord appears more than 8.2% of the time. Looking at these data, it is not immediately obvious that this kind of corpus analysis can show anything more than how complicated actual musical surfaces can be.

The Martian, however, is committed to figuring out how to relate this complicated harmonic hodgepodge to the simpler tonal vocabularies they read about in their textbook survey. Luckily, the Martian notices that certain set classes appear more frequently, and certain groups of chords with similar scale-degree constituencies seem to appear in the same contexts. Returning to Figures 3.2–3.4, our Martian notes that those sets outside of traditional Roman numeral–style vocabularies tend to be subsets or supersets of tertian chords and that the triads and seventh chords to which they are related tend to appear more frequently in the distributions. Figure 3.2, for instance, shows sets $<\hat{1}, \hat{3}>$, $<\hat{1}, \hat{5}>$, and $<\hat{3}, \hat{5}>$ each appearing less frequently than the tonic triad, their superset. Excluding singletons, recognizable chords like I, V, V^7, and IV appear more often than their subsets. Note, too, that the scale-degree sets shown in Figure 3.4 tend to have similar constellations of scale degrees. Indeed, these chords are all subsets or supersets of the tonic triad, dominant triad, or dominant seventh chord. For example, $<\hat{4}, \hat{5}, \hat{7}>$ is a subset of the V^7 chord, and $<\hat{1}, \hat{3}>$ is a subset of the tonic triad.[7]

If certain sets appear more frequently than others, and if sets with related scale-degree content occur in contextually similar locations, then it follows that we, along with our extraterrestrial scientist, could create groupings of chords based on contextual and scale-degree similarities. We could hypothesize that the musical surface – comprising the many specific behaviors of the vast diversity of possible scale-degree sets – could be organized into a smaller array of general cases by exploiting these similarities. If the surface provides a raw vocabulary, then this categorization would provide a "reduced" vocabulary, a smaller set of chord types to which each individual surface token might be related.

Let's consider an informal and intuitive application of these relationships to analysis. Imagine that our Martian researcher posits two rules for analysis: (1) that a chord can be mapped onto, or *reduced* to, another chord that is both more likely to occur in the same context as the original chord and that also is a subset or superset of the original chord; and (2) that repeated chords or subsets of a surrounding chord are not allowed. The Martian takes out (their version of) a pencil and sketches Figure 3.5, a series of YCAC slices from a

102 What Is Harmony?

FIGURE 3.5 A sample reduction using subset/superset relationships in Wolfgang Mozart, K. 279

YCAC scale degree events	1/3	3	2/4	4	5/7	2/5	1	1/5	1	5/7	1	1/5	3	3/5
Remove/combine adjacent subsets	1/3		2/4		5/7	2/5	1	5/7			1/5		3/5	
Add/subtract to increase contextual probability	1/3/5		2/4/6		2/5/7	2/5/7	1/3/5	2/5/7			1/3/5		1/3/5	
Remove repeats (and use R.N. annotations)	I		ii		V		I	V			I			

Mozart excerpt. The boxes show the slices and their scale-degree constituency in C major. Note that no resulting set is an actual triad; they are all dyads or singletons. Let's imagine that our Martian follows the second rule first, removing explicit repeats and adjacent subsets. This produces the progression in the second row of boxes. Following the Martian's first rule, these sets can now be reduced to more frequently occurring chords. The first two slices (<$\hat{1}$, $\hat{3}$> and <$\hat{2}$, $\hat{4}$>) have relatively high probabilities of occurrence in the raw dataset; they both appear in Figure 3.2. But by adding scale degrees to complete the common triads of which they are constituents, they will not only increase their probability of occurrence but will also produce chord progressions that occur more frequently. The third row of boxes in the example reflects this transformation of the observed sets into more probable supersets: the dyads <$\hat{1}$, $\hat{3}$> and <$\hat{2}$, $\hat{4}$> now become I and ii triads by adding $\hat{5}$ and $\hat{6}$ to the respective sets. Removing repetitions a second time, the Martian is left with the final row of the sequence, a series that uses chords and progressions that occur frequently in the YCAC's distribution.

Figure 3.6 provides another example. The second box in the top row contains the set <$\hat{1}$, $b\hat{3}$, $\hat{4}$, $b\hat{6}$>, i.e., iv⁷. This moment is a superset of the far more likely iv triad. <$b\hat{3}$>, which a musician would see as a dissonant seventh, can be deleted to produce the "reduced" iv chord. In a somewhat more sophisticated move, the <$b\hat{3}$, $\hat{5}$, $\hat{7}$> trichord in the next box is a superset of the more probable dyad, <$\hat{5}$, $\hat{7}$>, which is a subset of the following V⁷ chord.

The Martian strokes their (version of a) chin and considers how they might computationally automate this reduction process. After a brief moment, they come to the conclusion that these reductions involve two different kinds of formal relationships: similarities of context and similarities of content. Content

What Is Harmony? **103**

YCAC scale degree events	1 b3 5	1 b3 4 b6	b3 5 7	5 7 2 4	1 b3 5
Add/subtract to increase contextual probability	1 b3 5	4 b6 1	5 7	5 7 2 4	1 b3 5
Remove repeats (and use R.N. annotations)	i	iv	V7	i	i

FIGURE 3.6 A parsed version of Frédéric Chopin, Op. 28, no. 20, m. 1

similarities result from the scale-degree constituency of two sets being related in some way. For example, one chord may be a subset of another. Contextual similarities result when two sets occur in similar positions within progressions. Claiming an equivalence between the I and the $<\hat{1}, \hat{3}>$ nodes in Figure 3.4 relies on both concepts: both sets follow a V chord, and the latter is a subset of the former. Implementing this process into a computational algorithm would involve relating specific chords in the raw YCAC to sets that are more contextually probable and that have similar scale-degree content. A particular $<\hat{1}, \hat{3}>$ following a V chord could be "reduced" to a I chord, because the latter occurs in the same context with a greater probability while also sharing almost all scale degrees. In other words, certain sets seem to be favored within a vocabulary by their frequency of occurrence and grammatical positioning; they occur more frequently than their subsets and supersets, and they appear in the same contextual locations as their subsets and supersets. These favored sets, then, populate a reduced harmonic vocabulary.

There is much more to say about the computational reduction process, but I want to highlight two additional aspects of this reduction formalization that bear distinguishing: *replacement* and *prolongation*. Both concepts are well ensconced in music theory and analysis. The former involves the idea that a (raw) surface token stands in for some (reduced) type. When Riemann (1914) discusses *Scheinkonsonanzen* – whereby chords are only "apparent consonances" insomuch

104 What Is Harmony?

as they are transformations of (read: "stand-ins for") other triads – he is invoking the concept of replacement. Conversely, prolongation includes claims about various linear events instantiating the same underlying event. When Schenker (1935) discusses the process of *Auskomponieren*, in which several adjacent surface-level events "compose out" or contrapuntally elaborate some background event, he is invoking the concept of prolongation.

The same two concepts are at work here. In the Martian's version of replacement, a less frequent member of the raw vocabulary is swapped for a contextually similar and more frequent chord – when we interpret sets like $<\hat{1}, \hat{3}>$ or $<\hat{5}, \hat{7}>$ as incomplete I and V chords, we are engaging in this kind of logic. The Martian's version of prolongation, on the other hand, involves glomming together adjacent events to create a more expected chord. If they interpolate a $<\hat{1}, \hat{3}>$ dyad into the previous tonic triad or interpret a V triad followed by V^7 as a single harmonic event, they are engaging in prolongational logic.[8]

To this point, we have used subset/superset relationships and replacement/prolongational logic to produce a more manageable and familiar series of harmonies. While the preceding examples have been presented using an intuitive logic, we – along with our alien researcher – are interested in a computational system that can process a corpus of surface data and produce a textbook tonal vocabulary and grammar. In the following section, I formalize such a process by describing a general algorithm that parses a raw surface and outputs a reduced harmonic vocabulary and formal language.

Step 2b: A Formal Model for Reduction

We might imagine these content/context mappings and reductions metaphorically in terms of gravity and planet formation. Initially, each pitch set culled from the raw musical surface floats in a cloud of syntactic chaos, unrelated to any other simultaneity. Equivalencies like subset/superset relationships and contextual similarities introduce gravitational pulls between the sets. Chords that act the same way and share scale degrees are drawn toward each other, and they fuse to create classes of chords, like planets forming from a cloud of tonal space debris. These newly formed planetoids of contextually related simultaneities comprise a simpler syntactic system and a simpler vocabulary of chords that adheres more readily to traditional notions of harmony.

As described, there are two gravitational forces at play in this system: contextual similarities and overlapping scale-degree content. To create the contextual side of this logic – to determine what chords exert more contextual gravity than others – we can use a probabilistic model. This chapter uses the same two-chord progressions ("2-grams") as Chapter 1. The probability of a chord occurring at any given time point is contingent upon the number of times that the model has observed that particular chord following the previous chord within a corpus. On the other hand, to determine how much gravity is exerted by the second force, similarity of content, we can simply examine the scale-degree overlap between two chords: the greater the number of shared scale degrees between two chords, the more pull that connection has. (The computational and mathematical specifics of this model appear in White, 2013, 2016.)

While more details about of this process are found in the appendix, the algorithm's mathematics involve maximizing the probabilities being considered. This calculation uses the YCAC's raw transitions to combine the probability of a chord occurring given the preceding chord and the probability of that 2-gram succession occurring at all. Consider the progression (<$\hat{1}$, $\hat{3}$>, <$\hat{2}$, $\hat{5}$>). For this pair, we observe how many times <$\hat{2}$, $\hat{5}$> follows <$\hat{1}$, $\hat{3}$> in the raw YCAC data and divide that by the number of times <$\hat{2}$, $\hat{5}$> occurs overall. This proportion produces the probability of <$\hat{1}$, $\hat{3}$> appearing given the appearance of <$\hat{2}$, $\hat{5}$>. This calculation equals 1.8%. We then calculate the probability of that succession of two chords occurring at all by taking the count of that 2-gram divided by the count of *all* 2-grams in the YCAC. This calculation equals 0.04%. The product of the two probabilities is 0.072%: this product provides the value that the algorithm will try to increase in its reduction process. (Although, as we saw in Chapter 1's usage of entropy, this number is converted into a logarithm for the computational implementation.) The algorithm tries a variety of combinations of the original sets' subsets and supersets and finds that the progression between two supersets, I and V, not only produces the highest possible product, 2.1%, but it also adds only one scale degree to each set. The reduction process therefore "reduces" (<$\hat{1}$, $\hat{3}$>, <$\hat{2}$, $\hat{5}$>) to the succession (I, V).

Figure 3.7 shows the frequency of various chords by relative font size and their sub- and superset relations with arrows. Less probable chord structures map onto their more probable subsets and supersets, with multiple recursive steps creating a network of sets that all eventually map onto one central, most probable chord. For instance, <$\hat{2}$, $\hat{4}$> is a subset of the more probable vii°, which, in turn, is a subset of the yet more probable V^7, which is a superset of the most probable V chord. The V network therefore has the power to reduce a <$\hat{2}$, $\hat{4}$> dyad to a V triad through its scale-degree overlap with vii° and V^7.

But an event's context also needs to be taken into consideration. As Figure 3.7 shows, <$\hat{2}$, $\hat{4}$> is also a subset of the ii chord. We would intuitively imagine

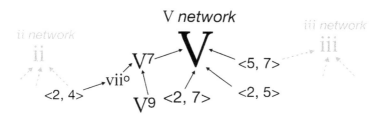

FIGURE 3.7 The V reduction network, with connections to the ii and iii networks

106 What Is Harmony?

this dyad being reduced to a V chord if it, for instance, followed a $<\hat{5}, \hat{7}>$ dyad and preceded a I chord. But if the dyad appears as a traditional predominant (as it does in Figure 3.5), we would likely prefer to relate it to the ii chord.

Let's now imagine the Martian applying the processes used in Figures 3.5 and 3.6 to every passage of every piece in the YCAC to produce a new, reduced series of chords which can be counted and collated to form a *reduced vocabulary*. Figures 3.8 through 3.11 show the results of implementing such an algorithm on the raw YCAC vocabulary. The most frequent chords in the reduced vocabulary are shown in Figure 3.8. Now these chords comprise almost all of the corpus's total probability mass, a far more limited vocabulary than that found in Figure 3.1. Where the I chord occurred slightly more than 8% of the time in the raw vocabulary, it now occupies almost 25% of the probability distribution. Taken together, the tonic and dominant triads comprise about 12% of surface events in the raw YCAC; in the reduced vocabulary, they occupy more than 66% of the probability mass. Figure 3.9 illustrates similar constraint within the prime forms of the reduced vocabulary, and Figure 3.10 shows the chords to which V progresses in the reduced vocabulary (showing only those progressions with >2% probability). Where Figure 3.4 presented 12 options, Figure 3.10 shows only 8. And the most probable transitions occur much more frequently than in Figure 3.4: V goes to I almost 40% of the time compared to 12% in Figure 3.3. (NB: Because I'm primarily interested in harmony and chord construction, these and subsequent analyses exclude passages of three or more adjacent singletons. I return to the issue of analyzing monophonic passages in Chapter 6.)

In sum, mapping chords onto their more contextually probable subsets and supersets produces a more limited chordal vocabulary that appears to heavily favor diatonic triads. This combination of corpus analysis and computational modeling yields two main insights into tonal corpora: First, diatonic triads tend to occur more frequently than do other sets. Second, their subsets and supersets appear less frequently but in contextually similar positions.

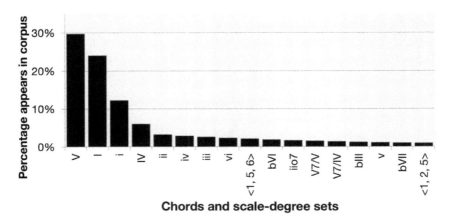

FIGURE 3.8 Chord vocabulary reduced from the YCAC (96% of all chord events)

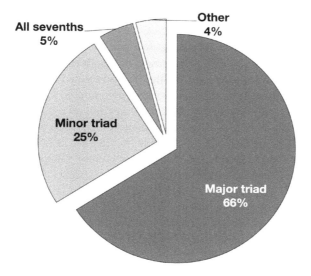

FIGURE 3.9 Reduced YCAC prime forms

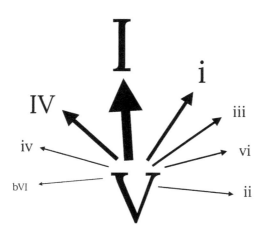

FIGURE 3.10 Reduced YCAC transitions from V

But am I not overcomplicating and overexplaining what music theory has known for centuries? On the contrary, this analysis uniquely formalizes the kinds of assumptions we make and which characteristics of a corpus we rely upon when we assume the syntactic supremacy of triads and seventh chords. By computationally modeling this reduction process, I am potentially identifying strategies used by listeners, composers, and learners when they parse and categorize the events of a musical surface.

108 What Is Harmony?

The unintuitive results produced by this modeling can also cause us to reconsider the hegemonic status that music theory affords the triad. Figure 3.8 provides a clear example. There, two non-triadic chords appear in the distribution, <$\hat{1}$, $\hat{5}$, $\hat{6}$> and <$\hat{1}$, $\hat{2}$, $\hat{5}$>. This means that both these structures and their subsets and supersets appear with enough frequency and contextual regularity to become vocabulary items through the reduction process. The chords ostensibly exhibit a traditional predominant function: they follow a variety of chords (I, i, IV, V, etc.), but <$\hat{1}$, $\hat{5}$, $\hat{6}$> overwhelmingly proceeds to V (98.14%), while <$\hat{1}$, $\hat{2}$, $\hat{5}$> moves to I, i, vii, or V (40.34%, 18.58%, 17.79%, and 16.92%, respectively). In the appendix to this chapter, I dive further into how these chords act, how they are derived, the interesting insights that they can yield about the inner workings of this model, and the surprising-yet-consistent properties of tonal harmony they might identify.

In addition to these two non-tertian sets, several applied chords (i.e., secondary dominants) are also present in the reduced vocabulary. Their inclusion means that these non-diatonic chords appear frequently enough and with sufficient contextual regularity that they have their own equivalency networks – their own "centers of gravity" – to which other chords are related by the reduction process. This result calls into question our general assumption that the members of the diatonic collection – the notes of the major and minor scales – have exclusive rights to express the vocabulary and grammar of tonality. In other words, this model views secondary dominants not as destabilizing forays into foreign keys but as standard and expected members of a key's harmonic vocabulary.

However, these chromatic and non-tertian sets are the minority. Most chords that recur with enough consistency in the same context as their sub- and supersets are diatonic triads and seventh chords. From a theoretical perspective, we can say that the focal points of context/content networks like those shown in Figure 3.7 capture something akin to "Roman numerals" in the music theory classroom: they describe the basic building blocks of a tonal composition and provide the vocabulary for a system of musical expression or communication. In other words, this reduction process suggests ways that triads and seventh chords might undergird something like a language of tonal music.

Step 3: A Sanity Check to Verify the Model Against Human-Made Models

At this point, the Martian scholar would be quite pleased with themself. They have taken the difficult and confusing hodgepodge that is the musical surface and derived a relatively simple vocabulary and grammar. But casting their (Martian version of a) glance back at their stack of harmony books, the alien begins to have doubts. Does this corpus-derived vocabulary and grammar actually cohere to human musical experiences, compositional intuitions, or expert theoretical knowledge? We can imagine our otherworldly spectator devising an extraterrestrial "sanity check" to compare the reduced vocabulary to models present in the looming stack of textbooks and treatises.

In what follows, I outline such a sanity check, comparing the output of the reduction method to corpora of human-produced analyses. I examine my reduction method against four models used in contemporary music theory and cognition research by seeing how well they each predict (i.e., assign probabilities to) a further chord-progression model derived from human-labeled analyses. This will allow me to observe whether the reduction process produces prototypical chord categories similar to those that musicians and theorists actually use and whether the process identifies how these prototypes move from one to another in a way approximating human analysis. (This sanity check is based on White, 2018.)

For this task, I selected models from the standard corpus analysis literature with the aim of including work that deals both with music of the Western European Common Practice Period and with music from a decidedly different repertoire: twentieth-century American popular music. Since the reduction method produces chord-to-chord probabilities, I selected models that also make use of 2-grams. I have named the chosen models by combining the authors' names with the sources behind their datasets. The two Common Practice models are the Tymoczko/Bach, and the Quinn/YCAC; the popular music models are the de Clercq-Temperley and the McGill/Billboard. Finally, the corpus that each model will be analyzing is the Temperley/Kostka-Payne.

First, the Tymoczko/Bach corpus uses the datasets reported in Tymoczko (2011). This source examines Bach chorales analyzed by hand with Roman numerals and tallies the frequency with which each diatonic chord moves to every other. This model's vocabulary includes triads on the standard major scale degrees with the addition of triads rooted on the lowered mediant and lowered submediant as well, producing a total of nine chords.[9] Second, the Quinn/ YCAC, the largest corpus model used here, is comprised of transitions between each raw chord in the YCAC. (Its moniker references Quinn, 2010, in which surface 2-grams are used to analyze a corpus of Bach chorales; I return to discussing Quinn's approach in Chapter 6). 2-grams that occurred less than three times in the corpus were discarded to simplify the model, following Quinn and Mavromatis (2011).

The two-chord transitions of the Temperley/Kostka-Payne corpus, as reported in Temperley (2009a), provide the chord progressions to be assessed by the other models. These 2-grams are drawn from the harmonic analyses found in the instructor's edition for the Kostka and Payne (2012) textbook. This corpus, totaling 919 annotations, involves only root information and the mode of the excerpt. Here, V^7, V, and v would all be represented as $\hat{5}$, conflating chords that are distinguished in several of the other models.[10]

I chose to include models derived from two popular-music corpora to create a richer assessment of the reduction method. Since American popular music

110 What Is Harmony?

uses a similar chord vocabulary to the Common Practice but deploys it in a very different way, comparing the reduction model's behavior to these popular-music models will give us a better picture of how accurately the reduced vocabulary situates within the norms and expectations of the Common Practice. (That is, because it was trained on Common Practice music, the reduced model should ideally perform closer to a Common Practice model than to a popular-music model when assessing the Temperley/Kostka-Payne data.) The first popular music model, the de Clercq-Temperley, uses the same annotations as the Temperley/Kostka-Payne corpus – that is, chord roots on chromatic scale degrees – but it is drawn from a corpus of popular music (de Clercq and Temperley, 2011). The McGill/Billboard corpus uses key-centered lead sheet notations, thereby introducing seventh chords, incomplete chords, and dissonances into its vocabulary, which includes 638 distinct chords (Burgoyne et al., 2011). Finally, I refer to the harmonic model produced using the procedure outlined already as the Reduced YCAC and use the top 22 chords from the reduced distribution and the 2-gram transitions between them.

For this "sanity check," I employ *cross entropy*. Recall from Chapter 1 that this process assesses some series of observations using a probabilistic model and then outputs a cross-entropy value. The higher the cross entropy, the more "surprised" that probabilistic model is by the event it is observing. Given that the Temperley/Kostka-Payne corpus represents something of a "textbook" model of tonal harmony, a serviceable model of Common Practice chord progressions should be able to predict that corpus's events relatively well: models that predict this corpus with a low cross entropy (and high probability) should more or less align with the Kostka and Payne (2012) textbook's approach to harmony. I can then track and compare the resulting cross entropies to see which models more closely adhere to this textbook corpus. If our reduction method does, indeed, produce an intuitive vocabulary and grammar of Common Practice tonal harmony, the Reduced YCAC model should return a cross entropy value comparable to other Common Practice models and should even outperform the models based on popular music.[11]

However, the varying sizes and components of each model's harmonic vocabulary make a single cross-entropy measurement insufficient: trying to compare apples to oranges requires multifaceted descriptors. Therefore, two different cross entropy measurements are reported, both representing two different ways to deal with zero-probability events, i.e., progressions in the Temperley/Kostka-Payne corpus that may not be present in the other corpora. (Since these models assign probabilities based on the number of times they've seen something before, when they observe something they have never encountered, that event is assigned a probability of zero, a value very difficult to work with in multiplicative and logarithmic computations!) The first solution uses what informatics researchers call "smoothing." This solution ascribes a very low probability – but not zero – to all such zero-probability events.[12] Because this approach ascribes these low probabilities to events that *do* occur in the Temperley/Kostka-Payne corpus but *do not* occur in some other corpus, the less that some corpus overlaps with the Temperley/Kostka-Payne corpus, the more of these very low probabilities will result. With more low probabilities in their array of assessments, models that have less overlap with the observed corpus will produce higher overall cross entropies.

The second cross-entropy measurement, which does not involve smoothing, ignores those 2-grams that the assessing model has never seen before, passing over them as probability assessments are made. This approach captures how well each model performs when its vocabulary and 2-grams overlap with those of Temperley/Kostka-Payne observations. However, if a model minimally overlaps with Temperley/Kostka-Payne but these few overlaps involve high-probability events, the resulting cross entropy will be relatively low, even though the process ignores most of the observed sequence. Therefore, to determine the amount of overlap between corpora, I calculate the percentage of 2-grams that this second cross-entropy measurement skips over and report this value as the *exclusion rate*. Finally, the size of each model's chord vocabulary is also reported.

With all these bits of technology in place, we can set our sanity check in motion, calculating the cross entropies resulting from each corpus assessing the Temperley/Kostka-Payne corpus. Figure 3.11 shows cross-entropy quantities for the six models used to assess the 2-grams drawn from the Temperley/Kostka-Payne corpus, allowing one to see how well the Reduced YCAC model measures up against each other model.

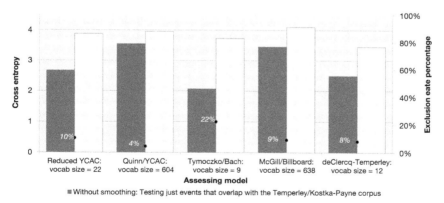

FIGURE 3.11 Cross-entropy results for each corpus-based model

112 What Is Harmony?

The Quinn/YCAC model provides the lowest percentage of exclusion, indicating that very few of the Temperley/Kostka-Payne 2-grams are not present in its model. This low exclusion rate is not surprising given that the model uses the YCAC's raw vocabulary and, therefore, includes a large number of chords. The model's size can also account for its relatively high cross entropies (3.4 and 4.0): because its probability mass is divided among a large vocabulary of slices, the probabilities it assesses will be relatively low on the whole compared to models with smaller vocabularies. In contrast, the Tymoczko/Bach model produces a high exclusion rate and considerably different smoothed (i.e., using only overlapping events) and unsmoothed (i.e., using all events) cross entropies (2.1 and 3.9, respectively). Since it uses only diatonic triads, the model can assess only diatonic progressions – it therefore excludes all non-diatonic progressions in the unsmoothed approach or assesses them as having very low probability in the smoothed approach.

The de Clercq-Temperley model – one of the models using a popular-music corpus – produces low cross entropies relative to the other corpora. This likely results from its use of the same method of annotation as the baseline Temperley/Kostka-Payne corpus. However, the difference between smoothed and unsmoothed values indicates that there are several chord progressions that simply don't overlap between the two musical styles. The McGill/Billboard corpus's unsmoothed and smoothed values (2.49 and 3.45, respectively, with an 8% exclusion rate) can be attributed to the relative size of its chord vocabulary combined with its contrasting syntax. Finally, the Reduced YCAC model returns an unsmoothed cross entropy of 2.7, a smoothed cross entropy of 3.9, and an exclusion rate of 10%.[13]

Given these results, the Reduced YCAC model seems to provide a method of organizing a musical surface into chords that approximate the 2-grams of the Temperley/Kostka-Payne corpus with precision similar to other published models. As a comparison with Quinn/YCAC shows, the not-smoothed cross entropy of the Reduced YCAC is lower than the non-reduced version of the same corpus, indicating that the reduction method siphons the complicated grammar of the YCAC into a system more in line with progressions found in the Kostka and Payne textbook. With smoothing, its cross entropy is similar to the much simpler triadic vocabulary of the Tymoczko/Bach model. While it is by no means a *perfect* match, the Reduced YCAC model seems to function within the range of other models when they assess the 2-grams of the Temperley/Kostka-Payne corpus and certainly does so better than a simple surface model.

Applying the Model I: Determining the Chords in a Short Passage of Free Composition

Relatively satisfied with the performance of the reduction model, our hypothetical Martian investigator soon becomes curious as to how the model

What Is Harmony? 113

EXAMPLE 3.1 (a, left) Mozart, Sonata in D major, K. 284, iii, mm. 1–2 and (b, right) the algorithm's reductions of the passage

fares when analyzing specific musical passages. While the sanity check tested how well the reduced vocabulary and grammar worked in comparison to other approaches, the Martian wonders how the model behaves when reducing specific musical moments and whether its behavior conforms to the intuitions they have developed through the study of harmony treatises and textbooks.

Example 3.1a contains the first two measures of the last movement of Mozart's Sonata in D major, K. 284. Example 3.1b shows the steps used by the algorithm to reduce the surface. For simplicity's sake, the process assumes a division at the half-note pulse; beginning with the eighth-note pulse would produce the same results but with several more steps. The left panel groups all surface pitch content into these half-note divisions. Here, the passing and neighbor tones in the melody produce chord structures that occur relatively rarely in the YCAC, creating less-probable 2-gram transitions between these half-note divisions. Using x-ed note heads, the right panel shows which pitches the algorithm would remove in order to increase the progressions' 2-gram probabilities.

Clapping their (Martian versions of) hands together, our alien is very pleased with this analysis. These are exactly the Roman numerals they expected given the procedures outlined in their library of earthly textbooks. They are also delighted to be able to represent the passage's chord usage and harmonic practice in two different ways: at the elaborate surface level and in a reduction to underlying vocabulary items. The Martian has reached their goal.

However, the extraterrestrial again thinks back to their earlier reading and recalls that in some of the more sophisticated treatises, the authors group chords into syntactic categories. In many of these texts, triads and seventh chords are grouped into even broader categories according to relations in voice leading proximity, similarities in grammatical behavior, and other myriad ways. With terms like "harmonic function" and "contrapuntal prolongation" swirling in the back of their mind, the Martian begins to investigate the possibility of further vocabulary reduction.

114 What Is Harmony?

Step 4: Grouping Chords by Their Behavior

Insomuch as the reduction process shows the contexts in which constellations of chords and scale degrees appear, it interacts with aspects of harmonic function. A chord network like the one in Figure 3.7 shows various pitch structures that can function like a V chord. The corpus analysis, then, demonstrates how diatonic triads can act as syntactic pillars or functional paradigms to which other chords are related. In other words, the gravitational pull and planetary orbits around the V chord in Figure 3.7 represent something like the "dominant function."

Figure 3.12 shows the 2-gram relationships between the eight most frequently occurring chords in the Reduced YCAC model (a choice that selects all chords that that appear with a frequency greater than 2.1% but also includes only diatonic triads).[14] The font size captures the chords' relative frequencies, and the weight of the arrows shows the relative 2-gram probabilities. (Again, only transitions greater than 2% are shown.) Additionally, I have bookended the diagram with the two most frequent chords – I and V – and placed the remaining chords in between these pillars.

While none of these chords have exactly identical grammatical properties, my arrangement of this space shows that certain groups of chords exhibit similar behaviors, something that will come as no surprise to music theorists. Figure 3.13 uses a cluster analysis (introduced in Chapter 2) to quantify this intuition. Here, each of the eight chords is represented by a series of numbers that reflect the chord's tendency to progress to every other chord, with each value in the series being the proportion of times that the chord in question moves to one of the other chords within the Reduced YCAC. The cluster

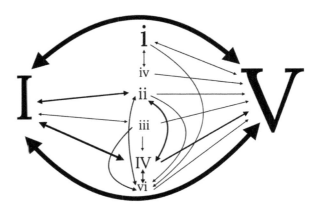

FIGURE 3.12 A 2-gram grammar of the Reduced YCAC distribution

What Is Harmony? **115**

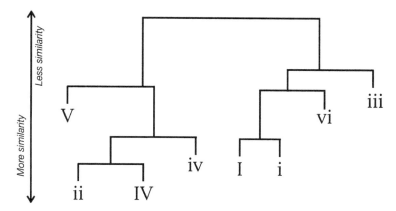

FIGURE 3.13 A clustering solution for the corpus-derived transitions of Figure 3.12

analysis considers these numbers as points in eight-dimensional space, measures the distance between the points, and reduces these distances to a two-dimensional representation. In the end, the greater the similarity of their behavior, the closer chords will be when mapped in the space. The diagram's divisions can be read from top to bottom, indicating greatest to least amount of difference between the chords and clusters. The first (highest) division cordons the space into two larger clusters (roughly tonic and non-tonic chords). The next division shows the mediant triad acting notably different from every other chord. Further divisions group the V chord separately from the IV-iv-ii cluster and remove vi from the I and i pair. Overall, we can read this clustering representing several broad syntactic relationships. Most broadly, the left-hand side contains chords that often progress to chords on the right-hand side and vice versa. But the diagram makes a further distinction between V (to which chords on the right-hand side all progress to and from) and a cluster of "predominant" chords (ii, IV, and iv, which all progress to V but to which V does not often progress). The right-hand side, then, marks vi and iii as having particularly unique progression capacities, neither acting exactly like a tonic triad, nor like the non-tonic predominant cluster.

Figure 3.14 attempts to reconcile the frequency-based layout of Figure 3.12 and the similarities expressed in the cluster analysis of Figure 3.13. While frequency continues to be represented by relative font size, I have now placed the major and minor tonic chords in the leftward category based on their syntactic similarities. Having a unique syntactic function and as one of the reduced corpus's most frequent chords, V dominates the rightward category. I then group

116 What Is Harmony?

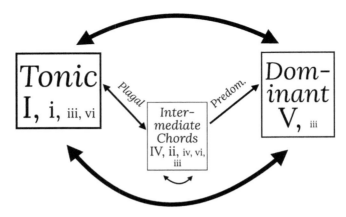

FIGURE 3.14 A syntactic categorization of the chord behaviors in Figures 3.12 and 3.13

the remaining chords into a single category, as they each tend to move to and from the pillar chords. Reflecting its capacity to both shuttle toward and follow from a V chord, the submediant appears within the intermediate and tonic groups.[15] Finally, iii – an infrequent chord that goes to and from many different chords – has been placed in all three categories.

I have also included labels on this diagram that are drawn from traditional music-theoretical notions of chord grammar. Here, I call the two main pillars "tonic" and "dominant," since they track with traditional conceptions of chord constituency and behavior. I then use the term "intermediate" to describe chords that shuttle between the two pillars. These chords exhibit two possible behaviors: First, they can move to and from tonic chords, a behavior that I label as "plagal." These intermediate chords can additionally move to dominant chords, although chords in the dominant category do not exhibit reciprocal behavior. I label this move as "predominant." (I return to the idea and history of the plagal function in Chapter 4, but in short: the term "plagal" generally indicates a IV-based function that expands tonic and does not lead to dominant.

There is nothing new about these categorizations. Schenker (1935) describes *intermediate* chords as progressing between *tonic* and *dominant Stufen* (or scale steps), and the distinctions between *plagal* and *predominant* functions have been variously described by theorists like Smith (1981), Swinden (2005), and Doll (2017). But the corpus modeling of these categories yields an interestingly subtle reading of chord function. Figure 3.14 uses two qualitatively different ways of describing and grouping chords: according to the way they progress and according to their frequency. Taken together, I and V comprise over half of the reduced grammar's probability mass. They also act very differently from one another. Their status as pillars is warranted by the combination of the two characteristics. Every other chord, then, is an intermediate chord by virtue of its membership in the remaining probability mass. However, the predominant and plagal functions are defined by how the intermediate chords act in relation to the tonic and dominant pillars.

In sum, by analyzing the corpus modeling, we can make claims about different ways that chords function within the corpus. In Chapter 4, I will examine other ways that corpora can express notions of harmonic function, but for now, I will delve into how voice leading proximity can be used to further reduce a chord vocabulary.

Step 5: Further Reduction Using Voice Leading Similarity

Our extraterrestrial researcher is not finished. Flipping through several historical and contemporary books and articles, they find recurrent claims that two chords often engage in the same grammatical behavior if they share constituent elements and especially so if their distinct elements differ from one another by a half or whole step. (See, for example, Hauptmann, 1853; Harrison, 1994; Agmon, 1995; Lerdahl, 2001; Kopp, 2002; Cohn, 2012.) The alien considers the functional theories of Hugo Riemann (1893) that involve privileging the I, V, and IV triads as the prototypical instantiations of three aptly named functions: tonic, dominant, and subdominant. The remaining triads in the diatonic system can be swapped for these prototypes according to the overlap of their content and their voice leading proximity to those prototypical triads. A iii chord can, for instance, function in the tonic or dominant orbits since two of its notes overlap the I triad and two overlap with the V triad, and the remaining note is related by a whole or half step to the remaining note of the respective prototype triad. (Here, the term "prototype" is drawn from Agmon, 1995, an approach I'll return to in Chapter 4.)

The alien scratches their (Martian version of a) head. Given that they derived *two* syntactic pillars in Figure 3.14, why would these humans make so much hullabaloo about *three* chord prototypes? Wondering whether there might be something special about these triads and how they relate to the corpus studies they have already performed, our alien takes out (their Martian version of) a pen and paper and doodles Figure 3.15. They draw the I, IV, and V chords as scale-degree sets, using boxes to note the sets' constituencies and their overlaps. Using size to denote the triad's frequency in the YCAC, they draw in the corresponding Roman numerals. Looking down, the Martian realizes that these three triads have minimal scale-degree overlap. The alien notates the remaining triads onto the space to find that they, conversely, all share two scale degrees with at least one prototype triad.

Studying their doodle, the Martian begins to consider a few characteristics of this space. First, it promotes the major triad – the YCAC's most frequent

118 What Is Harmony?

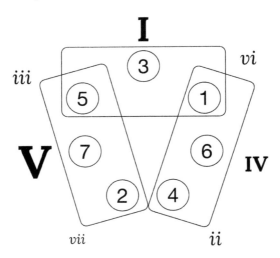

FIGURE 3.15 The scale-degree constituencies of the I, IV, and V triads as maximally distinct

set class — to prototype status. Second, the three iterations of the major triad prototype are maximally distinct within the diatonic set. The Martian also notices that this solution relegates the less frequent triadic set classes — minor and diminished triads — to points of maximal overlap with the more frequent prototypes. Additionally, they notice that they only need to move one note by step in any of the minor or diminished triads to produce one of the prototypical major triads. That is, the not-major triads are all related to major-triad prototypes both by their scale degree overlap and by the fact that the remaining note is only a step away from the corresponding note in the prototype. And, the Martian notes with delight, these properties are overdetermined. The diatonic system has all these properties simultaneously baked into it: there are only three major triads, they are maximally distinct within the system, and they are related by stepwise voice leading to the other (not-major) triads.

Convinced that humans rely on tactics that involve stepwise voice leading in their understanding of harmony, the extraterrestrial gets to work designing a new version of their reduction model, one that relates chords by voice leading relationships.

Following the same logic as our extraplanetary interloper, I modify the reduction model to include stepwise equivalencies in addition to subset and superset equivalencies. Through this modification, less probable chord structures will now be reduced to more probable chords that contain scale degrees a step away from the original chord.[16] For instance, relatively less frequent ii chords can now be reduced to more frequent IV chords when they occur in similar contexts, because ii shares two scale degrees with IV, and the remaining scale degree in ii ($\hat{2}$) is a step away from the remaining scale degree in IV ($\hat{1}$).

Similarly, minor tonic triads will generally be reduced to major tonic triads when they occur in similar contexts: they have two notes in common ($\hat{1}$ and $\hat{5}$), the remaining notes are related by step ($\flat\hat{3}$ and $\hat{3}$), and the major tonic occurs more frequently in the corpus than the minor.

Figure 3.16 represents the vocabulary and grammar produced by applying this procedure to the YCAC, showing those sets that occur more than 6% of the time in the resulting distribution as well as the transitions between them. The size of the font represents the frequency with which each chord prototype occurs in the reduced vocabulary, the thickness of the arrows represents the proportion of transitions from each chord, and the percentages represent the overall probability of each transition between the figure's chords.

In this grammar, most chords in the corpus transform into tonic, subdominant, and dominant triads.[17] All chords move between each other, but IV progresses to V more often than V moves to IV. (The V-IV progressions that do occur are generally non-cadential uses of traditional predominant chords, like V^7-IV^6-V^{65}-I progressions, vii° momentarily moving to an apparent ii, or V resolving to I with 6-4 ornamentation over $\hat{1}$). In terms of our gravitational metaphor, introducing the voice leading force into the system results in further planetary fusing. Where subset/superset equivalence and contextual relationships fused the surface-level chords of the raw YCAC into asteroids of tertian diatonic chords, stepwise voice leading relationships pull these asteroids together and fuse them into tonic, subdominant, and dominant planets, three large-scale reduction networks.

In sum, this step demonstrates that adding an additional force into the reduction model – namely, stepwise voice leading proximity – allows for fewer, larger chord networks. When the reduction model processes the YCAC, the centers of the largest networks are the I, IV, and V triads. The reasons for this are threefold: (1) I, IV, and V occur very frequently in the YCAC, making them

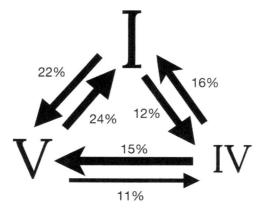

FIGURE 3.16 The YCAC's vocabulary and syntax with stepwise equivalencies added to the reduction process

the chords to which less frequent harmonies reduce; (2) there is minimal scale-degree overlap between these triads, so they do not reduce to one another; and (3) they are relatable to many other less frequent chords through stepwise voice leading transformations and will therefore be targets of the reduction process. Through this, the reduction process demonstrates corpus-based reasoning for treating the tonic, dominant, and subdominant triads as functional prototypes within this repertoire.

My broader model of tonal harmony now has three levels: the musical surface, a middleground reduction favoring triads and seventh chords, and a further reduction that brings three chord prototypes to the fore. In the middleground we find chords grouped around two syntactic pillars with a third category related to those pillars. On the prototype level, this intermediate group is roughly identified with the IV chord. Obviously, this model resonates with Riemannian three-function theory, but – importantly – it is rooted in corpus data and derived using computational processes. In other words, the model reveals the properties a corpus relies upon to produce a three-function model. It shows that grouping surface events into networks by balancing subset/superset relationships of scale degrees, voice leading proximity, and contextual similarities results in a system that favors triads that are optimally distinct in their scale-degree constituency and progress to one another in optimally distinct ways. Instead of beginning with the assumption that I, IV, and V chords underpin all tonal function in music of the Common Practice Period, this modeling employs corpus-based reasoning and results in a paradigm that privileges these three chords. (There is more to say about these topics; the following chapter is devoted to further explorations of harmonic function.)

Applying the Model II: Another Level of Reduction

Our alien now wants to see how the expanded reduction method behaves when confronted with a musical passage. Example 3.2 once again shows the first two

EXAMPLE 3.2 The reduction process applied to Example 3.1, now using voice leading equivalence

measures of the last movement of Mozart's K. 284, this time parsed using voice-leading reduction networks. In the left panel, the arrows and diamond note heads show how the algorithm maps these events onto the more probable chord prototypes. The right panel shows the results. The vi chord is recognized as prolonging the initial tonic harmony, and the ii chord is modified to complete a maximally probable I-IV-V progression. From this perspective, the musical surface expresses a rotation through the three grammatical prototypes identified in the corpus. Once again, the alien feels quite pleased with themselves, as their method tracks with the analytical intuitions gained from studying their music-theory library. Indeed, the Martian now has at their disposal a method of employing corpus statistics to derive not only a tertian analysis but one reliant on chord prototypes and harmonic function.

Step 6: Hierarchy, Consonance, Dissonance

Our Martian researcher pauses to reflect on their accomplishments. They have produced two strategies for mapping a musical surface onto a reduced vocabulary: one using concepts that echo traditional diatonic Roman numerals and the other similar to traditional function theory. The Martian is particularly pleased that their report on harmonic practice in Western classical music will include a general model that describes how humans potentially make sense of, learn about, and compose the complexities of a musical surface. But, having noticed that music theorists often frame tonal vocabularies and grammars in terms of hierarchy, stability, consonance, and dissonance, the alien continues to question their music theory texts, wondering, "Why do music theorists think of the tonic chord as an optimally stable sonority and attribute lesser amounts of stability to other harmonies?", "What gives a tonic triad its unique stance as a tonal *home*?", and, "Do notions of consonance and dissonance have some kind of statistical underpinning in this corpus?"

Relating the reduction model to what we know about how humans perceive stability can help answer these questions. First, frequency-based modeling resonates with how humans experience feelings of stability when presented with certain musical phenomena. In the reduction process, we imagined less probable chord events as prolonging or being replaced by more probable chord events. From a cognitive perspective, the frequency with which an observer has been exposed to an event heavily predicts how much that observer likes or prefers that event (Zajonc, 1968). In these terms, a corpus's most frequent event — here, the tonic triad — has the potential to be both the most syntactically central and maximally stable chord.

Connecting an event's frequency, its grammatical determinacy, and its position in a tonal hierarchy is not new. Theorists of scale-degree hierarchy have argued that pitches that are both more frequent and occur in more predictable contexts are perceived as more fundamental and consonant; theorists concerned

122 What Is Harmony?

with chord hierarchy similarly argue that pitch structures that occur more predictably and frequently are felt as more stable. (I return to these topics in Chapter 6.) Relying on these principles, we can more broadly approach the ideas of hierarchy and prolongation as they relate to corpus modeling.

Consider any of the reductions outlined already. Examples 3.1 and 3.2 or Figures 3.5 and 3.6 all prolong or replace surface events with more probable structures. Here, the reduction process potentially depicts a stable (more probable) framework undergirding less stable (less probable) surface structures. If we assume a connection between frequency and predictability and notions of stability and hierarchy, then we can consider the pitches that are removed or altered to be less fundamental to the progression. The reduction processes, then, produce not only a more constrained chord vocabulary but also progressively more stable and hierarchically deep structures.

Even though this reduction modeling does not involve any explicit definition of dissonance *per se* – it has no concept of neighboring notes, passing motion, etc. – it does suggest some conceptual overlap with the perception of certain notes as more or less consonant. Again: if probable, frequent, and predictable structures can be imagined as stable, and less frequent structures are considered unstable, then it stands to reason that when our process relates surface events to a more probable reduced vocabulary, we are parsing which aspects of the surface are more stable and which are unstable.[18] The unstable scale degrees that are removed or changed between levels of reduction can therefore be seen as dissonant pitches. This notion of dissonance is relative: surface pitches can be dissonant relative to the middle-ground reduction, and middle-ground pitches can be dissonant relative to the chord prototypes of the final reduction. (Subsets would follow a different logic. Adding chord members only increases the probability of the set, and so none of the subset members are "dissonant.")

I am not arguing against the standard concepts of dissonance and consonance in music theory, be they contrapuntal or functional. Rather, my model suggests a way that corpus data can support these theoretical constructs. When the reduction process is applied to a musical surface, the relatively less frequent non-tertian sonorities created by contrapuntal dissonances are removed. And applying voice leading equivalence reduces the relatively less frequent triads and seventh chords of functional dissonance to chord prototypes. In both cases, my model capitalizes on the overarching probabilistic features of dissonances in the reduction processes, giving rise to a more general definition of dissonance than could be applicable to any particular compositional tactic.

Step 7: Comparing Corpora

Before finalizing their report to the alien authorities, our Martian researcher decides to include a short addendum so the research community of their home planet will not get the impression that all human music works exactly the same way. This is wise: a corpus with different properties will output different reduced vocabularies. Consider Figure 3.17, a corpus of American popular music submitted to the same process applied to the YCAC above. The figure uses the McGill/Billboard corpus (Burgoyne et al., 2013). This corpus's annotations are very different from those of the YCAC. It consists of lead-sheet-style chord symbols provided by human analysts rather than simultaneities of scale-degree sets. These harmonic annotations provide the triadic root and chord quality and, if necessary, the bass note and any added tones. There are several noticeable divergences from the YCAC's reduced vocabulary and Figure 3.17. Among them, the subdominant triad overtakes the dominant in terms of frequency, and the subtonic triad (♭VII) is present in this distribution. <$\hat{1}, \hat{2}, \hat{5}$>, encoded as V^{sus}, is still present in this dataset, and it continues to act similarly, proceeding to I more frequently than to V. In line with previous corpus analyses of popular music (de Clercq and Temperley, 2011; Burgoyne, 2012), it seems that chords appearing in both styles have different frequency ranks in these corpora than in corpora representing the Common Practice Period.

This method of reduction can show deeper divisions than those found in comparing the basic chordal vocabularies. Figure 3.18 is analogous to Figure 3.16, in that stepwise voice leading equivalence has been added to the reduction process. Once again, only a few chord prototypes remain. (Only chords that occur more than 2% within the frequency distribution are represented.) The font sizes show chords' relative frequencies, arrows show the relative transition probabilities from each chord, and the percentage values indicate the probability of each transition. The resulting chord prototypes and the transitions between them are dramatically different from those in the YCAC. Instead of contextual categories based around three maximally distinct triads, the space is divided into

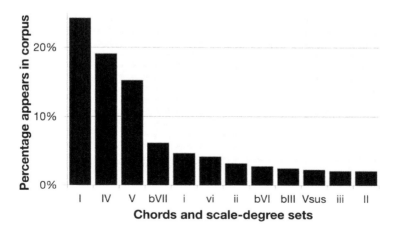

FIGURE 3.17 Top 85% of chords in the reduced McGill/Billboard corpus

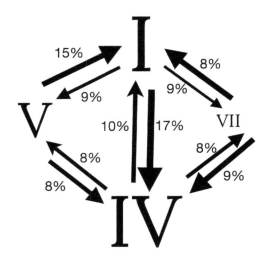

FIGURE 3.18 Chord prototypes in the McGill/Billboard corpus

four areas. ♭VII <$\hat{2}$, $\hat{4}$, ♭$\hat{7}$>, a chord that exists two stepwise changes from either IV or V, now occurs with enough frequency to create its own gravitational pull and to become its own voice leading prototype.[19] While I and IV move to every other chord, I moves most often to IV, and IV's transitions are equally divided. V and ♭VII transition to and from I and IV but not to each other (or, at least not sufficiently frequently to appear in the figure). This dynamic creates a syntactic space oriented around the I-IV axis, with V and ♭VII existing as medial points on either side of this central axis.

While harmonic function in popular music is hotly debated (Everett, 2004; Biamonte, 2010; Nobile, 2016; White and Quinn, 2018), these arguments remain somewhat outside the scope of this chapter. This figure simply highlights that subjecting a pop-music corpus and a Common Practice corpus to the same voice leading reduction produces different vocabularies and grammars.

Our Martian also decides that their addendum should address the variation that can exist within one musical tradition, in particular, the subtle differences they have noted in chronological divisions of the YCAC. Table 3.1 shows chord frequencies in reduced chronological subsets of the YCAC. Some interesting differences appear. The rise of V^7 as the dominant prototype, the changing role of v in the distribution, and the prominence of V^7/V between 1751 and 1850 are all evidence of changes in harmonic practice through different historical eras.[20]

These changes reflect the stylistic distinctions discussed in Chapter 2, and they will play a role in Chapter 6, where I model key orientation. But at this point, it will suffice to say that my reduction procedure reveals slightly different chordal vocabularies in different historical eras.

TABLE 3.1 Top 10 chords present in the reduced vocabulary of five subsets of the YCAC, ranked by frequency

Rank	1650–1700	1701–1750	1751–1800	1801–1850	1851–1900
1	V: 29%	V: 26%	I: 33%	V^7: 28%	V^7: 24%
2	I: 23%	I: 20%	V: 28%	I: 23%	I: 20%
3	i: 16%	i: 12%	i: 10%	i: 18%	i: 15%
4	IV: 7%	IV: 8%	IV: 7%	iv: 6%	iv: 7%
5	iv: 5%	ii: 4%	V^7/V: 5%	IV: 4%	IV: 5%
6	v: 4%	<$\hat{1}$, $\hat{5}$, $\hat{6}$>: 4%	vi: 4%	ii: 3%	ii: 4%
7	V^7/V: 4%	iv: 3%	ii: 3%	♭VI: 2%	♭VI: 3%
8	ii: 3%	iii: 2%	iv: 2%	<$\hat{1}$, $\hat{5}$, $\hat{6}$>: 2%	v: 2%
9	vi: 3%	♭VI: 2%	iii: 2%	V^7/V: 2%	ii°^{7}: 2%
10	♭VI: 2%	vi: 2%	ii°^{7}: 2%	♭VII: 2%	iii: 2%

Cognitive Considerations: Triads and Seventh Chords as Simplification; or, Why <$\hat{1}$, $\hat{5}$, $\hat{6}$>and <$\hat{1}$, $\hat{2}$, $\hat{5}$> May Not Appear in a Harmony Textbook

Our extraterrestrial begins looking for any loose ends that need tying up as they put the finishing touches on their report. From a cognitive and compositional standpoint, their work has revealed some properties of music that are available to listeners as they learn the norms and expectations of any given repertoire, and it has offered potential explanations for some common compositional choices. But there are still some observations that they are hard-pressed to connect to their collection of music textbooks and treatises. The alien researcher drums their (alien version of) fingers on the table and asks themself: What about the non-triadic structures in the reduced vocabularies? And what about chromatic and applied chords? If these structures occur so frequently and consistently, why don't they show up as part of a baseline tonal vocabulary in their library of books?

David Huron's (2006) concept of *heuristic listening* offers one potential explanation. Each step in this chapter has focused on a way of deriving a small group of privileged sets from some larger universe of possibilities. We can frame this kind of discernment as a listening strategy in which a listener privileges simple and serviceable patterns over more precise and complicated patterns. This is the very definition of heuristic listening (Huron, 2006, 94). A learner identifies a simpler system that works *most* of the time in place of more complicated systems that work *all* the time, balancing a model's complexity with its predictive power. Consider a model of musical learning that tallies, categorizes, and tracks the progression of every member of the enormous vocabulary of possible events that occur on a musical surface. This listening strategy would work well, but it would be immensely complicated. Creating a smaller vocabulary reduces the

126 What Is Harmony?

complexity of the model while sacrificing only a relatively small amount of predictive power.[21] This cognitive simplification could explain why traditional models favor diatonic tertian sonorities at the expense of non-triadic structures and applied dominants. While the use of these collections seems statistically important in Common Practice music, removing them from the system reduces complexity while forgoing minimal predictive power. That is: a learner can heuristically focus only on diatonic pitches and tertian sonorities when internalizing the properties of Common Practice music, because – after all – these are the most frequent scale degrees and sets in these corpora. In sum, a simplified vocabulary of diatonic triads or chord prototypes strikes a balance between surface-level complexity and the predictability and accessibility of tonal music.

Summary

Overall, this chapter has shown how relatively simple chordal vocabularies and grammars can be computationally learned by processing the contextual similarities, subset/superset relations, and voice leading proximity found in the musical surface of a corpus. I also related my findings to notions of harmonic function and dissonance treatment, and I showed how stylistic variation between corpora can result in different vocabularies and grammars. Finally, I suggested that this way of understanding chords interacts with theories of cognitive simplification insomuch as it offers a strategy for listeners to interpret the complexities of a musical surface with simplified templates and expectations.

This chapter is by no means a comprehensive study of all possible corpus-derived properties of harmony. For instance, further work remains to be done in algorithmically modeling more specific relationships between harmonic function, voice leading, and chord inversion. This chapter's references to music cognition are also generally speculative. Future work could aim, modify, or test these models in relation to human perception and cognition.

Notes

1. While a historical review of Roman numerals in music theory is outside the scope of this chapter, it bears noting that they have not always been so central to harmonic theory and pedagogy. Advocated by Vogler (1776), Weber (1817), and Reicha (1818), Roman numerals were vehemently challenged by Hugo Riemann, who lobbied for his own functional notation. In 1917, he wrote, "the Roman numeral method is being more and more marginalized as outmoded" (quoted in Cohn et al., 2001). Riemann's assessment turned out to be false, and Roman numerals have existed essentially in their Reicha-esque form, such that "the inessential notes of the piece are eliminated," leaving the triadic "essential notes" with the numerals showing "the fundamentals [roots] of the chord" (Reicha, 1818, quoted in Cohn et al., 2001).
2. There have been several corpus studies of Roman numeral syntax in the field of music theory, including McHose (1947), Pardo and Birmingham (1999), Huron (2006), Rohrmeier and Cross (2008), Temperley (2009a), and Tymoczko (2011).

Each of these uses datasets from human-made musical analyses or data mining procedures that assume a triadic Roman numeral vocabulary. As it is our goal to investigate the foundations of this generally assumed triadic vocabulary, I make no such assumptions. I instead use a series of unanalyzed surface verticalities.

3. I have included all slices that follow V at least 2% of the time. Also note that the raw transitions do not include points of modulation, such that a slice moving to a slice in another key would not be counted.

4. This modal agnosticism follows my preference for invoking as few musical assumptions as possible within my modeling; but mode is also a topic to which I will return later in this book. However, as one might expect, this choice will favor major mode vocabularies. 65% of pieces in our corpus begin in the major mode, and 82% of all non-ambiguous simultaneities are analyzed as being in a major key.

5. The specific peculiarities of the key-finding algorithm influence the chords in the distribution. For instance, the algorithm is not particularly aggressive in noting modulations to parallel and relative minor keys, which therefore means that lowered mediant, submediant, and subtonic scale degrees arise more in the YCAC than they might if the corpus used another key-finding method. Notably, Trevor de Clercq (2016) has identified several unintuitive key assessments within the YCAC as well as the presence of encoding errors in the original MIDI files. My stance is that the sheer size of the corpus will allow these errors to function as random noise in the signal, noise outweighed by reliable data.

6. When compiling the YCAC's harmonic slices for the raw vocabulary, three simplifying assumptions were made. First, if a set with fewer than three notes was adjacent to its superset, the subset was ignored. For instance, if the single pitch <C> preceded <C, E, G>, the former was deleted. Second, as mentioned, all repeated sonorities were ignored. Third and also discussed previously, each slice was compiled as an unordered set of scale degrees. This means that all inversions of, say, V would be considered equivalent, but V and V^7 would be distinguished. While this results in some problematic equivalencies – we would intuit that V^6 and V occur in different contexts – introducing chord inversions into the dataset creates a vastly more complicated model, making the following processes computationally prohibitive.

7. iii^7 provides a particularly interesting example, since it is a superset of its origin, V, and likely represents the introduction of a passing or neighboring $\hat{3}$ above some underlying V or V7 triad. A music theorist would recognize such an event not as a progression *per se* – this apparent iii^7 isn't moving from one harmonic location to another – but rather as a prolongation of the underlying V triad. I deal with the distinction between progression and prolongation in what follows.

8. I include two heuristics in the process designed to weight the final distribution toward *chord progressions* rather than singletons and repeated chords. If a set with fewer than three notes was adjacent to its superset, the subset was ignored. For instance, if the single pitch <C> preceded <C, E, G>, the former was deleted. Second, all repeated sonorities were ignored. Remaining orphaned singletons are then removed in the ensuing analyses.

9. Tymoczko delineates his models by mode, but since the current model operates by agglomerating both modes, I combine his two datasets into one to create the one employed here.

10. I discuss how I deal with these inconsistencies later, but two peculiarities should also be noted. First, the corpus includes chords with no discernible root: these are often augmented-sixth chords and passing chords and are designated as "miscellaneous." Such chords are removed from my calculations. Second, chords are designated by their

128 What Is Harmony?

root using chromatic scale degrees (i.e., the integers modulo 12). This means that events that might be distinct in diatonic space will be considered equivalent in my models (for instance, chords on the flat mediant scale degree and the raised supertonic would both be represented as having the same root).

11. Since many corpora had somewhat different definitions of "chord," the most frequent chord in the assessing corpus was identified with each of the Kostka-Payne chord roots. For instance, the most frequent chord with a root on scale degree 5 in the Quinn/YCAC was V^7. When subjected to the cross-entropy measurements, this was mapped onto each of the Temperley/Kostka-Payne $\hat{5}$ annotations. For the Tymoczko/Bach V was used, and so on. Also, by reconstructing 2-gram transitions using reported transition probabilities rather than using actual musical passages, we sidestep the thorny problem of modulation.

12. This was done using the Laplace smoothing method, with an additive factor of 1 (Jurafsky and Martin, 2008). This process simply means that I add "1" to all potential possibilities so that no possibilities have a zero probability.

13. These results show that cross-entropy values benefit from a shared chord vocabulary (as in the de Clercq-Temperley corpus) and a small vocabulary (Tymoczko/Bach), and that exclusion rates benefit from a large vocabulary (Quinn/YCAC and McGill/Billboard). The Reduced YCAC model produces results that somewhat balance these factors. Even though it uses the same underlying dataset as Quinn/YCAC, its cross-entropy rates approach the more constrained Tymoczko/Bach model but with less exclusion.

14. The vi chord has a somewhat fragile placement within this distribution. When you allow for mappings to sets of cardinalities less than 3, vi is mapped onto one of its subsets, <$\hat{1}$, $\hat{3}$> or <$\hat{1}$, $\hat{6}$>, which then map onto the far more frequent I or IV chords. This mapping has suggestive implications for our traditional understanding of vi chords as functioning comparably to the tonic or subdominant chords, and it has suggestive overlap with Riemann's *Scheinkonsonanz* concept. However, vi's position within this distribution is also chronologically fragile. As I address later in this chapter, the rank positions of less-frequent chords change between different chronological divisions of the YCAC. In this sense, excluding sets like ♭VII and V^7/V that some periods admit into their list of top-ranked chords is something of a compromise within (or an emergent property of) the long Western-European common practice.

15. In traditional classroom music theory, vi is not considered to have the plagal capacity to expand a I chord, at least not to the same extent as IV or even ii. However, recall that this chapter's methods are both based on surface data (in which an upper-voice $\hat{5}$–$\hat{6}$–$\hat{5}$ neighbor motion over a tonic triad could register as a I-vi-I progression) and do not take inversion into consideration (such that a vi triad followed by a cadential 6/4 would register as a vi-I progression).

16. Music theorists will recognize these relationships as the neo-Riemannian L, P, and R transformations and their non-triadic extensions.

17. Fully 97% of chords transform into one of these prototypes. The remaining chords transform either into some other prototype or map onto themselves. When graphed, these create a very thin tail of chords that are not related to a chord prototype. These low-probability chords are not pictured in Figure 16.

18. I am not the first to rely on this kind of logic. Temperley (2010) suggests that the concept of "metric dissonance" might be defined as rhythmic/metric events that occur at less probable moments given listener expectations of the musical style. A similar computational approach to the issue can be found in Temperley (2009b).

19. This does not seem to be specific to the minor mode, as $\flat$VII transitions to the major tonic as well as to the minor tonic. This aligns with Biamonte (2010), Burgoyne (2012), Moore (1992), and White and Quinn (2018).
20. The frequencies are also found to be significantly different ($p < 0.01$) in a χ^2 test, a statistical test that tracks whether categorical divisions of data exhibit significantly distinct behaviors and is outlined in Chapter 6's appendix.
21. While there appears to be a general consensus regarding the preference for simpler systems with fewer parameters in valuing computational or formal representations of human cognition (Pinker, 2000; Temperley, 2010; Mavromatis, 2009), some recent work suggests that our cognitive processes may *not* be biased toward simple systems and that they can accommodate large numbers of parameters and address low-probability events (Arnon and Snider, 2010; Priva and Arnon, 2013).
22. Combining transitional/conditional and non-conditional probabilities of n-grams is by no means my own invention but rather is used in related processes in information theory (Jurafsky and Martin, 2008) and in computational music theory (Duane, 2012). In fact, calculating the entropy of n-gram sequences generally uses this kind of approach. Recall the section "Other Equation Formats for Entropy and Cross Entropy" in Chapter 1's appendix. These equations used the log probability of some event but then weighted that log probability with the probability of that sequence occurring. Here, the transition probability would provide the log probability, while the occurrence probability would provide the weighting probability.
23. As outlined, I constrained the reduction process to reduce to chords of cardinality 3 or higher. This means that $<\hat{1}, \hat{2}>$, a set that occurs *higher* than $<\hat{1}, \hat{2}, \hat{5}>$, is edited to that set. In another model that allowed for dyads to be at the center of a reduction network, $<\hat{1}, \hat{2}>$ would be the parent of $<\hat{1}, \hat{2}, \hat{5}>$; the implications of that sort of result will remain for future work.
24. A further consideration about $<\hat{1}, \hat{5}, \hat{6}>$ is that its reduced version proceeds overwhelmingly to V. This is not the case with the tonic or subdominant triadic sets to which it could potentially reduce (i.e., if you delete $\hat{6}$ or $\hat{5}$, the set becomes a subset of the I and IV chords, respectively).

References

Agmon, E. 1995. "Functional Harmony Revisited: A Prototype-Theoretic Approach." *Music Theory Spectrum*, 17/2, 196–214.

Arnon, I., and Snider, N. 2010. "More Than Words: Frequency Effects for Multi-Word Phrases." *Journal of Memory and Language*, 62, 67–82.

Biamonte, N. 2010. "Triadic Modal and Pentatonic Patterns in Rock Music." *Music Theory Spectrum*, 32, 95–110.

Burgoyne, J. A. 2012. *Stochastic Processes and Database-Driven Musicology*. PhD dissertation, McGill University, Montreal, Canada.

Burgoyne, J. A., J. Wild, and I. Fujinaga. 2011. "An Expert Ground Truth Set for Audio Chord Recognition and Music Analysis." *12th International Society for Music Information Retrieval Conference (ISMIR 2011)*. Anssi Klapuri and Colby Leider, eds. Miami, FL, pp. 633–638.

Burgoyne, J. A., J. Wild, and I. Fujinaga. 2013. "Compositional Data Analysis of Harmonic Structures in Popular Music." *Proceedings of the 4th International Conference on Mathematics and Computation in Music*. Springer: Heidelberg, pp. 52–63.

130 What Is Harmony?

Cohn, R. 2012. *Audacious Euphony: Chromatic Harmony and the Triad's Second Nature.* New York: Oxford University Press.

Cohn, R., B. Hyer, C. Dahlhaus, J. Anderson, and C. Wilson. 2001. "Harmony." *Grove Music Online.* https://doi.org/10.1093/gmo/9781561592630.article.50818

de Clercq, T. 2016. "Big Data, Big Questions: A Closer Look at the Yale: Classical Archives Corpus (c. 2015)." *Empirical Musicology*, 11/1, 59–67.

de Clercq, T., and D. Temperley. 2011. "A Corpus Analysis of Rock Harmony." *Popular Music*, 30/1, 47–70.

Doll, C. 2017. *Hearing Harmony: Toward a Tonal Theory for the Rock Era.* Ann Arbor: University of Michigan Press.

Duane, B. 2012. "Agency and Information Content in Eighteenth and Early Nineteenth-Century String-Quartet Expositions." *Journal of Music Theory*, 56/1, 87–120.

Everett, W. 2004. "Making Sense of Rock's Tonal Systems." *Music Theory Online*, 10/4. https://mtosmt.org/issues/mto.04.10.4/mto.04.10.4.w_everett.html

Harrison, D. 1994. *Harmonic Function in Chromatic Music: A Renewed Dualist Theory and an Account of its Precedents.* Chicago: University of Chicago Press.

Hauptmann, M. 1853. *Die Natur der Harmonik und der Metrik.* Leipzig: Breitkopf und Härtel; trans. W. Heathcote as *The Nature of Harmony and Metre.* London: S. Sonnenschein, 1888.

Huron, D. 2006. *Sweet Anticipation: Music and the Psychology of Expectation.* Cambridge: The MIT Press.

Jurafsky, D., and J. H. Martin. 2008. *Speech and Language Processing: An Introduction to Natural Language Processing, Computational Linguistics, and Speech Recognition*, 2nd edition. Upper Saddle River, NJ: Prentice Hall.

Kopp, D. 2002. *Chromatic Transformations in Nineteenth-Century Music.* Cambridge: Cambridge University Press.

Kostka, S., and D. Payne. 2012. *Tonal Harmony with an Introduction to Twentieth-Century Music*, 4th edition. New York, NY: McGraw-Hill.

Lerdahl, F. 2001. *Tonal Pitch Space.* Oxford: Oxford University Press.

Lippius, J. 1612. *Synopsis Musicae Novae Omino Verae Atque Methodicae Universae.* Strassburg: K. Kieffer; trans. B. Bivera as *Synopsis of New Music.* Colorado: Spring, Colorado College Music Press, 1977.

Mavromatis, P. 2009. "Minimum Description Length Modeling of Musical Structure." *Journal of Mathematics and Music*, 3/3, 117–136.

McHose, A. I. 1947. *The Contrapuntal Harmonic Technique of the 18th Century.* New York: F.S. Crofts & Co.

Moore, A. 1992. "Patterns of Harmony." *Popular Music*, 11/1, 73–106.

Nobile, D. 2016. "Harmonic Function in Rock Music: A Syntactical Approach." *Journal of Music Theory*, 60/2, 149–180.

Pardo, B., and W. P. Birmingham. 1999. "Automated Partitioning of Tonal Music." *Technical Report, Electrical Engineering and Computer Science Department.* Ann Arbor, MI: University of Michigan.

Pinker, S. 2000. "Survival of the Clearest." *Nature*, 404, 441–442.

Priva, U. C., and I. Arnon. 2013. "More Than Words: The Effect of Multi-Word Frequency and Constituency on Phonetic Duration." *Language and Speech*, 56/3, 257–264.

Quinn, I. 2005. "Harmonic Function without Primary Triads." Paper delivered at the Annual Meeting of the Society for Music Theory in Boston.

Quinn, I. 2010. "What's 'Key for Key': A Theoretically Naive Key: Finding Model for Bach Chorales." *Zeitschrift der Gesellschaft für Musiktheorie*, 7/ii, 151–163.

Quinn, I., and P. Mavromatis. 2011. "Voice Leading and Harmonic Function in Two Chorale Corpora." *Mathematics and Computation in Music*. Carlos Agon, ed. Heidelberg: Springer, pp. 230–240.

Reicha, A. 1818. *Cours de Composition Musicale, ou Traité Complet et Raisonné d'harmonie Pratique*. Gambaro.

Riemann, H. 1893. *Vereinfachte Harmonielehre, oder die Lehre von den tonalen Funktionen der Akkorde*. London: Augener.

Riemann, H. 1914. *Katechismus der Harmonie- under Modulationslehre*. Leipzig: Hesse. (Revised from 1890, *Katechismus der Harmonielehre: theoretisch und praktisch*).

Rohrmeier, M., and I. Cross. 2008. "Statistical Properties of Tonal Harmony in Bach's Chorales." *Proceedings of the 10th International Conference on Music Perception and Cognition*. Sapporo: ICMPC, pp. 619–627.

Schenker, H. 1935. *Der freie Satz*, Wien, Universal Edition, 1935, trans. as *Free Composition* by E. Oster, New York, Longman, 1979; Pendragon Press, 2001.

Smith, C. 1981. "Prolongations and Progressions as Musical Syntax." *Music Theory: Special Topics*. Edited by Richmond Browne. New York: Academic Press, pp. 139–174.

Swinden, K. J. 2005. "When Functions Collide: Aspects of Plural Function in Chromatic Music." *Music Theory Spectrum*, 27/2, 249–282.

Temperley, D. 2009a. "A Statistical Analysis of Tonal Harmony." *Blog Post*. www.theory. esm.rochester.edu/temperley/kp-stats

Temperley, D. 2009b. "A Unified Probabilistic Model for Polyphonic Music Analysis." *Journal of New Music Research*, 38, 3–18.

Temperley, D. 2010. "Modeling Common-Practice Rhythm." *Music Perception*, 27/5, 355–376.

Tymoczko, D. 2003. "Function Theories: A Statistical Approach." *Musurgia*, 10/3–4, 35–64.

Tymoczko, D. 2011. *A Geometry of Music: Harmony and Counterpoint in the Extended Common Practice*. New York: Oxford University Press.

Vogler, G. J. 1776. *Tonwissenshcaft und Tonsetzkunst*. der kuhrfürstlichen Hofbuchdruckerei.

Weber, G. 1817. *Versuch einer geordneten Theorie der Tonsetzkunst*. B. Schott's Söhne.

White, C. W. 2013. "An Alphabet-Reduction Algorithm for Chordal N-Grams." *Proceedings of the 4th International Conference on Mathematics and Computation in Music*, Heidelberg: Springer, 201–212.

White, C. W. 2016. "Deriving and Evaluating SPOKE, a Set-Based Probabilistic Key Finder." *Proceedings of the International Conference for Music Perception and Cognition*, San Francisco, 68–73.

White, C. W. 2018. "Feedback and Feedforward Models of Musical Key." *Music Theory Online*, 24/2.

White, C. W., and I. Quinn. 2018. "Chord Content and Harmonic Function in Tonal Music." *Music Theory Spectrum*, 314–350.

Zajonc, R. B. 1968. "Attitudinal Effects of Mere Exposure." *Journal of Personality and Social Psychology*, 9/2, 1–27.

Zarlino, G. 1558. *Istitutioni harmoniche*. Venice: Pranceschi; Part III trans. G. Marco, ed. C. V. Palisca as *The Art of Counterpoint*. New Haven: Yale University Press, 1968.

APPENDIX TO CHAPTER 3

Balancing Content and Context

Equation A3.1 formalizes how I balance the content and context of chords to create reduction networks. The equation acts upon a series of scale-degree sets D with time points 1 to z such that $D = \left(d_1, d_2 \ldots d_z\right)$, where each individual d_j is the scale-degree set that appears at time point j in a piece of length z. In other words, D is the surface of the music, and each constituent d is a particular surface harmony. The equation's end goal is to reduce these sets to other scale-degree sets – the equation calls these reduced sets s. Since these new sets also correspond to time points in the same piece, we can say that the sequence of s's combine into the series S, such that $S = \left(s_1, s_2 \ldots s_z\right)$, where each s_j indicates the reduced set at each time point j in that same piece of length z. The equation produces these reduced chord s by maximizing the contextual probabilities through function C and the proximity of the two sets through function π. Here, C is a process that produces a contextual probability: $C\left(s_j\right)$ is the probability that a given s would occur given the context of time point j. The next function, π, is a process that produces a proximity value between two sets. $\pi\left(s_j, d_j\right)$ returns a value that captures the similarity of the original set that appears on the musical surface (d_j) and the reduced set (s_j). With the notation *argmax*, the equation is indicating that values for each of its variables should be chosen to produce the highest overall value. Several of the equation's variables are fixed: j is simply some time point within a series, and once some j is determined, the d_j is similarly determined – we can't change the actual notes that occur at a particular time point in a piece of music. The only variable that the equation can change in order to maximize the resulting value is s (and this is why s appears as the subscript of *argmax*). The equation is therefore attempting to solve for the scale-degree set *s* that produces the best contextual value *C* and the best proximity value π given the existence of some chord *d* within the context of point *j*. However, since this process occurs over all time points within the piece, the equation replaces all observed chords *d* with the best possible reduced chords *s* to best maximize the context- and content-derived values. In so doing, the equation reduces a series of surface (less probable) chords using these networks to produce a more likely progression with optimal similarity.

I specify how I implement the functions *C* and π in what follows, but it should be noted that any process that tries to maximize some contextual factor for each member of a sequence can get very complicated very quickly. Changing one event means changing the context of the surrounding events, which might affect how one deals with those surrounding events; how you deal with those surrounding events affects not only the context of the reciprocally surrounding events but that of the original event as well. Such considerations compound exponentially. I therefore employ a tool from machine learning called the *Viterbi algorithm* to implement the following maximization. A description of this tool lies outside the bounds of this book (but see, for instance, Jurafsky and Martin, 2008); however, suffice to say, it limits exponential growth in complexity to linear growth.

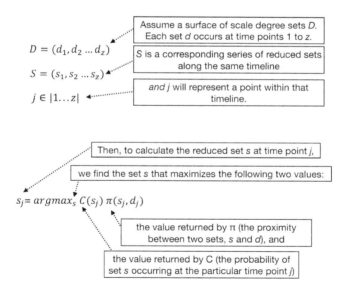

EQUATION A3.1 Relating a surface to a reduced series

Calculating Similarities of Context and Content

In principle, Equation A3.1 could be implemented in any number of ways, securing contextual values and content-based similarities using any pair of appropriate metrics. Equation A3.2 shows a formalization of how I implement this chapter's contextual values (C in Equation A3.1) using a combination of transition probabilities (i.e., how often an event occurs given past events) and the frequency (what I'll call the "occurrence" probability) of those events.

The **transitional probability** is calculated using the n-gram formulation I outlined in Chapter 1 and described in detail in that chapter's appendix. As with all probabilities, the count of some specific case is divided by the count of some general case: here, the specific case involves a sequence of length n ending with some particular chord s, and the general case is the sequence of length n ending with any chord. More formally: the transition probability of a set occurring at time point j in a sequence of length n is calculated as the number of times that sequence ends with set s_j (the specific case) divided by the number of times that sequence ends with any set (the general case). In this chapter, I use 2-chord progressions (i.e., 2-grams).

The **occurrence probability**, or what I'm labelling the **likelihood**, captures how probable that full chord sequence – here, the 2-gram – is within the corpus. Now, the specific case is the particular 2-gram and the general case is all 2-grams. We therefore calculate the likelihood by counting the number of times that 2-gram chord sequence is observed in the corpus and dividing by the count of all 2-chord sequences within that corpus.

Following norms of information theory, we use the negative logarithm of the product. This primarily bolsters against unusably small numbers that result from multiplying already-small probabilities together, but it is also a relic of this procedure's parentage in entropy and information theory.[22] (Further explanation of my use of logarithms appears in the appendix to Chapter 1.)

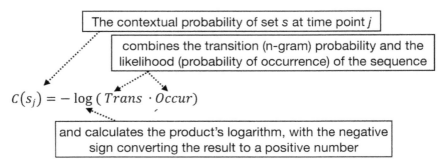

EQUATION A3.2 Balancing transitional probabilities and probabilities of an event occurring

Similarly, Equation A3.3 shows how the proximity measurement (π of Equation A3.1) is implemented. Quite simply, the value is derived from the overlap between the two sets. Sets with greater overlap will have greater values for π than sets with fewer members shared in common.

What Is Harmony? 135

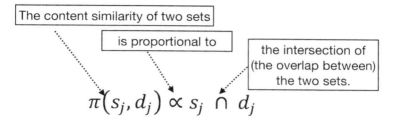

EQUATION A3.3 Quantifying the content overlap of two sets

Some Non-Traditional Chords

While most of the outputs of this chapter's reduction process are triads or seventh chords, two non-tertian chord structures occupy relatively high frequencies in the YCAC's reduced distribution: scale-degree sets $\langle \hat{1}, \hat{2}, \hat{5} \rangle$ and $\langle \hat{1}, \hat{5}, \hat{6} \rangle$. Illustrating the first of these, Example A3.1 shows two primary situations in which one finds $\langle \hat{1}, \hat{5}, \hat{6} \rangle$, as either a passing tonic expansion or a suspended dominant. $\langle \hat{1}, \hat{2}, \hat{5} \rangle$ is a somewhat more variable case. The structure arises in a variety of contexts, two of which are shown in Example A3.2: as a prolongation of a V chord and as an ornamentation of a cadential pattern.

EXAMPLE A3.1 G.F. Handel: Alla Hornpipe HWV 349: mm. 9–10

EXAMPLE A3.2 G.F. Handel, Bourée HWV 349: m. 8, Andante HWV 315: mm. 46–47

136 What Is Harmony?

EXAMPLE A3.3 Haydn Cello Concert in C major, Hob. VIIb:1, mm. 49–50.1

These sets rise to the top of the reduced distribution because – like triads and seventh chords – they occur frequently and their subsets and superset occur in the same contexts. They also appear relatively frequently in the raw YCAC distribution and are *not* subsets or supersets of structures that appear more frequently. For instance, the non-triadic scale-degree sets <$\hat{2}$, $\hat{4}$, $\hat{7}$>, <$\hat{4}$, $\hat{5}$, $\hat{7}$>, and <$\hat{2}$, $\hat{4}$, $\hat{5}$> are all subsets of the more-frequent V^7 set. <$\hat{1}$, $\hat{2}$, $\hat{5}$> and <$\hat{1}$, $\hat{5}$, $\hat{6}$>, however, are not proper subsets of more frequent chords and are therefore afforded the chance to rise relatively high in the reduced distribution. These sets become the center of reduction networks that attract related chords that appear in similar situations. For instance, <$\hat{1}$, $\hat{2}$, $\hat{5}$>'s superset <$\hat{1}$, $\hat{2}$, $\hat{4}$, $\hat{5}$> occurs less frequently but within similar harmonic contexts and therefore reduces to <$\hat{1}$, $\hat{2}$, $\hat{5}$>.[23]

Example A3.3 shows how a surface event would reduce to the scale-degree set <$\hat{1}$, $\hat{5}$, $\hat{6}$>. The first half of measure 49 outlines a dominant triad, potentially with an added seventh, and then beat 3 moves to a cadential 6/4, which is prolonged into the first eighth note of the fourth beat with a passing raised $\hat{4}$. The end of the measure, however, introduces $\hat{6}$ in addition to the raised $\hat{4}$ while retaining the dominant and tonic degrees. To a theorist's eye, this moment would likely be read as a vii°/V above a dominant pedal. The reduction process, however, identifies that moment as a superset of <$\hat{1}$, $\hat{5}$, $\hat{6}$>. The algorithm recognizes this set as similar to other <$\hat{1}$, $\hat{5}$, $\hat{6}$> sets: it's expanding a cadential 6/4 and moves to a V chord. Since the purely contrapuntal set <$\hat{1}$, $\hat{5}$, $\hat{6}$> occurs more frequently in this corpus than this observed set, the algorithm reduces that moment to the <$\hat{1}$, $\hat{5}$, $\hat{6}$> trichord.[24]

4

WHAT IS FUNCTION?

An Epistolary

This chapter consists of a series of eight letters that use the analytical techniques introduced in previous chapters to explore various definitions of harmonic function. The letters first identify aspects of harmonic function that were not addressed in the previous chapter, particularly that categorizing harmonies can involve different weightings of scale-degree content and the chord's harmonic context. The letters argue that not only can these different definitions be computationally modeled, but these formalizations and implementations can also illustrate various aspects of tonal harmonic practice. The letters then use this discussion to demonstrate that certain properties held in common between corpora suggest some generalizable properties of harmonic function and connect those properties to larger cognitive theories of categorization. Overall, the fast-paced, playful, and speculative nature of the analyses shows the capacity of corpus analysis to assist in the project of theory building, in drawing connections between music theory and cognitive theory, and in broader analytical conjectures.

Letter 1: "Function" Can Simply Refer to a Chord's Content

From the Correspondent to the Author

Dear Author,

Your last chapter, while entertaining, neglected several crucial aspects of harmonic function. In particular, you assumed a specific definition of function that grouped chords into categories based on a balance between their scale-degree contents and their contexts within chord progressions. The term "function," however, has its oldest provenance in a content-oriented

DOI: 10.4324/9781003285663-4

138 What Is Function?

definition. When Hugo Riemann originated the term in 1893, he was describing something structural about diatonic tonal music: there are three fifth-related major triads present in the unaltered diatonic system to which a key's other minor, diminished, and applied/chromatic triads can be related. Riemann would subsequently argue that aspects of function theory interact with harmonic syntax – namely that the symmetrical disposition of IV and V around a tonic triad within a cycle of fifths lends a certain amount of attraction between these harmonies.[1] However, in his approach, a chord's capacity to participate in a "function" resides in its scale-degree content. This content-based definition has precursors in thinkers like Hauptmann (1853) and finds contemporary analogues in theories like Harrison (1994) and Biamonte (2010); but Agmon (1995) is probably the clearest contemporary exemplar of this approach – I've reproduced his zone-based representation of function in Figure 4.1. The tonic, dominant, and subdominant functions are shown as distinct zones centered around the three major-mode triads: I, IV, and V. While these three triads have minimal overlap with one another, the remaining triads in this system share two scale degrees with at least one of these central harmonies and occupy the functional zones of the triads with which they overlap. The mediant triad (iii), for instance, overlaps with both the tonic and dominant zones, because that triad shares two scale degrees with the tonic and dominant triads.

Agmon's figure certainly overlaps with the work of your previous chapter. There, your more complex reduction system – the one that relied on both subset/superset relationships and voice-leading similarities – produced basically the same model as in Figure 4.1, prioritizing the I, IV, and V triads (here,

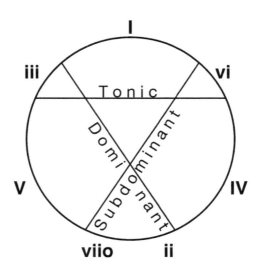

FIGURE 4.1 Agmon's (1995) content-based functional zones

I'm looking at Figure 3.16). You also partially ascribed this outcome to these triads' minimal scale-degree overlap (here, I'm looking at your Figure 3.15, which looks eerily like Agmon's functional zones).

You argued that this outcome was the result of a corpus model incorporating both a chord's scale-degree content and its context. But this is not strictly true. A corpus model that entirely removes harmonic context from consideration comes to the same Agmon-esque conclusions. Since I, IV, and V are maximally distinct in scale-degree space, are more frequent than their sub/supersets, and have scale-degree overlaps with other, less frequent chords, a version of your reduction process that takes *frequency only* into consideration — one that uses no contextual information — will produce networks similar to those in Agmon's circle. Figure 4.2 shows how this process would work for the 23 most frequent scale-degree sets in the major-mode portion of the YCAC, with font size showing the chords' relative frequencies, singletons excluded. (Recall that the YCAC represents its data as *salami slices* of every moment in which a pitch is added or subtracted from the texture, and these slices are used to tally this list of scale-degree sets.) The tonic triad is most frequent, followed by the dominant triad. Scale-degree set <$\hat{1}$, $\hat{3}$> is next most frequent, and being a subset of I, it maps onto the more-frequent tonic triad. As the process continues, three networks form around the tonic, dominant, and subdominant triads. With very few exceptions,[2] this process would map the entire vocabulary of the YCAC onto just three triads without ever considering the events' context.

The example shows two somewhat contentious mappings involving the ii and vi triads, which are ranked as the 22nd and 23rd most-frequent chords

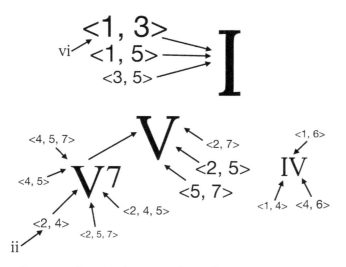

FIGURE 4.2 Content-only reduction networks in the YCAC

140 What Is Function?

in the distribution. The former maps onto the dominant function: its most probable subset being $<\hat{2}, \hat{4}>$, a member of the V network via V^7. The latter maps onto the tonic network as a superset of $<\hat{1}, \hat{3}>$. This is exactly why *context* becomes an issue: A music theorist's intuition would likely dictate that ii should somehow map onto the IV triad because of their shared subdominant-like syntactic capacities. Similarly, vi should map onto both the I and IV networks because of its multiple contextual roles.

However, regardless of these arguable mappings, the very fact that this purely content-based approach works *at all* tells us something about the concept of harmonic function: by dominating a chord distribution and by having minimal scale-degree overlap with one another, I, IV, and V have the opportunity to become the pillars of a model that relies purely on frequency and scale-degree similarity.

In other words: *"function" can be used to refer only to a chord's content*, and a corpus-derived model can represent such an approach.

Sincerely,

Correspondent

★★★

Letter 2: "Function" Can Simply Refer to a Chord's Context

From the Author to the Correspondent

Dear Correspondent,

It was with great interest that I received your previous letter, arguing that the concept of function could be based entirely on a chord's content. However, one doesn't need to look very far to find examples of the opposite approach: context-only definitions of harmonic function. Drew Nobile (2016), for instance, argues that a chord's function in American pop music can be defined purely by its position within a phrase.[3] To Nobile, a "tonic" is an event that indicates ending, and a dominant chord is one that indicates movement to the tonic. While most phrases that Nobile considers end with a V-I cadence, a penultimate IV chord would have a dominant function if it moves to a final tonic chord.

This type of discussion is not limited to popular music's harmonic syntax. For instance, in classroom teaching of Western European classical harmonic syntax, an Agmon-esque content-oriented "subdominant" function is often replaced with a "predominant" function, a contextually defined category of chords that appears prior to dominant chords (e.g., Laitz, 2012). Such an approach then uses a three-function system consisting of the predominant (P), dominant (D), and tonic (T) functions, with T-functioning chords progressing to chords of the P or D functions, P harmonies moving to harmonies in the D or T functions, and D-functioning chords only progressing to T-functioning chords. With the context/content dichotomy implied, Charles Smith (1981) argues that a "plagal" function should be distinct from the "predominant" function and reserved for IV chords that progress to tonic.[4] Kevin Swinden (2005) comes to the same conclusion, writing that because "harmonic function cannot be defined by pitch class alone" (253), chords like IV should be placed in different functional categories if they progress to I rather than move to V. From a behavioral standpoint, the collaborative work of Daphne Tan, David Baker, and Jenine Brown (Brown et al., 2021) have investigated the kinds of harmonies that participants hear as being drawn to V chords, finding the category to be constituted of such expected chords as ii, IV, and V/V but also chords like I and iii.

Computationally, my work with Ian Quinn (2018) takes this logic a step further, using a Hidden Markov Model to group together chords that act similarly within some corpus. Without getting too far into the computational weeds: our machine-learning technique groups chords into categories that tend to appear in similar locations relative to other categories. The process not only identifies the constituency of those categories but also how many categories (or how many "functions") are ideally applied to some corpus. When analyzing the Bach Chorales, the process produces two different solutions, with one solution using three functions and the other 13. For the simplicity of this letter, I enclose only my reproduction of our three-function model in Figure 4.3. Arrows show the probability of chords in the corpus moving between the chord categories, while the pie graphs show which chords appear in those categories. The sizes of the pies show the relative frequency of each category, with larger pies indicating the more frequently used functions. The letters are after-the-fact labels we provide to indicate reasonable analogies with the tonic, predominant, and dominant functions (using T, P, and D, respectively). The most-frequent T function (its pie is the largest) progresses to each of the two less frequent functions; P progresses to D (or expands itself with other P chords), and D progresses to T. T contains mostly I, vi, and iii chords, while V, V^7, vii°, and vii^{O7} are the most-frequent harmonies within the D function. P is a mixture of IV, ii, vi, and many other chords.

This three-function system somewhat conforms to many of the theories your brought up in your letter. These three categories group together chords that we've seen classified within a single function by other models. For instance, the motions between functions roughly track the T-P-D syntax you described. However, there are some differences between this model and a more traditional approach. Note that the P category not only transitions to itself quite often, but it does so between a great many different chords, even

142 What Is Function?

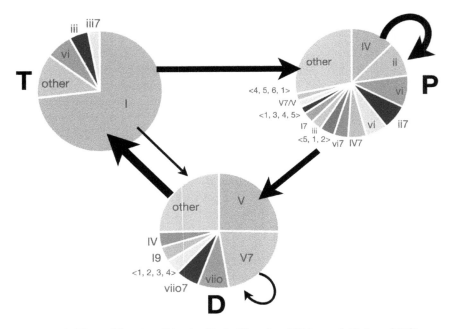

FIGURE 4.3 Three "functions" in the Bach Chorales (White and Quinn, 2018)

including several dissonant passing and neighboring non-triadic sets. The category would seem to be a bit of a "catch-all" in which phrases churn while waiting to proceed to the D function. Additionally, the dominant function – being the function that moves most often to I – includes not only traditional dominant harmonies but also a healthy dose of IV chords along with dissonant structures that anticipate I. For example, the D category contains I^9 chords, or the first part of a 9–8 suspension into a tonic triad.

From a contextual standpoint, however, these groupings make sense and highlight the properties of this definition of harmonic function: if D is simply a chord category that generally moves to I, then IV chords that move to I – "plagal" subdominants in Charles Smith's estimation – should be included in that category. Furthermore, there are a *lot* of harmonic events that happen before a phrase's dominant-to-tonic cadence, and the sundry churn of the P category captures this diversity. If a model eschews all scale–degree–based similarity measures, then the resulting functions will simply capture the sorts of chords that tend to appear at particular locations within phrases.

Notably, different styles produce different functions when using this contextual definition. Figure 4.4 shows my rendition of the four main categories that result from our context-only HMM model of 20th-century American

What Is Function? 143

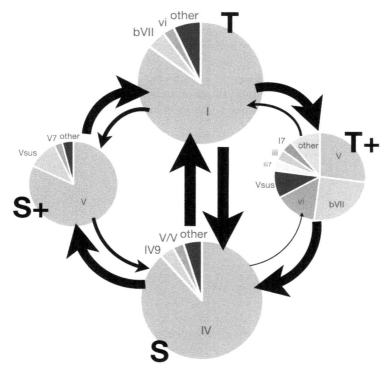

FIGURE 4.4 Four "functions" in White and Quinn (2018)'s 20th-century popular-music model

pop music's harmonic functions, using the major-mode section of the McGill-Billboard corpus (a corpus used in Chapter 3).[5] Again, the most frequent function is built around tonic triads (labelled as T in the diagram). Now, however, the second-most-frequent function (called S in the diagram) is mostly comprised of subdominant triads. A third function progresses from T to S (we label this function T+), and a fourth moves from S to T (we call this function S+). Progressions like I-V-IV-V, I-♭VII-IV-V, or I-iii-IV-V[7] would all traverse around a full T- T+-S-S+ cycle. Like the three-function Bach model, categories in this model appear to favor certain chord structures: the T and S functions favor the I and IV triads, respectively, and S+ favors the V triad along with other chords rooted on $\hat{5}$. But also like the Bach model, some categorizations are unintuitive in terms of the chords' scale-degree contents. T+ features a diversity of chords united only by the fact that they tend to appear between T and S chords in this corpus, while T contains some ♭VII chords.

This letter is neither the place to litigate the specific merits of these functional categories nor to argue about the value of purely contextual

144 What Is Function?

approaches to harmonic function. Rather, I simply intend to demonstrate that chord categories *can* be constructed using only contextual information and that this task can be accomplished using corpus methods. If – as you claimed in your letter – my previous chapter did not do justice to content-based notions of harmonic function, then it also did not do justice to contextual understandings either. In other words: *"function" can simply refer to a chord's context*, and such groupings can be justified using corpus statistics.

Sincerely,

Author

★★★

Letter 3: Corpus Models Can Show a Consistent Reciprocity Between a Harmony's Scale-Degree Content and Its Context

From the Correspondent to the Author

Dear Author,

My initial letter and your timely response were both adamant about distinguishing between context- and content-based approaches to harmonic function, especially when operationalizing those concepts within a corpus model. My initial reaction – like yours – was motivated by the frequent slippage between the roles of those parameters within discussions of harmonic function. However, this conflation is not surprising given that chord behavior is overdetermined by these two parameters. In this letter, I'll demonstrate this overlap by citing, discussing, and building contextual models that inform chord context along with content-based models that inform a function's scale-degree constituency.

Before diving into further corpus analysis, it's worth noting the ubiquitous content/context overlaps in the corpus models and music theories that we've already mentioned in our earlier correspondence. It's striking, for instance, that Figure 4.2's content-derived categories resonate with Figure 4.3's contextually derived categories. Additionally, many content-oriented theories tend to incorporate some aspects of harmonic context. For instance, function theories that incorporate a mixture of the identities of and roles played by scale degrees often exhibit this sort of overlap (see, Harrison, 1994; Doll, 2017). This content-but-with-an-eye-to-context approach suggests that a model could start with a content-oriented definition of harmonic function, and its results could be used to account for harmonic behaviors.

This content-to-context logic can be formalized in a computational model. I could, for instance, build a model that generates chord progressions with three simple rules that determine the contextual behavior of a chord's scale-degree content: (a) chord successions that involve $\hat{7}\rightarrow\hat{1}$ or $\hat{4}\rightarrow\hat{3}$ half-step motion are the most probable, (b) successions that involve other half-step motions ($\hat{1}\rightarrow\hat{7}$ and $\hat{3}\rightarrow\hat{4}$) are half as probable as the most probable transitions, and (c) all other chord transitions are half again as probable.[6] These rules could then be used to output a series of chords whose position relative to other chords – their context – is determined by their content. I could then perform a hierarchical cluster analysis on these chord transitions (as you introduced in your Chapter 2; the chord transitions for this model can be found in this chapter's online supplement). This analysis would group together chords that follow from and progress to similar chords and would produce my Figure 4.5, which is notably similar to your previous Figure 4.13. Because these contexts are determined by the chords' scale-degree constituency, the clusters can be described both by noting the chords' contents and by referencing their contexts. The two smaller clusters are defined by the presence of the strongest tendency tones within the triads, with the ii/IV cluster containing $\hat{4}$ and the V/iii cluster featuring $\hat{7}$; the final I/vi cluster is primarily defined by the presence of the resolution tones, $\hat{3}$ and $\hat{1}$. The larger ii/IV/V/iii cluster, then, contains chords whose tendency tones progress to chords of the I/vi cluster, while the latter may be more broadly defined as those events that are progressed to. We might further analogize between the I/vi, ii/IV, and V/iii clusters and the tonic, subdominant (or predominant), and dominant functions, respectively, given the chord constituencies of these groups. Indeed, scale degree–based definitions of function (like those advocated by Harrison, 1994) often

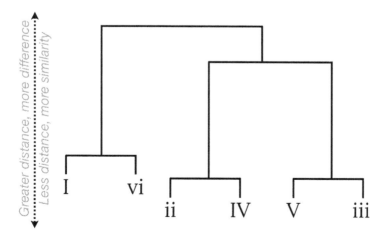

FIGURE 4.5 A hierarchical clustering of the transition frequencies of the content-to-context generative model

explicitly argue that the "tonic" function involves chords that contain $\hat{3}$ and $\hat{1}$ *because* these degrees provide expected resolutions for $\hat{4}$ and $\hat{7}$, with the subdominant and dominant functions then defined by the presence of those respective scale degrees.

Again, I do not wish to advocate for this particular approach.[7] This quick analysis is merely designed to point out that one *can* design a computational model of function that is primarily based on scale-degree content but is informed by the contextual tendencies of those scale degrees.

Analogously – as you suggest in your previous letter – a model can be based primarily on harmonic context and can be used to subsequently derive content-based information. You referenced the purely contextual models of harmonic function presented in White and Quinn (2018), and Figure 4.6 shows the scale-degree constituents of the two functional

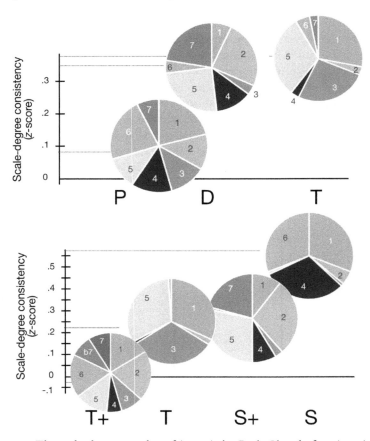

FIGURE 4.6 The scale-degree overlap of (a, top) the Bach Chorale functions (of Figure 4.3) and (b, bottom) the McGill-Billboard functions, plotted by their z-scores

models you mentioned: the three-function Bach model and the four-function pop-music model. The pies show the ratios with which scale degrees occur in the chords that occur in each category, and the vertical axis plots how consistently each function deploys these scale degrees. This is calculated using a measurement called *z-scores*, which quantify how different the scale-degree content of chords within a function are from the average scale-degree overlap between all chords within a corpus. That is, these scores ask whether pairs of chords within a function overlap more (resulting in a positive number) or less (resulting in a negative number) than the average pair of chords in the entire corpus. A more thorough description of the z-score formula can be found in this chapter's appendix; but the more positive the score, the more scale-degree overlap exists between the chords that constitute the function. In most functions, certain scale degrees dominate each of the respective pies. In the Bach model, chords in the tonic function use mostly scale degrees 1, 3, 5, and 6, reflecting the function's use of tonic and submediant triads. The S function in the pop-music model uses mostly scale degrees 4, 6, 1, and 2, reflecting the prevalence of IV and ii. Even the constellations of degrees within the more divided functions (those with lower z-scores) make intuitive sense from a content-based perspective. The Bach model's P function uses the degrees of a IV chord most frequently, but the next-most-frequent degrees reflect the function's use of vi and ii^7 chords.

But scale-degree constituency is not a perfect determinant of these context-based categories, as evidenced by the pop model's T+ function. Because the function contains a mix of V, ♭VII, and vi chords, the function's z-score is a negative value, meaning that this group of chords overlaps *less* than the average pair of chords in the corpus. The diversity of chords present in the Bach model's P function provides a similar example. That function's z-score is near to zero, or close to the corpus's average overlap. However, most of the study's context-based groupings receive an overall positive z-score, indicating that they each have more internal scale-degree consistency than appears between their corpus's chords on average. Grouping by context, in other words, tends to create bundles of chords with overlapping scale degrees. Here, a model that begins with purely contextual parameters produces an output with relatively consistent scale-degree content.

In this letter, I've demonstrated how a model that considers a chord's content can interact with a corpus's contextual information, and I've shown how a model that considers a chord's context can produce groupings with overlapping content. Given that the relationship between content and context appears to be a two-way street, it makes sense that most theories of harmonic

148 What Is Function?

function blend these two parameters. *Corpus models can show a consistent reciprocity between a harmony's scale-degree content and its context.*

Sincerely,

Correspondent

★★★

Letter 4: Models of Function Privilege Chord Frequency but Differ Based on the Type of Data Being Analyzed

From the Author to the Correspondent

Dear Correspondent,

It was with great interest that I read your previous letter. Upon studying your computational examples and reexamining my own contributions (both from our correspondence and from my previous chapter), I noticed three recurring properties of our corpus-based models of harmonic function: (1) they all rely on distinguishing a corpus's most frequent chords from those used less frequently, (2) functional categories are created around these most-frequent chords, and (3) other chords are subsequently related to those most frequent chords to populate the functional categories. The most frequent – i.e., most probable – chords in a corpus become cornerstones for their respective functions. Less frequent chords then group into functions that are situated in relation to these most frequent chords, creating orbits of harmonic function around some set of most frequent pillars. In other words: regardless of one's definition of *function*, chord frequency is likely to play a leading role in how harmonic events are organized.

Let me provide some examples. In my last chapter, I showed how a corpus's most frequent chords formed the centers of reduction networks to which less frequent chords were related by both context and content. The most frequent chords acted as the centers of those networks, with less frequent chords relying on contextual information to determine into which network they would be placed. The pure-content model of your first letter retraced this path, only using the chords' scale-degree content. Again, the corpus's most frequent chords sat at the centers of networks, and less frequent chords were related to these central nodes according to their scale-degree content. The blended model of Figure 4.5 traces a similar logical pathway, but trod from a different direction. Here, the "tonic" cluster is formed around the scale degrees to which other scale degrees transition more often, namely $\hat{1}$ and $\hat{3}$. Even though the tonic cluster is based on this simple contextual information, it implies information about chord frequency:

the tonic cluster will occur more frequently because its scale degrees are progressed to more often. Even the machine learning underpinning the pure-context models of Figures 4.3 and 4.4 follows a similar logic. Notice that the most frequent functions – those with the largest pies – have substantial slices dedicated to a single chord. The most frequent chords seem to congregate in individual pies, resulting in some functions being dominated by a single frequently occurring chord – I and V in the Bach model's T and D functions and I and IV in the pop model's T and S functions exemplify this tendency. Again, the engineering of the Hidden Markov Model is outside the bounds of this letter, but it should be noted that such models favor frequent and consistent relationships of events as they create their categories.[8] In each of these computational approaches, therefore, a corpus's most frequent events are used to create categories around which subsequent categories of less probable events are arranged.

The differences between content- or context-oriented models, then, can be framed in terms of how they analyze, organize, and define these most frequent events. If, as in your first letter, an analyst is concerned with chord identity, they would populate a model simply with the frequencies of individual chords, and the most frequent chords or scale degrees will define their functions. The model will privilege chord content because the underlying data privileges the identities and contents of a corpus's chords. If, on the other hand, an analyst populates a model with the frequencies of chord progressions, the model will be primarily concerned with the relationships between chords, and the output will favor the most consistent, predictable, and frequent chord sequences. The model will be a contextual one.

This is no earth-shattering revelation. As we have already discussed, theorists like Harrison (1994), Kopp (2002), and Nobile (2016) have been identifying the different roles played by a chord's identity and its syntactic position for decades. However, my point is that contextual and content-based models often share an emphasis on events' frequencies, privileging the sorts of things that happen most often in their creation of harmonic categories. Different corpus-based models of function, then, approach and organize a corpus in similar ways when deriving function, and the results differ depending on whether chord content or chord context is being modeled. *All models of function privilege chord frequency, but they differ based on how corpus data are used, defined, organized, and analyzed.*

Sincerely,

Author

★★★

150 What Is Function?

Letter 5: The Overlaps Between Computational and Cognitive Models of Harmonic Function Can Be Represented Using an Approach From Cognitive and Data Science Called the Entity/Relationship Dichotomy

From Correspondent to Author

Dear Author,

Upon reading your previous letter, I was initially puzzled by its simplicity. The fact that contextual understandings of function use relational probabilities and that content-oriented definitions use chord identities seems self-evident. Additionally, the idea that more frequent events exert greater force on a computational model is also not surprising. It makes sense that things that happen more often will receive more attention in corpus analyses of harmony because – at least in some respects – these analyses are all based on counting chords and relationships within some dataset.

After some reflection, however, I have come to believe that your points contain some fundamental insights into how corpus analyses of harmonic function can relate to broader questions of music cognition. More specifically, the way you describe the role of high-frequency chords resonates with some broader cognitive theories of categorization. In particular, there is a potentially strong analogy between what you are describing and what cognitive and data scientists have called the *entity/relational* dichotomy (hereafter, "E/R").

In E/R theory, every database, cognitive process, or organization of information involves two broad categories: *entities* and *relationships*.[9] Entities are kinds of objects, while relationships are links between objects. As conceptual categories, entities are defined by the essential characteristics of objects, while relationships are defined by how objects interact with one another. If a soccer player kicks a ball, we could model that situation using two entities – the player and the ball – and one relationship – the kicking. *Entity sets* are groups of entities that have some similarities between their attributes or relationships: each soccer player is an entity, while the team would be an entity set. Similarly, *relationship sets* are groups of similar relationships. The team/manager and team/owner relationships could all be a part of the team's administrative set of administrative relationships.[10]

E/R theory originated with the work of the computer scientist Peter Chen (1976), who argued that data can be efficiently and usefully organized by identifying entities and then mapping the relationships between them. This paradigm has been expanded over the past several decades to include research into database efficiency (e.g., Hull and King, 1987) and into ways to organize the vast amount of data available on the Internet (Chen et al., 2017).

This approach has also been adapted to language and cognition. Chen himself (1983) extended the scheme to describe natural language, analogizing nouns with entities and verbs with relationships, though this grammatical mapping is by no means without exception. Cognitive theorists and linguists have also wielded the E/R dichotomy to conceptualize ways that humans categorize and describe the world around them, investigating whether and how we differentiate entity and relationship concepts linguistically and cognitively (Sowa, 1984, 2000; Gentner and Kurtz, 2005).[11] Such research has shown some deep differences between how we approach, learn, and cognize entities versus relationships. Children, for instance, tend to first learn words associated with entity concepts before expanding their vocabulary to describe relationships (Gentner and Ratterman, 1991), and language speakers have more agreement when tasked with categorizing entity-like words and concepts than when tasked with categorizing relational words and concepts (Barr and Caplan, 1987; Asmuth and Gentner, 2017). In terms of music, Janet Bourne (2015) and Elliot Chun (Bourne and Chun, 2017) have suggested that listeners might understand themes, chord progressions, and textures in terms of the entity/relationship dichotomy, with listeners processing musical motifs that rely on their inherent characteristics differently than those that rely on relationships with other music.

With this dichotomy in hand, arguments and disagreements between various computational and theoretical models of harmonic function can mostly be reduced to whether and which functions are being described as entities versus relationships. If a theorist is concerned about the content of a function – if, for instance, their main definition of "dominant" is that it contains scale degrees 5, 7, and 2, for instance – then they are working with an entity-based definition. In this case, *dominant* is something a chord *is*. But if they use a contextual definition – if a dominant is that which progresses to tonic, for instance – the theorist is constructing a relational definition. Here, *dominant* is something a chord *does*.

The conceptual move that I am advocating for, however, involves connecting the probabilities and frequencies used in our corpus models to this E/R dichotomy. These connections can then link a model's computational engineering with claims about how listeners hear and use harmonic functions. My simple chord-frequency model would entail an entity definition, since the model is tallying the identities of different harmonies, building categories around a corpus's most frequent chords, and then creating entity sets around those chords' identities. A hypothetical listener using this model would conceive of chord categories as entity sets, with no relationships between them. A chord-progression model, on the other hand, would use a relational definition, since the model is now tallying relationships between chords. The most frequent chord progressions would create functional categories based on these relationships, with less frequent

152 What Is Function?

chords related or subsumed within those relationships. A hypothetical listener using this model would now hear chords categorized based on their relational positions. Figures 4.2 and 4.3 both have similar functional categories; the former represents an entity approach because its functions are derived from the frequency of its constituent chords and scale degrees, while the latter represents a relational approach because its functions rely on chord-progression information. However, regardless of their superficial similarities, the E/R dichotomy highlights the differences between how these models should be understood and heard.

We can also imagine relationship and entity functions existing within the same system. Some of the discussion in White and Quinn (2018), for instance, suggests such a blend. The article contends that each of its harmonic-function models all feature (1) a *tonic* function, which is created around the corpus's most frequent chord, (2) an *antitonic* function, which is created around a second-most-frequent chord, (3) at least one *pretonic* function that transitions overwhelmingly to the tonic chord, which is used to create cadences, and (4) further categories that precede, succeed, or expand these functions. According to this logic, in the Western European Common Practice, I and V tend to be the most- and second-most frequent chords, respectively, and V progresses overwhelmingly to I (see Figure 4.3). Therefore, the tonic function will be created around the I triad, and the dominant triad serves as the cornerstone for a harmonic category that functions as both antitonic and pretonic. In contrast, in mid-century American popular music, IV triads create the antitonic category, since IV is now the second-most-frequent chord, while chords like V and V^7 are still pretonic since they progress overwhelmingly to I (see Figure 4.4). In each of these corpora, the most frequent event is a tonic triad.

In this scheme, the tonic and antitonic are entity sets, because they are based on the identity of a corpus's most frequent chord. That is, in order to know what is tonic or antitonic, the model creates an entity set around the identity of a corpus's most and second-most-frequent chord. Pretonic, on the other hand, would be a relational category, because it is defined by how it relates to other entities. In order to identify a pretonic, the model concentrates on the contextual position of chords relative to the tonic category. Indeed, these concepts map onto our earlier correspondence about the content/context dichotomy, with the tonic and antitonic entities relying on the former and relational functions relying on the latter.

And as you described in your last letter, each of these models uses a corpus's most frequent events to make sense of less frequent events. Entity functions will privilege a corpus's most frequent chord identities to create their categories, while relationship functions will rely on the most frequent chord progressions for their definitions.

Now – my dear author – I can easily imagine your skeptical reaction. Am I not advocating new terms for old concepts? After all, your earlier citations on harmonic function make it clear that the sorts of distinctions I'm making between the role of content versus context in harmonic theory have been around for decades if not centuries.

But by connecting older ideas to E/R theory, I can now link definitions of function to how humans and machines organize and make sense of a large amount of data, thereby connecting corpus analyses to theories of cognition and learning. In database theory, the E/R approach describes how pieces of information relate to one another, how large amounts of data can be categorized in optimally efficient ways, and how this data can become accessible and manageable. Similarly, E/R cognitive theory shows ways that humans might parse and categorize the enormous – and what might otherwise be ungainly – amount of data present in the world around us. Comparably, a musical E/R approach can show how harmonic functions might represent a strategy that organizes, optimizes, and makes sense of the vast amounts of data present in a musical corpus.

Figure 4.7a is a broad approximation of your three-function model in Figure 4.3, now using standard E/R orthography to incorporate some of their novel conceptualizations of tonic/antitonic and pretonic. Square boxes indicate entities within the network, and diamonds represent relationships. A selection of the functions' constituent chords is connected to their respective nodes to create entity sets. The tonic function, for instance, is an entity set made of the entities like I and vi. I am using the designation "Other" for the batch of chords that is neither tonic nor antitonic, and the two possible relationships available to this entity set are designated plagal and predominant, the former relating back to the tonic category and the latter moving towards the dominant. The pretonic relationship then describes the cadential connection between tonic and antitonic. Note that unlike directed graphs like Figure 4.3, the connections are not represented by arrows but rather are described by the relationship node. In other words, these graphs rely on the attributes/definition of a particular relationship in order to navigate between the entities: the *plagal* relationship, for instance, would be bidirectional according to its definition, while the *pretonic* relationship would entail a progression into the tonic entity.[12] Figure 4.7b is a reworking of your previous chapter's YCAC functional diagram that resulted from your reduction processes (Figure 3.15). I additionally incorporate one of your reduction networks (the V network is drawn from Figure 3.7) while leaving the remaining reduction networks to the imagination.

The graphs are now somewhat more complicated, with several layers of entities and relationships. Each square node within one of these networks (i.e., the squares enclosing Roman numerals) represents a chord that either maps onto or is mapped onto another chord using your

154 What Is Function?

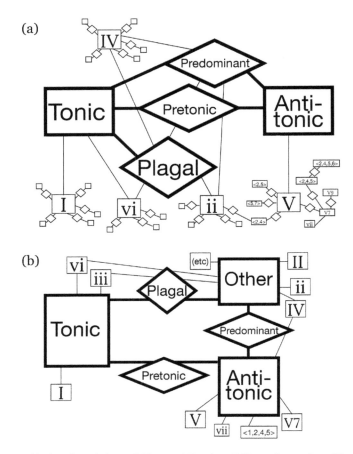

FIGURE 4.7 (a) A reimagining of Figure 4.3 using E/R orthography; (b) a similar reimagining of Figure 3.15

content/context reduction process. The intervening diamonds indicate the (subset/superset/voice leading) relationships that underpin the reduction process. (For instance, just as in Figure 3.7, the V^9 chord of Figure 4.7a maps onto the V^7 chord using a relationship in which the former is both a superset of and less frequent than the latter.) The centers of these networks then participate in larger entity sets or relationships. Eventually, chords of the I and V networks create the tonic and antitonic entities that are connected by the pretonic relationship. Additionally, in my representation of 4.7a, chords (or, more precisely, the reduction networks) connect directly to the predominant and plagal relationships, indicating that these chords all group together primarily because they behave in similar ways – they all participate in the same set of relationships. Here, these relational functions are something a chord *does*. Connecting to an entity set indicates that these chords have some similar identity or shared characteristics. These functions are something a chord *is*.

Again, I can anticipate your skepticism. These diagrams are simply representing the same information as existing models with mere orthographic differences. However, I see a fundamental benefit to this reimagining: these graphs show the link between how data are organized by a computational system and how they may be categorized within human cognition. To circle back to the topic of your previous letter: if computational models of harmonic function privilege a corpus's most frequent chords and then build categories around these chords' identities, the resulting categories will be entities and could be understood by listeners and analysts as such. If functions/categories are instead based on the roles chords play in relation to one another, those functions will be relationships and also could be cognized as such. Given that one of corpus analysis's main powers is to show how data can be organized in ways that yield some insight into a human's experience with that corpus, connecting data about chord frequency, harmonic context, and scale-degree content to E/R theory demonstrates exactly this overlap between analysis and cognition. By showing how these data can be organized via an E/R representation, we can make a generalization about how the complexities of a musical corpus can be corralled both by computation and by a human mind. In sum: *the overlaps between computational and cognitive models of harmonic function can be represented using an approach from cognitive and data science called the entity/relationship dichotomy.*

Sincerely,

Correspondent

★★★

Letter 6: In Tonal Music, Tonic and Antitonic Functions Are Entity Concepts, While Further Functional Categories Are Relational Concepts

From Author to Correspondent

Dear Correspondent,

Apologies for this lengthy response, but your previous letter has inspired me to pursue, research, and develop your ideas both conceptually and experimentally. After this work, I am quite convinced of your analogy

156 What Is Function?

between E/R theory and function theory. In fact, I would now advocate that certain functions *are* relational concepts and some *are* entity concepts. I've come to believe this somewhat surprising assertion because of the role that frequency distributions play within the computational models we've discussed thus far and because of some experimental data linking how we cognize harmonic functions in tonal music to how we cognize entity and relationship concepts. In this letter, I will rely on a mix of corpus analysis, behavioral analysis, cognitive theory, and even some pure speculation to make a provocative argument: part of what makes a corpus "tonal" is that it features tonic and antitonic *entity* functions, with further chord categories acting as *relationship* functions.[13]

My argument arises from two logical strains. For one, when you contrast the ways musicians interact with tonic and antitonic functions with how they interact with further functional categories, those differences resonate with behavioral data in the E/R literature. Second, categorizing chords into harmonic functions potentially relies on a consistent property of tonal musical corpora and natural languages in general, namely *Zipf's law*. It is to this latter property that I first turn my attention.[14]

Zipf's Law and Power-Law Distributions

Zipf's law describes a consistent property of written and spoken languages and states that the frequency of any word is inversely proportional to its position in list that ranks events from most to least frequent. These frequencies will specifically follow a *power-law distribution*, in which the distribution features an initial steep drop-off followed by a long tail. The formula for the curve that fits this distribution is described in depth in this chapter's appendix.

Within a piece of music, distributions of musical events (like those of pitches, scale degrees, and durations) tend to follow this same pattern (Zanette, 2006). Figure 4.8a shows the distribution of harmonic events within the raw YCAC (excluding singletons and using only major-mode data), while Figures 4.8b and 4.8c plot the chord distributions within the Bach-chorale corpus (on which Figure 4.3 is based) and within the Kostka-Payne corpus (see Chapter 3), respectively. I show the Kostka-Payne harmonic data in two different ways: the frequency ratio of each harmony (or the number of times each harmony occurs divided by the total number of chord events in the corpus) and a ratio using these harmonies' total durations within the corpus. Finally, Figure 4.8d plots the distribution of chords in the McGill-Billboard dataset (see Chapter 3). Each graph shows the corpus's most frequent events followed by a precipitous dip ending in a long tail. Within this power-law distribution, the first ranks occupy a huge proportion of the probability mass: much of the area under the curve appears under the first

What Is Function? **157**

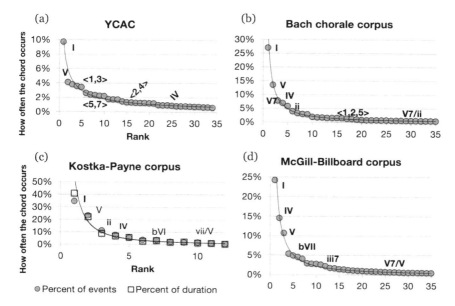

FIGURE 4.8 The frequency-rank distributions of four musical corpora

several ranks. For instance, in Figure 4.8a, the first 10 ranks represent 25% of events within the entire corpus – one quarter of all simultaneities within the YCAC use those 10 scale-degree sets. Similarly, over three quarters of the chords in the Kostka-Payne corpus use the four most frequent chord roots. Each of these frequency distributions also exhibit long tails. We can imagine these graphs extending asymptotically to the right far past the chords shown in these graphs. (The exception, of course, is the Kostka-Payne corpus, whose vocabulary is constrained to the 12 possible chromatic scale-degree roots.) Therefore, the chords that appear most frequently represent a very small proportion of the types of chords used in the corpus, but this handful of chord types are used vastly more often than any other chord or harmony within the corpus. Conversely, a great number of chord types appear only a handful of times. For instance, some three thousand different scale-degree configurations appear in the YCAC, but the 35 scale-degree sets shown in Figure 4.8a describe 66% of all simultaneities in that corpus.

As outlined in Chapter 1, the frequencies of musical events play a crucial role in how listeners learn about those events. There is much reason to believe that more frequent events are privileged within learning. For instance, my earlier chapters outlined research that shows that humans not only learn about music by being exposed to frequent and consistent events (Krumhansl, 1990), but we show a preference for events to which we have been exposed more frequently (Zajonc, 1968, 2001).

158 What Is Function?

While this research attests to the fact that frequent events play an important role in harmonic expectation and musical learning, there is also evidence that the contours of frequency distributions are crucial to how we recognize and internalize differences in the world around us. In 1866, Gustav Fechner built upon the experimental work of his mentor, Ernst Weber, to describe what would become known as the *Weber-Fechner law*. The law states that a perceived difference between two stimuli is not best described by the exact amount of difference but instead results from the proportion of difference (Fechner, 1860). For instance, if we heard two violinists playing a melody together and then two more joined in at the climax of that melody, the increased loudness and intensity at that moment would be quite noticeable. However, if we heard 20 violinists playing that melody, the addition of 2 more violinists at the climax might not even be detectable. Even though the exact amount of change is the same in both examples – both add two violinists – we would perceive each situations quite differently. The noticeable difference is a result of the *proportional* change: where there's a 100% increase in the former situation, there's only a 10% change in the latter. (To be sure, there are further acoustical factors in the total loudness output in these situations, but role of proportional increase is central.) While the Weber-Fechner law advocates for plotting these proportional differences using what's known as a logarithmic distribution (another type of sharply rising curve), subsequent research has shown that power-law distributions – the curves I used to describe Figure 4.8 – can also plot noticeable differences in certain stimuli (Staddon, 1978, 2016; Weiss, 1989). Concerning the topic of harmony specifically, in a recent collaboration with Emily Schwitzgebel (2021), we demonstrated that listeners harbor reliable expectations about chords and chord progressions that happen most frequently in tonal corpora and are less sensitive to norms and violations involving less frequent events. We additionally showed that the relationships between more and less frequent chords can be modeled using exponential distributions.

We may speculate, then, that the exponential differences between chord frequencies might ensure that these differences are salient to listeners and learners. If, for instance, a human is to notice and internalize the fact that some harmonies occur more frequently than others, then distributing those chords along a power-law curve might guarantee that the differences are noticeable and learnable.

The privileges that a power-law distribution afford to its top-ranked events fundamentally connect to the divergent ways that different harmonic functions are constructed in both corpus analyses and music theory in general, and these differences can be aptly described using E/R theory. For one, in a power-law distribution, the top chords will "stand out" simply due to their occurring so much more than other chords, with the chord atop the distribution being particularly privileged. Recalling that models of function tend to begin by identifying a corpus's most frequent events, this exponentially most frequent chord will be particularly privileged in this process. I would argue that this set of conditions – assessing a musical parameter that follows a power-law distribution with an approach that favors a corpus's most frequent events – allows a tonic function to always be built around a corpus's exponentially most frequent chord. The next-most-frequent chord can then create a contrasting category: what you referred to in your previous letter as the antitonic. This second-most-frequent chord will occur less frequently than the tonic but will still occur noticeably more than the remainder of the corpus's chords – so much so that a system of categorization that relies on chord frequencies will likely also treat this chord as a categorical cornerstone. The tonic and antitonic functions therefore are defined by the identity of these two vastly most-frequent chords. With their definitions grounded in chord identities (rather than some kind of relationship), these frequency-based categories will produce entity sets centered around the tonic and antitonic harmonies' identities. In other words, a corpus's most frequent chords are entities – they are objects – and these functions based on these objects will be entity sets. In the YCAC, the Bach-Chorale and the Kostka-Payne distributions, I and V are the two most frequent chords and would therefore become the entities around which the tonic and antitonic entity sets are built.[15] In the McGill-Billboard corpus, I and IV create the tonic and antitonic entity sets as the two most frequent chords in that corpus.

After the initial most frequent events, the distributions in Figure 4.8 begin to even off into their tails. If tonic and antitonic entity categories were based on chords' capacities to "stand out" in a distribution, the remaining chords – with their lower and more similar frequencies – become distributional wallflowers, making it less obvious whether these chords should exert themselves as the loci of entity sets. Instead, we can imagine that these less frequent chords either become subsumed into the tonic and antitonic categories because of their similarities to those chords or become organized into categories by their placement relative to (i.e., by their relationship to) these more frequent entity sets. For instance, consider the V^7 chord in the Bach corpus or the <$\hat{1}$, $\hat{3}$> set in the YCAC corpus within Figure 4.8. Both of these chords will be subsumed into their corpus's respective antitonic and tonic entity sets because of the chords' similarities to the two most frequent chords in those corpora. However, consider the $\flat$VII chord in the McGill Billboard corpus or the IV chords within the other corpora. Because these chords appear both exponentially less frequently than the top-ranked chords, its identity will be less marked. If the chords are not categorized into the tonic or antitonic categories, their role will rather be defined by their contextual relationships to these more-frequent chords. In this frame, $\flat$VII or IV would not participate in an entity function but rather would participate in relationship functions in their respective corpora.

160 What Is Function?

To summarize my argument thus far: (1) distributions of harmony in tonal music generally follow Zipf's law; (2) in these distributions, the most frequent chords appear exponentially more often than less frequent chords; (3) because they appear so much more often than the remaining harmonies, models of harmonic function that privilege chord frequency will create functions around these very frequent chords; (4) the most frequent chord will create what music theory has come to know as the *tonic* function, and the second-most-frequent chord will produce the *antitonic* function; (5) the tonic and antitonic functions will be entity sets because they are defined by these most frequent chords' identities; and (6) subsequent less frequent chords will then either be subsumed into these functions to create larger entity sets or will carve out positions relative to these functions, organizing into relationship categories.

To this point, I have connected some aspects of this argument to human cognition — I suggested that the power-law contours underpinning these corpora help listeners internalize chords' positions within these distributions. However, by arguing that certain functions are entities and others are relationships, I am implying that there exists some sort of fundamental difference in how listeners learn about and conceptualize different functions. Additionally, by describing the two most frequent chords as the pillars around which the tonic and antitonic entity functions will be constructed, I have implied a boundary between a corpus's two most frequent chords and its remaining chords, essentially arguing that the former are sufficiently marked within a frequency distribution to warrant entity status while the remaining chords fail to qualify. This boundary, however, seems potentially arbitrary. Indeed, privileging IV in the Bach corpus or ii in the Kostka-Payne corpus would seem to be plausible, creating a "subdominant" entity set on par with tonic and dominant.

The next portion of my letter addresses these questions by unpacking the different ways that entities and relationships are learned and cognized, making analogies between existing E/R experimental data and function theory and introducing two new experiments that use a mix of corpus and behavioral data to investigate aspects of these analogies.

Hearing Entities and Relationships in Musical Data

To outline some potential connections between E/R theory and harmonic function, Table 4.1 summarizes some differences between how E/R categories behave (this summary is generally drawn from Gentner and Kurtz, 2005, and Asmuth and Gentner, 2017). Table 4.2 then outlines musical characteristics that I would argue analogize with Table 4.1. I'll take each point in turn, considering the established characteristics of Table 4.1 and my corresponding analogies of Table 4.2.

What Is Function? **161**

TABLE 4.1 A summary of entity/relationship differences (from Gentner and Kurtz, 2005; Asmuth and Gentner, 2017)

Entity Concepts/Stable Nouns	Relationship Concepts/Verbs and Relational Nouns
Acquired easily in language learning	Acquired with more difficulty in language learning
Given relatively fewer meanings (in dictionaries and in meaning-solicitation tasks)	Relatively more meanings
Categorized with consistency (in categorization tasks)	Categorized with less consistency
Easy to translate between languages	Hard to translate between languages

TABLE 4.2 Analogies with entity and relationship functions

Entity Functions: Tonic & Antitonic	Relationship Functions: All Others
Prominent in frequency distributions	Less prominent in frequency distributions
Relatively more definitional agreement	Relatively less definitional agreement
Chords and scale degrees are categorized into these functions with consistency	Chords and scale degrees are categorized into these functions with less consistency
Relatively stable between tonal styles	Relatively unstable between tonal styles

Entity Functions Are Easier to Learn About (and This Learning Relies on Their Prominence in a Frequency Distribution More) Than Relationship Functions

From various different standpoints, words and concepts associated with entities are easier to learn. Kloos and Sloutsky (2004), for instance, show that entity concepts are learned more quickly via passive exposure than are relationship concepts: this dynamic extends more generally to the relative ease with which language learners remember and internalize nouns (which are primarily associated with entity concepts) versus the relative difficulty with which they learn verbs (which are primarily associated with relationship concepts; Gentner, 1982). Further reflecting this dichotomy, infants generally learn several object-based words and concepts first before learning relational words (Gentner, 1982; Golinkoff and Hirsh-Pasek, 1990; Imai et al., 2005; E. Markman, 1989; Waxman and Markow, 1995).[16] Taken as a whole, this linguistic research suggests that entity concepts provide a foundation upon which a learner can build their initial understanding of language, while relationships are second-order concepts that we learn subsequent to the entities to which they relate.

I would argue that there is an analogy between the sheer overwhelming frequency of what we're calling the tonic and antitonic functions and the ease of learning entity categories. Intuitively, it stands to reason that it should be easier to learn about chords that happen more often – musical listeners should be able to learn more quickly about the identities and behaviors of more frequent events than about less frequent events. Having internalized some characteristics of these most frequent events, learners could then proceed to relate less frequent chords – those chords that are harder to learn about – to these most frequent events as they add greater sophistication to their understanding of some musical grammar. Just as children first learn entity concepts and then build relationships between them, so too might we first learn harmonic entity categories associated with a corpus's most frequent chords and then proceed to relate the remaining chords in that corpus to those entities. In this analogy, when our computational models created functional categories by first centering a corpus's most frequent chords and then relating less frequent chords to those central pillars, the processes were paralleling aspects of E/R learning.

As noted earlier, these claims are, at their foundation, related to how we understand and cognize musical categories. Again in collaboration with Emily Schwitzgebel (2019), I designed a study to investigate whether some of these corpus-based analogies with E/R theory are indeed reflected in musicians' behavior. For this experiment, we created chord progressions with only I, V, IV, and ii triads and used their associated 2-gram probabilities (drawn from the Bach-chorale corpus) to create progressions of these triads. We created a bank of these progressions and selected a handful of sequences whose internal distributions of chord frequencies roughly matched the power-law distribution associated with the whole corpus (that is, the excerpt's chord distribution approximated Figure 4.8b). Next, we ciphered those progressions by replacing chord symbols with nonsense shapes, with each shape corresponding to a single triad. Figure 4.9a shows an example of a chord progression generated from this process, and Figure 4.9b shows the ciphered version.

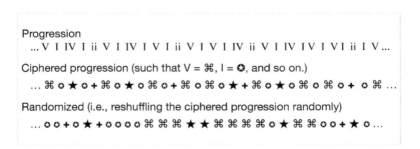

FIGURE 4.9 An example of the (a, top) original, (b, middle) ordered ciphered, and (c, bottom) randomized ciphered chord progressions used in this experiment

With these ciphered examples in hand, we could ask musicians familiar with this style to decode the ciphers, challenging them to determine which symbol meant which Roman numeral. However, we could also manipulate the ciphers to see what aspects of the cipher were more or less useful in the decoding task.[17] One such manipulation is shown in Figure 4.9c. The original cipher (4.9b) uses the original progression's ordering: with this version, a participant could use the chords' contexts to complete the task. The cipher of 4.9c, however, completely randomizes the sequence: in this version, only the symbols' frequencies could be used to complete the task. After recruiting a group of musicians (who would be familiar with Common Practice harmonics; see my *methods* footnote), we divided them into two categories, presented them with the ciphers of either the ordered or randomized variety, and explained the task, including whether their ciphers were ordered or randomized. The participants were instructed to view these ciphers as snippets from a larger progression of chords – the beginnings and endings did not necessarily represent the boundaries of a piece or phrase. We hypothesized that the participants would be able to decode the chords with greater consistency when they are ordered. But more fundamentally, we hypothesized that randomizing the ordering would reduce how well participants decoded ii and IV more than I and V. (After all, in this style, ii and IV are situated similarly within the frequency distribution yet have the notable contextual distinction that IV often progresses to ii, but ii infrequently moves to IV.) If musical learners rely on frequency to make sense of this corpus's entity functions (namely, the functions based on the I and V chords), then removing a sequence's ordering and retaining chord frequency should make identifying I and V easier and identifying ii and IV harder.

And this is exactly what happened. Figure 4.10 shows the results of this survey, with 4.10a showing the difference in correct/incorrect answers for each chord under the randomized and ordered conditions. I and V have smaller differences (with responses to V actually slightly *improving* in the randomized condition!), and ii and IV have larger differences. The last two groups of white/black bars pool together the I and V and the ii and IV data. Pooled, the I/V bars have a smaller difference between them compared to the ii/IV bars. Figure 4.10b then divides the responses into each ciphered chord type in both conditions, showing the responses grouped by the correct (unciphered) answer. I've bolded the correct answers and added a glow to the *incorrect* response provided most often. As before, when I and V are the correct answer, there's little difference between the ordered and randomized conditions, while there is a greater difference between conditions when ii and IV are the expected answers. More strikingly, however, is that when incorrect answers are given, participants appear to confuse I and V for one another and ii and IV for one another: when a mistake is made, the mistake tends to be within the hypothesized entity pair or relationship pair of triads.[18]

164 What Is Function?

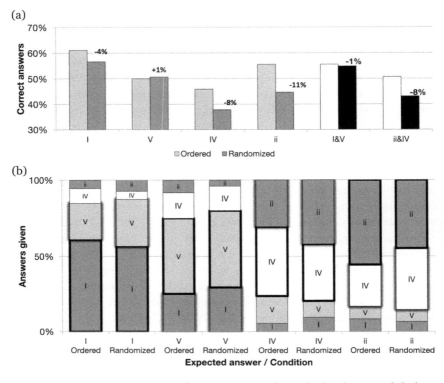

FIGURE 4.10 (a, top) Percentage of correct answers for each chord type and (b, bottom) proportion of answers given for each chord type

Of course, this experiment involves musicians solving a puzzle rather than actually listening to and responding to music. Such a design also uses a very conscious and intellectual task rather than one based on an internalized and/or preconscious hearing of these different chord categories. Regardless, if these musicians' interactions with tonal music did not encourage them to weight chord frequency and context differently for different chords, they would not have had different reactions to each harmony. These different behaviors show that (a) I and V triads can be identified by frequency alone better than ii and IV triads, (b) ii and IV benefit more from contextual information than do I and V in this recognition task, and (c) if, as they decode, a participant confuses one triad with another, they are likely to swap either between I and V or between ii and IV. In sum, the two chords that we would associate with tonic and antitonic functions are identified with frequency information with more reliability than are the remaining chords, while these remaining chords can be better identified by their contexts within a progression.

These findings nicely analogize with the relative ease with which entity concepts are learned and the relative difficulty with which relationship concepts are learned. Recalling that I and V are the most frequent triads in the Bach-chorale corpus, these findings indicate that the more straightforward parameter (frequency) is more useful when decoding these more frequent triads. The more complex parameter (ordering) is more useful when decoding the corpus's less frequent triads, ii and IV. In sum: not only are these strategies evocative of the E/R dichotomy (with contexts used to identify the chords within the hypothesized relationship set and chord identity used for the entity-set harmonies), but it would also seem that I and V are identified with the simplicity of an entity concept, and ii and IV are identified with more complex strategies, reminiscent of relationship concepts.

There Exists Relatively More Definitional Agreement Concerning Entity Functions Than Relationship Functions

When simply counting the number of definitions attributed to words in dictionaries, nouns – a rough linguistic proxy for entities – tend to have about half the definitions associated with them as do verbs – a rough linguistic proxy for relationships (Gentner and Kurtz, 2005). This complexity also manifests in how language speakers conceptualize these definitions. If you ask participants to define certain words, their definitions of relational concepts tend to be more mutable and changeable than entity concepts (Gentner and France, 1988). I would argue that the relative slipperiness of relationship concepts manifests in how theorists write about relationship functions in their research. Conversely, if entity concepts are easier to define than relationship concepts, then there should be fewer disagreements in the literature about entity functions than about relationship functions. In Common Practice tonality, this means that tonic and antitonic/dominant functions should see more agreement than concepts like predominant, plagal, and subdominant; in mid-century American popular music, this means that tonic and that corpus's antitonic – the subdominant – should have more consensus than other functions.

A cursory examination of the scholarship on harmonic function – much of which we've discussed earlier – would support these speculations. In studies of Western European Common Practice music, there is little argument about the constituency of the antitonic function – theorists tend to agree that the "dominant" function involves chords that look and act like the dominant triad. Additionally, no substantive argument has arisen around the constituency of the tonic function. (The one exception might be the contentious role of second-inversion tonic chords – "cadential 6/4 chords" – that precede authentic cadences.) However, there is a reasonably large controversy about further functions. The previously cited authors (like Smith and Swinden) are not the only authors who propose their own

166 What Is Function?

reading of what we might refer to as subdominant, plagal, or predominant functions. These readings can involve adding other functional categories (Lerdahl and Jackendoff, 1983; Kopp, 2002), focusing on the different roles played by specific chords (Aldwell and Schachter, 2011; Kostka and Payne, 2012), restricting the notion of function to cadential patterns (Laitz, 2012), or accounting for different contexts, contents, and behaviors for various "predominant" chords (Brown et al., 2021). Also, in contrast to the tonic and dominant functions, there are arguments about these further functions' prototypes and constituency. For instance: is IV the prototypical predominant harmony (Harrison, 1994; Agmon, 1995) or is ii (Kostka and Payne, 2012; Quinn, 2005)? Furthermore, there has even been evidence that the constituency and behavior of a predominant function might change within different Western European Common Practice styles (Brown et al., 2021).

Pop-music scholarship concerning harmonic function has a shorter history than its Common Practice correlate, yet many of its disagreements can also be mapped onto the entity/relationship dichotomy. As in Common Practice scholarship, pop-music discourse contains almost no arguments about the definition and constituency of the tonic function. However, arguments abound about the function expressed by dominant triads.[19] These disagreements include theorists advocating for a revised definition of the "dominant" function in this repertoire (Doll, 2017; Nobile, 2016) or for including non-traditional chords within the auspices of a "dominant" function (Biamonte, 2010). On the other hand, there is a general consensus that the subdominant triad plays a greater role in many popular music styles than in Common Practice classical music (de Clercq and Temperley, 2011). Recalling that dominant triads are *less frequent* than the IV triads in the McGill Billboard dataset and that our earlier discussion suggested that IV (rather than V or V[7]) serves as the prototype for this corpus's antitonic function, it is no surprise that more controversy and disagreement surround the constituencies and definitions of the dominant triad's function rather than this repertoire's antitonic (or IV-based) entity function. Here, the V chord attracts the contention and disagreement of a relationship function, while the IV chord now enjoys the relative stability of an entity function.

These paragraphs have provided an admittedly cursory (and potentially unsatisfying) overview of these disputes. However, it is the very fact that these arguments exist – not the details and specifics of the arguments – that supports my analogy between entity/relationship concepts and harmonic functions. If relationship concepts naturally have more slippery and mutable definitions than do entity concepts, we should expect commentators to have more disagreements over relational functions than the tonic/antitonic entity functions.

Chords and Scale Degrees Are Categorized Into Entity Functions With Greater Consistency Than Relationship Functions

In language, we categorize the components of entity sets more easily and consistently than those of relationship sets (Barr and Caplan, 1987). Asking participants to freely generate instances of entity sets (like providing examples of "animals" and "fruits") versus instances of relational sets (like providing examples of "barriers" and "filters") results in entity responses having more agreement between participants than do relationship responses (Gentner and Kurtz, 2005). If tonic and antitonic functions are cognized as entities while further functions are cognized as relationships, then there should be a comparable discrepancy in how consistently chords and scale degrees are categorized into these functions.

This inconsistency manifests in both computational and behavioral domains. The computational perspective can be seen by glancing back at Figure 4.6: throughout, the tonic and antitonic categories tend to have their pies divided into fewer, bigger slices and are plotted higher on the z-score axis (our proxy for consistency). Notice that the tonic functions tend to be dominated by the scale degrees of the I triad, and the antitonics are dominated by degrees of the V^7 or IV triad (in the cases of the Bach and pop-music models, respectively). In contrast, functions like T+ in the pop model and S in the Bach chorale model are more divided. Similarly, in my last chapter's models of harmonic function (particularly Figure 3.12), the tonic and dominant categories were primarily chords that looked and acted like I and V, while what I called "intermediate" chords were far more varied.[20] In sum, we see more consistency in the kinds of chords and scale degrees that are categorized into the tonic and antitonic (entity) functions versus the remaining (relationship) functions.

But again, these corpus-derived claims invite connections to human behavior and cognition. Therefore, I ran another experiment, now prompting participants to categorize chords into functions. Participants were either undergraduates who had completed at least three semesters of a theory sequence or were graduate students in a music program, and I assumed that these backgrounds entailed a certain amount of knowledge about harmonic function. The survey included 11 chord progressions of diatonic triads, with each progression containing eight chords. Chord sequences were generated in the major mode using the same 2-gram data as my previous experiment but now included all diatonic triads; I selected sequences that contained a diversity of these triads. Examples of the prompt given to participants can be found in this chapter's online supplement. Progressions were presented as chord symbols (upper- and lowercase letters with accidentals) with the key indicated at the beginning of the progression and with Roman numerals annotated underneath the chord symbols. Participants were instructed that these chord progressions were designed to approximate traditional Common Practice syntax, and they were asked to assign each chord either T, S, or D to indicate its function. While I did not provide them with any definition of those functions, these letters were meant to evoke the tonic, dominant, and sub/predominant functions generally introduced in undergraduate music-theory classrooms.[21] I hypothesized that participants' responses should show more consistency, reliability, and agreement when using the T and D designations (what would be entity functions in this corpus) than when using S (what would be a relationship function in this corpus).

This is indeed what occurred. S responses were more variable than T and D responses. This variability can be attributed to two causes: more chord types were associated with S than the other two designations, and there were more between-participant disagreements when they used the S label than when applying T or D.

Figures 4.11a and 4.11b demonstrate the first of these causes. On the top left (4.11a), each function is shown divided into its constituent chords with portions of the bars corresponding to the proportion of each function-label assignments given to each chord. On the top right (4.11b), each chord is now divided into the proportion it was assigned to each function. Figure 4.11a shows the T and D annotations to be far less divided between chords than the S annotations, with the former functions being primarily

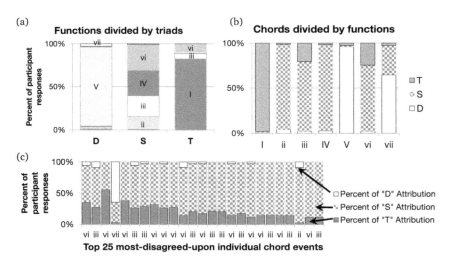

FIGURE 4.11 Responses to the function-identification survey, (a) as Roman numerals grouped into their functional annotations, (b) as annotated functions divided by their Roman numerals, and (c) isolating the individual moments in the survey that elicited the most variance between participants

composed of I and V chords, respectively, and the last being divided between vi, IV, ii, and even iii.[22] Figure 4.11b also shows the consistency with which I and V dominate their respective functions: these two chords are overwhelmingly labeled with the T and D designations, respectively. While the chart shows that IV and ii are also consistently categorized as S, it also shows the iii and vi chords are also often placed in that category. In other words, while T and D are each dominated by a single triad (with D admitting the secondary vii° triad with some consistency), four different chords are consistently assessed as S. (This variability would seem to resonate with Brown et al. (2021), a study that explicitly shows the diversity of chords that exhibit predominant tendencies.)

Figure 4.11c illustrates the second cause of variability: between-participant disagreement. The figure's horizontal axis shows the Roman numerals of the 25 moments in the survey that elicited the most variation between participants, ordered from left to right by their level of disagreement.[23] The bars show the proportion of responses that assigned each function: bars that divide the chord more evenly indicate greater disagreement and variation between participants. Perhaps most strikingly, most of these disagreed-upon chords are iii and vi. The results show a tension about whether these chords are T or S in the case of the latter, and T, S, or D in the case of the former. Specifically, the tension appears to arise from whether respondents use S to denote *anything* that occurs before V (often including iii and vi in that category) versus some stricter definition of S. For instance, the first most-divided event – the figure's most leftward vi chord – is a deceptive cadence that (somewhat unusually) progresses to a tonic chord: participants appear to be divided as to whether the chord substitutes for a tonic, is simply a subdominant, or even prolongs the previous dominant function. (I've highlighted this moment in the online supplement.)

Importantly, each of these ambiguous chords encourages at least some of the respondents to label the moment with an S. The checkered pattern of Figure 4.11c indicates S responses: note its overwhelming ubiquity within the chart. With the exception of the third and fourth ranks (involving vi and vii° triads), each of these disagreed-upon events involves more than 50% of respondents annotating the triad with an S. And even in those two exceptional instances, the second-most-assigned annotation is S. In other words, when a group of participants disagree on how to categorize a chord, one of the contentious categories is S.

In sum, analogous to entity categories, the T and D labels appear to have stable and consistent definitions, while the S designation involves more disagreement and fluidity. When prompting participants to assign chord labels that approximate tonic (T), antitonic (D), and a further category (S), the former two receive a consistency that the last does not. Again, this experiment relies on explicit knowledge acquired in classroom

170 What Is Function?

settings. Indeed, the variation within the S responses could be a relic both of participants negotiating their own slippery definitions of that category and also of different participants having been taught different definitions of the sub/predominant function. Furthermore, some of the variability associated with S annotations could also be the result of participants simply misremembering the definitions of sub/predominant categories they learned in their undergraduate education. However, these multifaceted variations and explanations are a feature of the study rather than a bug: relationship categories should have more overall mutability, complexity, and disagreement than entity categories on many levels and from various perspectives.

Entity Functions Are Relatively Stable Between Styles, While Relationship Functions Vary Between Styles

The final analogy I wish to draw between E/R theory and harmonic function involves the relative ease with which entity and relationship concepts can be translated between languages/styles. While entity nouns tend to have exact correlates between different languages, relational verbs are less likely to have exact translations (Gentner, 1981). Similarly, words indicating relationships are less likely to be borrowed between languages than words indicating some kind of entity (Sobin, 1982). I would argue that the same kinds of dynamics can be seen when comparing corpora from different musical styles: it is easier to locate analogous tonic and antitonic functions in two contrasting corpora, while it is harder to "translate" relational functions between different styles.

Consider Table 3.1, in which I trained my harmonic-reduction algorithm on different chronological divisions of the YCAC. In the table, the I and $V^{(7)}$ reduction networks – the pillars for this corpus's tonic and antitonic functions – always occupy the top two ranks. In other words, the reduction networks associated with the two entity functions remain stable throughout the chronological divisions of the YCAC. The further reduction networks, however, are variable not only in their placement in the distribution but also in whether they even occur at all: II^7 (or, V^7/V), for instance, changes its position within the distribution quite a bit and is not even present in one of the time periods' distributions. This moment shows that, while these styles' tonic and antitonic reduction networks remain somewhat constant through these decades and centuries, the usage of further chords is variable.

But an even more general argument could be made. Throughout this letter, I have argued that any corpus of tonal harmony will involve a tonic and an antitonic function built around the corpus's two most-frequent harmonies. Because these functions are stable aspects of tonal harmony, it is easy to analogize one corpus's tonic and antitonic functions with those of another corpus: one can simply relate the functions built around the corpus's two most frequent harmonies, whatever they may be. In my last chapter and in this current letter, I identified the V chord as the pillar of the antitonic function in the Bach-chorale corpus. I then "translated" that observation to the McGill-Billboard corpus by identifying that corpus's second-most-frequent IV chord as analogous to the Common Practice V chord. Mapping between these two antitonic chords was a relatively straightforward endeavor.

The same, however, cannot be said of relational functions. Comparing my previous chapter's Figure 3.16 and 3.18 and our earlier letter's Figures 4.3 and 4.4, it is not obvious what comparisons to make between the functions that are neither tonic nor antitonic. Each of these different repertoires returns different numbers and kinds of relational functions. Analogous to relationship concepts, the behaviors and categorizations of chords that are *not* tonic or antitonic will be far more variable between styles, making intercorpus and interstylistic comparisons of these functions difficult if not impossible!

A Summary of a Long Letter

In sum, the fact that the harmonies of tonal corpora consistently follow a power-law distribution means that a corpus's most used chords will occur vastly more frequently than its less used chords. The overwhelming frequency of this handful of chords will allow for a tonic function to be built around a corpus's exponentially most frequent chord and an antitonic function to be built around the second-most-frequent chord. The remaining chords will either be subsumed into those functions or coalesce into functions that are defined by how they relate to the tonic and antitonic functions. I argued that this process not only describes the workings of computational and machine-learned modeling of harmonic function but that it may also describe aspects of how humans cognize harmonic function. In particular, I relied on entity/ relationship theory to explore connections between corpus properties and the ways harmonic function might be understood by musical listeners and practitioners. Using a combination of existing literature and the results of two new behavioral experiments, I explored this analogy. Most broadly, because the tonic and antitonic functions are defined by the identities of a corpus's most frequent chords, I suggested that they can be considered entity sets, while further functions are defined by their relationships to these entities. Aligning with the definitional clarity and ambiguity associated with entity and relationship concepts, respectively, we saw that musicians and research-ers showed relatively more definitional agreement when using tonic and antitonic functions than when using other functions, while computational models – as well as musicians – categorized chords and scale degrees into tonic and antitonic functions with more consistency compared to other func-tions. Furthermore, I suggested that because the definitions of tonic and antitonic were tethered to a generalizable statistical property of tonal corpora, these functions remain stable (and translatable) between different corpora and

172 What Is Function?

styles, while further relationship-based functions are more mutable. In other words, this letter has used a mixture of theory, corpus analysis, and behavioral data to argue that *in tonal music, tonic and antitonic are entity concepts, while further functional categories are relational concepts.*

Sincerely,

Author

★★★

Letter 7: Connecting Harmonic Function to E/R Theory Shows Ways That Corpus Analysis Can Interact With Broader Theories of Music Learning, Cognition, and Analysis

From Correspondent to Author

Dear Author,

I am impressed by the scope and commitment of your previous letter. I appreciate its provocative ideas, but I think we can both acknowledge that many of these points are – while compelling – speculative. However, I believe that your motivation was not to *prove* some kind of connection between E/R theory and harmonic function but rather to plumb interesting and exciting meaning from your corpora, enrich our understanding of a few music-theory topics, challenge our understanding of some basic aspects of tonality, and suggest potential connections between corpus statistics and larger theories of musical learning and cognition.

This sort of playful and challenging speculation heralds back to several arguments you made in Chapter 1. There, you suggested that humanities-oriented corpus analysis has the power to interpret corpus data in the service of producing interesting readings. Using your Meaningful Corpus Model, you suggested that empirical data can participate in a logical flow in which a corpus analysis can support some broader interpretative claim. You also warned that while corpus data constitute testable facts, connections to broader interpretative ideas are harder (if not impossible) to prove. You then argued that researchers – especially those in the humanities – should lean into the interpretive aspects of this logic, carving out a space for creative analysis and speculative theory building. To my mind, your letter followed this very paradigm. Your arguments did not *prove* that listeners use corpus data to cognize harmonic function in terms of entities and relationships, but it did weave a captivating story involving musical corpora, models of harmonic function, and human cognition. While not proven, analyses like yours have the potential to deepen our understandings of some musical phenomena, challenge us to reconsider how we approach theoretical ideas, and help us synthesize the insights of divergent domains of disciplinary discourse. In other words, even if your conclusions are not provable, they can be *useful*.

Let me elucidate a few ways your argument has the potential to activate provocative connections between theory, corpus data, and cognition and ways it might challenge us to reconsider our understanding – and even our teaching – of some theoretical concepts.

First, and most salient to the project of your last chapter, E/R theory distinguishes the specific roles of content and context in harmonic function by equating content with entities and context with relationships. It then clearly defines two distinct cognitive lanes for understanding these roles, each with its own behavioral characteristics and corpus properties. Second, your arguments lay out ways we might make sense of musical corpora using strategies that parallel those used in other media. Insomuch as E/R theory shows ways that enormous amounts of corpus data can be organized into more manageable and reference-able categories, the theory shows provocative parallels between music, language, and even data organization in general. Third, these sorts of discussions act as a sort of meta-theory of harmonic function, accounting for both the variation in and similarities between different theorists' approaches to the topic. In other words, the E/R approach provides a potential account of why arguments about harmonic function occur and within which topics we should expect disagreements to arise.

Also – both more abstractly and more fundamentally – E/R theory shows a non-tautological definition of concepts like "tonic," "dominant," and "predominant." One might say that the definition of *tonic* is a function constructed around the most stable triad, but one might also say that the tonic triad is the most stable triad because it underpins the tonic function. Your framing of the tonic function, however, defines it by its position within a power-law frequency distribution. Notions like predominant and pretonic are therefore also untethered from potentially tautological definitions. ("The ii chord is predominant because its scale degrees often move toward V; ii's scale degrees often move toward V because ii is predominant.") Because these chords are lower in the frequency distribution, we make sense of them by relating their usage to more frequent chords, creating relationship functions that describe the actions of these harmonies. (I believe that your Chapter 6 will return to the importance of these distributions, arguing that they are fundamental to the very definition of *tonality* itself.)

Finally, I think these ideas are particularly important given how they interact with arguments about musical meaning. Because our correspondence has thus far only focused on musical corpus analysis and behavioral correlates, I hesitate to even enter into the thorny and murky thicket of musical semantics and syntax. However, let me attempt to hew a narrow pathway through these weeds.

174 What Is Function?

Certainly, some portion of musical meaning involves connecting musical events to extramusical ideas. Here, I'm thinking of projects like topic theory (Ratner, 1980; Agawu, 1991) in which certain gestures have specific associated meanings (e.g., horn calls evoking images of hunting). However, some other portion of musical meaning is purely self-referential. Here, I'm thinking both of the centuries-old work of Hanslick (1854) and also of research showing that the fulfillment/deferral of musical expectations elicits meaningful responses in listeners (Arthur, 2016; Huron, 2006; Temperley, 2007; Schwitzgebel and White, 2021; among many others). In this latter approach, researchers argue, for instance, that a tonic triad attains a feeling of stability because it occurs most often, appears in predictable locations, and begins and ends phrases, while a dominant triad elicits a certain tension in the classical style because of consistent corpus-based expectations for that harmony to resolve to the tonic.

The E/R model contributes to this self-referential approach. The tonic function can be seen as stable not only because of its statistical frequency and predictability but also because it forms a foundational pillar within a larger system. Similarly, tonic and antitonic events might have a feeling of power and arrival because we identify them as entity functions, while a chord we might label as "predominant" might communicate a feeling of motion because of its relationships to other functions.

I can also imagine several ways that your ideas could be further tested. Researchers could directly investigate whether very young children learn entity functions first, perhaps testing whether they are more sensitive to alterations in I and V chords in standard nursery/folk songs than to alterations of less frequent chords. One could also test the specific role of power-law distributions, teaching participants an artificial non-tonal harmonic syntax (following Louie, 2012, for instance) using different frequency distributions and testing whether those differences affect the efficacy of participants' learning. Furthermore, more work could be done studying how tonic and antitonic chords that are *not* the corpus's two most frequent chords are situated in your model. For instance: are "tonic" submediant chords cognized as relationships because their defining characteristic is their *relationship* to the I chord, or are they cognized as entities because they participate in an entity set, or are they understood using some mixture of these two tactics? However, regardless of the potential for more behavioral work, your investigations do present a compelling starting point for this line of research.

Your analogies and arguments about E/R theory are speculative – to be sure – but they show the potential of connecting corpus analysis, music theory, and cognitive theory. Your previous letter jumped between observations about musical corpora, cognitive theory, linguistic behavioral studies, and musical behavioral studies to make a fairly complicated point about the different ways that harmonic functions are theorized and cognized.

What Is Function? **175**

Even if one does not agree with all aspects of your arguments, it shows a larger potential of corpus analysis: that it can connect music theory and theories of cognition to make broader claims about the way music is heard and learned and can underpin larger projects of speculative system building. Even if your argument contains holes and inconsistencies,[24] it shows ways that corpus analysis can nimbly negotiate and participate in broader and interdisciplinary discourses. In other words, *connections to E/R theory show the ways that corpus analysis can interact with broader theoretical and speculative points about music learning, cognition, and analysis.*

Sincerely,

Correspondent

★★★

Letter 8: Representing the Complexities of a Corpus via an Orthographic Model Shows Further Ways That Corpus Analysis Can Engage With the Historical Project of Music Theory

From Author to Correspondent

Dear Correspondent,

Thank you for your thoughtful response. The enthusiasm of my previous letter needed some methodological positioning, and I am grateful for your gracious efforts on that front.

I want to offer two final points before we close our correspondence, first about how this work might connect corpus analysis to network- and graph-based music theories and how these analyses instantiate my goal of reading musical corpora akin to individual texts (see Chapter 1).

First, I want to argue that orthographic representations of a corpus's properties have the power to illustrate ways that data analysis actively engages with music theory's historical research methods. While we could likely find precursors, Allen Forte (1973) and David Lewin (1987) pioneered and popularized the idea of representing a piece of music using a series of nodes and directed arrows, with the nodes representing musical events and arrows representing the transformations or operations that create or relate those events. This approach has been formalized and extended by various scholars, including Steven Rings (2011), whose work connects musical graphing to contemporary network theory. The appeal of this approach makes a lot of sense – after all, music is a phenomenon that unfolds over time, and a network of nodes and transformations allows us to represent linear musical events with the immediacy of visual representation (White, 2016).

176 What Is Function?

Importing E/R theory – or really any strategy for visually representing data structures – into corpus analysis is analogously beneficial. The statistical properties of a corpus are multifaceted and complex, and their totality cannot be viewed and grasped at a single moment any more than can a piece of music. Representing corpus statistics in, say, the manner of Figure 4.7b affords a birds-eye view and immediate representation of what is otherwise an unwieldy morass of data. By reducing the enormous array of corpus analyses of the previous chapter, of our earlier letters, and of other corpus-based models of harmonic function into a single network of entities and relationships, I am packaging the complexities of these analyses into one immediately observable representation.

Finally, this sort of speculative and cumulative analysis treats a corpus as a text to be read. In my first chapter, I argued that music analysis and corpus analysis are similar activities that use different texts, with the former reading musical pieces and the latter reading the statistical properties of large musical corpora. I would suggest that my E/R analyses acutely show this capacity of corpus analysis. Again, whether you agree with my arguments or not, this work not only shows that corpus analysis can engage with notions of music theory and cognitive research, but it also shows how it can summarize these insights using graphs and networks that are native to music analysis to produce (hopefully!) creative and insightful readings of broad swaths of data. In other words: *representing the complexities of a corpus via an orthographic model shows ways that corpus analysis can engage with aspects of the historical project of music theory.*

Sincerely,

Author

Notes

1. A deeper dive into Riemann's theories shows an even greater gap between how we currently motivate discussions of chord syntax and how Riemann would have imagined this topic. Riemann interpreted the relationships between I, IV, and V as illustrating a dialectic: "*These ist die erste Tonika, Antithese die Unterdominante mit dem Quartsextakkord der Tonika, Synthese die Oberdominante mit dem schliessenden Grundakkord der Tonika; thetisch ist die Tonika, anti-thetisch die Unter-, synthetisch die Oberdominante*" (Riemann, 1900, 3). ("The first tonic is the thesis, the subdominant followed by the cadential 6/4 is then the antithesis, and the dominant with the final root-position tonic is the synthesis. The tonic is thetic, the subdominant antithetic, and the dominant synthetic." My translation.)
2. The process would orphan a few smaller chords: without including singletons, sets like $<\hat{1}, \hat{2}>$ and $<\hat{1}, \hat{5}, \hat{6}>$ would not map onto any one higher-probability event.
3. Nobile's argument is quite sophisticated and an excellent deep dive into the concept of function. He investigates no fewer than 14 historical definitions of the term and

argues that there are three broad approaches: function-as-category, function-as-progression, and function-as-syntax. The first more or less maps onto my content-oriented approach, and the second more or less aligns with my context-based models. To Nobile, "syntax" means "position in a phrase," something that also comes under the auspices of my conception of "context," although this book's modeling does not address phrase position independently, at least not in the way Nobile frames the concept.

4. Tymoczko (2003) notes that the concept of plagal function might find its roots in the Boulanger tradition.

5. The original model actually returns eight total "functions" when trained on the full (non-mode-delineated) corpus, with one pair devoted primarily to jazz-influenced songs and another pair devoted to minor-mode songs. For simplicity, I've included only the non-jazz-influenced major-mode nodes in this discussion.

6. These rules basically follow textbook descriptions of scale-degree grammars (for instance, Laitz, 2012) but also find support in corpus studies of scale-degree motion (Huron, 2006). Historical theorists like Francois-Joseph Fetis and Alexandre Choron also highlight the tendencies of the tritone-related fourth and seventh scale degrees in their theories of tonal syntax (Simms, 1975). There has also been some substantial work done in the domain of scale-degree attraction, including Lerdahl (1996)'s melodic attraction model and the "taxicab metric" of Rogers and Callender (2006), the latter of which simply sums the semitonal motions between two chords as an approximation of the attraction between those two chords. Additionally, some behavioral research supports the particular directedness of the semitone motions I use in this model, including Brown and Butler (1981), Brown et al. (1994), and Matsunaga and Abe (2005, 2009). The actual perceptual salience of the unidirectional tendencies of particular diatonic half steps, however, is a bit contentious (Krumhansl, 1990; Vega, 2003).

7. Brown et al. (2021) undertake an in-depth study of the expectations associated with "predominant" scale degrees. They test the strength of participants' expectations that various chords progress to V and find a strong connection between certain scale degrees and predominant attraction. Showing a link between chord context and content, they find that chords containing chromatic degrees like $\#\hat{4}$ and $\flat\hat{6}$ exhibit the strongest pull toward V.

8. Specifically, the machine-learning of the HMMs in White and Quinn (2018) rely on what is called an expectation maximization (EM) algorithm that favors solutions of higher probabilities. Because these musical datasets have some events that occur much more frequently and consistently (i.e., they are associated with higher probabilities) than others, the EM process will try to preserve and leverage those initial high probabilities, creating functions around those events and then creating functions relating to those high-probability events.

9. Strictly, E/R theory also involves a third category: *attributes*. Attributes can be roughly analogized to the adjectives and adverbs that describe entities and relationships. I'm not going to spend a lot of time on this aspect of E/R theory, but I can imagine several fruitful pathways in applying the idea of "attributes" to harmonic function.

10. There is some disagreement about the definition of a "martini." You will find some people argue that a martini is defined by the recipe: gin (or, in more permissive circles, vodka) with some proportion of vermouth. People making this argument rely on an entity-based definition: a drink with a fixed set of components *is* a martini. In contrast, some people will argue that any elaborate and expensive mixed drink

178 What Is Function?

that appears in a raised conical glass is a "martini." This definition of martini is relational, as it depends upon its relationship to a particular kind of serving vessel and to a particular social context. Arguments about "what *is* a martini," therefore, hinge not exactly upon the definition *per se* but rather upon your method of defining. But the very fact that these arguments are ongoing means that there's value in both entity and relational definitions of the martini. Winston Churchill would order entity martinis; a chocolate-strawberry-espresso martini is a relational martini.

11. Certainly, these types of theories about categorization did not arise out of whole cloth in the past several decades. Barr and Caplan (1987), for instance, discuss a similar *intrinsic/extrinsic* dichotomy, in which the former has features considered in isolation (such as "wings" can define a bird) and the latter expresses some relationship or action (such as "hammers" being defined by the kind of work they do). And indeed, a historical outline of this approach – something far outside the bounds of this footnote – would likely reference Charles Sanders Peirce, Gottlob Frege, and even Aristotle's *The Categories*. Furthermore, E/R theory has no particular monopoly on categorization theory. Computationally, the work of Emilios Cambouropoulos (2001) and Darrel Conklin (2010) has overlaps with this type of work. Cambouropoulos, for instance, develops algorithms to classify musical cues into categories using their internal characteristics and then measures the resulting algorithm's behavior against that of human participants. These notions of similarity would be similar to the "entity" class of relationships discussed here. For a contrasting approach applied to musical categorization, see Zbikowski (2002).

12. Because of these changes, we lose the immediate visual clarity of a directed graph. In an earlier footnote, I discussed "attribute" objects within E/R theory, and I could easily imagine an addendum to my orthography that adds attributes to define transitional probabilities, chord constituencies, or even qualitative descriptions of an entity or relationship (attributes are generally represented as circles attached to that which they describe). See Rings (2011) for more on graph and network theory in musical representations.

13. Please keep this letter between us: its arguments are embarrassingly flamboyant.

14. I'm broadly arguing that different functions have different sorts of E/R properties. My current framing will be one way to express those differences, but I could imagine other framings. For instance, in a database, a piece of data is an entity rather than a relationship if it is a "thing" that can be discretely identified; in contrast, a relationship is some association. From this approach, every chord or group of chords is an entity, since they are "things" and have thing-like attributes: they have scale degrees, positions within a phrase, bass notes, durations, etc. Following this logic, every function is an entity, since it is a group of things. And so while I'm tracing a different logic in this letter, I could imagine making a parallel E/R-based argument that identifies all functions as entities, but different types of entities. For instance, functions like predominant and subdominant could be "weak entities," a concept from E/R theory in which an entity is defined by its internal attributes, but those attributes are associated with multiple entities. Because attributes are shared between different weak entities, databases need to reference multiple attributes of a weak-entity object to know into which category that object should be classified. To identify a player on a soccer team, one needs to reference both the team's jersey color and the number, since neither attribute would specify an individual player. Similarly, while you can classify a I chord into the tonic category using only its scale degree content (thus making "tonic" a strong entity), one would need both the scale-degree content and

the context of a IV chord to determine whether it's functioning as a plagal or pre-dominant chord. In this framing, plagal or predominant chords, then, would be considered weak entities.

15. The YCAC has two singletons (the tonic and dominant scale degrees) within the initial ranks of the distribution; however, as the previous chapter illustrates, prioritizing sets of scale degrees over singletons makes for more manageable constructions of harmonic function. Additionally, singletons likely arise from passages with unaccompanied melodies and, as such, have limited relevance to a discussion about harmony. Finally, if one graphs the distribution of these singletons, they produce a power-law distribution in and of themselves, suggesting there could be a parallel melodic phenomenon existing in tandem with the distribution I am describing here.

16. Indeed, this literature suggests that children first learn relational words *as entities* and then add complexity and sophistication to their initial definitions until they create a relational definition. As an example, my son's first word was "Go." However, this word initially only meant one specific thing – a prompt to throw a ball. He then expanded the definition to have other specific meanings, like turning on the tub's faucet at bath time and tossing him into the air. Finally, these specific entity-based definitions all expanded into an abstract relational definition of "Go": to move from one place to another.

17. *Methods:* In this experiment, I used the transitions between chords in the Bach-chorale corpus as reported by Rohrmeier and Cross (2008) but used only transitions between I, V, IV, and ii. I used that transition table to generate 100,000 chords and selected windows of chords of lengths between 25 and 35 chords long that approximated the power-law distribution of Figure 4.8c. After consenting to the protocol and reading a description of the task, each participant saw three ciphered series; all three were either ordered or randomized. There were six versions of the cipher, each with different shapes associated with different chords. There were six versions of the survey, three in each condition. Each question within the survey used a different version of the cipher so that the shapes changed their meanings in each example. Forty-eight music majors from the University of Massachusetts, Amherst took the survey in return for a snack of their choice, with eight people taking each version. Given that the test both involved specialized knowledge and relied on a familiarity with Western European Common Practice harmonic syntax, it was important to use musicians in this study. There are examples of the ciphers in this chapter's online supplement. This research was first presented in White and Schwitzgebel (2019).

18. According to χ^2 tests, the only significant difference between responses to a particular expected chord when divided by ordered and unordered conditions occurs when ii is the expected answer: $p = 0.047$. However, dividing correct answers by chord provided an overall significant result $\chi^2(3) = 7.9$, $p = 0.038$. Dividing correct answers by entity chords (I and V) and relationship chord (ii and IV) provides a significant result as well $\chi^2(1) = 3.9$, $p = 0.048$. Isolating I and V chords, there was no significant difference of correct answers between the two conditions $\chi^2(1) = 2.47$, $p = 0.62$, but there was a marginally significant difference between the conditions for the ii and IV chords $\chi^2(1) = 2.59$, $p = 0.064$. Chapter 6's appendix provides a description of the χ^2 test.

19. My outline here ignores some of the arguments around the "antitonic" function in this repertoire that would seem to arise from the improper importation of Western European classical functional paradigms into American popular music.

180 What Is Function?

20. This appears to be the case in other computational models of harmonic function as well: the modeling of Jacoby et al. (2015) often (but, to be fair, not always) produces categories that can be described as tonic, dominant, and then "everything else."

21. *Methods:* Thirty-five upper-level undergraduate and graduate students at the University of Massachusetts, Amherst participated in this task. My chord-progression selections favored triads that had the potential to be functionally ambiguous, so while there were 29 I chords, 5 ii chords, 10 IV chords, 20 V chords, and 1 vii chord, there was a disproportionate number of iii and vi chords (10 and 13, respectively), chords shown to exist in multiple functional categories in several of the models reviewed in this chapter (see Figures 4.1 and 4.3, for instance). Progressions were in C, D, F, G, Bb, A, and Eb. The letters T, S, and D were printed under each chord, and participants were instructed to circle the one that best described the function of the chord within its context.

22. Of course, this finding can be partially attributed to there being more I and V chords than other chords. Since the greater frequency of these chords is part of my larger entity/relationship logic, I view this as part and parcel of my argument rather than a confound.

23. There are a handful of mistakes and misunderstandings – or highly unconventional approaches – within these answers, including S-labeled I chords and T-labeled V chords. (I imagine most of these mistakes simply involved misunderstanding what key the series of triads was in.) However, a table of chords and the number of times participants labeled them as each function indicated a significantly consistent categorization: $\chi^2(12) = 4640.63$, $p < 0.001$

24. Which it does. A more thorough discussion of E/R theory would add more nuance to the dichotomy between entity functions and relationship functions. E/R cognitive theorists, in fact, do not generally advocate a strict separation between these two categories but rather a sliding scale between them, a scale which can manifest diachronically and synchronically. A concept, for instance, might essentially exist in some grey area between an entity and a relationship. I could imagine, for example, that a function built around a third-most-frequent chord like IV might exist within this gray area. Learners, also, might first comprehend the easier-to-learn entity concepts available within some corpus and then sophisticate their understandings by revising these concepts into relationships. I could imagine an argument in which the Common Practice's second-most-frequent $V^{(7)}$ chord is first understood as an entity by a musical learner, while its capacity to participate in the pretonic relationship would be learned later. In this formulation, a learner might develop their understanding of, say, the Common Practice "subdominant" function in a manner similar to how my son developed his understanding of the word "Go" (see my earlier footnote on the subject). Initially, the listener might equate the function solely with the IV chord – that is, as an entity – and then expand their definition to include other chords with similar scale-degree content. They might then finally cognize those chords using their relationships to the tonic and antitonic functions. This insight was brought to my attention by Morgan Patrick, a graduate student at Northwestern University.

References

Agawu, V. K. 1991. *Playing with Signs: A Semiotic Interpretation of Classic Music.* Princeton: Princeton University Press.

Agmon, E. 1995. "Functional Harmony Revisited: A Prototype-Theoretic Approach." *Music Theory Spectrum*, 17/2, 196–214.

Aldwell, E., and C. Schachter. 2011. *Harmony and Voiceleading*, 4th edition. Boston, MA: Schirmer.

Arthur, C. 2016. *When Leading Tones Don't Lead: Musical Qualia in Context.* Ph.D. Dissertation, The Ohio State University.

Asmuth, J., and D. Gentner. 2017. "Relational Categories Are More Mutable Than Entity Categories." *The Quarterly Journal of Experimental Psychology*, 70/10, 2007–2025. DOI: 10.1080/17470218.2016.1219752

Barr, R., and L. Caplan. 1987. "Category Representations and Their Implications for Their Category Structure." *Memory & Cognition*, 15/5, 397–418.

Biamonte, N. 2010. "Triadic Modal and Pentatonic Patterns in Rock Music." *Music Theory Spectrum*, 32, 95–110.

Bourne, J. 2015. *A Theory of Analogy for Musical Sense-Making and Categorization: Understanding Musical Jabberwocky*. PhD diss., Northwestern University.

Bourne, J., and E. Chun. 2017. "Using Analogical Processing to Categorize Musical Patterns." *Proceedings of the 39th Annual Meeting of the Cognitive Science Society*, London, UK, 16–29.

Brown, J., D. Tan, and J. D. Baker. 2021. "The Perceptual Attraction of Pre-Dominant Chords." *Music Perception*, 39/1, 21–40.

Brown, J., D. Tan, and M. Lin. 2021. "A Context-Sensitive Analysis of Pre-Dominant Chords in Sonata Movements by Mozart." Paper delivered at the International Conference for Music Perception and Cognition, online, Sheffield, UK.

Brown, H., and D. Butler. 1981. "Diatonic Trichords as Minimal Tonal Cue Cells." *In Theory Only*, 5/6–7, 37–55.

Brown, H., D. Butler, and M. R. Jones. 1994. "Musical and Temporal Influences on Key Discovery." *Music Perception*, 11/4, 371–407.

Cambouropoulos, E. 2001. "Melodic Cue Abstraction, Similarity, and Category Formation: A Formal Model." *Music Perception*, 18/3, 347–370.

Chen, L., J. M. Jose, H. Yu, and F. Yuan. 2017. "A Hybrid Approach for Question Retrieval in Community Question Answering." *The Computer Journal*, 60/7, 1019–1031. https://doi.org/10.1093/comjnl/bxw036

Chen, P. 1976. "The Entity-Relationship Model: Toward a Unified View of Data." *ACM Transactions on Database Systems*, 1/1, 9–36.

Chen, P. 1983. "English Sentence Structure and Entity-Relationship Diagrams." *Information Sciences*, 29/2, 127–149.

Conklin, D. 2010. "Discovery of Distinctive Patterns in Music." *Intelligent Data Analysis*, 14, 547–554.

de Clercq, T., and D. Temperley. 2011. "A Corpus Analysis of Rock Harmony." *Popular Music*, 30/1, 47–70.

Doll, C. 2017. *Hearing Harmony: Toward a Tonal Theory for the Rock Era*. Ann Arbor: University of Michigan Press.

Fechner, G. T. 1860. *Elements of Psychophysics [Elemente der Psychophysik]*. New York: Holt, Rinehart and Winston. (Translated in 1966 by H.E. Adler).

Forte, A. 1973. *The Structure of Atonal Music*. New Haven: Yale University Press.

Gentner, D. 1981. "Some Interesting Differences between Nouns and Verbs." *Cognition and Brain Theory*, 4, 161–178.

Gentner, D. 1982. "Why Nouns Are Learned before Verbs: Linguistic Relativity versus Natural Partitioning." *Language Development: Vol. 2: Language, thought and Culture*. S. Kuczaj, ed. Hillsdale, NJ: Erlbaum, 301–334.

182 What Is Function?

Gentner, D., and I. M. France. 1988. "The Verb Mutability Effect: Studies of the Combinatorial Semantics of Nouns and Verbs." *Lexical Ambiguity Resolution: Perspectives from Psycholinguistics, Neuropsychology, and Artificial Intelligence.* S. L. Small, G. W. Cottrell, and M. K. Tanenhaus, eds. San Mateo, CA: Kaufmann, 343–382.

Gentner, D., and K. J. Kurtz. 2005. "Relational Categories." *APA Decade of Behavior Series: Categorization Inside and Outside the Laboratory: Essays in Honor of Douglas L. Medin.* W. Ahn, R. L. Goldstone, B. C. Love, A. B. Markman, and P. Wolff, eds. Washington, DC, US: American Psychological Association, 151–175.

Gentner, D., and M. J. Ratterman. 1991. "Language and the Career of Similarity." *Perspectives on Thought and Language: Interrelations in Development.* S. A. Gelman, and J. P. Bryes, eds. London: Cambridge University Press, 225–277.

Golinkoff, R. M., and K. Hirsh-Pasek. 1990 "Let the Mute Speak: What Infants Can Tell Us about Language Acquisition." *Merrill-Palmer Quarterly,* 361, 67–91.

Hanslick, E. 1854. *Vom Musikalisch-Schönen.* Translated as *The Beautiful in Music* by Gustav Cohen, edited with an introduction by Morris Weitz. New York: The Liberal Arts Press, 1957.

Harrison, D. 1994. *Harmonic Function in Chromatic Music: A Renewed Dualist Theory and an Account of its Precedents.* Chicago: University of Chicago Press.

Hauptmann, M. 1853. *Die Natur der Harmonik und der Metrik.* Leipzig: Breitkopf und Härtel; trans. W. Heathcote as *The Nature of Harmony and Metre.* London: S. Sonnenschein, 1888.

Hull, R., and R. King. 1987. "Semantic Database Modeling: Survey, Applications, and Research Issues." *ACM Computing Surveys,* 19/3, 201–260. https://doi.org/10.1145/45072.45073

Huron, D. 2006. *Sweet Anticipation: Music and the Psychology of Expectation.* Cambridge: The MIT Press.

Imai, M., E. Haryu, and H. Okada. 2005. "Mapping Novel Nouns and Verbs Onto Dynamic Action Events: Are Verb Meanings Easier to Learn Than Noun Meanings for Japanese Children?" *Child Development,* 76/2, 340–355.

Jacoby, N., N. Tishby, and D. Tymoczko. 2015. "An Information Theoretic Approach to Chord Categorization and Functional Harmony." *Journal of New Music Research,* 219–244. DOI: 10.1080/09298215.2015.1036888

Kloos, H., and V. Sloutsky. 2004. "Are Natural Kinds Psychologically Distinct from Nominal Kinds? Evidence from Learning and Development." *Proceedings of the meeting of the Cognitive Science Society,* Chicago.

Kopp, D. 2002. *Chromatic Transformations in Nineteenth-Century Music.* Cambridge: Cambridge University Press.

Kostka, S., and D. Payne. 2012. *Tonal Harmony with an Introduction to Twentieth-Century Music,* 4th edition. New York, NY: McGraw-Hill.

Krumhansl, C. 1990. *The Cognitive Foundations of Musical Pitch.* Oxford: Oxford University Press.

Laitz, S. 2012. *The Complete Musician: An Integrated Approach to Tonal Harmony, Analysis, and Listening,* 3rd edition. Oxford and New York, NY: Oxford University Press.

Le, X., I. Lancashire, G. Hirst, and R. Jokel. 2011. "Longitudinal Detection of Dementia through Lexical and Syntactic Changes in Writing: A Case Study of Three British Novelists." *Literary and Linguistic Computing,* 26/4, 435–461.

Lerdahl, F. 1996. "Calculating Tonal Tension." *Music Perception,* 13/3, 319–363.

Lerdahl, F., and R. Jackendoff. 1983. *A Generative Theory of Tonal Music: A Generative Theory of Tonal Music.* Cambridge: MIT Press.

Lewin, D. 1987. *Generalized Musical Intervals and Transformations*. New Haven: Yale University Press.

Louie, P. 2012. "Learning and Liking of Melody and Harmony: Further Studies in Artificial Grammar Learning." *Topics in Cognitive Science*, 4, 1–14.

Markman, E. M. 1989. *Categorization in Children: Problems of Induction*. Cambridge, MA: MIT Press.

Matsunaga, R., and J.-I. Abe. 2005. "Cues for Key Perception of a Melody: Pitch Set Alone." *Music Perception*, 23/2, 153–164.

Matsunaga, R., and J.-I. Abe. 2009. "Do Local Properties Function as Cues for Musical Key Identification?" *Japanese Psychological Research*, 55, 86–97.

Nobile, D. 2016. "Harmonic Function in Rock Music: A Syntactical Approach." *Journal of Music Theory*, 60/2, 149–180.

Quinn, I. 2005. "Harmonic Function without Primary Triads." Paper delivered at the Annual Meeting of the Society for Music Theory in Boston.

Ratner, L. 1980. *Classic Music: Expression, Form, and Style*. New York: Schrimer.

Riemann, H. 1900. *Präludien und Studien III*. Leipzig: Hermann Seemann.

Rings, S. 2011. *Tonality and Transformation*. New York: Oxford University Press.

Rogers, N., and C. Callender. 2006. "Judgments of Distance between Trichords." *Proceedings of the 9th International Conference on Music Perception and Cognition*. Mario Baroni, Anna Rita Addessi, Roberto Caterina, and Marco Costa, eds. Bologna, Italy: University of Bologna, pp. 1686–1691.

Rohrmeier, M., and I. Cross. 2008. "Statistical Properties of Tonal Harmony in Bach's Chorales." *Proceedings of the 10th International Conference on Music Perception and Cognition*, Sapporo: ICMPC, 619–627.

Schwitzgebel, E. and C. W. White. 2021. "Effects of Chord Inversion and Bass Patterns on Harmonic Expectancy in Musicians." *Music Perception*, 39/1, 41–62.

Simms, B. 1975. "Choron, Fétis, and the Theory of Tonality." *Journal of Music Theory*, 19(1), 112–138.

Smith, C. 1981. "Prolongations and Progressions as Musical Syntax." *Music Theory: Special Topics*. Edited by Richmond Browne. New York: Academic Press, 139–174.

Sobin, N. 1982. "Texas Spanish and Lexical Borrowing." *Spanish in the United States: Sociolinguistic Aspects*. J. Amastae and L. Elias-Olivares, eds. New York: Cambridge University Press, 166–181.

Sowa, J. F. 1984. *Conceptual Structures: Information Processing in Mind and Machine*. Boston: Addison-Wesley Longman.

Sowa, John F. 2000. *Knowledge Representation: Logical, Philosophical, and Computational Foundations*. Pacific Grove, CA: Brooks/Cole Publishing Co.

Staddon, J. E. R. 1978. "Theory of Behavioral Power Functions." *Psychological Review*, 85/4, 305–320.

Staddon, J. E. R. 2016. *Adaptive Behavior and Learning*. Cambridge: Cambridge University Press.

Swinden, K. J. 2005. "When Functions Collide: Aspects of Plural Function in Chromatic Music." *Music Theory Spectrum*, 27/2, 249–282.

Temperley, D. 2007. *Music and Probability*. Cambridge: The MIT Press.

Tymoczko, D. 2003. "Function Theories: A Statistical Approach." *Musurgia*, 10/3–4, 35–64.

Vega, D. 2003. "A Perceptual Experiment on Harmonic Tension and Melodic Attraction in Lerdahl's Tonal Pitch Space." *Musicæ Scientiæ*, 7/1, 35–55.

Waxman, S. R., and D. B. Markow. 1995. "Words as Invitations to Form Categories: Evidence from 12- to 13-Month-Old Infants." *Cognitive Psychology*, 29, 257–302.

184 What Is Function?

Weiss, D. J. 1989. "Psychophysics and Metaphysics." *Behavioral and Brain Sciences*, 12, 251–320.

White, C. W. 2016. "Review of Tonality and Transformation." *Music Theory Spectrum*, 38/2, 265–270.

White, C., J. Pater, and M. Breen. 2022. "A Comparative Analysis of Melodic Rhythm in Two Corpora of American Popular Music." *Journal of Mathematics and Music*. 16/2, 160–182. TBD.

White, C. W. and I. Quinn. 2018. "Chord Content and Harmonic Function in Tonal Music." *Music Theory Spectrum*, 314–350.

White, C., and E. Schwitzgebel. 2019. "Harmonic Grammar, Chord Frequency, and Database Structure." Paper presented at the Society for Music Perception and Cognition, New York City.

Zajonc, R. B. 1968. "Attitudinal Effects of Mere Exposure." *Journal of Personality and Social Psychology*, 9/2, 1–27.

Zajonc, R. B. 2001. "Mere Exposure: A Gateway to the Subliminal." *Current Directions in Psychological Science*, 10/6, 224–228.

Zanette, D. H. 2006. "Zipf's Law and the Creation of Musical Context." *Musicae Scientiae*, 10, 3–18.

Zbikowski, L. 2002. *Conceptualizing Music: Cognitive Structure, Theory, and Analysis*. New York: Oxford University Press.

CHAPTER 4 APPENDIX

z-Scores

Equation A4.1 outlines the formula for *z*-scores, the values used to quantify scale-degree overlap in Figure 4.6. The formula is designed to compare the averages of multiple datasets when the absolute values of variables in the different datasets might involve different scales. In Figure 4.6, different corpora will have chords of different sizes, and the underlying corpora will be of different scopes, and therefore comparing the average overlap between different corporas' functions would be comparing proverbial apples to oranges. However, a *z*-score normalizes between these corpora by representing each value as the number of standard deviations from a corpus's overall average. Each corpus might contain different averages and different standard deviations from that average, but by representing these differences as the number of standard deviations, *z*-scores strip away these differences and use a value that has the same meaning across different datasets.

For example, let's imagine corpus #1 has an average of 2 scale degrees of overlap between each of its constituent chords with a standard deviation of 1 scale degree, and corpus #2 has an average overlap of 4 scale degrees with a standard deviation of 2. (Perhaps, for instance, this difference could be because corpus #2 contains larger chords than corpus #1, and larger chords will simply have more opportunities to overlap with one another.) If Function *A* in corpus #1 has an average of 3 scale degrees overlapping between its constituent chords, the difference between that function's average and the global average is 1 scale degree, or one full standard deviation in corpus #1. The *z*-score would therefore be 1. If Function *B* in corpus #2 had an average overlap of 5 scale degrees,

186 What Is Function?

the difference from that corpus's global average would also be 1 scale degree, but 1 is now only one half of that corpus's standard deviation: the z-score would be .5. And so, because corpus #2 has a higher baseline expectation of scale-degree overlap (as represented by its average and standard deviation), even though Function B in corpus #2 had a higher absolute number of scale degrees overlapping, the z-score shows that result is less impressive than the overlap in corpus #1's Function A.

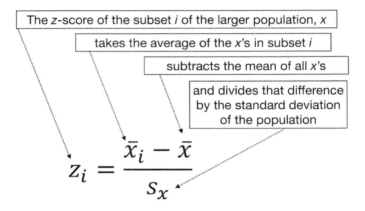

EQUATION A4.1 z-scores

Zipf's Law

In spoken language, when a word appears in a text, that word is very likely to appear again in the text. Additionally, the more often a word appears, the more likely it is to be used again. This phenomenon is described by Zipf's Law: the compounding probabilities of reused words creates the exponential distribution of a power-law curve. Figure A4.1 shows the frequency distribution of words in my previous chapter (Chapter 3). "The" is exponentially more likely to occur than "of," which is exponentially more likely to occur than "and," and so on.

I've added the equation for the line that traces this distribution: the frequency y can be predicted by the rank of the word x when multiplied by 0.07 and raised to the power of −.08. I've broken down the roles of these two values in Equation A4.2. The exponent k will act as a slope for the curve, with the negative value indicating that the values decrease as the ranks increase. The larger the number used for k, the steeper the slope. The first value a functions

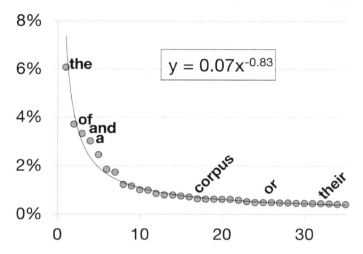

FIGURE A4.1 The frequency-rank distribution of words in Chapter 3, along with its power-law curve

akin to an intercept, showing the value on the curve when $x = 1$. I have provided an example of this distribution in the online supplement for this chapter, along with an example of another type of distribution curve referred to in this chapter, the logarithmic curve.

While this chapter focused on *whether* the chords within musical corpora follow a power-law curve, the curve's actual slope can be used for other means. For example, some forensic linguists claim that a higher slope can be seen in speakers manifesting a cognitive decline, since a steeper slope will indicate that the speaker reuses a few words more frequently and uses less diversity in their words overall (see Le et al., 2011, for instance). As another example: along with my collaborators Joe Pater and Mara Breen, I have used this curve to quantify the diversity of rhythms used in premillennial versus postmillennial popular music (White et al., 2022).

188 What Is Function?

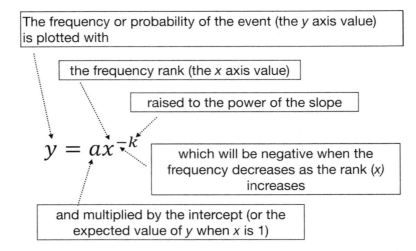

EQUATION A4.2 The power-law curve

5

WHAT IS METER?

A Dialogue

In this scene, Aloysius and Josephus discuss some ways that computational corpus analysis can be used to test, challenge, and enhance our understanding of musical meter. Aloysius is a consummate musician and deeply aware of the nuance and complications behind metric theory but is generally skeptical of computational approaches. Josephus, on the other hand, is an energetic and knowledgeable proponent of computational corpus analysis but often overstates their findings. We join them as they reminisce about their evening and follow their conversation as they ruminate about some corpus-based approaches to meter-finding.

Aloysius: (*enters, catching his breath*) What a night! I had forgotten how much I thoroughly enjoy discotheques. I was very impressed with how seamlessly the DJ mixed each song into the next by matching their meters.

Josephus: Are you referring to how the DJ matched the grooves and accent patterns of each pair of tracks with one another as they transitioned between songs?

Aloysius: (*suddenly pedantic*) Well, yes, but that is essentially the definition of meter, isn't it . . .

Josephus: (*laughing*) Aloysius, I would be very interested to hear your nuanced definition of meter in a moment. But it was not the DJ who was mixing the tracks with one another: it was actually a computer! While this kind of mixing was originally done using two records on alternate turntables (see Butler, 2006; Greasley and Prior, 2013, for instance), the process is now digitally lubricated by computational models that look for peaks in loudness that occur with a certain regularity in the two tracks and then align those peaks.

A: How interesting! But wouldn't you agree that such a computational model would essentially be a model of meter? (*They pass a street sign labelled . . .*)

DOI: 10.4324/9781003285663-5

190 What Is Meter?

Metrical Corpus Analysis: Musical Surfaces versus Metric Templates

J: (*annoyed but excited that the conversation has turned academic*) To my mind, computational analyses, especially those that rely on data from musical corpora, either need to import some external definition of meter or are limited to analyzing surface patterns. In the course of our conversation, I'll lay out the conceptual framework for this claim, introduce a computational tool that can identify patterns within musical corpora, and then I will apply that tool to four corpora. After observing the output of these corpus analyses, we'll be able to see the power and limits of corpus analysis within studies of meter and clearly articulate how corpus analyses can link with larger cognitive and music theories to contribute to a richer understanding of meter within various repertoires and musical traditions. I'll argue that corpora of musical surfaces do not, in fact, express musical meter and therefore computer models that rely on raw, uninterpreted corpus data will be greatly limited in the kinds of claims they can make about musical meter. I will additionally argue that a full accounting of meter requires some kind of human interpretation of a musical corpus. My analyses will show that the frequent equation between surface events and meter is the result of isomorphisms present in Western European classical music and that allowing for more flexibility in how we relate corpus data to musical meter is necessary for culturally sensitive and socially responsible analysis.

   (*catches breath*) Perhaps we can start with a working definition of *meter*?

A: Certainly. To be technical, *meter* is a phenomenon that: (a) arises from a series of consistently paced pulses (Krebs, 1999; Lerdahl and Jackendoff, 1983), (b) involves listeners' expectations that the pacing will continue into the future (Hasty, 1997; London, 2004; Long, 2020), (c) groups adjacent pulses by either twos or threes to form a robust hierarchy of stronger and weaker pulses related by duple or triple ratios (Yeston, 1976; Lerdahl and Jackendoff, 1983; Cohn, 2001), and (d) draws listeners' attention to events commensurate with their place in the hierarchy (Jones and Boltz, 1989; Jones et al., 2002; London, 2004). Importantly, a bodily experience of meter will feature the phenomenon of *entrainment*, a combination of the expectation of the second component and the attention of the fourth. In entrainment, a person feels isochronous pulses in a preconscious or bodily manner – entrainment is the phenomenon that allows us to tap our foot, feel a groove, or even dance to a piece of music (Patel, 2007; London, 2004). While the stronger beats in a meter do not always need to be manifestly louder or accented (Brochard et al., 2003), the overall accent pattern of some passage gives rise to an emergent metric framework of felt pulses. (Here, "accent" means a musical moment that is heard as relatively stronger or more marked than other surrounding moments: Cooper and Meyer, 1960; Jones, 1987). Entrainment additionally gives rise to *metric accents* (Lerdahl and Jackendoff, 1983): in contrast to *phenomenal accents*, which have some sort of manifestly marked quality about the sound itself (a moment that is louder has a phenomenal accent, for instance), metrical accents are the peaks of awareness that accompany an entrained pulse. In fact, in the repertoire to which we were just dancing, we often heard a clear pattern of phenomenal accents, something like a "*BOOM boom BOOM boom*," a sequence that alternates strong and weak accents. This pattern features a quick isochronous pulse (all booms, big and small) that are grouped equally by a slower, more-accented isochronous pulse (the bigger BOOMS). The consistency and isochrony of this pattern allowed us to feel and move to the beat. Even when the pattern altered in some way, we still continued dancing to that isochronous pulse – we had entrained to the pulse and felt the consistent metric accents.

(*Pauses and draws a dot diagram with his toe on the sidewalk*). Perhaps you'll recall the coffee-bean approach that our friends Florestan and Eusebius showed us in our local coffee shop several weeks ago; I've modified their approach into a "dot-notation" where the number of dots correspond to the structural accents of a metric level in Figure 5.1a (Lerdahl and Jackendoff, 1983). If we consider a sequence with five different levels of loudness (loudest, loud, medium, soft, and softest), and these events were deployed in the nested isochronous patterns indicated by the figure, the pattern would indicate the metric levels shown by the dots. This pattern would represent the 16th divisions of a quadruple measure, with the downbeat being the most accented, the offbeat 16th notes being the least accented, and so on. Here, the loudest moments create the broadest metric pulse, and the medium accents create a pulse that is both twice as quick and divides the loudness/broadest pulse in half. Finally, the quickest pulse underpins all events, including the softest moments. As multiple commentators have noted (London, 2004; Cohn, 2021), such patterns are generally cyclic, insomuch as the metrical accents repeat in the same sequence with the same isochronous periodicities over and over. To illustrate this aspect of meter, Figure 5.1b represents the content of Figure 5.1a as a circle (somewhat combining the circular diagrams of London, 2004, and the dot diagrams of Lerdahl and Jackendoff, 1983.)

J: (*furrowing their brow*) Aloysius, I would argue that when a computer finds a pattern in a musical sequence of signal, that does not mean it's found a hierarchy of accents or even any relationships between pulses. In fact, I would go so far as to argue that your definition of meter is not sensitive to variations between musical corpora and does not account for the potential flexibility between expectations harbored by listeners and the events of a musical corpus. To turn our conversation explicitly to the topic of metrical corpus analyses, I would argue that an approach to meter that is sensitive both to the variations between musical corpora and to the differences in listeners' metric expectations will have two components: (1) at least one recurrent pattern on a musical surface and (2) a method of organizing those patterns by imposing beginnings, endings, accents, and hierarchies onto that pattern. Importantly, these two components are distinct and, I would argue, represent two sides of the meter learning, hearing, and identifying process. While recurrent patterns can be observed in and derived from a corpus of musical surfaces the organizing method is *not* learned from a corpus.

192 What Is Meter?

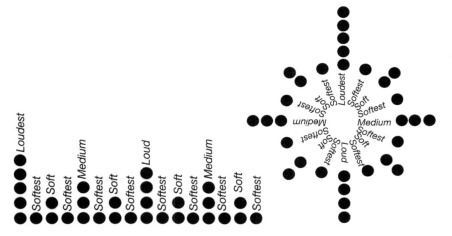

FIGURE 5.1 (a, left) A basic dot diagram expressing the meter of an accent pattern and (b, right) the same pattern shown as a cycle

    Now, to be clear, I'm arguing about what's available on a musical surface or in some most-basic definition of musical materials — notions like the sounds hitting a listener's ears, notes streaming over a computer's cursor, or the punctures of a piano roll. Because of this, I'll be talking about datasets of raw surface events: pitches, durations, dynamics, and other basic musical attributes. For now, this excludes explicit metric notations like barlines and time signatures that are not available to the listener (an audience doesn't "hear" a time signature, nor does a piano roll have barlines). We can litigate these choices later, but for now my arguments stands as such: a full accounting of "meter" cannot be learned from this type of data. Instead, patterns can be learned from these corpora, but these patterns need to rely on some outside, non-corpus-based definitions to organize into a full meter, definitions potentially imported from some theoretical, cognitive, or bodily understanding.

A: (*somewhat surprised*) From this perspective, you would be arguing that corpus analysis of meter is fundamentally constrained to observing surface patterns, not analyzing *meter* . . .

J: To illustrate what I mean, Figure 5.2a converts your cycles of loudness into a series of letters: the loudest event is converted to the letter *X*, *A* becomes the softest events, *Y*'s are the medium events, and so on. The overall pattern now involves four sequences of *ABA* (what were the softest/soft/softest sequences of Figure 5.1), the first beginning with *X* (what was the loudest event), the second and fourth beginning with *Y* (medium), and the third beginning with *Z* (loud). Were we to look at this sequence from a completely naïve vantage point (and as argued in Chapter 1, that such a vantage point is one of the strengths of computational corpus analyses), we would find several ways in which this broader pattern repeats its component patterns. In particular,

What Is Meter? **193**

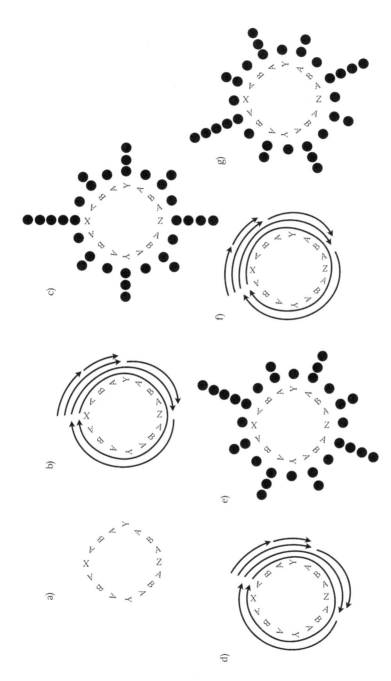

FIGURE 5.2 Different potential divisions and metric interpretations of the same cyclic pattern

194 What Is Meter?

given its internal repetition, the larger sequence can be divided in half and then divided into quarters – for instance, the four appearances of *ABA* support the quadruple divisions, and the two repetitions of *Y* support this duple division. Furthermore, given that A repeats every other event, a final division of the sequence into local groups of two seems reasonable as well.

However, while it is clear that this larger pattern has some components that repeat four times, some sequences that repeat twice, and a letter that repeats every other event, it is not clear where these groups should begin and end. In other words, it's not obvious where we should divide the larger 16-member pattern into two groups of 8, how to divide those divisions into further subdivisions of 4, and how to finally construct the smallest groups of 2.

Figure 5.2 illustrates this ambiguity. We *could* define our patterns as beginning with the sequence's most unique (i.e., least frequent) letters, *X*, *Y*, and *Z*; I show some of these patterns with the arrows in Figure 5.2b. I can then import your dot diagram and align greater metric accents with the longer cycles to produce Figure 5.2c. However, I could also define the patterns as beginning with the most frequent sequence, *ABA*. This definition would result in the patterns shown in Figure 5.2d and the hierarchical representation of Figure 5.2e. Finally, we could imagine the end of the *ABA* sequence initiating the beginnings of patterns, a definition that would produce Figures 5.2f and 5.2g. Looking simply at the pattern, there is no clear way to decide between these solutions.

A: I couldn't disagree more. When your example abstracts the sequence to letters, it obscures its essential and obvious components. For one, louder events are more accented, which makes for an obvious placement of metric pulses and a clear beginning and ending of the larger pattern and each component pattern. For another, similarities in loudness levels allow for the sequence to be first divided in half, then in quarters, and then in eighths at these specific points of similarity.

J: While these alignments may be intuitively obvious, your intuition is still importing a definition of accent onto the musical surface: your "obvious" analysis required referencing particular assumptions about how meter aligns with surface events, specifically that louder events are more accented and that these phenomenal accents should generally align with metric accents. In other words, your pronouncements do not rely on the structure of the patterns themselves but on some suite of *a priori* assumptions about how to map a meter onto these patterns.

To be sure, the distinction I am trying to draw between surface events and cognitive processes has been evoked by earlier researchers. Justin London's (1990, 2004) dichotomy of *period extraction versus template matching* similarly describes the process of molding a musical pattern into a meter. London argues that a listener's experience of meter involves two complementary processes – one in which they identify periodic regularities in a musical signal and the other applying some preexisting understanding of metrical structure onto those regularities. This approach also analogizes with David Huron's (2006) dichotomy between the *perceptual* and the *cognized* in musical experiences. Huron argues that pitches, for instance, are perceived – they are stimuli

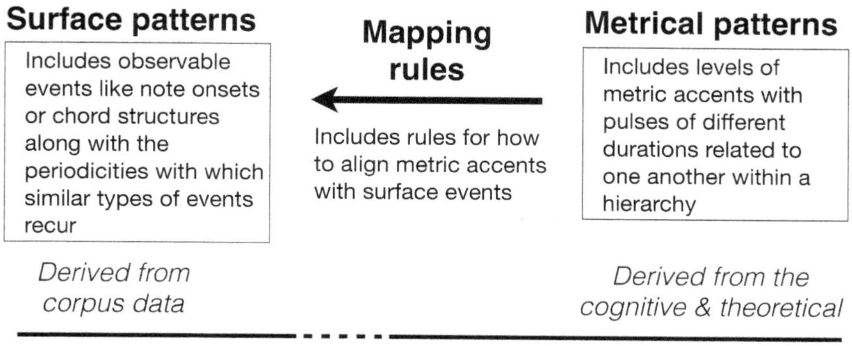

Surface patterns

Mapping rules

Metrical patterns

Includes observable events like note onsets or chord structures along with the periodicities with which similar types of events recur

← Includes rules for how to align metric accents with surface events

Includes levels of metric accents with pulses of different durations related to one another within a hierarchy

*Derived from
corpus data*

*Derived from the
cognitive & theoretical*

FIGURE 5.3 Generic Corpus Analysis of Meter Model (GCAMM)

that exist in the world – while scale degrees are cognized – our own minds work to interpret the pitch stimulus in some way to produce scale degrees. In much the same way, patterns are a simple property of the musical phenomenon, but meter is a way of interpreting that phenomenon.

I recognize that there are several issues in my analysis of Figure 5.2 that we could interrogate, contest or dispute— from the potential musical attributes of each letter to the unique positions of each letter within the ordering of the larger sequence. However, I want to table these concerns for a moment to outline a more bird's-eye view of the kind of argument I'm trying to make.

Figure 5.3 summarizes my corpus-based approach to meter, using a flow-chart I call the Generic Corpus Analysis of Meter Model, or GCAMM. The figure shows surface patterns and metrical patterns as two distinct components, along with what I'm calling "mapping rules." On the left, I show the surface patterns. These are items that can be observed directly from a musical surface, can include patterns of any sort, and are derivable from corpus data – they are akin to the inner circles of Figures 5.1 and 5.2. On the right are metrical patterns. These are akin to the outer cycles of Figures 5.1 and 5.2 and are frameworks of metrical accents or entrained pulses that organize a musical surface. I want to remain agnostic as to the constituency of these patterns, but throughout this conversation, I'll adopt the definition of meter you outlined earlier. The mapping rules then determine how to align a surface pattern with a metrical pattern, potentially defining what should be considered metrically accented, what kinds of events should begin patterns, and so on.

J: *(continues)* From this perspective, much theoretical work on meter concerns metrical patterns and their corresponding mapping rules. Lerdahl and Jackendoff (1983), for instance, present metrical well-formedness rules that outline the kinds of hierarchies and relationships that can be considered a *meter* in their theory (e.g., in their theory, meter contains nested hierarchies with duple and triple relationships between levels): these rules are theories about the figure's rightward pane, the constituency of metric patterns. Their

196 What Is Meter?

metrical preference rules then outline the kinds of musical events that should align with metric accents, where a metric pattern should begin, how to resolve ambiguities, and so forth: these preference rules correspond to my mapping rules or the ways that metrical patterns map onto surface patterns. Indeed, any theory concerned with the sorts of patterns humans can feel as metric – be it the ground rules for human entrainment (London, 2004) or the mathematical underpinnings of a metrical hierarchy (Cohn, 2001) – concerns the figure's metrical patterns pane. Any theory that concerns how a notated or felt meter should aligns with the events and patterns of a musical surface actual musical events – be it studying what events humans hear as relatively accented (e.g., Acevedo et al., 2014; Fraisse, 1946; Iversen and Patel, 2008; Repp et al., 2008) or even how poetic texts should be aligned with a metrical pattern (Long, 2020) – concern the GCAMM's mapping function.

A: (*annoyed*) And the left-hand pane?

J: The *surface patterns* pane then describes events as they appear on a musical surface, and these are often a focus of music analysis. When Krebs (1999) describes the kinds of accent and harmonic patterns present in the music of Robert Schumann or Long (2020) shows the kinds of regular chord progressions that arise in 16th- and 17th-century vocal music, they are studying surface patterns.

A: The annotations below the chart suggest that you believe corpus analysis to have a well-defined territory in this metric trifecta.

J: Indeed! In my estimation, corpus analysis's strength lies primarily in describing the surface patterns present in some repertoire. These patterns can then be potentially linked to the meters of a corpus's constituent music, but how and why those mappings are made are the domain of cognitive and theoretical research. Additionally, some feedback may occur between mapping rules and a corpus's events, a topic to which we'll return momentarily and which is indicated by the dotted line between the corpus and cognitive/theoretical poles of the GCAMM.

But before we progress into larger issues, I should note that the GCAMM is related to another dichotomy often invoked in metric analysis: the distinction between *rhythm* and *meter*. Like surface patterns, the former involves durational, onset, and accent patterns that are immediately observable (Lerdahl and Jackendoff, 1983; Rothstein, 1989). My surface-pattern concept, however, specifically stipulates a regularity in the event series and, in that sense, emphasizes the periodicity and recursion in the musical surface more than the rhythmic and durational events themselves. Additionally, *grouping* versus *meter* serves as another foundational dichotomy in meter studies that resonates with the GCAMM: indeed, Cohn (2021) locates the "birth of modern metric theory" to when scholars began to make distinctions between meter and musical groupings (or the boundaries and nesting of musical motives, harmonic durations, and phrases). I'm sure we'll return to the role of grouping in our analyses in the course of our walk, but suffice to say: the dicey notions of where phase groups begin and end along with their lackadaisical regularity have been primary points of distinction between this concept and a rigorous definition of meter. Finally, from a more philosophical perspective, Mariucz Kozak (2019) has argued that musical meter should be located within the body's engagement with musical sounds. To Kozak, concepts like *accent* or *entrainment* do not derive from musical phenomena *per se* but are rather located in cognitive predilections or bodily metaphors or are simply taught. In this way, Kozak makes precisely the same distinction I am, isolating embodied human experience as the location of metrical patterns, patterns imposed onto some set of observed musical phenomena.

A: (*exasperated*) Again, I find your distinctions and arguments needless and petty to the point that they obscure how music expresses meter. To my mind, meter can easily be pinpointed within a score: we don't need to impose the meter; the patterns *are* the meter because of ways they consistently deploy events like accent and chord change. After all, deducing meter from musical events is a frequent exercise of music analysis (Krebs, 1999; Guerra, 2018; Mirka, 2009; Murphy, 2007). Additionally, it's important to also note that London also uses his period-finding/template-matching dichotomy as something of a progression, with templates being learned by listeners after being exposed to a number of periodic patterns: the regularities of musical stimuli teach listeners how meter works rather than meter involving some external suite of necessary characteristics imposed upon a musical experience!

J: I believe I can best argue my viewpoint by undertaking some basic pattern-finding corpus analysis.

A: I'll look forward to it. Let's turn down this street, and you can begin to describe your corpus-based models. (*Aloysius points to a street sign that reads . . .*)

Autocorrelation as a Basic Tool for Corpus-Based Metrical Analysis

J: To the best of my knowledge, the first foray into corpus analysis and meter-finding was undertaken by Palmer and Krumhansl (1990), who noticed that the number of note attacks that occur at a particular event is correlated to the metric strength of that pulse: more note attacks occur on stronger metric pulses in Western European art music, while less metrically accented moments host fewer note attacks. In this correlation, note attacks are proxies for loudness: all things being equal, if more instruments enter or more notes are sounded at a particular moment, that event will be louder. Again reflecting the assumptions underpinning Figure 5.1, these researchers assume that phenomenal and metrical accents should — on average — coincide. In other words: the more note attacks that simultaneously occur, the louder the proverbial *BOOM* is, and the more likely that moment is to express a strong metrical pulse.

To illustrate this phenomenon, Figure 5.4 shows the first two measures from Fanny Mendelssohn-Hensel's song "Die Mainacht" and then shows the

198 What Is Meter?

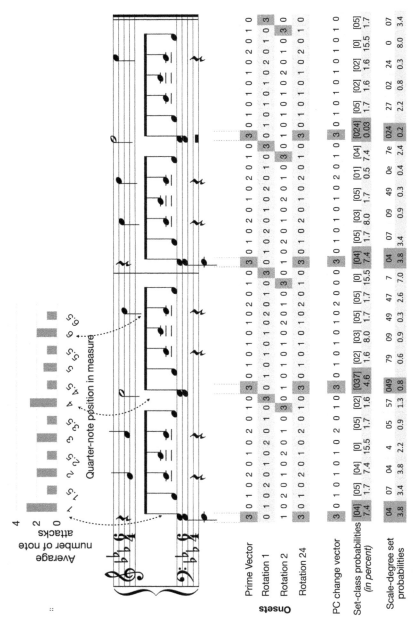

FIGURE 5.4 Josephus's adaptation of Fanny Mendelssohn-Hensel's "Die Mainacht," Op. 9 no. 6, mm. 1–2; along with the prime note-onset vector, three example vector rotations, and three further prime vectors showing pitch-class change, set-class stability/probability, and scale-degree set stability/probability

average number of note onsets on each pulse throughout the song, with arrows orienting which metric pulse each datapoint refers to. The note attacks parallel the contours of your Figure 5.1: the peaks and valleys of note attacks are isomorphic with the relative metric accent of each pulse.

Judith Brown (1993) computationally operationalized this observation using a relatively simple statistical process called *autocorrelation*. Brown showed that peaks and valleys in the numbers of notes beginning at each timepoint can predict the notated time signature of a piece of music with surprising accuracy. Several researchers have created sophisticated modelings to better represent the relationship between note onsets and loudness, sophistications that improve the performance of this approach to meter-finding (Eerola and Toiviainen, 2004; Eck, 2006), while other applications have extended and supplemented autocorrelation with such additions as expectation maximization (de Haas and Volk, 2016) and Shannon entropy (Eck and Casagrande, 2005) to increase the process's utility and precision.[1] The connection between note onset and metrical accent has also been subsequently tested and verified by computational (e.g., Gouyon et al., 2006) and behavioral research (e.g., White, 2019a).

A: This sort of modeling sounds compelling, but has this work had much influence on broader music theory research?

J: Honestly, not very much. From my perspective, mainstream music theories of meter have not been influenced by computational and corpus-based research in the same way as, say, the topics of harmony and style have been. The exception that proves the rule is the work of Graham Boone (2000), who used the counts of note attacks to identify isochronous pulses in Renaissance music in order to investigate differences in various mensural notations. This publication remains something of an outlier in investigations of meter by music theorists and musicologists.

A: Your emphasis on the autocorrelation method belies your interest in it. I'd like to hear how this computational approach might be useful to our discussion of meter. But first, I think you should explain how autocorrelation works.

J: To be clear, autocorrelation is a relatively simple procedure – something of a "lowest common denominator" in computational meter-finding. By no means does it represent the state-of-the-art, nor is it the most efficacious computational model for this task. However, the benefit of an autocorrelation model is that it imports no preexisting understanding of accent, downbeat, or any other kind of metrical structure to its meter-finding process and relies solely on the regularities of a musical surface to create its output. As such, any results obtained from the method can be considered surface patterns and properties of the basic musical data of the corpus – in other words, it will serve as a good approximation of the leftward pane of the GCAMM. Additionally, as a lowest common denominator, we can use autocorrelation to observe the sorts of patterns that might be used in more complex state-of-the-art approaches . . .

A: (*becoming exasperated*) I'll be sure to remind you to talk more about the pros and cons of other meter-finding approaches later, but only after you explain the inner workings of autocorrelation! (*Aloysius points them down a side street called . . .*)

200 What Is Meter?

Autocorrelation: Methods

J: Autocorrelation identifies the basic recurrent patterns within a passage along with the periodicities at which those patterns repeat. Under Figure 5.4's score of "Die Mainacht," I show a long string of boxed numbers. The boxes slice each measure into sixteenth-note durations, representing the occurrences at each sixteenth pulse. The first box corresponds to the downbeat and has three note attacks, the next corresponds to the following offbeat sixteenth pulse at which no new note attacks occur, followed by the single note attack of the next eighth note, and so on. In this initial series – what I'll call the *prime note-onset vector* – I highlight the beginnings of the dotted-half pulse articulating the measures and half-measures.

A: (*squinting at the vector*) Yes, I notice that these highlighted points include the most prominent and consistent peaks in note onsets: they all have three note attacks. Other less prominent and less consistent peaks occur at the quarter-note and eighth-note pulses, with the intervening sixteenth pulses having no onsets.

J: The autocorrelation process relies on the aggregate patterns that you are noticing and identifies these patterns by comparing the prime vector to its rotations. Below the prime vector, I've shown three rotations of the series, what I'll call *secondary* vectors. These rotated vectors move all members of the previous rotation to the left, with the first value being appended to the end, creating something of a conveyor belt of numbers. The second rotation then moves the numbers one more position, and so on.

In autocorrelation, the prime vector is compared to each of these secondary vectors, assessing their similarities and differences. In Figure 5.2, if we compare the prime vector to the first rotation, the numbers do not align particularly well. This rotation shifts the vector one sixteenth note, such that every event in the prime vector is aligned with the event that happens one sixteenth note removed; in the current example, this aligns events with no onsets in one vector with events that have at least one onset in the other. The resulting mismatch makes sense: events on metrically strong pulses tend not to have much in common with the metrically weak offbeats surrounding them. Rotation 2 continues this process by shifting the values two positions – or by one eighth note. Now, zeros are aligned with one another, as are integers. Again, this makes sense: events separated by an eighth note are more similar in the current example than events separated by a sixteenth note. The rotation process continues in the same manner. The last secondary vector in the figure rotates the prime vector by 24 sixteenth notes. This rotation aligns the beginning of the second measure in the secondary vector with the beginning of the first measure in the prime vector. At this rotation, these two vectors are quite similar: the largest peaks of accent align with one another, medium peaks align with one another and so on. Such a similarity once again makes sense: events that are one measure away from one another (that is, they appear at the same place in their respective measures) should look quite similar on average.

I can then run *correlations* to quantify these similarities and differences. Correlations show how similar two series of data are to one another. A correlation will return a coefficient of 1 when two series of numbers perfectly match, 0 in a completely random and unaligned pairing, and −1 when opposite values align. *Autocorrelation* specifically refers to the process of comparing a prime vector to each of its incremental rotations. (Correlations can be run on any computational interface, including standard spreadsheet software; I'll post spreadsheets that undertake each step underpinning the autocorrelation of the Mendelssohn-Hensel example in our online supplement.)

A: I think I understand: the autocorrelation method returns high coefficients when it aligns moments that have similar note-onset patterns with one another and lower coefficients when pulses with more note onsets align with pulses with fewer onsets. For instance, even though every single quarter-note pulse in the example does not host more note attacks than every single intervening eighth-note pulse, the procedure notices that events separated by a quarter note tend to look alike, at least more alike than events separated by a single eighth note. In other words, the method relies on recurring patterns separated by consistent intervals.

J: Exactly. Figure 5.5 shows a graph of the autocorrelations at each rotation of the "Die Mainacht's" prime vector (again, I'll post these calculations in the online supplement). The perfect correlation at the zero-th mark on the horizontal axis indicates the perfect comparison between the prime vector and itself with no rotation; the next position shows the low correlation of the rotation of a single sixteenth note, followed by the middling correlation of an eighth-note rotation, and so on. Scanning the example, we see peaks

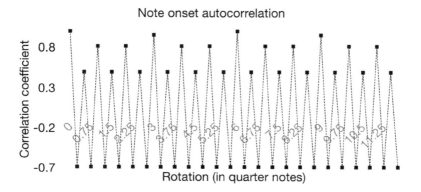

FIGURE 5.5 Correlations resulting from all rotations of the note attacks of Figure 5.4

202 What Is Meter?

at each quarter note, higher peats at the half measure, and then even higher peaks at the full measure. Comparing this to the music of Figure 5.4, these larger values make sense: the greatest numbers of attacks appear at the half-measure (i.e., the dotted-half-note rotation), and the highest correlation at the measure (i.e., the dotted-whole-note rotation).

A: I can then imagine that you use this series of correlations to identify a piece's meter. Visually, Figure 5.5 has a lot in common with the dot diagrams of Figure 5.1: the size of the peaks corresponds to the strength of the metric pulses. The example should have the strongest metric accents at the beginning of each of its six-quarter-note-long measures, and indeed the highest correlation appears at the six-quarter-note rotation; middle-sized peaks then occur at durations corresponding to the middling metric accents of the half-measure, and so on.

J: The actual meter-finding step identifies peaks of similar sizes that recur at consistent intervals.[2] The process starts by identifying the highest consistent correlations, then the next highest, and so on. In the excerpt from "Die Mainacht," the dotted-whole-note periodicity has the highest values, and so the autocorrelation meter-finding procedure would return this as a metric pulse. It would then identify the next-highest consistently paced correlations at the dotted-half-note level, then the quarter-note, and finally the eighth-note periodicities.

A: As you say, this example aligns the relative magnitude of note attacks with levels of metric accent. Does this hold for pieces across large corpora?

J: Figure 5.6 averages several parameters for all pieces in 4/4 within a portion of the music21 corpus, showing average note onsets with the solid black line. The music21 programming library (Cuthbert and Ariza, 2010) includes several collections of pieces, and for these analyses, I use musicXML files (a file format with well-curated and reliable metric and tonal information) from those composers in the corpus who were writing music in Western Europe between 1600 and 1900. (This includes Claudio Monteverdi, Johann

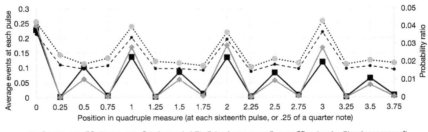

FIGURE 5.6 Average distribution within quadruple measures in the music21 tonal corpus for a variety of musical parameters

Sebastian Bach, Arcangelo Corelli, George Handel, Joseph Haydn, Ludwig Beethoven, Wolfgang Mozart, Robert Schumann, Clara Schumann, and Franz Schubert.) The contour of the solid black line shows downbeats to have the most events, followed by the half-note pulse, then quarter pulses, the intervening eighth notes, and finally the offbeat-sixteenth pulses. Because this consistency exists, we can expect that – in aggregate – an autocorrelation procedure will be able to notice that in quadruple meter, events have a certain similarity with those events four quarter notes in the future and four quarter notes in the past. Similarly, because the first half of the figure looks somewhat the same as the second half and because each quarter and each eighth pulse also feature similarities, an autocorrelation would notice a half-note, quarter-note, and eighth-note pulse in pieces with these sorts of properties.

A: In other words, it returns the quadruple metric hierarchy!

J: Well . . . not exactly. (*distracted*) Before we litigate this topic once again, let me demonstrate how this procedure acts on a corpus. Because note attacks are certainly not the only parameter important to meter-finding, you'll notice that I've included several other parameters in both Figure 5.4 and Figure 5.6. While parameters like duration, pitch height, linear intervals, harmonic change, motivic repetition have variously been.[3] I've done some previous work with several of these parameters (White, 2018, 2019b, 2021); however, for our current conversation, I'm using pitch-class change, set-class probabilities, and scale-degree set probabilities.

The first of these – pitch-class change – is a proxy for harmonic rhythm. Many commentators have noted that harmonic change interacts with metrical periods in Western European art music, suggesting that harmonic changes generally align with metric accents (Lerdahl and Jackendoff, 1983; Hannon et al., 2004; London et al., 2009; Prince and Rice, 2018; Smith and Cuddy, 1989; Dawe et al., 1993, 1994, 1995; Ellis and Jones, 2009). A pitch-class change vector identifies how many new pitch classes are introduced at each moment when compared to the previous moment. In Figure 5.4, I show the pitch-class changes underpinning the Mendelssohn-Hensel passage. For instance, two pitch classes are introduced on the first downbeat (E-flat and G). Because these are held over into the following sixteenth-note slice, zero new pitch classes are introduced, while the following B-flat eighth note introduces one new pc. Then, the E-flat/G sonority at the entry of the melody only introduces one new pc, because the bass's E-flat had been held throughout the full previous quarter-note duration. While the results of this process are similar to a note-attack approach – after all, in order to change pitch classes, you need to attack a new note – the vector will express the amount of harmonic change occurring at each moment. The benefit of this

204 What Is Meter?

method is that dramatic harmonic changes will receive larger values than more subtle changes or harmonic prolongations – for instance, a IV triad moving to a V triad would receive a value of 3, adding a seventh onto a V triad would receive a value of 1, and a pianist's right-hand arpeggiation of the triad they are sustaining in the left hand would receive values of zero.

A: If I recall my undergraduate partwriting tutelage – and I vividly do – I believe that textbooks often indicate that harmony changes should align with barlines and metrical accents. *(closing their eyes to recall the wording and paginations of their citations)* For instance, Aldwell and Schachter (2011) note that students should write progressions such that "changes of chord support the meter" and that these progressions should "avoid repeating a chord from a weak to a strong beat" (p. 93), while Laitz (2012) similarly encourages his readers to use "the speed of harmonic change" to reinforce the meter (p. 27). The fact that the magnitude of pitch class changes in Figure 5.5 tends to track the metric hierarchy, then, is not surprising!

But my intuition is also that specific types of harmonies tend to indicate strong beats, and others indicate weaker beats. In our earlier conversation with Florestan and Eusebius, I believe they mentioned some historical theorists who discuss which sorts of chord structures occur on strong versus weak beats?

J: They did! This idea is quite old. The overarching claim is that consonances tend to appear on metrically accented events in this style, while dissonances are native to metrically weak moments, with early descriptions of this dictum found in the *Discantus positive vulgaris* (c. 1230), John of Garlandia's *De Mensurabili Musica* (c. 1240), and Franco of Cologne's *Ars cantus mensurabilis* (c. 1250).[4] Indeed, one of our earlier dialogues (Fux, 1725) teaches explicit connections between certain intervals and metric strength.

A: The work of more recent thinkers similarly connect consonance, tonal structure, and meter. The work of Heinrich Schenker (1935), Carl Schachter (1999), and Maury Yeston (1976) each adopt some alignment between metric emphases and tonal design.

J: Computational studies on the topic often rely on the connection between stability and probability. Recall from our previous chapters that countless cognitive experiments have found that chords and scale degrees that appear more frequently in a corpus are usually heard as most stable by listeners (Krumhansl, 1990; Huron, 2006). Prince and Schmuckler (2014) and White (2018), for instance, both find that a corpus's most frequent chords tend to occur on stronger pulses, at least in corpora of Western European art music.

A: I imagine this logic underpins the two final parameters of Figures 5.3 and 5.5?

J: Indeed. As this research suggests, the frequencies of chords within the corpus can act as proxies for chord consonance. On the left of Figure 5.7, I've calculated the distribution of set classes in our tonal corpus, and on the right, I show the distribution of scale-degree sets. For the latter distribution, I used

What Is Meter? 205

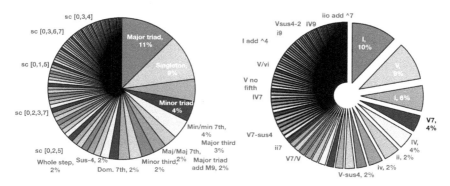

FIGURE 5.7 Distributions of set classes and scale-degree sets in the music21 Western Art Music corpus

the xml files' designations for the piece's opening tonic (a piece of metadata usefully included in the music21 corpus's xml files) and then applied that information to the first eight measures of each file to translate those measures' constituent pitches into scale degrees. For both set-class and scale-degree-set tallying, I divided these measures into each moment a pitch is added or subtracted from the texture (*salami slicing* in the manner of Chapter 2 and Chapter 3). I also ignored rests in these distributions. (NB: Rests were also ignored in the averaging done in Figure 5.6.) In both graphs of Figure 5.7, I've used standard nomenclature for familiar sets (e.g., set class [0, 4, 7] is labelled as a major triad, and the scale-degree set <$\hat{5}$, $\hat{7}$, $\hat{2}$> is labeled as V), and while I label all sets that occur 2% of the time or more, I've added a few labels for less frequent chords later in the distributions. Notice that, as we've seen throughout our discussions, dissonant structures (like, the set classes [0, 2, 5] and [0, 2, 6], and the scale-degree sets IV^9 and I with an added $\hat{4}$) occur much less frequently than consonant sets.

A: I see that Figure 5.6 shows the average probability of both these parameters as they appear in your corpus's 4/4 measures. The averages generally track with the metric accents, with higher probabilities occurring on pulses with greater metric accent. (Although there are some notable fluctuations and incongruities in some of the offbeat sixteenth pulses. I imagine this is due to some accented downbeat dissonances resolving into the following pulse.) On the whole, these probability contours are isomorphic with metric accents.

J: In Figure 5.4, I show how to integrate these values into the autocorrelation procedure. The figure includes prime vectors for the set-class and scale-degree-set probabilities in the Mendelssohn-Hensel passage. The process follows the note-onset approach, populating the vectors with probabilities that correspond to each moment in the music. The probabilities align with where harmonies begin, and zeros show moments of stasis or rest.[5]

206 What Is Meter?

A: To recap, we have four ways of representing musical passages as vectors in which each value of the vector represents sequential sixteenth-note slices. We can then perform an autocorrelation procedure on these vectors, which will indicate the durations at which the same sorts of events recur. However: how do we know whether your model produces the correct answers? How do we know whether the process has identified the correct durations for a piece of music in your corpus?

J: By using the piece's time signature. Our analysis of "Die Mainacht" identified patters at the duration of the dotted-whole note, dotted-half, quarter note, and eighth note. These pulses are precisely those suggested by the piece's 6/4 time signature. We can consider the autocorrelated patterns a success because they align with the time signature.

A: (*suddenly irritated*) Of course, equating time signatures with meter is a vast oversimplification. Time signatures can be ambiguous: 6/4 *could* be both a simple triple or compound duple meter! Furthermore, the same periodicities of 6/4 meter could arise in a piece with a 3/4 time signature with a two-bar hypermeter. And, Western Classical music often uses time signatures more for notational convenience or convention than metric designation – for instance, J.S. Bach's music in 4/4 and 2/4 time signatures are notoriously quite similar if not identical. Additionally, by their very definition, time signatures do not capture events like hemiolas and displacement dissonances (Krebs, 1999). Contemporary theorists are usually very hesitant to equate a piece's meter solely with its time signature and instead see it as an imperfect shorthand designed to indicate only the most basic of metrical characteristics (Cohn, 2021). It's hard to imagine a time signature acting as a kind of infallible truth against which you can measure your model's performance.

J: (*carefully*) You mentioned that time signatures can be a "shorthand for performers" – and this is the sense in which I intend to use them. As a shorthand, they represent a choice made by the composer to communicate some baseline about the piece's metric organization. When a composer notates a piece in 3/4 rather than 4/4 or 6/8, that choice is not arbitrary. The time signature means *something*. If we relax the expectation that a time signature should show us *everything* about a piece's meter, we can focus on the things a time signature *can* show us. And we can then compare that – admittedly limited – information to the assessments given by my autocorrelation model.

In this case, I can simply compare my autocorrelation's groupings of various notated rhythmic durations to the groupings that the time signature suggests. If my analysis indicates a dotted-quarter pulse in a piece with a 6/8 time signature, then that pulse would align with the time signature. If instead the method indicates quarter-note and half-note pulses in a 6/8 piece, the autocorrelation's assessment would not align with the time signature. We, however, won't be able to address durations outside of the notated time signature. For instance, a piece's hypermeter (or metric levels longer than the notated measure) will not be able to be assessed with this approach.

A: (*after a long pause*) I think your use of time signatures makes sense in this limited framing. How will you measure the model's performance?

J: An *F*-score. These values capture how many correct answers the model gives while penalizing it both for wrong answers and for missing pulse levels indicated by the time signature.[6] The value runs between 0 and 1, with 1 indicating a model that perfectly identifies all possible correct answers and produces no incorrect answers. (A more in-depth explanation of the *F*-score calculation is found in this chapter's mathematic appendix.) In a very broad way, we can consider an *F*-score above 0.5 to be "fair" and a score above 0.667 to be "good." (*waving their hands vaguely*) These values *roughly* indicate the model to be right more than half the time and more than two-thirds of the time, respectively.

To make the prime vectors for the autocorrelation analysis, I take each piece's first 32 quarter notes (eight measures within a piece in 4/4), and divide that passage into its constituent sixteenth pulses, just as in Figure 5.2. I find the pitch content that occurs within each of those pulses and create note attack, pc-change, set-class-probability, and scale-degree-set-probability values from that content. To see how this model performs differently in different styles, I run the autocorrelations for the entire corpus but then also on the sub-corpora of the four composers with the most pieces in the music21 corpus (Monteverdi, Bach, Mozart, and Beethoven). The results are shown in Table 5.1. (*Josephus guides them onto a main thoroughfare labeled . . .*)

Autocorrelation: Results

A: Table 5.1 shows each parameter to perform well overall! Note onsets, pc changes, set classes, and scale-degree sets each seem to be good ways of indicating the periods indicated by time signatures.

TABLE 5.1 *F*-scores for the music21 corpus

Composer	Note Onsets	PC Changes	Set-Class Probs.	S.D.-Set Probs
Total	**0.75**	**0.77**	**0.74**	**0.73**
Monteverdi	0.82	0.71	0.81	0.79
Bach	0.72	0.78	0.74	0.72
Mozart	0.83	0.83	0.57	0.63
Beethoven	0.73	0.76	0.67	0.59

208 What Is Meter?

J: There are two notable points I want to highlight about these results. First, pitch-class changes are surprisingly efficacious! Perhaps as a testament to the importance of harmonic changes to the expression of meter in this repertoire, it slightly outperforms other parameters in the overall corpus. Second, there are some notable fluctuations between composers. Note onsets and pitch-class changes are much more efficacious than set classes and scale-degree sets in the music of Mozart, while pitch-class changes are more useful in the Bach corpus than the other parameters. These differences likely indicate that certain parameters are more pronounced (i.e., with greater differences between accented and non-accented moments) and more regular (i.e., with more reliable isochrony within the emergent patterns) in some styles compared to others. (These ideas align with those of prior computational experiments; see, for instance, Gouyon and Dixon, 2005 and Gouyon et al., 2006). It's not surprising that the Bach corpus – being made primarily of his chorales – will express its meters more reliably with harmonic parameters than with the note-onset approach. After all, the chorales' homophonic texture will result in a consistent array of note attacks, while their clear successions of four-voice harmonies will make their harmonic outlines quite clear.

A: Overall, the autocorrelation process does quite often find a piece's meter using the recurrent patterns in these domains! (*The pair turns back onto a side street labeled . . .*)

Three Brief Analyses

J: (*sighing*) Perhaps now is the time to discuss how these models support the GCAMM's distinction between metrical patterns and the patterns we find on the musical surface. To my mind, three important and interrelated chasms exist between the output of the autocorrelation models and meter: (1) the patterns do not exhibit metric strength, (2) there is no indication of where the patterns begin, and (3) patterns derived from the same passage are not related to one another in any type of duple or triple relationship.

To the first: it is tempting to make an equation between the metric accents of Figure 5.1, the correlations of Figure 5.5, and the patterns of Figure 5.6 – that when the autocorrelation method finds a dotted-whole-note pattern in the Mendelssohn-Hensel passage, for instance, it aligns phenomenal accents or harmonic stability with metric accent. It does not. By identifying a dotted-whole-note pattern, an autocorrelation process simply states that events separated by that duration are quite similar; it does not claim that any point within a dotted-whole-note span is more emphasized than any other.

A: (*flummoxed*) But the process *does* match phenomenal accents with metric accents! As clearly shown in Figure 5.6, autocorrelation is only possible in this repertoire because predictable points in the measure feature greater numbers of note attacks and more harmonic stability than other portions of the measure. This consistency is what allows for autocorrelation to detect metric patterns.

J: While that is true, the autocorrelation is not finding accents, it is simply finding patterns, something that ties into my second point: that autocorrelation does not identify where measures – or any of the pulses it identifies – begin. When the procedure identifies the dotted-whole-note pulse in the Mendelssohn-Hensel, it is making no claims about where that dotted-whole-note pulse starts or ends. For instance, consider Figure 5.8's recompositions of that passage. In the first, I've added an upbeat, while in the second, I've placed the greater number of note attacks one eighth note later than the original example. For both, the autocorrelation procedure would produce the same autocorrelations, a graph identical to that of Figure 5.5, and would identify the same time signature: it would still find the dotted-whole, dotted-half, quarter, and eighth pulses. There would be no indication that there's an upbeat or that the accent pattern has shifted. After all, the passage still exhibits patterns separated by a dotted whole, dotted half, quarter, and eighth! The patterns, however, now begin on what we intuitively feel as less accented events, but this intuition is not available to the autocorrelation process.

A: *(annoyed at how simple it would be to refute Josephus's straw-man argument)* Well . . .

J: Before your retort, let me quickly outline the third chasm: the lack of a clear duple or triple hierarchy. Most music and cognitive theorists agree that – all things being equal – Western enculturated musicians will intuitively divide longer spans of isochronous pulses into groups of two or three. A listener who hears a metric span of eight pulses will divide those into two groups

FIGURE 5.8 Two recompositions of the Mendelssohn-Hensel passage, (a) with an added upbeat and (b) with a shifted accent pattern

210 What Is Meter?

of four, which they will subsequently divide into two groups of two (Cohn, 2001; Murphy, 2009; Sadakata et al., 2006; Jacoby and McDermott, 2016).

A: (*Rummages around in their coat for Book 3 of Monteverdi's madrigals.*) Autocorrelation demonstrates how surface patterns have no such loyalty to these strictures. Figure 5.9 shows the opening measures of Monteverdi's "O Primavera," an instance in which the autocorrelation finds pulses at the eighth note, the quarter note, and the double whole note. The process does not detect a reliable recurrence at the whole-note or half-note level. Considering only the events of the musical surface, this result makes sense. After all, the primary motive of the example is imitated between voices at the distance of the double whole note, ensuring that similar events will appear every two notated measures. Of course, singers performing this piece are nearly certain to feel the measure and half-measure pulse as they subdivide the broader points of imitation, and listeners would also likely divide any two-measure metric pulse into its constituent duple sub-pulses. However, the autocorrelation process highlights the fact that these divisions are imposed by the listeners and performers and do not necessarily exist within the actual notated musical surface.[7]

A: (*holding their tongue but clearly wanting to contest these points*) Are there any more issues to outline before we debate these topics?

J: Yes. Can I borrow your score of the first prelude from Bach's *Well Tempered Clavier*?

A: (*momentarily distracted from their annoyance, they open their score to its first pages*) Certainly. I've reproduced the first measure in Figure 5.10. Obviously, a note-attack approach would be useless on this prelude, given that there are

FIGURE 5.9 "O Primavera" (Book 3 of Madrigals), Claudio Monteverdi, mm. 1–4

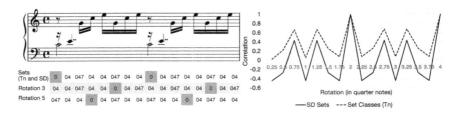

FIGURE 5.10 J.S. Bach's *Well-Tempered-Clavier*, Book 1, Prelude 1, m. 1

single onsets on every sixteenth pulse – an undifferentiated string of identical events allows for no periods or groupings to emerge.

J: But, scanning the example, a musician would see plenty of parameters that point to the quadruple meter indicated by the time signature: the half measures always sound the lowest and longest notes, and the melodic patterns change every measure. Because of these patterns, the set-class and scale-degree-set approaches identify similarities at the half-note, whole-note, and even the four- and eight-measure levels in this piece. (White, 2021 analyzes this prelude in some depth.)

A: (*once again frustrated*) Yes, the fluctuations between the *F*-scores for different composers highlighted that different parameters are better suited for different styles and situations. What makes this example unusual?

J: The autocorrelation method does not identify a consistent quarter-note or eighth-note pulse but rather finds non-isochronous units. I've added the autocorrelation chart for this piece in Figure 5.10: notice that the medium-sized peaks articulate the points three and five sixteenths away from the downbeat and half measure. In Bach's pattern, the first three pitch classes are the same as the next three, and the last six sixteenth notes rotate through the same three pitch classes twice. Additionally, whatever pitch class is lowest in the right hand often appears every three subsequent sixteenth notes (m. 1, 4, 6, 9, etc.). Set classes and pitch-class sets also often recur every three and five sixteenths in Bach's patterning. Conversely, these patterns lack similarities at regular intervals of two and four sixteenths; the method therefore does not identify the quarter and eighth periodicities and rather finds peaks at the third and fifth sixteenth pulse.

A: Your computer isn't the first one to notice that Bach uses non-isochronous patterns within an ostensibly duple framework. For instance, in his 1968 analysis of this piece, Edward T. Cone argued that the prelude's arpeggiated pattern encourages exactly the types of patterns you are describing.

J: Like the Monteverdi passage, this example shows an instance in which surface patterns do not reliably divide a longer pulse into its expected divisions. Unlike the Monteverdi passage, however, this example *does* divide the longer pulse, but not into isochronous divisions. (*after a pause*) Now that I've outlined the primary issues as I see them, perhaps we can discuss their broader implications? (*They pass into a neighborhood with a prominent sign that reads . . .*)

The Disconnect Between Meter and Surface Patterns

A: (*Relieved they can finally answer*) To first summarize your contentions: you are arguing that an aggressively surface-oriented program that identifies meter using recurrent patterns will have three main deficits when compared to theoretical and cognitive models of meter: it will not identify

212 What Is Meter?

metric strength, it will not identify where those patterns start and end, and it will not reliably express a nested metric hierarchy of duple and triple relationships.

J: Indeed, and these deficits specifically articulate the differences between what I described as *surface patterns* in Figure 5.3's GCAMM and what that figure labelled *metric patterns*.

A: But the solution is simple! Your model simply needs to learn concepts of accent and hierarchy either from observing the corpus or from observing connections between the corpus and human behavior. We've seen these associations between corpus data and external non-musical information used numerous times in our previous chapters, from connecting musical events to composers' identities to linking chords and harmonic function.

From a corpus-centered perspective, we need to look no further than Figure 5.6. To create this graph, you took measures of 4/4 in your corpus and found the average of different parameters at each position in the measure. In other words, you used information from the corpus – how events are annotated within each measure – to make generalizations about each pulse within quadruple meter. These generalizations can be considered a template for quadruple meter: they show the types of patterns that express 4/4 meter and the types of accents and harmonies that we should expect to appear at different points in a measure of quadruple meter. If your pattern-finding method, then, begins to identify quadruple patterns of a whole-note duration, you can be reasonably sure those whole-note pulses will start at the moment of most note attacks and greatest stability. Given the regularities in the quadruple template, you can also reasonably look for pulses that divide the whole-note duration into subsequent duple divisions of half notes, quarter notes, and eighth notes, each with the properties evident in Figure 5.6. You'd prefer to align the second-most-accented/stable moments with the half measure whenever possible and the next-most-accented/stable moments with quarter pulses, each because of the expectations provided by your template. In other words, you can simply use these corpus-derived connections between quadruple surface patterns and quadruple metric patterns to map between the two. By making these connections, we would effectively unite the two sides of your GCAMM using only corpus data!

J: *(carefully interjecting)* What you're describing resonates with several computational models that do, in fact, derive metric templates from a corpus, especially machine-learning approaches like Hidden Markov Models (Khadkevich et al., 2012; Papadopoulos and Peeters, 2011), support vector machines (Durand et al., 2014), recurrent neural networks (Durand et al., 2015; Böck et al., 2016), and temporal convolutional networks (Böck and Davies, 2020). Each of these models trains on some corpus to create templates, and individual pieces can then be aligned with these templates to identify their meter. These approaches have proven to perform quite well against a ground truth and represent the current state of the art in meter detection within the music information retrieval literature. However, each of these . . .

A: (*interrupting*) Furthermore, the supposed "problem" about identifying phenomenal accents is not a problem at all! There's no mystery about what we hear as accented versus not accented. We need only glance at the cognitive and theoretical literature to know that there are very predictable ways that we hear accent. As we discussed earlier, accent has been shown to reliably arise from a number of different musical parameters – loudness, harmonic change, contour change, and so on. (Indeed, the list of citations in your Endnote 3 is quite ample!)

J: (*producing a dog-eared copy of* Music Perception) Again, this information has been put to good use in the computational literature. One well-known example is the work of Large et al. (2015) and Large et al. (2016). Their model uses a computational system that mimics the ways that energy cycles within the brain identify and represent metric accents. The model relies on neurodynamics research to create a precise and efficacious model of musical meter using a physical and neuro-scientific understanding of accent. (*fishing out several pages torn from a conference proceedings*) Another example might be Rohrmeier's (2020) computational system that translates between surface rhythms and larger metric hierarchies using rules about duration and accent adapted to a language-like grammar: once again, this more complex model performs impressively well in mimicking human behavior when meter-finding.

A: All these instances you've cited derive metric templates either from a corpus or from behavioral data. In so doing, these models solve the problems produced by your autocorrelation approach and show the GCAMM's chasm between surface patterns and metric patterns to be based on a false dichotomy.

J: (*quickly*) No. Let me take these corpus-based and behavioral issues in turn.

Corpus solutions – like the machine-learning models I cited earlier – use some process to identify the norms of some corpus, but they are still simply learning patterns. For argument's sake, let's again imagine that the contours of Figure 5.6 represent some underlying norm for quadruple meter, such that a corpus-based model might learn to identify pieces in quadruple meter by matching them to the peaks and valleys of this template: a piece is in the same meter as the pieces being averaged in Figure 5.6 if that piece's events correspond to that figure's contours. However, in this instance, a metric hierarchy is not being imposed upon a pattern; rather, two patterns are simply being matched with one another – in such a method, the quadruple meter of a passage isn't assessed because it expresses some particular hierarchy of metric accents but simply because its events correspond to an expected pattern. This matching process involves no metric accents, no relationships between metric levels, and no beginning/end to the patterns. Such processes are more sophisticated than a simple autocorrelation model, but they are still models of surface patterns.

On the other hand, a corpus-based model could learn associations between time signatures or metric annotations and particular patterns of events. We could, for instance, use a corpus of music notated in 4/4 to study the properties of downbeats versus offbeats. Here, we would be able to identify and describe the properties of metrical accents, and this information could easily be used to interpret surface patterns with accents, upbeats, beginnings, endings, and the like. In other words, knowing what often occurs on beat 1 within a corpus would help us know that the first event of the Mendelssohn-Hensel example is not, in fact, an upbeat but rather the beginning of that piece's first measure.

While these sorts of endeavors would be completely legitimate – and we've certainly indulged in similar observations in the course of our conversation – such studies are not corpus analyses of a musical surface but rather of human annotations. As we noted earlier, barlines, measure placement, and time signatures might provide a useful shorthand for performers, and they might even yield a blunt insight into a composer's understanding of the piece's meter, *but these annotations aren't available to listeners.* Barlines and time signatures are not part of the perceived musical surface; they are additions for the benefit of the score's users. Conceptually, using such annotations in a corpus model is akin to explicitly teaching a student about meter, drawing their attention to specific events as being metrically accented and to other events as being un-accented: external information is used to connect surface information with metric information. In contrast, using only the surface patterns is akin to a listener learning about meter simply by being exposed to metric music, learning about meter by observing musical events. In sum: the sequence of peaks and valleys in Figure 5.6 represents the surface patterns of a subset of music in our corpus; associating these patterns with positions within a measure (or Figure 5.6's horizontal axis) imports notational information that is conceptually separate from raw musical data.

To be clear, metric annotations can be an important part of corpus analysis. Figure 5.6 shows useful information about how surface patterns are deployed within our corpus's notated measures. And while I used time signatures when calculating the F-scores for our meter-finding model, they were not used to construct the model, only to test it. There are plenty of research questions in which it is useful to observe the kinds of events that appear on moments of different notational accent – Prince and Schmuckler, 2014; Prince et al., 2009; White, 2018, for instance, all explicitly study the properties of notated strong versus weak beats. However, a corpus analysis that strives to learn meter solely from a musical surface cannot reference the notated meter; it should *not* learn meter from its method of notation.

Finally, a similar issue arises when we import cognitive understandings of accent into a corpus analysis. Certainly, there are important and interesting research questions that can be studied by analyzing events that cognitive

What Is Meter? **215**

science suggests are heard as accented. Large et al.'s model, for instance, shows how a neurodynamic approach to accent will respond to the events within musical stimuli. However – again – such a study would *not* be investigating the corpus patterns in and of themselves but rather would be investigating cognitive phenomena and how they interact with a corpus. In other words, approaches that rely on cognitive understandings of meter may model a listening experience of a corpus – but they do not model the corpus itself. Once again, adding an *a priori* definition of accent will teach the corpus model about meter; in contrast, a surface-only model lets the corpus teach us about how meter manifests within it.

In sum: attempts to use more sophisticated models or notational/cognitive information to fill the GCAMM's chasm either will be inadequate or will import data external to the musical surface. On the one hand, machine-learning algorithms that learn metric templates may be more sophisticated than my basic pattern-finding autocorrelation approach, but they still simply output patterns that lack accent and hierarchy. On the other hand, relying on notational information (like barlines and time signatures) or cognitive definitions of accent uses information that is outside the boundaries of a strict analysis of musical surfaces. To my mind, the musical surface simply does not contain the kinds of information needed to supply a robust model of meter with accent and hierarchy. These issues are generalizable to metric corpus analysis and not specific to an autocorrelation approach – metric models that draw solely on a musical surface for their analyses will produce patterns that lack boundaries, hierarchies, and accents. Instead, external definitions and human intervention would be needed to create a full accounting of these parameters within a meter.

A: (*after a long pause*) So, to review, we can simply return to your Figure 5.2. You're claiming that corpus analyses based solely on a musical surface can find isochronous patterns, what are the inner circles of Figure 5.2. However, some external definition of meter must be imposed upon these patterns for the patterns to express any boundaries, accents, relationship, or hierarchies.

J: Precisely. As outlined in the GCAMM, surface patterns do not *create* meter but instead have a metric hierarchy imposed upon them. The inner surface-pattern cycles of Figure 5.2 do not indicate a particular alignment with the outer metric cycles in and of themselves; rather, this alignment requires some set of definitions about accent and hierarchy that are neither present in nor learnable from those surface patterns.

Importantly, I'm not indicting metrical corpus analysis or charging machine-learning with intellectual fraud or advocating for some embargo on cognitive models of musical meter. I just mean to be very specific about what a surface-oriented musical corpus analysis can do and what it cannot. The benefit of this distinction is twofold. First, it clearly delineates the role of a musical corpus in metric analyses and, indeed, the role of the musical surface in general. While we can learn certain aspects of meter from a musical surface, we need some human component – be it behavioral data, notation, an expressive performance, or even sheer musical intuition – to create a rich definition of meter. If meter requires accent and hierarchy, then a group of isochronous musical patterns becomes a meter only under human intervention.

Second, by acknowledging the disconnect between surface patterns and metric patterns, we allow space for different corpora, repertoires, and cultural traditions to express different relationships between meter and surface patterns. If the ways that meter is imposed upon surface patterns is a function of some external suite of mapping rules, then different repertoires may well have different mapping rules.

A: This claim is intriguing. From this perspective, assuming that all musical cultures connect musical surfaces and meters using the same mapping rules as Western European art music does a disservice to those cultures, misrepresents their metrical practices, and even reflects the hegemony of Western classical music in music theory (Ewell, 2020).

J: Correct, and I specifically believe that the field of music theory often falls into the trap of equating "how meter works in Western music" with "how meter works in general" because of certain isomorphisms present in Western art music's surface patterns. To illustrate this phenomenon, Figure 5.11a shows the average note attacks within Mendelssohn-Hensel's "Die Mainacht," along with a contour line showing those pulses with the most, second most, and third most onsets. The figure then converts this line into a cycle, and overlays that line onto a cycle that represents the measure's metric hierarchy. Note that the metric accents and magnitudes of note onsets are commensurate – they are isomorphic. Figure 5.11b then generalizes this isomorphism by converting the graph of Figure 5.6 into a cycle, with the end of the graph wrapping back onto its beginning. The peaks and valleys are again quite similar to those of the quadruple cyclic metric hierarchy I've reproduced in Figure 5.11c, and 5.11d shows the overlap. It is naturally tempting to assume that the peaks within surface events necessitate peaks in the metrical accent – that moments with more onsets, change, and stability should align with moments with more dots. After all, the contours within both domains look the same! This kind of equation generally holds in Western European art music: throughout the literature we've cited in the course of our conversation, we've seen arguments that loudness, onsets, chord change, and harmonic stability align with metric accents in this repertoire.

This assumption, however, does not take into account the diversity of expressions and experiences of other repertoires: surface patterns could align with meter in other ways. In what follows, I'll demonstrate instances in which the peaks and valleys in surface patterns do not indicate greater and lesser metric accent with the same isomorphism as in Western art music.

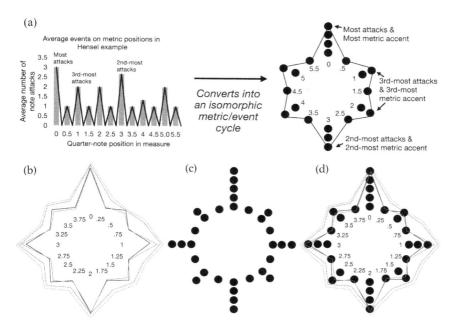

FIGURE 5.11 (a) The onsets of Mendelssohn-Hensel's "Die Mainacht" at each point in a measure, first as a linear graph and then overlain onto a metric cycle, (b) the data of Figure 5.5 presented as a cycle, (c) a quadruple metrical framework, (d) the overlap of the two

I'll show how non-isomorphic surface patterns can indicate metric emphasis with regularity and robustness. In doing so, I'll not only illustrate the diversity of relationships between surface patterns and metric patterns but also argue that this diversity evidences the GCAMM's gap between the musical surface and hierarchical meter. Indeed, recognizing this gap will not only more clearly show the distinct role of the corpus and human experience in the creation of musical meter but will show how relationships between surface patterns and metric patterns are not universal, but are instead culturally defined.

A: I must admit, I am fascinated by this turn in our conversation. (*pointing*) Let's take this boulevard. (*Aloysius points to a street sign that reads . . .*)

An Analysis of a Popular-Song Corpus

J: (*fishing around in their pockets*) Yes, I believe I have several other corpora on hand. The first corpus is a subset of the Million Song database (Bertin-Mahieux et al., 2011), a collection of one million songs that represents an enormous swath of 20th- and 21st-century popular music from the Americas and Europe; the subset we're using includes 2,197 songs converted to MIDI and whose accuracy and metadata have been checked and curated, dubbed the Lakh MIDI dataset (Raffel, 2016). The dataset is largely 20th-century pop and rock music but contains other songs representative of a Western listener's generic experience – the corpus includes popular classical and folk tunes like "Greensleeves" and "O Fortuna" from Carl Orff's *Carmina Burana*, for instance. Because key-finding in rock and pop music is anything but straightforward (de Clercq, 2021), this analysis does not use scale-degree sets for its approximation of harmonic consonance, only set classes. Note-onset and pitch-class-change vectors are still used.

Figure 5.12a shows the distribution of all set classes in the Lakh MIDI dataset, labeling all sets that occur more than 2% of the time and sparsely labeling the remainder. (These types of graphs will help orient us toward which events are probable and improbable as we shuffle between corpora.) As in the Western Common Practice corpora, the most probable sets are those we would intuitively associate with stability – major and minor triads, fourths/fifths, thirds/sixths, and seventh chords – with more dissonant sets being less frequent. Figure 5.12b then shows how each parameter is distributed within

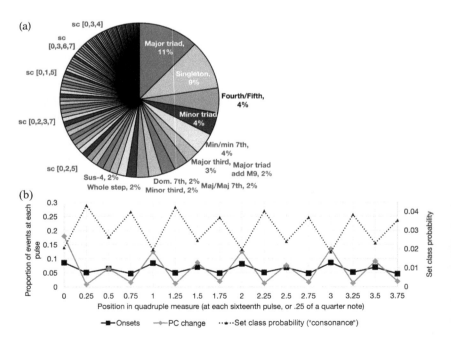

FIGURE 5.12 (a) The distribution of set classes in the Lakh MIDI corpus; (b) the profiles of each parameter within pieces in that corpus notated in quadruple meter

music notated in quadruple meter in this corpus. (We'll return to how these averages differ from the music21 corpus momentarily.)

I applied the same autocorrelation procedure to this corpus and used the same *F*-score analysis as we applied earlier. I, however, made two modifications to accommodate this corpus's peculiarities. A quick perusal of the corpus showed that many files begin with extended periods of rests/silence; I therefore discarded the events of the first 8 notated quarter notes in each file. The autocorrelation procedure was then performed on the following 64 quarter notes (i.e., the subsequent 16 measures if the piece were notated in quadruple meter). Then, for the corpus's ground-truth, each files' MIDI metric information was used. Importantly, this ground truth will involve some manner of imprecision: time signatures in this corpus not only can be used to indicate the overall meter of a song but also can be modified to indicate pauses or fermatas within songs. (Additionally, songs that might otherwise be a compound meter are sometimes notated in a simple meter with underlying triplets in this corpus.)

A: These seem like reasonable modifications. Additionally, because of the corpus's size, any errors could be considered "noise" in the sense we introduced in Chapter 1.

J: Table 5.2 shows the *F*-scores that result from this corpus, along with the scores resulting from the two other corpora we will be discussing. All parameters work quite well in the Lakh MIDI corpus, but the set-class probability works remarkably well – it even slightly outperforms the note-onset approach – while the pc change is the most successful parameter.

A: The contours of Figure 5.12b help explain these *F*-scores. Onsets have a somewhat even distribution throughout the measure – it's no wonder this parameter has a relatively low *F*-score. In contrast, the distribution of pc changes clearly articulates the various levels of pulse present in a quadruple meter – it's also no wonder this parameter returns such a high *F*-score.

J: (*studies the profiles*) The particulars of Figure 5.12b also show some notable characteristics of this corpus's surface patterns, some of which contrast with those in our earlier studies. While on balance, stronger metrical pulses do host more note attacks than do weaker pulses, the difference is markedly less than the European art-music profiles we observed earlier. This evenness is

TABLE 5.2 *F*-scores for three further corpora

Corpus	Onsets	Change	Set Class Probability
Lakh MIDI	0.69	0.81	0.70
Drum Grooves	0.74	0.71	0.69
Malian Jembe	0.90	0.90	0.88

220 What Is Meter?

almost certainly due to the increase in syncopation in American and European popular music (Tan et al., 2018; Temperley, 2018, 2019). In contrast, the pitch-class-change profile is much more similar to that of the Common Practice profile, with peaks and valleys more clearly articulating metric strength. These findings suggest that the simple conflation between note onsets and metric strength that often holds in European art-music corpora (Palmer and Krumhansl, 1990) begins to fail in more syncopated corpora (a finding suggested by London et al., 2017).

A: Similarly, the peaks in set-class probability do not align with metric accents – peaks of probability/consonance occur on offbeats rather than metrically accented moments. Yet according to our *F*-scores, this parameter predicts this corpus's time signatures quite well. The contour of these probabilities would also seem to express the syncopated nature of this repertoire – many strong pulses host some kind of dissonant/improbable set, while offbeats sound the more probable consonances. Notice, for instance, that the most probable events are on the sixteenth pulse following the downbeat. On the one hand, it is remarkable that these patterns allow for the autocorrelation procedure to engage in meter-finding. However, the relative success of the procedure indicates that these offbeat consonances are consistent enough that they can express reliable periodicities: you can garner isochronous pulses from this vector even if its peaks and valleys are not isomorphic with the metric accents. On the other hand, the set-class probabilities add a nuanced understanding to how syncopations manifest in this corpus. Peaks in pitch-class change – peaks that appear on metrically accented pulses – correspond to valleys in set-class probability and vice versa: if pitch-class change indicates the music's harmonic rhythm and set-class probability indicates consonance, then this repertoire would seem to change harmonies on metrically accented pulses, with these changes often involving dissonant harmonies. These dissonant harmonies then resolve via minimal pitch-class change to the surrounding weaker pulses. In other words, harmonies change on metrically strong pulses, but these changes introduce some dissonance. The surrounding weaker pulses, then, contain consonant structures that are part of the same chord as the strong-beat dissonances – they share a large amount of pitch classes with the adjacent low-probability set classes.

Figure 5.13 excerpts a few measures from the corpus that illustrates this combination of syncopation, chord change, and dissonance. In Natalie Imbruglia's "Torn," her syncopated vocal line will often weave through the underlying chord content, hitting chord tones on offbeats (see the vocal line of m. 15 and 32), while chord changes occur on the measures' downbeats. Additionally, the highly syncopated guitar pattern ensures that note-onset patterns are distributed between metrically stronger and weaker positions.

J: I am impressed with how committed you're becoming to our analyses! Before we discuss these results and how they relate to my broader contentions about patterns and meter, let's turn here. (*points to a sign that reads . . .*)

What Is Meter? 221

FIGURE 5.13 Simplification of the MIDI representation for two portions of "Torn" by Natalie Imbruglia (*Left of Middle*, 1997), (a) mm. 14–15.1, (b) mm. 31–32.1

An Analysis of a Drum-Groove Corpus

J: (*removing another corpus from their coat*) Our next corpus is a collection of 1,824 grooves derived from online repositories of live drum-set performance encodings. The files represent attacks on three drum set instruments: the bass drum, high hat, and snare drum (Hosken et al., 2021). The corpus includes microtiming for each drum attack but also metric alignments for each attack, snapping each event to the closest sixteenth note. We'll use the latter in our analyses. In the same way as our other corpora, onsets were calculated as the number of simultaneous attacks. But given that there is no pitch-based harmony in this corpus, I treated combinations of drums as "harmonies." Computationally, I considered each moment as a three-member set, with each member of the set representing whether or not a particular instrument was being struck, with bass drum, snare drum, and high hat occupying the three positions in the set. For instance, [1,1,1] would mean all instruments are being struck, [1, 0, 0] would mean only the bass drum is being played, [1, 1, 0] means bass drum and snare are simultaneously sounding, etc. I then treated these as akin to the set classes in our other corpora

222 What Is Meter?

and calculated the probabilities that each drum combination occurs. While the analogy between probability and stability is more tenuous in this corpus, such an approach at least provides a heuristic method for tracking drum sequences – I show the resulting distribution in Figure 5.14a. In the place of pitch-class changes, I simply tracked the change in the instrumentation from one event to the next: switching or adding a drum to the texture would each constitute one unit of change, while repeating attacks on the same drum would involve no change. To illustrate the kinds of simultaneities and changes that occur in the corpus, Figure 5.14b shows how events at each sixteenth pulse in a quadruple measure are apportioned to each instrument.

In terms of a ground truth, we assumed the corpus to be primarily in 4/4. Time signature information was provided for many – but not all – of the grooves, but all indicated time signatures were 4/4. (Furthermore, most pop music is in a simple duple or quadruple signature: 96.6% of the Lakh MIDI corpus was in 2/4 or 4/4).[8] Autocorrelations were then run on the entirety of the groove.

A: I see the resulting *F*-scores are in Table 5.2. I've taken the liberty of averaging the vectors for this corpus in Figure 5.14c.

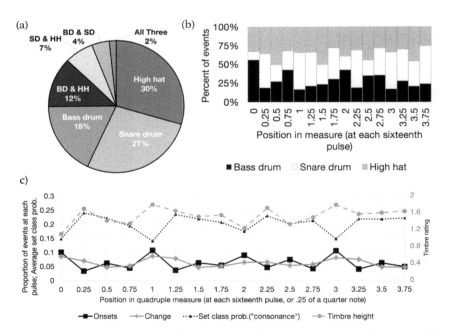

FIGURE 5.14 Events in quadruple measures in the Groove Corpus, shown as (a) simultaneities, (b) instruments occurring at each metrical position, and (c) profile of averaged events

J: (*studying the table*) Looking at the *F*-scores, onsets seem to be the best indicator of quadruple patterns, followed by the amount of instrumental change and the set-class probability. Perhaps not surprisingly for a percussion corpus, the parameter most associated with loudness seems to align most strongly with the notated meter.

A: I took the initiative and modified your machines to add a further parameter to Figure 5.14c – what I've labeled *Timbre*. Here, I simply assigned a value of 1, 2, and 3 to the bass drum (the lowest timbre), snare drum (the midrange timbre), and high hat (the highest timbre), respectively, and averaged the values appearing at each moment. The value – very heuristically and bluntly – represents the aggregate percussive timbre appearing at each moment. Given our experience in the discotheque earlier this evening, I wondered whether deeper sounds ("boomier booms") might more strongly align with downbeats . . .

J: . . . an intuition supported by some computational work (Gouyon et al., 2006) . . .

A: . . . and that higher timbres might be associated with the *backbeat*, or beats 2 and 4 in quadruple measures in popular music . . .

J: . . . an intuition supported by the abundant literature on backbeats (Tamlyn, 1998; Stephenson, 2002; Attas, 2014; Toiviainen et al., 2009; Toiviainen et al., 2010). This literature suggests – as does our intuitive experience with music in the pop/rock genres – that backbeats in this repertoire should have consistent accents, and those accents should generally involve the snare drum.

A: (*shrugging their shoulders*) But, at least in how I've framed this parameter, it returns a roughly identical *F*-score to that of the set-class probability. (I haven't added these to Table 5.2 for this reason.) Scanning Figure 5.14c, this similarity is not surprising given that the average timbre scores mostly track the contour of the set-class probabilities throughout quadruple measures.

J: I am again impressed by your initiative, Aloysius. It seems to me your figure also shows why the onsets appear to be the most successful, along with some distinctive characteristics of this corpus. To the first: the onset profile shows the greatest differentiation between pulses, and these peaks and valleys recur at regular isochronous intervals. The larger number of note attacks occurs on the backbeat (positions 1 and 3), followed by the downbeat (position 0), the half measure (position 2), the intervening eighth-note pulses, and, finally, the offbeat sixteenths. This differentiation allows for the autocorrelation to notice similarities at the remove of the whole note (i.e., at the measure level), at the half measure (for instance, the backbeat pattern peaks every half measure), and so on.

A: (*emboldened*) Looking at Figure 5.14, we can see characteristic features of this corpus's surface patterns. Most basically, this corpus is the first in which we've found the greatest number of note attacks *not* occurring on the downbeat. Instead – as you note – they occur on the backbeats; and, referencing the

224 What Is Meter?

timbre profile and the instrumentation distributions of Figure 5.14b, these events do indeed specifically feature the snare and high hat and *not* the bass drum. The bass drum, however, has its own distinctive pattern: Figure 5.14b shows the bass drum to favor the downbeat, the sixteenth before beat 2 (event .75), and the half-measure (event 2). The high hat, then, appears to characterize intervening eighth-note pulses (event 0.5, 1.5, 2.5, and 3.5) – nearly 50% of events at each of those positions involve a high-hat hit.

The drum change profile also acts very differently from our earlier pitch-class-change profiles: likely because there are only three types of events, there is a more uniform distribution of change. (Indeed, the rolling and smooth contour of the change profile is evocative of the drummer's body parsimoniously shifting between the drum arrays in front of them; de Souza, 2017). There are, however, mild peaks on the downbeat and the backbeats and small dips at the intervening eighth-note pulses – the drum played on these off-beat-eighths are likely present in the previous event and are simply repeated into these metrically weak moments. In fact, comparing the change profile of Figure 5.14c to the proportional events of Figure 5.14b, it would seem that the ubiquity of the high hat specifically contributes to this dynamic: given that the instrument often appears on every position, those pulses on which the high hat may be the only instrument are unlikely to introduce a change from the previous pulse.

A: This observation resonates with my intuition that rock/pop drummers often articulate most pulses within the measure on the high hat and use other drums to articulate composite rhythms on top of that underlying pulse.

J: Finally, your timbre and my set-class profiles generally track one another, suggesting that their constituent values are capturing roughly the same information about the kinds of events that appear on each position in the measure. The one exception to this synchrony is the backbeat: beats 2 and 4 seem to host relatively high-timbral events but low-probability events. Figure 5.14a suggests that the most probable events in this corpus are solo drum articulations; if, however, backbeats are characterized by the most amount of onsets, then these events will also be more likely to host the lower-probability drum combinations. Figure 5.14b indicates these combinations will involve the snare and high-hat, the two highest instruments in terms of timbre. These two complimentary tendencies result in the inverse peaks and valleys in the probability and timbre profiles on the backbeats.

J: You are becoming quite the master at interpreting computational data!

A: (*somewhat interrupting*) One thing continues to concern me. Given the consistency of the patterns we've been discussing, why are the *F*-scores not higher?

J: Well, as we've seen throughout this walk, the existence of an overall trend in a corpus does not mean every piece adheres to that trend. Figure 5.15 shows an excerpt where a three-sixteenth rotation (a dotted-sixteenth pulse) is identified by the note-onset method, while the set-class method identifies a

FIGURE 5.15 Measure 2 of the file 93_hiphop_75_beat_4–4 in Google's Magenta database

quarter-note pulse. (The excerpt is specifically from Google's Magenta database of drum-set grooves.) As shown in the Figure, the syncopations of the bass drum create a pattern of either one or two note onsets every three sixteenth notes, while the set-class probability method would notice the similarities in probability associated with solo bass drums and snare drums at the quarter-note pulse.

A: This example provides an excellent reminder that – even though a corpus might express prevailing norms – individual examples may deviate from, be more complex than, or play with the wider norms. But before we dive into a larger discussion, perhaps we can explore our final corpus? (*points to a street sign that reads . . .*)

An Analysis of a Malian Drum Corpus

J: Our final analysis involves a corpus of Malian jembe drum ensemble performances. Compiled by Polak et al. (2018), the corpus contains several performances of three different tunes, all using a four-drum ensemble made of two higher-pitched jembe and two lower-pitched dundun. Each tune features its own characteristic rhythms; however, each tune in the corpus is understood by its performers as being in a meter analogous to a compound quadruple feel (i.e., a 12/8- or 12/16-type organization), with a metrical unit every 12 pulses, which itself divides into four groups of three (Anku, 2000; Polak et al., 2016). The music also frequently accompanies dancing, and participants generally articulate these compound-quadruple pulses with their bodies (Polak, 2010). I used this meter as the ground truth for the F-scores.

Figure 5.16 summarizes the events of the overall corpus (additionally, note-onset distributions for each individual tune can be found in London et al., 2017). To attempt to not import the baggage of notated/measured musical traditions onto this repertoire, I've referred to units of 12 pulses as "cycles" rather than "measures" in this analysis, beginning from the downbeat (at point zero) and continuing with integers representing the remainder of the 12 cycle (points 1 to 11). To represent events in this dataset, I use the same methods as used in the Groove corpus, with sets representing which of the drums are being played (given that there were four drums, the sets now consisted of four members), and changes capturing the entry of new drums.

Figure 5.16a shows the distribution of drum combinations in the corpus, while Figure 5.16b shows how often each position in the cycle contains each instrument. In both representations, jembe 1 features as the most ubiquitous instrument used in the corpus – the most probable event in this corpus is a solo hit of jembe 1, and jembe 1 appears prominently on each point in the cycle. The remaining instruments also favor specific positions in this cycle. In particular, the coincidence of jembe 2 and dundun 1 at points 2, 5, and 8 in the cycle would appear to create the peaks we observed in the onset and change profiles (note that points 1, 4, and 7 do *not* generally host jembe 2 attacks, making the subsequent entry of that instrument a consistent textural change). Figure 5.16c then shows the aggregated patterns of onsets and changes in the corpus's three tunes. The average distributions include peaks at a cycle's beginning at its third, sixth, and ninth pulses (points 2, 5, and 8 in the cycle), with a secondary peak at the 12th pulse (point 11). The set-class

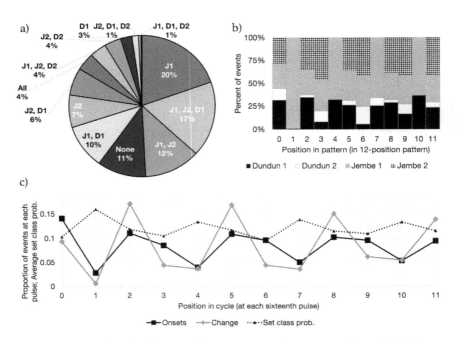

FIGURE 5.16 (a) The distribution of instrument combinations in the Malian Drum Corpus, (b) the distribution of instruments on each position in the 12 pulses used in this repertoire's underlying cycles, and (c) the average profiles for each parameter in this corpus

probability distribution shows peaks at different points, notably the first off-beat in the cycle (point 1), likely because this point often hosts a solo strike of jembe 1, the corpus's most frequent instrumental event.

A: (*after studying the figure for a moment*) Examining Figure 5.16 shows there to be consistent triple patterns within the profiles, but their peaks do not always align with the beginning of the cycle or with metrical accents. Indeed, the onset profile is the only parameter with its highest peak aligning with position 0 in Figure 5.16c. For instance, the change profile has its primary peaks every three events starting at position 2, while the probability distribution has peaks every three events start at position 1.

J: This consistency accounts for the high F-scores associated with this corpus. As shown in Table 5.2, the scores are the higher than those in any other corpus we've evaluated thus far. In other words, the autocorrelation procedure easily finds patterns of 3 and 12 within this corpus.

A: To show some further notable characteristics of this corpus, Figure 5.17 shows the distributions associated with individual performances of the tunes "Woloso" (Figure 5.17a) and "Maraka" (Figure 5.17b), along with the auto-correlations resulting from each tune's onset profiles. The autocorrelation method shows patterns of 3 and 12 events in the former. "Woloso's" profiles (Figure 5.17a) show clear triple patterns in each vector: the up/down/up contours of the onsets, and the up/down/down contours of the change patterns. Furthermore, these smaller triple patterns combine into a larger 12-event pattern detected by the autocorrelation procedure. Like "Woloso," "Maraka" exhibits recurrent patterns accessible to the autocorrelation procedure; however, the autocorrelation finds patterns in this tune that do not align with the ground truth more so than in any other member of the corpus. For instance, while the onset profile features up/down/up patterns starting at positions 0 and 9, this pattern is not extended across the whole cycle: indeed, a competing pattern of up/down pairs begins on positions 0, 2, 4, and 6 in this profile, with a complementary down/up pattern beginning at positions 8 and 10. This combination results in high correlations at three and nine rotations but then also shows high correlations at duple intervals between those positions.

J: Importantly, *many* analysts have commented upon the non-isochronous pulses in this repertoire (Pressing, 1983, 2002; Rahn, 1996; Toussaint, 2003). The underlying rhythmic motives in these repertoires in the two tunes of Figure 5.17 are themselves built on non-isochronous patterns: "Woloso," for instance, is based on a 2+3+3+3+1+3+3+3+3 rhythm that spans over two rotations of the 12 cycle, while "Maraka" exhibits a 2+4+3+2+1 pattern (London et al., 2017). Nor would we be the first to notice that peaks in the surface patterns' note onsets do not regularly align with metric accents in this corpus, even though these patterns still express metrical accents to this repertoire's practitioner. In the words of London et al. (2017), in this corpus,

228 What Is Meter?

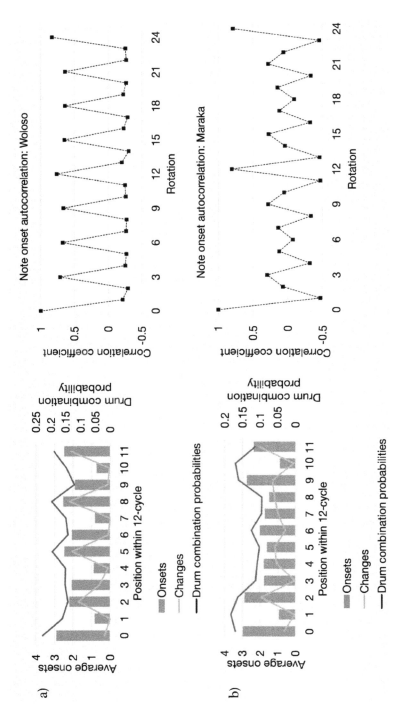

FIGURE 5.17 Onset, change, and set-class probabilities for the tunes (a) Woloso (file Woloso_5 from the dataset) and (b) Maraka (using file Maraka_2)

"the relative frequency of note onsets in a given metrical position does not correspond to patterns of metrical accent, though there is a stable relationship between onset frequency and metrical position" (474).

Notably, these patterns, their variations, the non-isochronous metric motives, and the ensemble's rhythmic accompaniment create aggregate vectors with peaks and valleys that are not isomorphic with the peaks and valleys of a metric hierarchy. Yet these surface patterns do express consistent isochronous periodicities, and the non-isomorphic relationship between the surface and metric patterns is consistently felt by performers, listeners, and dancers of this repertoire. Even though this corpus may not consistently express the strong-weak-weak accent pattern a Western-oriented theorist might expect in a piece in 12/8, it does consistently express recurrent patterns every 3 and 12 pulses, and this repertoire's users reliably map metrical accents onto these patterns.

A: To review, we've looked at three additional corpora, each of which featured patterns in the domains of note onsets, change, and set-class probability (along with the *ad hoc* timbre parameter tailored to groove corpora) that align with the patterns expected given the corpora's notated or assumed meters. In contrast to the Western European art-music corpus we observed earlier, these corpora featured patterns with peaks in onsets, changes, and probabilities that sometimes did not coincide with metric accents. Let's now turn onto this larger thoroughfare and discuss how these analyses relate to your larger contentions about meter. (*points to a sign that reads . . .*)

Surface Patterns, Metric Patterns, and Mapping Rules

J: (*taking a breath*) When we began this walk, I made a somewhat bold claim. I argued that meter requires two components – surface patterns and metric patterns. In the course of our discussions, I've suggested that the former are discoverable from a musical signal and are therefore detectable to a corpus analysis, while the latter requires some sort of external definition of accent, regularity, or entrainment. These definitions can be based on a variety of sources – be it cognitive/behavioral, theoretical, neurological, or mathematical – but they are not located in the corpus. If a theorist approaches meter using nested duple and triple relationships (Cohn, 2001), then they would be imposing a mathematic definition of meter upon patterns of a musical surface. If neuroscientists argue that the physical properties of electric oscillations in the brain cause humans to entrain to high-energy isochronous pulses (Large et al., 2015), they would be referencing a physical definition of metric pulses that is then imposed upon musical patterns. If a meter-finding algorithm uses the highest number of note onsets to find the beginning of a measure (Brown, 1993; Boone, 2000), it would be importing the assumption that the loudest events should align with the beginning of the broadest metrical pulses. In each of these cases, the ways that metric pulses connect to

230 What Is Meter?

surface events are not learned from a corpus but from some external source – be it mathematical, physical, or cognitive – and those connections are used to metrically interpret surface patterns.

A: *(interjecting)* You then argued that this distinction can become muddled when focusing on Western European corpora, because peaks in several musical parameters – numbers of onsets, amount of harmonic change, level of harmonic stability – often track the amount of metric accent attributed to an event, at least on average: the surface patterns and metric patterns are isomorphic. We then subsequently observed three corpora, each of which feature regular and observable patterns, but whose patterns have different relationships with metric patterns.

J: *(pauses and carefully draws several diagrams)* In Figure 5.18, I show the vectors of each corpus we've analyzed in our walk this evening, now represented

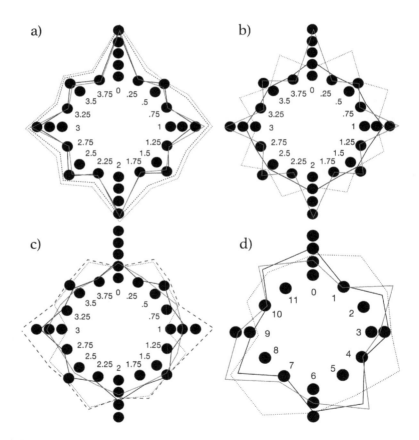

FIGURE 5.18 Surface patterns and metric patterns arranged cyclically in (a) the music21 corpus, (b) the Lakh MIDI corpus, (c) the Drum Groove corpus, and (d) the Malian Jembe corpus

cyclically and imposed on metric hierarchies. (In other words, I take Figures 5.6, 5.11c, 5.13c, and 5.15c and overlap them onto the diagram of Figure 5.1.) In terms of Figure 5.3's GCAMM, the profile lines represent the surface patterns, while the dots represent the metrical organization communicated by the notation or the musicological analysis underpinning these repertoires. The Western European corpus's surface patterns and metric patterns are isomorphic; the other corpora have varying degrees of non-isomorphography: the peaks in their surface parameters do not necessarily align with metric emphasis.

A: (*somewhat confidently*) Each in their own way, these corpora illustrate how an organizing metrical pattern can be aligned with regular surface patterns using some set of external definitions and rules and that these alignments can change from corpus to corpus. In Figure 5.3's GCAMM, you argued that surface patterns are properties of musical corpora, while a metric hierarchy and its alignment with surface patterns are not properties of the raw musical data. These corpora would seem to drive home the mutability of this relationship: given what we know about how their metrical organizations are understood by the composers, listeners, and performers of these repertoires, each corpus features patterns that are both regular and have different relationships to the meters.

J: To return to the GCAMM, we can imagine these different corpora having different mappings between surface and metric patterns – different ways of aligning the dot portions the Figure 5.18 with the inner vectors. The mapping protocol of Western European art music would seem to be one of isomorphism: peaks in metric accent should be commensurate with peaks in loudness, consonance, and harmonic change. Other corpora would seem to have different protocols: the rock/pop corpus maps downbeats onto harmonic change and onto moments immediately preceding consonance, while the drum-set corpus maps downbeats onto bass drum hits and second and fourth beats onto snare/high-hat simultaneities. The jembe corpus then has more complex mapping protocols, with peaks in several parameters often indicating the moments directly preceding a metrically accented pulse.

A: Again, there are theoretical precedents for your stance. For instance, you suggested earlier that Lerdahl and Jackendoff's (1983) "Metric Preference Rules" exemplify your idea of a mapping rule, insomuch as they discuss the kinds of events that an analyst should prefer to align with metric accents in Western art music. Showing how these mapping rules can change between repertoires, Temperley (1999) explicitly modifies these preference rules to account for the syncopation within rock and pop music.

Dance repertoires like the jembe and drum groove corpora provide a further – if more speculative – instance of your mapping rules' mutability. As we noted when introducing the jembe corpus, commentators often locate metrical accents within those dance motions that accompany this repertoire. It is not impossible that learners are taught the dance steps that accompany the tunes, and these dance steps literally choreograph a metric grid on top of the ensemble's surface patterns. Were such an explanation true, it could potentially mean that mappings between surface patterns and metrical patterns were musically arbitrary and instead the result of learned motions: the mapping protocol here would be one of choreography and not of phenomenal accent. It's similarly possible that the same phenomenon ocurred during our earlier excursion into the discotheque: we felt downbeats associated with certain drum sounds because we had learned to dance and move to that music in a particular way – dipping our bodies to the bass drum and clapping and moving our shoulders with the snare (Attas, 2014). While such an explanation is pure speculation as regards any corpus – deep ethnographic and cognitive studies would have to be conducted to test my hypothesis – the structure of my argument is sound: one *could* arbitrarily impose a metrical pattern onto a surface pattern via clearly metric dance steps!

J: (*nodding along*) Relatedly, the research on *groove* (Câmara and Danielsen, 2020) shows ways that misaligning phenomenal accents with metric accents can create effects that are both pleasurable and expected in certain musical styles. Indeed: the literature around this concept is rich and multifaceted and often demonstrates how predictable patterns can misalign or play with a metrical/hierarchical reference structure (Ashley, 2021; Danielsen, 2010; Toiviainen et al., 2009). This work often describes ways that misaligned phenomenal/metrical accents do not undermine the meter – dancers, listeners, and performers still "know where the beat is" – but instead creates a compelling mismatch between these two domains. This mismatch can lead to an accentual vertigo that in turn increases the "want to move" and danceability associated with this music (Janata et al., 2012). In terms of the GCAMM, the mapping protocols of these repertoires would involve this kind of expectation for misalignment. The patterns observed in Figure 5.18 would certainly seem to evidence this sort of grooviness!

A: I want to hone your points with two summarizing observations. First, these discussions of mapping rules imply some feedback from the corpus: the syncopation from a rock corpus necessitates different metric alignments, groovy styles teach certain expectations for accents, and the jembe corpus might map its meter onto its tunes via dance. This corpus dependency is precisely why Figure 5.3's GCAMM shows mapping protocols to be partly the property of musical corpora. By using consistent and observable patterns, a corpus can teach a listener how to impose a metric hierarchy onto it or at least provide guidance. For instance, by placing probable chords directly before and after events with the greatest number of onsets and greatest harmonic change, pop/rock music might "teach" its listeners to expect downbeats to appear misaligned with consonant chords.

Second, it's worth repeating that the surface patterns of Figure 5.18 are still regular, predictable, and mostly isochronous. In each of these corpora, your

What Is Meter? **233**

autocorrelation method consistently found periodicities that aligned with the time signature in each domain in each corpus. It would seem, then, that a consistent property of the music we've analyzed this evening still expresses consistent patterns, even if those patterns have diverse relationships to their underlying meters.[9]

J: (*noticing the landmarks of a familiar neighborhood*) I think we're arriving near your flat, but I have one further point to add before we draw our conversation to a close. We must acknowledge that not all surface patterns participate in metric patterns. For instance, a listener would be well within reason to hear the *Well Tempered Clavier* excerpt of Figure 5.10 in purely quadruple meter, excluding the 3- and 5-sixteenth pulses from participation in the piece's meter. Here, the GCAMM's metric patterns do not map onto all the patterns available on the surface. Instead, there exists an excess of surface patterns – more patterns in the music than participate within the meter.

To my mind, such excesses of surface patterns fall into the domain of non-metric *grouping*. Earlier, I referenced Lerdahl and Jackendoff's (1983) famous dichotomy between the concepts of meter and grouping; in my estimation, grouping represents the superset of patterns available on the musical surface, with *meter* selecting those patterns that map onto a metrical hierarchy. In sum: patterns that do not contribute to the prevailing meter that a listener imposes onto a musical passage can be considered grouping.[10]

A: And finally, we should briefly return to the ground rules of metric patterns. At the onset of our discussion, you mentioned that you did not want to litigate the subtle definitions of meter; subsequently, we used straightforward metric hierarchies suggested by the pieces' time signatures or by other data connected with the corpus, more or less accepting my initial definition of meter as a nexus of consistent, isochronous, and hierarchically nested pulses, with pulse layers related to one another by duple and triple relationships. However, other definitions of meter could certainly be used without harming your broader argument;[11] the GCAM simply stipulates that some definition of meter – any definition – must be "plugged in" to organize surface patterns into metric patterns.

J: I believe we're turning onto the street on which your flat is located. (*points to a sign that reads . . .*)

Summary

A: We began our discussion by showing how we intuitively align metric accents with phenomenal accents, especially in computational and corpus studies – bigger average "booms" should indicate greater metrical weight. You challenged this equation by arguing that a corpus-based understanding of meter will have three components: (1) surface patterns that will be derived from a

234 What Is Meter?

corpus, (2) a definition of meter, and (3) rules and protocols to map meter onto the corpus's patterns. You argued that while the first of these is eminently available to a corpus analysis of unannotated musical surfaces and the last of these can partially interact with such a corpus analysis, a definition of meter cannot be derived from these corpora and is instead the domain of cognitive and music theory.

We then began to use the computational tool of autocorrelation to identify surface patterns within several corpora, beginning with a corpus of Western European art music. Here, we saw patterns of note onsets, pitch-class change, and chord probabilities generally recur with the same periodicity/duration as those indicated by the pieces' time signatures. Further investigation indicated that those patterns tended to feature peaks or marked moments in their content that aligned with their notated metric strength. You argued that this isomorphism – relative accent correlating with relative metric emphasis – can lead corpus analysts to equate surface patterns with metric patterns. However, these two domains should be kept conceptually separate: corpus-derived surface patterns contain no inherent connection with metric organization, and an analyst needs to import some definition of meter or accent to align a surface pattern with a metric hierarchy.

J: I then emphasized this point by broadening the range of corpora being analyzed, first subjecting the Lakh MIDI popular-music corpus to the same autocorrelation analyses. We found that the corpus still produced isochronous surface patterns, but its syncopated nature meant that these patterns differed in how they related to metric patterns when compared with the Western art-music corpus. We similarly found consistent patterns in both a corpus of drum-set grooves and in a corpus of Malian jembe ensemble music, and each showed their own individualized relationships with their meters. These corpora each had unique surface patterns and unique ways that metric accents mapped onto those patterns.

A: The various examples clarify corpus analysis's relationship with musical meter. A computational analysis of musical surfaces can find recurrent patterns. It can also reference metric annotations like measured notation or time signatures to show how these patterns map onto meter. However, these patterns are *not* meter. Instead, meter is located outside the musical surface and in the expectations and cognition of a listener, performer, composer, or analyst. While identifying surface patterns can describe the kinds of events that tend to recur in a repertoire, the musical data – the sequences of pitches, rhythms, timbres, and duration that make up a corpus – does not indicate which events will be heard as accented where patterns begin and end, or the hierarchical relationships between patterns. Instead, some external definitions of which events are more and less accented, what types of events are heard as initiating patterns, and how pulses should relate to one another needs to be imported to organize surface patterns into musical meters.

J: In sum, *meter* cannot be learned from corpus data, at least not a corpus's surface patterns. Instead, corpus analysis can show the types of patterns that are present on a musical surface. A full account of meter requires reference to a human experience – how dancers move to a repertoire, what moments evoke a feeling of accent and emphasis, or how groovy a particular pattern feels. Computers might show patterns, but you need a human for meter.

A: I believe we've reached my flat. Thank you for a lovely conversation, Josephus.

J: Goodnight, Aloysius.

<Exeunt>

Notes

1. Brown, for instance, weighted longer notes more strongly and converted these note attacks into an "amplitude." While durational accents are not explicitly modeled in this chapter, some of my approaches do indeed interact with notions of duration: I discuss some of these below, in particular concerning the role of zero spans present in my vectors.

2. There is not a standard way of undertaking this task, and the parameters for doing so depend on how sensitive a meter-finder one desires. On the one hand, we could simply define a "peak" as a moment higher than surrounding values, or we could undertake a Fourier transform to identify salient periodicities in our peaks. I take a somewhat middle-ground approach by calculating the standard deviation of the correlations and then identifying recurrent peaks within the range of these standard deviations: if peaks are within some fraction of a standard deviation from one another, then I group peaks within that window as part of the same periodicity. Here, I use 1/10 of a standard deviation, but this choice depends on how strict one wants to be.

   Additionally, I should acknowledge that my autocorrelation compares primary and secondary vectors of the same length, something ensured by the "conveyor belt" approach I described earlier. However, this choice will mean that the resulting series of correlations will be symmetrical.

3. Accent has been shown to reliably arise from a number of different musical parameters, including changes in loudness (Lerdahl and Jackendoff, 1983; Repp, 1995; Tekman, 2002; Woodrow, 1911), timbre change (Cusack, 2000), variations in duration (Vos, 1977; Woodrow, 1951), melodic contour (Creston, 1961; Huron and Royal, 1996; Monahan et al., 1987; Thomassen, 1982, 1983; Graybill, 1989; Jones, 1993; Prince, 2014), melodic patterns and grouping (Acevedo et al., 2014; Fraisse, 1946; Repp et al., 2008; Steedman, 1977; Temperley and Bartlette, 2002), and chord change (Dawe et al., 1994; London et al., 2009; White, 2019a).

4. Many thanks to Julie Cummings for drawing my attention to these writers; these passages appear in McKinnon (1998).

5. White (2019a) examines various ways to represent probabilities within an autocorrelation's prime vector, including representing probabilities not only when events begin but for each moment they are sustained as well. This approach essentially creates vectors with no zeros, with each position in the vector capturing the probability of the set or the pitches occurring at that moment (whether they be note attacks or sustained events). However, my study showed that explicitly representing moments of stasis with zeros increases the performance of this process, likely because it embeds the duration of events into the vectors, with a series of zeros showing how long an event lasts.

236 What Is Meter?

6. *F*-scores are particularly useful in this context because autocorrelation is not forced to give an answer for each pulse level (it could, for instance, identify an eighth-note grouping, a whole-note grouping, and nothing in between), nor is it preprogrammed to identify levels that express proper hierarchies (nothing prevents it from identifying simultaneous periodicities of half notes and dotted quarter notes). I return to how this property of autocorrelation interacts with traditional concepts of meter in what follows.

7. At this point, I must note two things. First, the handful of parameters I'm using covers a wide range of events that contribute to meter finding but certainly not all possible events that contribute to meter finding. It is possible that using a parameter like contour or duration might find a measure-long period in the Monteverdi example. However, I am not arguing that the example contains no possible measure-long pulses, only that a surface-based naïve meter-finding model does not *need to* find a measure-long pulse. Second, by invoking performers and listeners in my argument, I am once again slipping between the score and the performed sound signal as my object of analysis. It's very possible – if not likely – that the subtle accents of the performers would highlight additional pulses. My argument, however, is that such a situation still adds components not present in the score.

8. We again can presume some minimal error/noise in this assumption, but not enough to significantly affect our results. Some spot-checking between the corpus and its source files found one piece to be indicated as being in 4/4 while its original source file was seemingly in 3/4, but this was the only error found. One further act of curation was undertaken to remove very long or very short grooves. The median groove was 16 quarter notes long (four measures in quadruple meter), but the longest groove was 584 quarter notes long, and the shortest was only two quarter notes long. For consistency, I used grooves that were greater than or equal to 8 quarter notes long (2 measures) and less than or equal to 256 quarter notes (64 measures) long, a stipulation that excluded less than 1% of the corpus.

9. Kvifte (2007) argues that some musical traditions – particularly northern European folk traditions – function foundationally different than any of the repertoires I've examined here. Kvifte would describe my models as assuming a common fast pulse, or a common denominator for all metrical groups. Indeed, by slicing my repertoires into some quickest duration (usually the 16th pulse), my autocorrelation model is built on the assumption of such a pulse. Other computational work (Misgeld et al., 2022) has been developed to represent corpora without a common fast pulse.

10. In contrast, when a consistent pattern emerges that conflicts with a broader pulse, we could alternately describe the pattern as exhibiting a *grouping metric dissonance* (Krebs, 1999). A grouping dissonance arises when some series of events causes a quicker pulse layer to be grouped into consistent patterns that conflict with or challenge an established grouping of these pulses. We might even distinguish between *rhythmic dissonances* that do not normally disrupt the meter (Krebs's "submetrical dissonances," 1999, 30), with *metric dissonances* that "disrupt the bar and the conducting pattern" – that is, they confuse how the broader hierarchy is organized (Biamonte, 2014, ¶ 1.3). But distinguishing between recurrent motives, metric dissonance, and rhythmic dissonance is famously subjective (Imbrie, 1973) and is the domain of the mapping rules a listener uses to relate metric and surface patterns.

11. Importantly, some researchers do relax such strict hierarchical definitions when analyzing phrasing and grouping: see Capuzzo (2018), for instance.

References

Acevedo, S., D. Temperley, and P. Q. Pfordresher. 2014. "Effects of Metrical Encoding on Melody Recognition." *Music Perception*, 31/4, 372–386.

Aldwell, E., and C. Schachter. 2011. *Harmony and Voiceleading*, 4th edition. Boston, MA: Schirmer.

Anku, Willie. 2000. "Circles and Time: A Theory of Structural Organization of Rhythm in African Music." *Music Theory Online*, 6/1.

Ashley, R. D. 2021. "Music, Groove, and Play." *Behavioral and Brain Sciences*, 44. https://doi.org/10.1017/S0140525X20001727

Attas, R. 2014. "Meter and Motion in Pop/Rock Backbeats." *Society for Music Theory Annual Meeting*, Milwaukee, WI.

Bertin-Mahieux, T., D. P. W. Ellis, B. Whitman, and P. Lamere. 2011. "The Million Song Dataset." *Proceedings of the 12th International Society for Music Information Retrieval Conference*. Miami, FL, 591–596.

Biamonte, N. 2014. "Formal Functions of Metric Dissonance in Rock Music." *Music Theory Online*, 20/2. www.mtosmt.org/issues/mto.14.20.2/mto.14.20.2.biamonte.php

Böck, S., and M. Davies. 2020. "Deconstruct, Analyse, Reconstruct: How to Improve Tempo, Beat, and Downbeat Estimation." *Proc. of the 21st Int. Society for Music Information Retrieval Conf.* Montreal, Canada (virtual), 574–582.

Böck, S., F. Krebs, and G. Widmer. 2016. "Joint Beat and Downbeat Tracking with Recurrent Neural Networks." *Proceedings of the 17th International Society for Music Information Retrieval*, New York.

Boone, G. M. 2000. "Marking Mensural Time." *Music Theory Spectrum*, 22/1, 1–43.

Brochard, R., Abecasis, D., Potter, D., Ragot, R., and Drake, C. 2003. "The 'Ticktock' of Our Internal Clock: Direct Brain Evidence of Subjective Accents in Isochronous Sequences." *Psychological Science*, 14, 362–366.

Brown, J. C. 1993. "The Determination of Meter of Musical Scores by Autocorrelation." *Journal of the Acoustic Society of America*, 94/4, 1953–1957.

Butler, M. 2006. *Unlocking the Groove: Rhythm, Meter, and Musical Design in Electronic Dance Music*. Bloomington: Indiana University Press.

Câmara, G. S., and A. Danielsen. 2020. "Groove." *The Oxford Handbook of Critical Concepts in Music Theory*. A. Rehding and S. Rings, eds. New York: Oxford University Press.

Capuzzo, G. 2018. "Rhythmic Deviance in the Music of Meshuggah." *Music Theory Spectrum*, 40, 121–137.

Cohn, R. 2001. "Complex Hemiolas, Ski-Hill Graphs, and Metric Spaces." *Music Analysis*, 20/3, 295–326.

Cohn, R. 2021. "Meter." *Oxford Handbook of Topics in Music Theory*. New York, NY: Oxford University Press.

Cone, E. T. 1968. *Musical Form and Musical Performance*. New York: W.W. Norton.

Cooper, G., and L. B. Meyer. 1960. *The Rhythmic Structure of Music*. Chicago: University of Chicago Press.

Creston, P. 1961. *Principles of Rhythm*. New York, NY: Franco Columbo.

Cusack, R., and B. Robens. 2000. "Effects of Differences in Timbre on Sequential Grouping." *Perception and Psychophysics*, 62, 1112–1120.

Cuthbert, M. S., and C. Ariza. 2010. "Music21: A Toolkit for Computer: Aided Musicology and Symbolic Music Data." *Proceedings of the 11th International Society for Music Information Retrieval, (ISMIR)*. J. S. Downie and R. C. Veltkamp, eds. Utrecht: Netherlands, 637–642.

Danielsen, A. 2010. "Here, There, and Everywhere: Three Accounts of Pulse in D'Angelo's 'Left and Right'." *Musical Rhythm in the Age of Digital Reproduction*. A. Danielsen, ed. Farnham, Surrey: Ashgate/Routledge, 19–36.

Dawe, L. A., J. R. Platt, and R. J. Racine. 1993. "Harmonic Accents in Inference of Metrical Structure and Perception of Rhythm Patterns." *Perception & Psychophysics*, 54, 794–807.

Dawe, L. A., J. R. Platt, and R. J. Racine. 1994. "Inference of Metrical Structure from Perception of Iterative Pulses within Time Spans Defined by Chord Changes." *Music Perception*, 12/1, 57–76.

Dawe, L. A., J. R. Platt, and R. J. Racine. 1995. "Rhythm Perception and Differences in Accent Weights for Musicians and Nonmusicians." *Perception & Psychophysics*, 57, 905–914.

de Clercq, T. 2021. "How Should Corpus Studies of Harmony in Popular Music Handle the Minor Tonic?" *Proceedings of Future Directions in Music Cognition*. J. Albrecht, L. Warrenburg, L. Reymore, and D. Shanahan, eds., 43–48. Columbus, Ohio. https://doi.org/10.18061/FDMC.2021

de Haas, W. B., and A. Volk. 2016. "Meter Detection in Symbolic Music Using Inner Metric Analysis." *Proceedings of the 17th Conference of the International Society for Music Information Retrieval*, New York, USA, 574–582.

De Souza, J. 2017. *Music at Hand: Instruments, Bodies, and Cognition*. New York: Oxford University Press.

Durand, S., J. P. Bello, B. David, and G. Richard. 2015. "Downbeat Tracking with Multiple Features and Deep Neural Networks." *IEEE International Conference on Acoustics, Speech and Signal Processing (ICASSP)*, Brisbane, 409–413.

Durand, S., B. David, and G. Richard. 2014. "Enhancing Downbeat Detection When Facing Different Music Styles." *IEEE International Conference on Acoustics, Speech and Signal Processing (ICASSP)*, Florence, 3132–3136.

Eck, D. 2006. "Identifying Metrical and Temporal Structure with an Autocorrelation Phase Matrix." *Music Perception*, 24(2), 167–176.

Eck, D., and N. Casagrande. 2005. "Finding Meter in Music Using an Autocorrelation Phase Matrix and Shannon Entropy." *Proceedings of the 6th International Conference on Music Information Retrieval*, London, 01, 504–509.

Eerola, T., and P. Toiviainen. 2004. "MIR in Matlab: The Midi Toolbox." *Proc. 5th International Conference on Music Information Retrieval*, Barcelona, Spain.

Ellis, R. J., and M. R. Jones. 2009. "The Role of Accent Salience and Joint Accent Structure in Meter Perception." *Journal of Experimental Psychology: Human Perception and Performance*, 35, 264–280.

Ewell, P. 2020. "Music Theory and the White Racial Frame." *Music Theory Online*, 26/2. https://mtosmt.org/issues/mto.20.26.2/mto.20.26.2.ewell.html DOI: 10.30535/mto.26.2.4

Fraisse, P. 1946. "Contribution à l'étude du rhythme en tant que forme temporelle." *Journal de Psychologie Normale et Pathologique*, 39, 283–304.

Fux, J. J. 1725. *Gradus ad Parnassum*. Translation and commentary by Mann, A., and Edmunds, J. as *The Study of Counterpoint from Johann Joseph Fux's Gradus ad parnassum* (1965). New York: W.W. Norton & Co.

Gouyon, F., and S. Dixon. 2005. "A Review of Automatic Rhythm Description Systems." *Computer Music Journal*, 29, 34–54.

Gouyon, F., G. Widmer, X. Serra, and A. Flexer. 2006. "Acoustic Cues to Beat Induction: A Machine Learning Perspective." *Music Perception*, 24/2, 177–188.

Graybill, R. 1989. "Phenomenal Accent and Meter in the Species Exercise." *In Theory Only*, J 1, 11–43.

Greasley, A. E., and H. M. Prior. 2013. "Mixtapes and Turntablism: DJs' Perspectives on Musical Shape." *Empirical Musicology Review*, 8/1.

Guerra, Stephen. 2018. *Expanded Meter and Hemiola in Baden Powell's Samba-Jazz*. PhD diss., Yale University, New Haven, CT.

Hannon, E. E., J. S. Snyder, T. Eerola, and C. L. Krumhansl. 2004. "The Role of Melodic and Temporal Cues in Perceiving Musical Meter." *Journal of Experimental Psychology: Human Perception and Performance*, 30, 956–974.

Hasty, C. F. 1997. *Meter as Rhythm*. New York and Oxford: Oxford University Press.

Hosken, F., T. Bechtold, F. Hoesl, L. Kilchenmann, and O. Senn. 2021. "Drum Groove Corpora." *Empirical Musicology Review*, 16/1. http://dx.doi.org/10.18061/emr.v16i1.7642

Huron, D. 2006. *Sweet Anticipation: Music and the Psychology of Expectation*. Cambridge: The MIT Press.

Huron, D., and M. Royal. 1996. "What Is Melodic Accent? Converging Evidence from Musical Practice." *Music Perception*, 13, 489–516. http://dx.doi.org/10.2307/40285700

Imbrie, A. 1973. "'Extra' Measures and Metrical Ambiguity in Beethoven." *Beethoven Studies*. Alan Tyson, ed. New York: W. W. Norton, 45–66.

Iversen, J. R., and A. D. Patel. 2008. "Perception of Rhythmic Grouping Depends on Auditory Experience." *Journal of the Acoustical Society of America*, 124/4, 2263–2271.

Jacoby, N., J. H. McDermott. 2016. "Integer Ratio Priors on Musical Rhythm Revealed Cross-Culturally by Iterated Reproduction." *Current Biology*, 1–33. http://dx.doi.org/10.1016/j.cub.2016.12.031

Janata, P., S. T. Tomic, and J. M. Haberman. 2012. "Sensorimotor Coupling in Music and the Psychology of the Groove." *Journal of Experimental Psychology: General*, 141, 54–75.

Jones, M. R. 1987. "Dynamic Pattern Structure in Music: Recent Theory and Research." *Perception & Psychophysics*, 41, 621–634.

Jones, M. R. 1993. "Dynamics of Musical Patterns: How Do Melody and Rhythm Fit Together?" *Psychology and Music: The Understanding of Melody and Rhythm*. T. J. Tighe and W. J. Dowling, eds. Hillsdale, NJ: Erlbaum, pp. 67–92.

Jones, M. R., and M. Boltz. 1989. "Dynamic Attending and Responses to Time." *Psychological Review*, 96/3, 459–491.

Jones, M. R., H. Moynihan, N. MacKenzie, and J. Puente. 2002. "Temporal Aspects of Stimulus-Driven Attending in Dynamic Arrays." *Psychological Science*, 13/4, 313–319.

Khadkevich, M., T. Fillon, G. Richard, and M. Omologo. 2012. "A Probabilistic Approach to Simultaneous Extraction of Beats and Downbeats." *IEEE International Conference on Acoustics, Speech and Signal Processing (ICASSP)*, Kyoto, 445–448.

Kozak, M. 2019. *Enacting Musical Time: The Bodily Experience of New Music*. New York: Oxford University Press.

Krebs, H. 1999. *Fantasy Pieces*. New York: Oxford University Press.

Krumhansl, C. 1990. *The Cognitive Foundations of Musical Pitch*. Oxford: Oxford University Press.

Kvifte, T. 2007. "Categories and Timing: On the Perception of Meter." *Ethnomusicology*, 51/1, 64–84.

Laitz, S. 2012. *The Complete Musician: An Integrated Approach to Tonal Harmony, Analysis, and Listening*, 3rd edition. Oxford and New York, NY: Oxford University Press.

Large, E. W., J. A. Herrera, and M. J. Velasco. 2015. "Neural Networks for Beat Perception in Musical Rhythm." *Frontiers in Systems Neuroscience*, 9, 159–173.

Large, E. W., J. C. Kim, N. Flaig, J. Bharucha, and C. L. Krumhansl. 2016. "A Neurodynamic Account of Musical Tonality." *Music Perception*, 33/3, 319–331.

Lerdahl, F., and R. Jackendoff. 1983. *A Generative Theory of Tonal Music: A Generative Theory of Tonal Music*. Cambridge: MIT Press.

London, J. 1990. *The Interaction between Meter and Phrase Beginnings and Endings in the Mature Instrumental Music of Haydn and Mozart*. Ph.D. dissertation, The University of Pennsylvania, Philadelphia, PA.

London, J. 2004. *Hearing in Time: Psychological Aspects of Musical Meter*. New York: Oxford University Press.

London, J., T. Himberg, and I. Cross. 2009. "The Effect of Structural and Performance Factors in the Perception of Anacruses." *Music Perception*, 27/2, 103–120.

London, J., R. Polak, and N. Jacoby. 2017. "Rhythm Histograms and Musical Meter: A Corpus Study of Malian Percussion Music." *Psychonomic Bulletin and Review*, 474–480. DOI: 10.3758/s13423-016-1093-7

Long, M. K. 2020. *Hearing Homophony: Tonal Expectation at the Turn of the Seventeenth Century*. New York: Oxford University Press.

McKinnon, J., ed. 1998. *Strunk's Source Readings in Music Theory, Vol. 2: The Early Christian Period and the Latin Middle Ages*. Leo Treitler, general ed., revised edition. New York: W.W. Norton and Co.

Mirka, D. 2009. *Metric Manipulations in Haydn and Mozart: Chamber Music for Strings, 1787–1791*. New York: Oxford University Press.

Misgeld, O, A. Holzapfel, P. Kallioinen, and S. Ahlbäck. 2022. "The Melodic Beat: Exploring Asymmetry in Polska Performance." *Journal of Mathematics and Music*, 16/2, 138–159.

Monahan, C. B., R. A. Kendall, and E. C. Carterette. 1987. "The Effect of Melodic and Temporal Contour on Recognition Memory for Pitch Change." *Perception and Psychophysics*, 41, 576–600. http://dx.doi.org/10.3758/ BF03210491

Murphy, S. 2007. "On Metre in the Rondo of Brahms's Op. 25." *Music Analysis*, 26, 323–353.

Murphy, S. 2009. "Metric Cubes in Some Music By Brahms." *Journal of Music Theory*, 53/1, 1–56.

Palmer, C., and Krumhansl, C. L. 1990. "Mental Representations for Musical Meter." *Journal of Experimental Psychology: Human Perception and Performance*, 16, 728–741.

Papadopoulos, H., and G. Peeters. 2011. "Joint Estimation of Chords and Downbeats from an Audio Signal." *IEEE Transactions on Audio, Speech, and Language Processing*, 19/1, 138–152.

Patel, A. 2007. *Music, Language, and the Brain*. New York: Oxford University Press.

Polak, R. 2010. "Rhythmic Feel as Meter: Non-Isochronous Beat Subdivision in Jembe Music from Mali." *Music Theory Online*, 10/4. www.mtosmt.org/issues/mto.10.16.4/mto.10.16.4.polak.html

Polak, R., N. Jacoby, and J. London. 2016. "Both Isochronous and Non-Isochronous Metrical Subdivision Afford Precise and Stable Ensemble Entrainment: A Corpus Study of Malian Jembe Drumming." *Frontiers in Auditory Neuroscience*. DOI: 10.3389/fnins.2016.00285

Polak, R., S. Tarsitani, and M. Clayton. 2018. "IEMP Malian Jembe: A Collection of Audiovisual Recordings of Malian Jembe Ensemble Performances, with Detailed Annotations." *Open Science Framework (OSF)*. DOI: 10.17605/OSF.IO/M652X

Pressing, J. 1983. "Cognitive Isomorphisms between Pitch and Rhythm in World Musics: West Africa, the Balkans and Western Tonality." *Studies in Music*, 17, 38–61.

Pressing, J. 2002. "Black Atlantic Rhythm: Its Computational and Transcultural Foundations." *Music Perception*, 19/3, 285–310.

Prince, J. 2014. "Pitch Structure, But Not Selective Attention, Affects Accent Weightings in Metrical Grouping." *Journal of Experimental Psychology: Human Perception and Performance*, 40, 2073–2090.

Prince, J. B., and T. Rice. 2018. "Regularity and Dimensional Salience in Temporal Grouping." *Journal of Experimental Psychology: Human Perception and Performance*, 44, 1356–1367.

Prince, J. B., and M. A. Schmuckler. 2014. "The Tonal-Metric Hierarchy: A Corpus Analysis." *Music Perception*, 31/3, 254–270.

Prince, J. B. William, F. Thompson, and M. A. Schmuckler. 2009. "Pitch and Time, Tonality and Meter: How Do Musical Dimensions Combine?" *Journal of Experimental Psychology*, 35/5, 1598–1617.

Raffel, C. 2016. *Learning-Based Methods for Comparing Sequences, with Applications to Audio-to-MIDI Alignment and Matching*. PhD Thesis, Columbia University, New York, NY.

Rahn, J. 1996. "Turning the Analysis Around: Africa-Derived Rhythms and Europe-Derived Music Theory." *Black Music Research Journal*, 16/1, 71–89.

Repp, B. H. 1995. Detectability of Duration and Intensity Increments in Melody Tones: A Partial Connection between Music Perception and Performance." *Perception & Psychophysics*, 57, 1217–1232.

Repp, B. H., J. R. Iversen, and A. D. Patel. 2008. "Tracking an Imposed Beat within a Metrical Grid." *Music Perception*, 26, 1–18.

Rohrmeier, M. 2020. "Towards a Formalization of Musical Rhythm." *Proceedings of the 21st Int. Society for Music Information Retrieval Conference* (virtual), Montreal, Canada, 621–629.

Rothstein, W. N. 1989. *Phrase Rhythm in Tonal Music*. New York: Schirmer.

Sadakata, M., P. Desain, and H. J. Honing. 2006. "The Bayesian Way to Relate Rhythm Perception and Production." *Music Perception*, 23, 269–288.

Schachter, C. 1999. *Unfoldings: Essays in Schenkerian Theory and Analysis*. Edited by J. N. Straus. New York: Oxford University Press.

Schenker, H. 1935. *Der freie Satz*. Wien: Universal Edition, 1935. Trans. as *Free Composition* by E. Oster, New York, Longman, 1979; Pendragon Press, 2001.

Smith, K. C., and L. L. Cuddy. 1989. "Effects of Metrical and Harmonic Rhythm on the Detection of Pitch Alternations in Melodic Sequences." *Journal of Experimental Psychology: Human Perception and Performance*, 15, 457–471.

Steedman, M. J. 1977. "The Perception of Musical Rhythm and Metre." *Perception*, 6, 555–569.

Stephenson, K. 2002. *What to Listen for in Rock: A Stylistic Analysis*. New Haven: Yale University Press.

Tamlyn, G. 1998. *The Big Beat: Origins and Development of Snare Backbeat and Other Accompanimental Rhythms in Rock 'n' Roll*. Ph.D. thesis, University of Liverpool.

Tan, I., E. Lustig, and D. Temperley. 2018. "Anticipatory Syncopation in Rock: A Corpus Study." *Music Perception*, 36, 353–370.

Tekman, H. G. 2002. "Perceptual Integration of Timing and Intensity Variations in the Perception of Musical Accents." *The Journal of General Psychology*, 129, 181–191.

Temperley, D. 1999. "Syncopation in Rock: A Perceptual Perspective." *Popular Music*, 18/1, 19–40.

Temperley, D. 2018. *The Musical Language of Rock*. New York: Oxford University Press.

Temperley, D. 2019. "Second-Position Syncopation in European and American Vocal Music." *Empirical Musicology Review*, 24/1–2. https://doi.org/10.18061/emr.v14i1-2.6986

Temperley, D., and C. Bartlette. 2002. "Parallelism as a Factor in Metrical Analysis." *Music Perception*, 20, 117–149. http://dx.doi.org/10.1525/mp .2002.20.2.117

Thomassen, J. 1982. "Melodic Accent: Experiments and a Tentative Model." *The Journal of the Acoustical Society of America*, 71, 1596–1605. http://dx.doi.org/10.1121/1.387814

Thomassen, J. M. 1983. "Erratum: 'Melodic Accent: Experiments and a Tentative Model'." *The Journal of the Acoustical Society of America*, 73, 373. http://dx.doi.org/10.1121/1.389590

Toiviainen, P., G. Luck, and M. R. Thompson. 2009. "Embodied Meter: Hierarchical Eigenmodes in Spontaneous Movement to Music." *Cognitive Processing. Special Issue: Neuroscience Today: Neuronal Functional Diversity and Collective Behaviors*, 10/Supp2, S325–S327.

Toiviainen, P., G. Luck, and M. R. Thompson. 2010. "Embodied Meter: Hierarchical Eigenmodes in Music-Induced Movement." *Music Perception*, 28/1, 59–70.

Toussaint, G. T. 2003. "Classification and Phylogenetic Analysis of African Ternary Rhythm Timelines." *Proceedings of BRIDGES: Mathematical Connections in Art, Music, and Science, University of Granada, Granada*, 25–36.

Vos, P. 1977. "Temporal Duration Factors in the Perception of Auditory Rhythmic Patterns." *Scientific Aesthetics/Sciences de l'Art*, 1, 183–199.

White, C. W. 2018. "Meter's Influence on Theoretical and Corpus-Derived Harmonic Grammars." *Indiana Theory Review*, 93–116.

White, C. W. 2019a. "Influences of Chord Change on Metric Accent." *Psychomusicology*, 29/4, 209–225.

White, C. W. 2019b. "Autocorrelation of Pitch-Event Vectors in Meter Finding." *Mathematics and Computation in Music*. Heidelberg: Springer: LNCS, v. 11502, pp. 287–296.

White, C. W. 2021. "Some Observations on Autocorrelated Patterns within Computational Meter Identification." *Journal of Mathematics and Music*, 15/2, 181–193.

Woodrow, H. 1911. "The Role of Pitch in Rhythm." *Psychological Review*, 18, 54–77. http://dx.doi.org/10.1037/h0075201

Woodrow, H. 1951. "Time perception." *Handbook of Experimental Psychology*. S. S. Stevens, ed. New York, NY: Wiley, pp. 1224–1236.

Yeston, M. 1976. *The Stratification of Musical Rhythm*. New Haven: Yale University Press.

APPENDIX TO CHAPTER 5

F-Scores

Relative to other mathematical formalisms we have encountered in this book, *F*-scores (also called F1 scores) are straightforward. Equation A5.1 outlines the *F*-score calculation as the combination of two other values, *precision* and *recall*. These values describe the relationship between true positives (correct answers), false positives ("false alarms" that incorrectly assess something as correct), true negatives (wrong answers), and false negatives (incorrectly assessing something as incorrect). An ideal model should only ever return true positives and true negatives, and precision and recall capture the ways a model might deviate from this ideal.

As Equation A5.1 illustrates, *precision* divides the number of correct answers given (true positives and true negatives returned by the model) by all answers given (the set of true and false positives and true and false negatives). More precise models will have fewer false positives/negatives and therefore return fractions closer to 1. *Recall* divides the number of true positives/negatives given by the model by the total number of expected true positives/negatives. Models with higher recall will return a greater fraction of the expected array of correct answers.

The *F*-score is then the average between these. Instead of the arithmetic mean, the harmonic mean is used (the harmonic mean is specifically appropriate for comparing multiple different rates or fractions). Higher *F*-scores, then, indicate models that return both greater proportions of correct answers within all given answers and greater fractions of the expected correct answers.

244 What Is Meter?

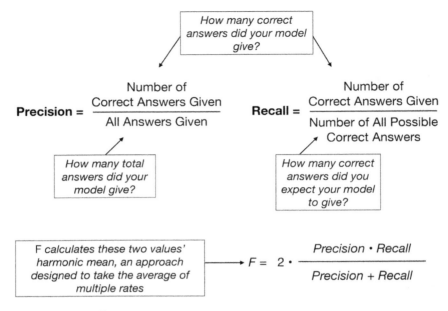

EQUATION A5.1 *F*-scores

6

WHAT IS KEY?

A Diatribe

The following chapter presents a series of contentions that sequentially build an argument about how corpus analyses represent the concepts of key and tonality through noticeable and learnable connections between surface events and scale degrees.

Contention #1: "Musical Key" Results From the Connections Between Pitches and Scale Degrees

At its core, the notion of tonal orientation involves some mapping between pitches and scale degrees. Using this mapping, music's *key* translates the raw pitch events of a musical surface into scale degrees organized around a central tonic pitch class. To once again evoke Huron's (2006) perceived/cognized dichotomy, pitches – their organization and the intervals between them – can be considered the basic events that are perceived, while mapping a tonic or key onto those events is a cognitive process that imposes some order and interpretation onto those perceived events.[1] In this framing, the key-finding process is an interpretive operation, with scale degrees being actively imposed upon some basic set of pitch data.

To illustrate a simple manifestation of this process, Example 6.1 shows the opening to the trio from Clara Schumann's *Romance No. 2*, Op. 11. A classical musician scanning over this excerpt would assess the passage as solidly in B-flat major. Except for the F-sharp passing tone, the notes are all part of a B-flat major scale, the phrase begins on a B-flat major triad, and it ends with an V^7-I authentic cadence in that key.

Each of these observations connects some aspect of the musical surface to an expectation about scale degrees. Example 6.1 isolates one such connection,

DOI: 10.4324/9781003285663-6

246 What Is Key?

B-flat major: I   vi   V7   I

EXAMPLE 6.1 *Romance No. 2*, Op. 11, Clara Schumann: Trio, mm. 51–52

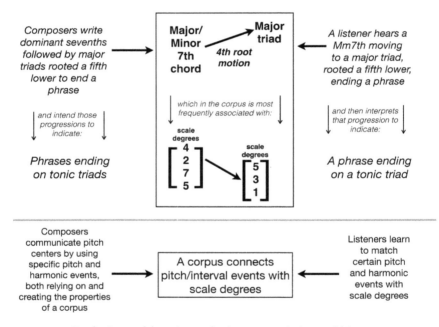

FIGURE 6.1 Producing and learning scale-degree associations within a corpus

linking an authentic cadence to its scale degrees. In the center of the diagram, a major/minor seventh chord progresses to a major triad rooted a fourth higher, and these events are associated with the scale degrees of a V^7 and I chord, respectively (or: <$\hat{5}, \hat{7}, \hat{2}, \hat{4}$> resolving to <$\hat{1}, \hat{3}, \hat{5}$>).

The remainder of the figure schematizes this connection's relationship to listeners, composers, and corpus data, with composers communicating scale degrees through these pitch events, listeners then interpreting those scale degrees, and a corpus containing pieces with these connections. By including the music's creators and consumers, the figure becomes a version of Chapter 1's noisy channel: we can imagine a composer encoding a key into a series of pitches and pitch sets, which becomes a message that communicates a tonal center, and listeners then decode these messages. However, as I demonstrated with Chapter 1's Meaningful Corpus Model, corpora play crucial mediating roles in this relationship, and I schematize some of these issues below the figure. In terms of Example 6.1, we imagine Clara Schumann being aware of the key orientation expressed by her musical choices – she is embedding a scale-degree message in her music. However, these choices not only inform the music being created but are informed by larger musical traditions – by larger musical corpora. If one is to write legible music that conforms to a standard stylistic practice, the music will reflect the norms of some musical corpus: Schumann needs to embed scale-degree information in ways her audience will expect. This adherence to norms and expectations creates a feedback loop that ensures a consistency in musical practice, a consistency that in turn aids in musical learning. For instance, if composers consistently produce music with phrases closing on tonic-ending authentic cadences, the connection between these surface events and tonic closure will be easily learned and internalized. Schumann's authentic cadence will clearly communicate B-flat major to such enculturated listening, and this enculturation is accomplished via exposure to a musical corpus.

In both these viewpoints, the pitches and intervals are not themselves scale degrees; rather, they acquire scale-degree associations through their regular usage within a corpus, associations that allow for composers and listeners to encode scale degrees into raw perceived events. This generalization is shown at the bottom of Figure 6.1, with composers embedding the connections between pitches and scale degrees into a corpus and learners gleaning these connections from a corpus. In terms of the noisy-channel dynamics: just as a message is made of raw ciphered materials from which encoders and receivers can glean meaning – the meaning is not *in* the message but is rather deduced *from* the message – so too are scale degrees and key orientations not explicitly present in some musical passage but are rather interpreted from the events of some passage.

In this chapter, I will describe a corpus-based approach to musical key using the dynamics of Figure 6.1. I will outline several ways that corpus models have been used to identify key centers in pieces of music, and I will outline the strengths and weaknesses of each. Throughout, I will also describe how corpus analysis can enrich our understanding of musical key, arguing that the ways that scale degrees are imposed on pitch events changes by repertoire, style, and corpus; however, I will also argue that certain distributional properties are shared throughout different styles, suggesting a statistical and corpus-oriented definition of musical key. The chapter will progress as a series of contentions that I will investigate through corpus modeling and reviews of existing corpus-based and psychological research.

These topics interact with many larger music theory topics, not the least of which includes the thorny definitions of *key* itself. While I will periodically return to these larger topics throughout the chapter, a few definitional

248 What Is Key?

boundaries are in order. First, when I refer to *key* and *key-finding*, I will *not* simply mean the identification of a central tonic note but – following the definitions of "key" given in Hyer (2002) and "tonic" in Rings (2020) – I will instead mean the ways in which pitch classes array themselves in an order or hierarchy around a tonic pitch. However, I will not restrict myself to one specific definition of key. Hynes-Tawa (2020), for instance, paints a rich historical epistemology of the notion of *tonic* as necessarily including a relationship with the fifth above the tonic note and the half step below the tonic note: while many of my corpus-derived models may produce results that align with this historical approach, I will not adopt such definitions *a priori*.

Furthermore, the notion of key undoubtedly overlaps with the concept of *tonality*. Theorists have argued for many diverse definitions of this concept, and many such definitions address how pitch classes organize around some central tonic. These theories range from the collection-oriented theories of Fétis (1958) to the dualist approaches of Riemann (1893) to prolongational theories of Schenker (1935) to the metrical/poetic observations of Long (2020). Additionally, several scholars explicitly list several interacting parameters that are necessary for tonality. Tymoczko (2011), for instance, argues that conjunct melodic motion, acoustic consonance, harmonic consistency, limited macroharmonic collection, and key centricity are foundational components (a list presaged by Straus, 2005), while Harrison (2016) constructs a theory of Common Practice tonality containing an overlapping confluence of well-worn phrase rhetoric, clear harmonic fluctuations between consonance and dissonance, metrical regularity, and linear voice leading.

And music cognition is not immune to such diversity of thought: the basic mechanics around the perception of key have been a point of contention in music psychology. Centering around the work of Carol Krumhansl (1990), one camp of research points to behavioral evidence that the most reliable accounting for how humans hear key within a passage turns on the amount that each pitch is used in the passage – if the pitches of a C-major scale are most frequently used, then listeners will hear a tonal center of C (Huron and Parncutt, 1993; Temperley, 2007; Temperley and Marvin, 2008; I will engage more thoroughly with this topic in my discussion of key-profile analyses later). A second camp finds its epistemological forebearer in Richmond Browne's (1981) "rare interval hypothesis," an explanation of tonal orientation that relies on the unique disposition of intervals within the diatonic set. If a melody leaps upward by a tritone and continues by a half step (e.g., F→B→C), the final pitch must be the tonic, given that this sequence of intervals occurs at a single unique position in the major scale (i.e., no other scale degrees besides <$\hat{4}$–$\hat{7}$–$\hat{1}$> contain that series of intervals). Accounts of tonality in this vein have been behaviorally tested by Brown and Butler (1981), Brown (1988), Butler (1989), Brown et al. (1994), Matsunaga and Abe (2005, 2009), and Matsunaga et al. (2012). (I will also engage with this topic more fully in what follows.)

Again, while my corpus-oriented models may ultimately resonate with various historical approaches – and while my argument will culminate in larger, qualitative descriptions of tonality – my initial perspective will be agnostic toward these broader ideas. Instead, I will hew closer to the approach of Quinn (2020), in which *tonal harmony* is any sequence of musical events that can be made sense of in terms of scale degrees (rather than by contrapuntal designs, absolute-pitch-based information, etc.). Starting from this theory-neutral stance will allow for clear demonstrations of what properties of musical key and tonality can be observed from musical corpora.

As I've done throughout this book, this chapter will slip between the notion of *hearing* a key versus *writing in* a key versus *analyzing* a key. When I noted that a listener, analyst, and Schumann herself would understand Example 6.1 "in B-flat," this statement will mean different things from different viewpoints: an analyst reading the score would explicitly be aware that the tonic note is B-flat, while a listener with relative pitch would not necessarily be aware of the absolute pitch of the tonic. Additionally, as I belabored in my first chapter, listeners and composers (and, to a certain extent, learners and performers) potentially use different methods when producing and interpreting a corpus. However, I also argued that the Meaningful Corpus Model can capture how these various viewpoints relate to one another. Throughout this chapter, I will heuristically use phrases like "in B-flat" to capture the diversity of relationships various actors will have with regard to key, embracing that diversity and locating their shared nexus in musical corpora.

Contention #2: Mapping Scale Degrees Onto Pitch Events Is an Activity Learnable From a Corpus and Representable by Corpus Analyses

In the previous section, I argued that scale degrees were an interpretation that musical listeners, composers, or performers impose on the raw pitch and intervallic events of a musical surface. Figure 6.1 also indicated that these mappings were learnable from – and observable in – a musical corpus. In this section, I will outline various ways that key-finding has been undertaken using corpus statistics, each of which connects a corpus's pitch events to scale degrees in some way.

In what follows, I provide a brief tour of two broad categories of corpus-based key-finding, beginning with what is perhaps the most straightforward: key-profile analysis.

Model #1a: Key-Profile Analysis

Key-profile analysis is not only the most straightforward approach to corpus-based key-finding but also the most widely used (Krumhansl, 1990; Aarden, 2003; Albrecht and Shanahan, 2013; Albrecht and Huron, 2014; Napolés and Arthur, 2019; Temperley, 2007, to name just a few!). This approach's engineering undertakes its key-finding by matching a passage's pitch-class distribution – the number of times each pitch class occurs in the passage – to an expected scale-degree distribution, or *key profile*. In other words, a key-profile analysis asks, "Given its pitches, in what key is this passage?"

250 What Is Key?

To create key profiles, we generally first observe passage with known keys. In this vein, Figure 6.2a shows the relative frequencies of scale degrees in the first 20 salami slices of each major-mode piece within the YCAC (see Chapter 2 for a discussion of salami slices; the corpus's curators notated the opening key and mode of each piece, and these annotations are used to assign scale degrees). The resulting key profile then represents the expectations for how often each scale degree should occur given these events in the YCAC. In Figure 6.2a, the tonic degree occurs the most frequently, followed by other members of the tonic triad, followed by other diatonic degrees, and with chromatic degrees occurring the least often.

This key profile can then be compared to unanalyzed passages of music in order to assess their keys. Figure 6.2b shows the pitch–class distribution for Example 6.1, noting which pitch classes occur the most. In this passage, B-flat occurs most often; D and F are tied for second/third place, followed by E-flat, G, and A. Computationally, a key-profile analysis rotates the pitch–class distribution twelve times to produce each possible scale-degree interpretation of the passage. Rotating the pitch–class distribution of the Schumann passage such that B-flat is aligned with scale degree 1 – we can imagine Figure 6.2b's bars either shifting 2 positions to the right or 10 to the left – produces Figure 6.2c. This rotation places B-flat in the profile's first slot, aligning that pitch-class with tonic; D becomes the mediant, E-flat the sub-dominant, and so on. Figure 6.2d shows another sample rotation, now with F oriented with $\hat{1}$. This process is repeated for all possible key interpretations, and the rotation that best aligns with the key profile shows the passage's key. In 6.2c's B-flat-as-tonic rotation, the most frequent pitch-class, B-flat, is placed in the position of $\hat{1}$, and the next-most-frequent degrees, D and F, are aligned with $\hat{3}$ and $\hat{5}$. Notice that this alignment isn't perfect – after all, the very fact that D and F have the same frequency in this passage means that no orientation of this distribution will exactly line up with the ordering of the key profile. But a B-flat orientation is the best of all options: while Figure 6.2d's F-as-tonic rotation aligns one of the most frequent pitch classes with $\hat{1}$, the passage's other frequent pitch classes do *not* align with the key profile's expected most frequent scale degrees. To quantify these similarities, we can import a technique introduced in Chapter 1: the correlation coefficient. Recall that correlation expresses how similar two series are to one another, returning a value between 1 and −1, with 1 indicating a perfect fit, 0 arising from a random relationship, and −1 indicating all values are the opposite/inverse of one another. Correlating the percentages of the key profile with the percentages of the B-flat-as-tonic rotation of Figure 6.2c will let us know how similar these two series are. Correlating this pair produces a correlation value (or "coefficient") of 0.94, while correlating the key-profile with the values of 6.2d results in a much-lower coefficient of 0.23. In sum: using a key-profile process, B-flat is the passage's tonic because the key profile best aligns (is most correlated) with the passage's pitch-class distribution when the distribution's B-flat is placed in the profile's tonic position. (This chapter's online supplement includes a spreadsheet that walks through these rotations.)

What Is Key? 251

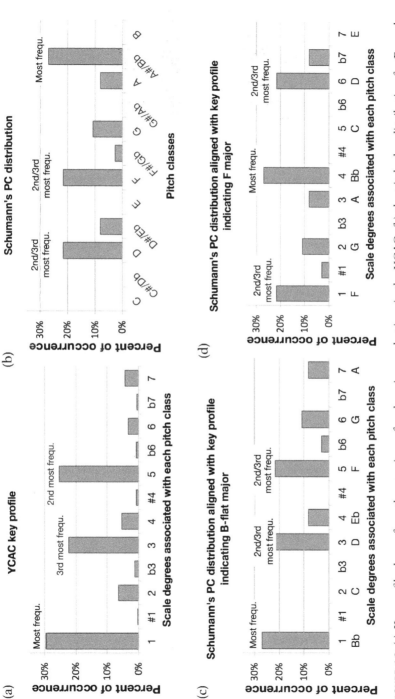

FIGURE 6.2 (a) Key profile drawn from the openings of each major-mode piece in the YCAC, (b) the pitch-class distribution for Example 6.1, (c) the distribution rotated to align the pitch-class B-flat with $\hat{1}$, and (d) the distribution rotation with F as $\hat{1}$

252 What Is Key?

Other applications of key-profile analysis follow the same general format as the one outlined, with some variation in how they are compiled and how they are applied. Similar to my approach with the YCAC, Temperley (2007) creates key profiles by identifying the key of pieces in a corpus and then simply counts the scale degrees contained in those tonally determined passages. In contrast, other researchers do not simply count scale-degree occurrences but count their durations (Krumhansl, 1990). While many approaches focus on melodies (e.g., Temperley and Marvin, 2008), others count all pitches in polyphonic passages (Albrecht and Huron, 2014), and others use only chord roots (Bellman, 2005). Furthermore, comparing the pitch-class profile (or, the particular ordering of a pitch-class distribution to align with the key profile, the expected distribution of scale degrees) of a passage to the key profile can be done in a number of ways. For instance, Krumhansl (1990) uses correlation, Albrecht and Shanahan (2013) treat the profiles like points in 12-dimensional space and calculate their distance, Yust (2017) performs a Fourier analysis on the distribution, while Temperley (2007) uses Bayesian probability.

Additionally, most key-profile analyses also compile minor-mode profiles, which can be used to assess the keys of minor-mode pieces. For simplicity's sake, I will mostly demonstrate major-mode key-finding in this chapter; however, I discuss minor-mode key profiles in the appendix.

Regardless of approach, however, key profiles of Western European tonal music look remarkably similar, following the same contour as my YCAC profile. Additionally, when compared with a ground truth of listener's key assessments (Temperley and Marvin, 2008), composers' key annotation (Longuet-Higgins and Steedman, 1971), and analysis by music scholars (Aarden, 2003; Temperley, 2007; Albrecht and Shanahan, 2013; Albrecht and Huron, 2014), these models are quite efficacious: most align with the ground truth more than 80% of the time.[2] Figure 6.2a's key profile, for instance, can be used to predict the keys assigned to the YCAC's pieces. To demonstrate the efficacy of this particular profile, I compiled the distribution using a random three-quarters portion of the YCAC; I'll refer to this portion as the *training set*, as the model learns its key profile by observing how often each scale degree occurs in this dataset. I then used that profile to assess the key of the corpus's remaining pieces; this portion is the *test set* of the corpus, as it provides the opportunity for the model to be tested. (In other words, a training set is used to create the analytical model – here, the key profile with its expected distribution of scale degrees – which is then applied to a test set, finding the keys of pieces in that set.) These assessments aligned with the key labels from the test set a respectable 79.4% of the time.

Model #1b: Bass Profiles

In principle, a model could take any distribution of pitch events, associate that with a distribution of scale degrees, and use those connections for a key-finding task. Using different categories of pitch events as potential key-finding tools allows computational researchers to compare how strongly different musical events seem to indicate a passage's key. The previous section's key-profile analysis indicated that counting all pitches in the YCAC predicts the annotated key nearly 80% of the time. However, if one wanted to test whether the pitch contents of bass lines were better or worse indicators of key, for instance, one could do so with a few modifications to the key-profile method. The results could then be compared to those of a key-profile method to see which method better predicts key in some corpus.

Figure 6.3a shows the scale-degree distribution of the bass lines in the YCAC. To create this *bass-note key profile* (or, what I'll refer to as the "bass profile") I followed the same procedure as that of the key profile but only counted the scale degrees with the lowest pitch height at each salami slice, excluding those above C5 (MIDI pitch 72; the C above middle C). (In other words, the bass profile becomes a key profile that only uses the lowest notes of a passage.) The distribution is a more extreme version of that of Figure 6.2a, indicating that bass notes favor the tonic and dominant degrees overwhelmingly more than other scale degrees. To assess the key of a passage, this bass profile can then be compared to the pitch-class distribution of a passage's bass line. Because it so strongly represents the tonic and dominant scale degrees, this key-finding process effectively identifies the most frequent scale degrees in a bass line separated by fifth and associates the lower pitch class with tonic. Figure 6.3b shows this process applied to the music of Example 6.1. The passage's bass line articulates the B-flat, F, and G pitch classes, with the first being most frequent. The best way to align this distribution with the bass profile is to associate B-flat with $\hat{1}$ and F with $\hat{5}$. While this rotation makes for a higher frequency of $\hat{6}$ (G) than expected, it is more similar to the bass profile than any other rotation: accordingly, the model assesses the passage to be in B-flat. I can test this method in the same way as I did the YCAC key-profile analysis but using only bass notes in the training and test sets. The method performs slightly worse than the full key-profile method: 71% of assessments matched the YCAC's ground truth. However, this performance is quite good considering its simplicity – even with restricting itself to only bass lines, much of the predictive power of the key-profile method is maintained. I'll return to some implications of this observation in later contentions; however, this exercise suggests that full key profiles do find key more reliably than bass profiles, but bass profiles do highlight the particular role of the $\hat{1}$-$\hat{5}$ relationship within the key-finding process.

Model #1c: Chord Profiles

In 1943, Helen Budge's dissertation at Columbia Teacher's College investigated Common Practice harmony by annotating and then tallying the chords used in a corpus of well-known selections of Western art music. While Budge's original research project focused on the normative harmonic practice of various Western European composers, Hector Bellman (2005) used this study to propose the idea of a *chord profile*, in which the expected frequencies of chords or chord roots would function akin to the expected frequencies of scale degrees in a key profile. Figure 6.4a shows this as applied to the YCAC, again tallying the opening salami slices of

254 What Is Key?

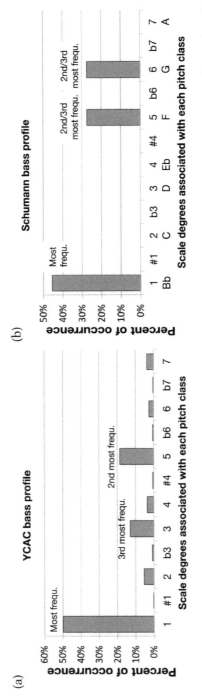

FIGURE 6.3 (a) the distribution of scale degrees in YCAC bass lines, and (b) the distribution of the bass pitch classes of Example 6.1 aligned with B-flat major

What Is Key? **255**

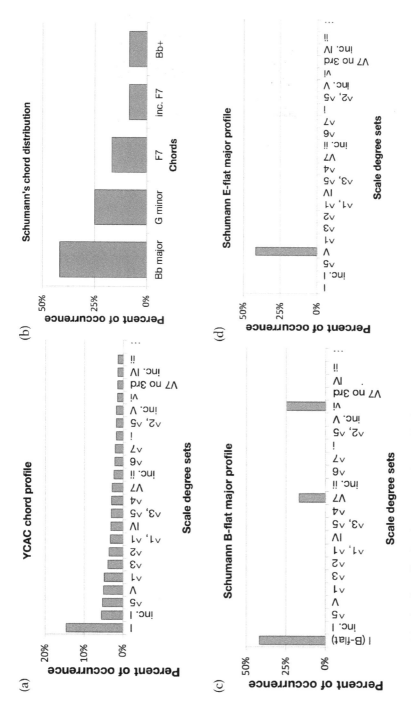

FIGURE 6.4 (a) Chord profile for the YCAC, (b) profile for the Schumann excerpt, rotated to the keys of (c) B-flat and (d) F

256 What Is Key?

each piece. The most frequent event is a I chord, followed by a I chord without a fifth. Singletons like $\hat{1}$ and $\hat{3}$ are prominently featured in the profile, as are V, V^7, and other diatonic triads and sevenths. The figure's graph stops at the ii chord, but the full profile extends to less frequent scale-degree sets, including less-used diatonic chords (like iii), dissonances, chromatic chords, and so on. While key-finding that uses a key profile or bass profile aligns a passage's most frequent pitch classes with most frequent scale degrees, a chord-profile method aligns a passage's most frequent chords and pitch-class sets with a corpus's most frequent scale degree sets – and, as we saw in Chapter 3, these will often be recognizable diatonic triads and their sub/supersets. Figure 6.4b shows the chords Schumann uses in Example 6.1: the B-flat major triad is the most frequent, followed by a G-minor triad, and so on. Just as in the key-profile method, we can rotate the passage's distribution for each possible key and observe which rotation best aligns with the chord profile. Figure 6.4c shows the resulting profile that would interpret B-flat as tonic by aligning the B-flat major triad with tonic triad and thereby orienting the most frequent event in the passage with the corpus's most frequent event. Additionally, the passage's less frequent pitch-class sets aligning with less frequent scale-degree sets in the chord profile (these less-frequent sets are not shown in the figure). For instance, the scale-degree set for an incomplete V^7 is the 33rd-most-frequent scale-degree set, and an augmented tonic set is 239th most frequent. Figure 6.4d shows an F-major interpretation of the passage, an orientation that aligns the B-flat triad with the IV triad, the G-minor triad with the ii chord, the dominant seventh with V7/IV (not shown in the chart but ranked 64th most frequent), and the augmented triad with IV+ (not shown in the chart but ranked the 498th most frequent set). Compared to other rotations, the B-flat interpretation would seem to maximize the alignment between the frequent events in the excerpt with frequent events in the chord profile. As before, this intuition can be quantified by using correlation. Of all rotations, the B-flat orientation correlates most highly with the chord profile, with a correlation value of 0.71: the passage is in B-flat. Applying the chord-profile method to the YCAC corpus produces a 69% success rate – lower than the key-profile method and comparable to the bass-profile method.

Model #2a: Salami Slice 3-Grams

In their 2008 contribution to *Music Perception*, David Temperley and Elizabeth West-Marvin argue that there are two broad ways of categorizing key-finding processes: they are either distributional or structural. The former category relies on the frequencies of single events (i.e., their distributions) to make key judgments: the key-, bass-, and chord-profile methods instantiate this approach. From a cognitive and theoretical perspective, distributional approaches frame key-finding as a process that observes a musical series, internalizes which events happen more than others, and use that information to determine a passage's key. In contrast, *structural* approaches use sequences of events – like melodic successions or chord progressions – to make key judgments. When I argued that example 6.1's authentic cadence evoked a dominant-to-tonic progression, I was making a structural claim. From a cognitive and theoretical perspective, a structural approach judges tonic based on the relationship between previous, current, and future events. The following sections outline several structural approaches to key-finding.

Figure 6.5 associates Example 6.1's cadence with scale degrees using 3-gram successions from the YCAC. Recalling from previous chapters that 3-grams are chains of three events and that salami slices are the pitch contents of each moment that a note is added or subtracted from the texture, the 3-gram comprising the example's authentic cadence is shown on the left side of Figure 6.5, beginning with an F-major-minor seventh, followed by an incomplete seventh on the same root (i.e., it omits C, the chordal fifth), and ending on the B-flat major triad. I'll call this sequence the *pitch-class 3-gram*, as the 3-gram <F7, F7-no-5th, B-flat major triad> represents the pitch-class sets of the three sequential salami slices. The middle of the example abstracts this sequence to its chord structure, showing its transpositionally equivalent set-class structure: this sequence's intervallic structure outlines a major/minor seventh, followed by an incomplete version of the same chord, concluding with a major triad rooted a fifth lower/fourth higher. (This type of structure is described as "transpositionally equivalent" because it remains the same regardless of key or transposition level; the sequence would have the same structure in C-sharp major as in B-flat major or any other key; Straus, 2005). I'll call this sequence the *set-class 3-gram*. In this chapter, the 3-grams do not include information about which pitch is in the bass – all chords in different inversions will be included in the same pitch-class set. However, some recent work (Schwitzgebel and White, 2021) has shown pitch-class content as playing a role in listeners' harmonic expectation in chord progressions.

The pie graph concluding the figure represents a corpus analysis of the YCAC. Recalling that the YCAC includes the pitch content, scale-degree interpretation, and set class for each of its slices, an analyst can tally how often

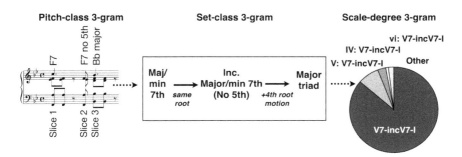

FIGURE 6.5 Associations between 3-grams and scale degrees

258 What Is Key?

sequences of set classes are associated with sequences of scale degrees. In this corpus, most (89%) of this type of set-class 3-gram is associated with the scale-degrees sets <$\hat{5}$, $\hat{7}$, $\hat{2}$, $\hat{4}$> (or a V⁷ chord), <$\hat{5}$, $\hat{7}$, $\hat{4}$> (or an incomplete V⁷), and <$\hat{1}$, $\hat{3}$, $\hat{5}$> (or a tonic triad). We can use these scale-degree connections to make key judgments about set-class sequences. The most likely scale-degree interpretation of Figure 6.5's sequence is <V⁷-inc.V⁷-I>, an interpretation that aligns B-flat with tonic.

This type of analysis was initially proposed by Ian Quinn (2010) in an article challenging the centrality key-profile analysis had enjoyed within cognitive and computational discussions of musical key to that point. There, Quinn showed that a system analogous to Figure 6.5 had a 100% accuracy rate on assessing the keys of the J.S. Bach four-part chorales.[3] While an *n*-gram chordal approach is markedly less used than key-profile analysis in corpus scholarship, several authors have adapted it to their own research, including myself (White, 2014, 2018) as well as Sears (2015), and Sears et al. (2017a, 2017b).

This approach can be tested in much the same way as I tested the key, bass, and chord profiles. Using only major-mode pieces and excluding those pieces whose openings are primarily monophonic, I create probabilistic scale-degree associations with each set-class 3-gram: the more times a set-class 3-gram is connected to a particular scale-degree 3-gram, the more probable that scale-degree orientation is. As before, I can use these probabilities to assess the key of pieces in the remaining test set.

The top rows of Figure 6.6 step through the entire key-finding process in the beginning of the Schumann excerpt. The figure's first row shows the pitch-class sets of each salami slice, represented by their common labels (i.e., the set <B-flat, D, F> is shown as a "B-flat major triad"). The second row shows the set classes, again labeled using traditional chord types (i.e., the set [0, 4, 7] is shown as a "major triad" in the figure, just as the set [0, 2, 6] is shown as an "incomplete major/minor seventh"). I additionally show the distance between each set using the shorthand of root relationships. For instance, the final pair of chords – the incomplete F-major/minor seventh moving to the B-flat major triad – are registered as two sets whose roots are separated by a perfect fourth.[4]

To be sensitive to the kinds of scale-degree sets that begin pieces, *blank positions* are added to the beginning of each piece in both the training set and test set. Figure 6.6's third row shows each set-class 3-gram, and the first of these is <__, __, major triad>, an indication that nothing occurs before the initial B-flat triad. Below these 3-grams, I show the number of times each of these 3-grams has been observed in the training portion of the YCAC. This initial set-class trigram expresses a tonic triad 258 times in that training set (i.e., the associated scale-degree trigram was <__, __, I >), while 60 times, the first triad in a piece was a V triad (i.e., the associated scale-degree trigram was <__, __, V>). If a B-flat major triad is interpreted as a tonic chord, the passage is in B-flat: 258

What Is Key? 259

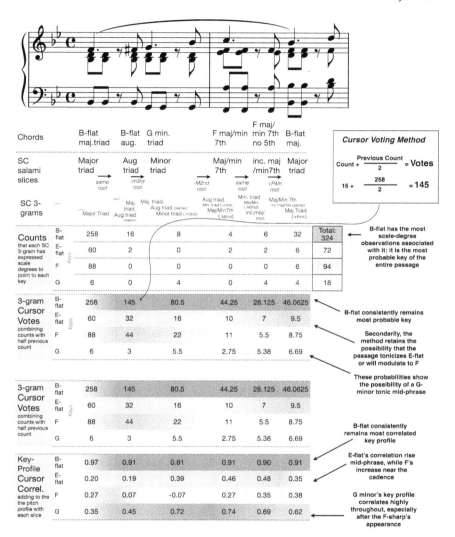

FIGURE 6.6 An outline of the 3-gram voting method and cursor-voting methods

observations in the training set support a tonic of B-flat given that the passage begins on a B-flat major triad, while 60 observations point to E-flat (the tonic if the first chord were a V triad).[5]

Below the first several rows, Figure 6.6's *Counts* table is populated with the number of observations each 3-gram associates with each key. (There are several observations from the corpus that point to more exotic tonal centers of this passage; for simplicity, I have restricted the table to those four keys that received the most observations.) Several approaches can be used to calculate the final

260 What Is Key?

key assessment of the passage; in this example, I use a simple *voting* method such that the key with the most overall observations is "elected" the passage's tonic. The voting method is not only simple, but it is also intuitive: moments that occur frequently in a corpus (for instance, beginning a piece on a major triad) contribute more weight to the final key assessment than more unusual progressions (i.e., the use of a passing augmented triad). The last column of the Counts table sums up the observations for each potential key center: B-flat received the most votes and would be assessed as the passage's tonic. (NB: the *Cursor Votes* table is applied in the next section and does not participate in the current key voting process.) Using this method results in a 72.5% success rate in the YCAC test set: while less successful than the key-profile approach, it is within the range of the bass-profile performance.[6]

Model #2b: Moment-to-Moment Key Analysis and Tonal Inertia

In David Lewin's widely cited 1986 article "Music Theory, Phenomenology, and Modes of Perception," he argues for the concept of *cursor time* in music analysis. Cursor time accounts for the vantage point a listener or analyst has within a score: like a cursor scrolling through a page of text or through lines of a computer program, a cursor's viewpoint absorbs the information it has already passed but does not yet have access to future information. (Notably, the concept is heavily indebted to work in artificial intelligence theory being done in the 1980s; Kane, 2011). Given that a salami-slicing 3-gram approach to key-finding makes assessments at nearly every moment in a piece of music, the method can capture these moment-to-moment changes in tonal perspective.

Figure 6.6's *Cursor Votes* table shows an adaptation of the previous section's voting method, but this method runs a tonal election at every salami slice – each cursor position – in an example. Following a similar approach used in Huron and Parncutt (1993), Quinn (2010), and White (2014), each moment in the analysis combines the scale-degree assessments of the current 3-gram with *tonal inertia*, importing the key assessments of the past into the current cursor-moment's calculation. This combination can be done in a number of ways; as I show in Figure 6.6, my approach simply adds half the votes that each key garnered in the previous cursor moment into the current one. Because each sequential moment will also have imported earlier information, past key assessments will continue to exert pressure on the present key assessments but with increasingly less force. (In Figure 6.6, for instance, you can see the high initial certainty associated with B-flat cascading through subsequent moments in the example.) While the same final result attains from both the Counts table and Cursor Votes table, the latter shows the ebbs and flows of secondary/possible tonal centers in the passage.

Finally, for comparison, Figure 6.6 also shows how Model 1a – the key-profile method – might be adapted to a cursor-time approach. For the calculations, I use the YCAC's major-key profile but also add the minor-key profile (again, this chapter's Appendix includes discussion of minor-mode key-finding). In this approach, the pitch-class profile expands with each consecutive chord: the pitch-class profile used for the first column in the *Key Profile Cursor Correlation* table uses only the first B-flat major chord, while the second assessments add the pitch classes of the B-flat augmented to the profile, the third adds the G-minor triad, and so on. Again, a B-flat tonic consistently correlates the highest with the key profiles, although G-minor is a strong secondary contender, especially mid-phrase. Additionally, the F-major assessments behave somewhat differently than the votes cast in the 3-gram cursor method, with F's key profile producing a negative correlation mid-phrase. I'll return to the differences between the behavior of key-profiles versus 3-gram methods; however, this example illustrates that a cursor approach to both methods can show the differing and shifting secondary key possibilities throughout this passage. (NB: Because the YCAC's opening-key labels do not note modulations or provide secondary/possible keys, I do not compare the cursor-time method to the corpus's ground truth.)

Model #2c: Harmonically Reduced 3-Grams

In my 2018 essay in *Music Theory Online*, I argued that key-finding involving harmonic successions includes a feedback loop between key-finding and chord-finding. *Chord-finding* involves grouping a musical surface into recognizable scale-degree sets, organizing the raw events of a musical surface into arrangements that align with some vocabulary of harmonies. Underneath the Schumann excerpt in Example 6.1, for instance, I noted a Roman-numeral progression: I-vi-V^7-I. To make this analysis, I implicitly decided that the augmented triad that precedes the vi chord is *not* a I$^+$ but rather a momentary passing dissonance and that the incomplete V^7 that precedes the final tonic triad is not a distinct event from the prior harmony. In both instances, I determined that an augmented tonic chord and an incomplete V^7 were not members of the underlying harmonic vocabulary of the passage and were subsumed into (or explained as prolongations of) their preceding harmonies. Importantly, I could only make these decisions by knowing the key of the passage – I needed to know the passage is in B-flat to know that the events beginning measure 2 all prolong a V^7. However, as I schematized in Figure 6.2, I also used measure 2's V^7-I authentic cadence as evidence of the passage's key. Even this simple exercise represents the feedback between chord-finding and key-finding: I needed to know the key to know the chords, but I needed to know the chords to find the key.

In Chapter 3, I outlined methods that identify underlying reduced harmonic vocabularies in musical corpora. The method alters chord progressions by combining adjacencies and by adding or subtracting notes from a progression's constituent pitch-class sets to create more probable/frequent successions. I also

262 What Is Key?

showed that applying such a reduction process on the YCAC produces a vocabulary of chords roughly analogous to diatonic triads and sevenths: broadly speaking, because diatonic triads and sevenths occur more frequently and consistently than do dissonant, incomplete, and chromatic structures, the former can be treated as the corpus's underlying harmonic vocabulary, and the latter can be reduced to these vocabulary items.

This very same process can be used to reduce a series of salami slices to conform to a corpus's vocabulary of chords. Figure 6.7 shows how the Schumann excerpt's salami slices would be parsed into vocabulary items, using Chapter 3's YCAC-derived Roman-numeral-like vocabulary. Using B-flat scale degrees, the process would notice that removing the augmented triad's F# would make that moment a subset of the preceding I chord, that the incomplete V^7 can be subsumed into the complete V^7, and that the seventh can be removed from the resulting dominant chord to make a V triad. Each of these modifications allows

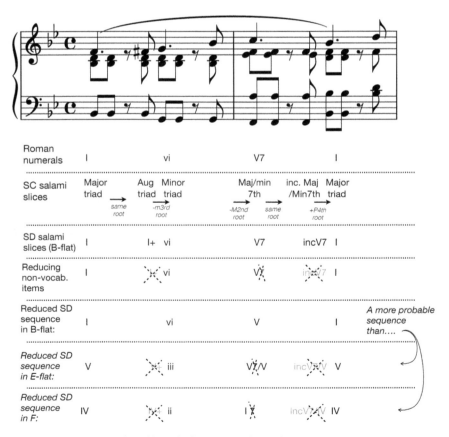

FIGURE 6.7 An example of key-finding using the reduction process

What Is Key? **263**

for the 3-gram <I, I+, vi> to become the more-probable <I-vi-V> (the latter occurs 15 times more often than the former in the corpus) and the 3-gram <V7, inc.V[7], I> to become the more-probable <vi-V-I>.

This reduction process can then be applied to the key-finding task in much the same way as the other processes I've outlined. Each potential reduction of the set-class 3-grams – and each potential scale-degree interpretation of those reductions – can be assessed, and the solution that contains the most probable/frequent 3-grams indicates the key of the passage. Figure 6.7's final rows show this method reducing the passage in the keys of E-flat and F; these scale-degree orientations, however, produce less probable sequences than those that orient B-flat with tonic. The resulting B-flat 3-grams occur 3 times more frequently than those in F and 50 times more frequently than E-flat major. The passage is therefore analyzed as being in the key of B-flat. (While this chapter's appendix describes this process in more detail, Chapter 3's online supplement also included pseudocode that outlines my computational implementation.)

I can add this reduction step to the 3-gram key-finding procedure used in the previous sections to analyze key in the YCAC. This chapter's appendix outlines this procedure in greater detail, but the process applies the first reduction method described in Chapter 3 (i.e., the process that edits chords using additions, deletions, and combinations of adjacent chords with subset and superset relationships) to three-quarters of the YCAC to create a baseline chord vocabulary. Analogous to earlier sections, I treated these reductions as my training set, and – just as in Figure 6.5 – I tallied how frequently each set-class 3-gram was instantiated by each scale-degree 3-gram. I then used those 3-grams to both reduce and assess the keys in the remaining quarter, analogous to the process in Figure 6.7. The process returned keys that aligned with the corpus's ground truth 78% of the time, a success rate that outperforms the salami-slice 3-gram method and is comparable to the key-profile analysis.

★★★

Each of these approaches represents a slightly different way of imagining musical key as being derived from surface data, and each links surface events to scale degrees very differently. Each connection between scale degrees and surface events was learned from a corpus: throughout, I derived probabilities, frequencies, and statistics from the YCAC to analyze pieces in that corpus. Importantly, in my discussion of Figure 6.1, I located the corpus as the nexus between listeners/learners and composers: listeners learn how to associate scale degrees with surface events by being exposed to a corpus, and composers ensure their key centers will be legible to listeners by adhering to the norms of corpora. By learning scale-degree associations from musical corpora, each of these models can potentially model this relationship – to represent how listeners might learn key from a corpus and how tonal norms are embedded in those corpora. In my next contentions, I follow this logic to one of its natural conclusions: if

264 What Is Key?

key orientations can be learned from corpora, then different corpora may express keys differently.

Contention #3: Because Key-Finding Models Are Corpus Dependent, They Will Change Between Styles, Time Periods, and Repertoires

In my previous contention, I demonstrated ways that corpus statistics can be used to associate pitch classes with scale degrees and thereby align a passage to some key. It follows, then, that these associations are dependent on the properties of a particular corpus and therefore can potentially change between datasets. Indeed, in Chapter 2, I introduced a method of stylistic categorization that relies on the internal consistencies and similarities within subsets of a larger corpus. There, I suggested that these kinds of groupings provide a certain understanding of *style*, insomuch as the process assembles musical pieces that are maximally similar to one another while being maximally distinct from pieces in other stylistic groupings. If these styles rely on corpus statistics to distinguish themselves from one another, and key-finding uses corpus statistics to associate surface events with scale degrees, it follows that a key-finding model trained on two statistically differentiated corpora or sub-corpora may feature two statistically different tonal behaviors.

Figure 6.8 shows several expressions of these inter-corpus differences. Figure 6.8a derives key profiles using four of the YCAC's stylistic groupings from the seven k-means clusters outlined in Chapter 2, heuristically referring to the groupings by their historical epochs. (For instance, the "Classical" cluster is that which includes Haydn and Mozart, while the "Late Romantic" cluster is that which includes Tchaikovsky and Saint-Saens.) I have also added the profile of the McGill-Billboard corpus – a corpus of 20th-century American rock and pop music analyzed in Chapters 3 and 4 – to the figure as well. While the overall contours of each distribution are similar, they are each significantly different from one other according to a X^2 test ($p < 0.01$). (I outline the details of this statistical test in this chapter's appendix, but a X^2 test determines whether the amount of events in different categories differ significantly from one another.) Figure 6.8b undertakes the identical comparison but now using bass profiles. In both profile types, the rock/pop profile presents the largest amount of difference. For instance, compared to the YCAC sub-corpora, the McGill-Billboard corpus's key profile uses markedly less $\hat{3}$ and $\hat{5}$ and more $\hat{4}$, $\hat{6}$, and $\flat\hat{7}$. Additionally, in the bass lines, the sub-dominant degree occurs more frequently in the pop/rock corpus than does the mediant, while this relationship is opposite in the YCAC distributions.

Figure 6.8c and 6.7d show how the YCAC and McGill-Billboard datasets provide different scale-degree associations for the same set-class 3-grams. Figure 6.8c compares the scale-degree associations of a major triad sandwiching an intervening major triad rooted a perfect fourth down. The most probable

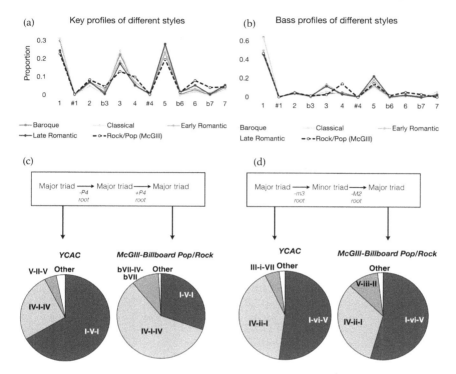

FIGURE 6.8 Some stylistic differences (a) in the key-profiles for the YCAC's subcorpora and the McGill-Billboard corpus, (b) in their bass profiles, (c) in the scale-degree associations of I-vi-V's set-class 3-gram, and (d) in the scale-degree associations of I-V-I's set-class 3-gram

interpretations of this progression are different depending on the style: the rock/pop corpus finds the most likely interpretation of that sequence to be the scale-degree 3-gram IV-I-IV, while the YCAC assesses the sequence as a I-V-I. In other words, the same corpus model trained on different datasets would assess the progression in two different keys: a C-G-C progression would be assessed in the key of C by the YCAC and in G by the McGill-Billboard corpus. Figure 6.8d shows a more subtle example: the scale-degree 3-grams associated with a major triad progressing to a minor triad by descending third root motion followed by a major triad rooted down a major second. Given these three events, both corpora identify I-vi-V and IV-ii-I as the two most-likely scale-degree 3-grams. However, while the YCAC assigns the next-most-possible sequence of scale degrees to a modulation to the relative minor, the McGill-Billboard corpus identifies a modulation to the dominant as the more plausible explanation. These different options could potentially have implications in key-finding model's final assessment of a passage – the different corpora would allocate different secondary votes to different key centers, something that might produce a different final result in particular contexts. In what follows, I demonstrate precisely this

266 What Is Key?

phenomenon: using two often-analyzed examples of tonal ambiguity, I show how different corpus-derived expectations result in different key assessments.

Corpus Analyses of Ludwig Beethoven's *Eroica* Symphony: A Case Study in Key/Corpus Connections and Historically Situated Cognition

Figure 6.9 shows a reduction of the opening passage from Ludwig Beethoven's Symphony #3, *Eroica*, including the famously colorful and evocative C-sharp fully diminished seventh of bar 7. In his landmark dissertation and

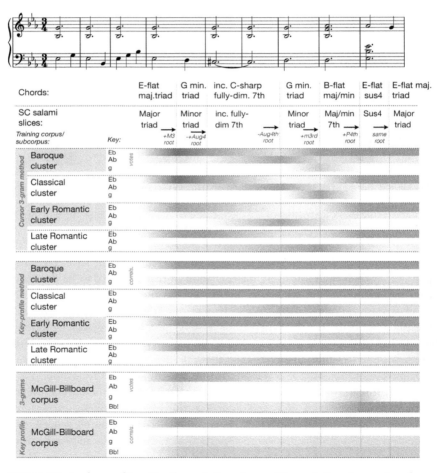

FIGURE 6.9 Analyses of L.v. Beethoven's Symphony #3, m. 3–9, using various key-finding methods trained on the YCAC sub-corpora and the McGill-Billboard rock/pop corpus

in subsequent work (Byros, 2009, 2012), Vasili Byros marshals an exhaustive review of how this moment has been interpreted over the last two centuries. In parallel with this review, he also demonstrates that the chord progression of measures 4–7 instantiates a harmonic pattern that was used quite frequently in European art music of the early 19th century. With a small army of musical examples, he shows this combination of harmony and bass line to express what he calls the *Le-Sol-Fi-Sol schema*, a musical lick designed to encircle a key's dominant with chromatic upper and lower neighbors. His examples also show this schema as falling from prominence after Beethoven's use of the progression, being used less and less as the century progresses. Returning to his examples from historical criticism, he shows that Beethoven's contemporary 19th-century listeners describe this pattern in ways that align with the *Le-Sol-Fi-Sol* pattern: they hear the <E-flat, D, C-sharp, D> succession as evoking a tonal center of G. He then shows that as the 19th century comes to a close – and the use of the *Le-Sol-Fi-Sol* pattern fades from memory – listeners are less apt to hear a momentary evocation of G-minor and instead are more likely to hear generic tonal ambiguity. In other words, as listeners become exposed to repertoires with fewer instances of the pattern, they are less likely to hear G-minor within this passage. Byros calls this kind of tethering between a musical interpretation and a repertoire *historically situated cognition*, or the approximation of what someone at a certain place and time might have understood. Crucially, by connecting listeners' key assessments of this passage with the historical use of the *Le-Sol-Fi-Sol* schema, historically situated cognition becomes another instance of corpus statistics acting as a foundational connection between listeners and composers. And by identifying changes in tonal hearing with changes in musical corpora, Byros's argument resonates with my own: how one hears Beethoven's C-sharp depends on the corpus one is using to interpret it.

Using the four YCAC sub-corpora as training data (the same sub-corpora outlined in Figure 6.8), Figure 6.9 shows the results of both a cursor 3-gram key-finding approach and a cursor key-profile analysis for measures 3 through 11 of a reduction of the symphony. Instead of populating the chart with votes or percentages, I use shading to show which keys are exerting the most dominance at each cursor point. (For the analysis, I now use both major and minor profiles and 3-grams; again, I discuss minor-mode key-finding in the appendix. A rendition of this analysis appears in White, 2014.) Each version of the key-profile method returns essentially the same results: using this method, the passage is in E-flat major, with a G-minor as a secondary possibility. The 3-gram approach, on the other hand, shows both more fluctuation in keys and more variation between sub-corpora. Each assessment begins solidly in E-flat major, and the large number of votes cast for this key in the opening measures provides E-flat some inertia throughout the example. However, the sub-corpora diverge in their approach to the famous C-sharp harmony of bar 7. The two Romantic training sets suggest G-minor emphasis as a strong possibility in that bar, a

268 What Is Key?

possibility strengthened by the arrival of the G-minor triad in bar 9. (This sequence approximates Byros's *Le-Sol-Fi-Sol* schema.) The classical and Baroque corpora, on the other hand, contain more tonal ambiguity. These models' interpretation of bars 7 and 9 invoke several different keys, indicating a fog of uncertainty that only begins to dissipate in bar 10. Both contain a fleeting smudge of G-minor in bar 9, but both also entertain A-flat as a possible tonicization in bar 7, "hearing" the C-sharp as a D-flat. (Notably, Beethoven himself activates this enharmonic interpretation in the movement's recapitulation when this moment is respelled as a V_2^4/IV and resolves to an A-flat harmony.)

Importantly, these tonal variations arise because of the differences in the sub-corpora: the datasets contain different associations between successions of set classes and scale degrees. For instance, the Romantic sub-corpora contain sufficient examples of Byros's *Le-Sol-Fi-Sol* pattern for measures 6 through 9's scale-degree sequence to solidly manifest a G-minor interpretation. Reflecting Byros's argument that exposure to music of different time periods results in familiarity with different musical patterns – a familiarity that informs how a listener hears musical key – these models morph and shift their key assessments as the tonal practices of their underlying styles morph and shift.

Finally, Figure 6.9 also contains analyses trained on the McGill-Billboard rock/pop corpus. This model finds B-flat a much stronger tonal contender than any of those trained on the YCAC. (I've placed an exclamation mark next to that key to indicate its unique role in this corpus's analysis.) Because the sub-dominant degree is more pronounced in this corpus (see Figure 6.8a and 6.8b) and the sub-dominant triad rivals the dominant triad for frequency (see Chapters 3 and 4 and Figure 6.8c), music that highlights he pitch classes E-flat and B-flat in this corpus is quite plausibly in the key of the latter. Additionally, because tonic sevenths are relatively frequent in the rock/pop corpus, the B-flat seventh chord can potentially function as a tonic within this style. Finally, while G does assert itself within the key-profile approach, the key plays a markedly minor role in the 3-gram approach when using this corpus. Indeed, the rock/pop corpus has no frame of reference for measure 7's C-sharp harmony – the corpus contains no instances of the *Le-Sol-Fi-Sol* schema nor any other set-class 3-grams that use this chord structure. No tonal judgments can be made at this point; no votes are cast, and only tonal inertia contributes to the key assessments at this cursor point. In sum, while the subtle differences in the YCAC's sub-corpora result in variations in how measures 6 through 9 are read, the greater stylistic differences of the McGill-Billboard corpus produce even greater variations in the keys being assessed within this example.

A Chordal and Key Analysis of the Prelude to Tristan und Isolde

The stylistic fluctuations we've seen in the analyses thus far can potentially affect the kinds of chords a model uses for its analyses: in my earlier review

What Is Key? 269

(Model 2a), I outlined an approach that united the 3-gram key-finding process with the harmonic reductions introduced in Chapter 3. If chords and keys are tethered to a corpus for their identity, then the same piece of music might not only be analyzed with different keys depending on the corpus, but it might also be analyzed using different chords.

Figure 6.10 excerpts another often-analyzed moment that combines both harmonic and tonal ambiguity, the opening of Richard Wagner's Prelude to *Tristan und Isolde*. The passage begins with a rising minor sixth that, after descending by a half step, blooms into the half-diminished chord that will come to signify the protagonist Tristan throughout the opera. After some half-step squirming through two different augmented-sixth sonorities, the passage ends on an E-dominant seventh, ostensibly a half-cadential gesture in the key of

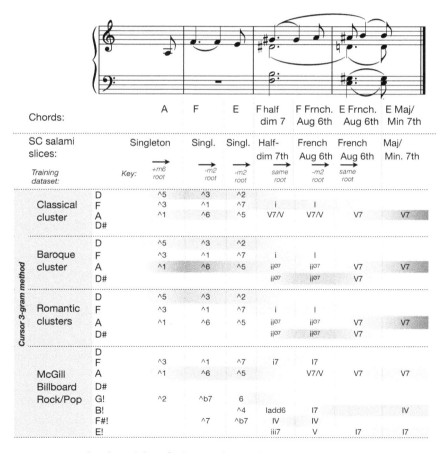

FIGURE 6.10 Chord- and key-finding analyses of the opening of Richard Wagner's Prelude to *Tristan Und Isolde*, using both the YCAC and McGill-Billboard corpus

270 What Is Key?

A-minor. Commentators have argued for more than a century and a half about the multifaceted ambiguity that accompanies the Tristan chord, disagreeing about which pitches are heard as chord tones, which are heard as incidental dissonances, and what keys are evoked throughout. Kurth's (1920) reading, for instance, hears a modified V^7/V in A minor – he hears the second measure expressing a B^7 harmony, with the expected F-sharp appearing as an F-natural. On the other hand, Arend (1901) and D'Indy (1903) hear the measure as a $ii^{\varnothing7}$ in A-minor, with the expected D-natural appearing as a D-sharp. Even more exotically, Rothgeb (1995) shows an identical passage in measures 35 and 36 of Beethoven's Piano Sonata Opus 31, no. 3, i; however, while the passage is "at pitch," it appears enharmonically in E-flat, respelling the D-sharp, G-sharp, and B-natural as E-flat, A-flat, and C-flat, respectively (or a $ii^{\varnothing7}$ in the key of E-flat). Furthermore, if one similarly reinterprets the downbeat of measure 3 enharmonically, the harmony is very close to a B-flat dominant seventh (i.e., the A-sharp becomes a B-flat, and the E-natural could be considered a potential dissonant chromatic neighbor to an F). In other words, Rothgeb's Beethoven citation suggests that this sequence could enharmonically be analyzed as a momentary $ii^{\varnothing7}$-V^7 in the key of E-flat.

Underneath the musical excerpt of Figure 6.10, I show the results of the YCAC sub-corpora and the McGill-Billboard corpus's chord/key-finding analyses using a 3-gram cursor method. Again, I use shading to indicate a key's strength and show the harmonies to which each moment is reduced in the charts' cells. Now, because the early- and late-Romantic training sets produced nearly identical results, I've folded them into the same row in the figure; as in the Beethoven analysis, I use both major and minor training data. For the harmonic reduction, I now allow for chords to be edited by moving pitch classes by a half step, a process I described at the end of Chapter 3. (I provide a more-detailed explanation and demonstration of this key-finding process in my appendix.)

These analyses indeed show different combinations of chords and keys arising from different corpora and sub-corpora. Throughout the example, none of the analytical models produces particularly clear tonal orientations – until the final cadence, no key casts an overwhelming number of votes. This tonal indeterminacy produces a certain fragility around the key centers, a fragility that magnifies the variations in the different corpus models: because no single key center exerts a domineering presence in the excerpt, small changes between different datasets' 3-gram probabilities can produce marked differences in which key is assessed as the "tonic" at each moment.

Initially, the opening solo melody is analyzed differently across different models. While the Baroque and pop/rock datasets more often associate this gesture as beginning on tonic, the Classical and Romantic datasets associate such a beginning more strongly with the dominant; the rock/pop corpus even finds this melody to begin on $\hat{2}$ sufficiently frequently to entertain the key of G. The "Tristan" chord – the half-diminished sonority of measure 2's downbeat – is also interpreted in several different ways. Using the reduction process to edit the chord's B-natural to a C and removing the D-sharp, each model briefly considers the chord to possibly function as a minor tonic chord in the key of F, although this key is quickly abandoned as the phrase moves forward. Evocative of Kurth's reading, as the phrase moves into measure 3, the classical sub-corpus edits measures 2 and 3 into a <V^7/V, V> progression, with the reduction process shifting measure 2's F and G-sharp to F-sharp and A, respectively, and removing measure 3's A-sharp. Because of different prevailing frequencies in their sub-corpora, the Baroque and Romantic models favor a ii$^{\varnothing7}$ chord in A-minor (replacing the D sharp with a D) at the cadence, similar to Arend and D'Indy. However, resonating with Rothgeb's enharmonic Beethovenian reading, both these models also favor a momentary shift to E-flat/D-sharp: both models read the F half-diminished seventh as a ii$^{\varnothing7}$ in that key and edit the following downbeat's <E, G#, D, A#> set into an A-sharp dominant seventh (or, the enharmonic dominant seventh in E-flat; I show these edits explicitly in my appendix). Finally, the rock/pop model continues to have difficulty conforming the cadential sequence to its corpus's expectations. Additionally, because this style contains frequent seventh chords of various stripes on each degree of the scale, the model finds several plausible scale-degree alignments for the passage's seventh-y surface texture but produces no single overwhelming key orientation for the cadence.

Summary of Contention #3

Five broad points arise from the preceding analyses. First, these examples illustrate connections between key and corpus, and even between chord and corpus. For instance, the different frequencies of the *Le-Sol-Fi-Sol* schema in various sub-corpora contributed to varying assessments of tonal ambiguity, and the different amounts that ii$^{\varnothing7}$ and V^7/V participate in cadences within the YCAC's sub-corpora resulted in different harmonic and tonal analyses of the "Tristan" chord. Second, it is remarkable how well the keys and chords identified in the YCAC's various epochs reflect the historical commentary surrounding the analyzed passages. In the Beethoven example, the disagreements primarily concern the tonal orientation of the C-sharp diminished chord in measure 7, and these disagreements parallel historical commentary. In terms of the Wagner example, analysts argue whether measure 2 is better heard as an applied dominant or a supertonic seventh, just as our corpus models reduce this measure to these two possibilities. Third, as I note in Chapter 3, there exists some overlap between the model's reduction process and notions of consonance and dissonance. This topic is most clearly demonstrated in the harmonic reductions of the "Tristan" example. When a model identifies the downbeat of bar 3 as an A-sharp dominant seventh in the key of D-sharp, that A-sharp is being treated as a chord tone; however, when that measure is treated as a V^7 in the key of A, that same A-sharp is treated as a non-chord tone. My models' behavior, then, not only emphasizes the connections between key, chords, and corpus but provides a reminder that the notions of consonance, dissonance, and chord tone are similarly constructed from corpus-derived expectations.

Fourth – and perhaps most salient to this chapter's larger argument – the behaviors of these models reinforce the role of style in musical communication, especially in communication involving key. Each of the key-finding models I use is trained on stylistic groupings derived in Chapter 2, groupings designed to be internally coherent while being unique from one another. In that chapter, I argued that such a corpus-based approach to style supported musical communication: with a consistent and predictable musical practice, listeners can learn clear expectations, and composers can rely on these expectations when writing music. If key is a connection that listeners make between scale degrees, pitch classes, and sets, and if that connection can be learned from a corpus, and if composers rely on these expectations to embed key orientations in their music, then the consistency and stability of a coherent and unique style would aid in this connection. Indeed, the evident difficulty that the rock/pop corpus has when analyzing key in the "Eroica" and the *Tristan* Prelude serves as a case in point: as a corpus removed from the style of the original compositions, the McGill-Billboard corpus produces tonal assessments that neither conform to historical readings, nor – frankly – to my musical intuitions about the passage. (Indeed, cognitive evidence strongly suggests that listeners have different tonal expectations in classical music versus rock music: Vuvan and Hughes, 2019.)

Finally, I should stress that these corpus analyses are not making specific historical claims. Figure 6.10 is not claiming that a listener from 1750 Vienna would certainly hear the antepenultimate chord of the *Tristan* except as V^7/V. Even with its relative size, the YCAC is nowhere near sufficiently large to make generic cognitive claims, nor is it sufficiently historically informed to account for the wide variety of listening experiences that individuals might have. Instead, using different corpora from different historical periods shows that tonal expectations *can* shift and change between styles. Once again reflecting Byros's notion of historically situated cognition, different historical situations will engender different listening experiences, producing listeners with different tonal expectations.

Contention #4: Corpus-Based Key-Finding Algorithms Lay Bare Our Assumptions About How Tonal Orientation Works

Participating in a decades-long slow-burning argument over computational key-finding, David Temperley (1999) asks the question "What's key for key?" – what musical events are most important for listeners and composers when they interpret pitch events as scale degrees? In this and in subsequent work (e.g., Temperley and Marvin, 2008), he argues for key-profile analysis as the ideal model for identifying music's tonal orientation. Pitting key-profile analyses against other models (e.g., a melodic 2-gram model), Temperley concludes that aligning scale degrees with a passage's distribution of pitch classes will find key with more precision, elegance, and greater alignment with human behavior than will other models. Responding to this proverbial gauntlet, Ian Quinn (2010) – using the salami slice model I outlined earlier – retorts that chord progressions might instead be more accurately described as "key for key." My own work (2018) has entered this fray by showing my reduction-based key-finding process to not only align with human assessments but also mimic the cognitive key-finding process itself. Indeed, by pitting various methods against one another – the key-profile, the bass-profile, the salami-slice, and the harmonic-reduction methods – I am engaging in precisely this sort of argument. Throughout, I reported how often each model's results aligned with the keys annotated in the YCAC, and in so doing, I measured the relative efficacy of each key-finding approach.

While I will return to the merits of various key-finding approaches in a moment, the very fact that such a battle can be fought using code and corpora illustrates one of corpus analyses strongest powers. As I outlined in Chapter 1 in my discussion of the Martian effect, a corpus model requires a researcher to make explicit their assumptions, to operationalize their process, and to limit how their own biases affecting the resulting analysis. In other words: *corpus models of musical key lay bare assumptions about how tonal orientation works in an objective, testable, and observable way.* If a computational researcher wishes to show how listeners can garner key from a musical surface's distribution of pitch classes, they must show how those distributions are learned and then how the resulting profiles are deployed in the service of key-finding, choosing which pitches are represented, how they are represented, and how they are related to scale degrees. Similarly, if a researcher wishes to argue that chord progressions are crucial to key-finding, they must define the length of those progressions, determine how sequences of chord progressions combine, and even specify what is meant by "chord." In corpus-based computational key-finding, each choice and decision can be a potential claim about the inner workings of musical key, and the explicitness of these claims makes such methods very useful for litigating and theorizing this concept.

And these investigations connect to higher-stakes topics in tonal theory: debates over how music communicates its key centers are debates over the nature of tonality itself. Earlier, I noted that the two competing accounts of musical key have been debated within the music cognition literature, with one camp pointing to evidence that pitch distributions primarily account for a listener's perception of a key, while the other advocates for the role of intervals (indeed, the Temperley/Quinn exchange is part of this wider debate). As I noted, the different key-finding models used in this chapter can be grouped into these two categories, with key- and bass-profile approaches modeling the former approach and *n*-gram models instantiating the latter. By modeling scale-degree relationships, these key-finding procedures operationalize notions like hierarchy and key relationships in very specific manners. The distinctive amounts of frequency given to each scale degree in a key profile specifically derives a scale-degree hierarchy from a corpus while also showing the potential changes to this hierarchy between corpora: while notes of the tonic triad are the most frequent in the YCAC, the subdominant is among the most frequent degrees in the rock/pop McGill-Billboard corpus. Similarly, the concept of tonal relationships within a piece of music might also be observed in the inner workings of these models, particularly in the secondary and tertiary key areas produced in a key-finding process. The analyses of Figure 6.6, for instance, identified B-flat as the prevailing key within the Schumann excerpt, but also noted F, E-flat, and G-minor as potential tonal contenders: in this example, we can imagine these keys as "close" or "related" to the tonic. (The idea that key relationships arise from statistical or behavioral similarities is present in Carol Krumhansl's earliest work on key profiles: Krumhansl and Shepard, 1979; Krumhansl and Kessler, 1982; Krumhansl, 1988).

The list of overlaps between tonal theories and these computational models is long. As I argued in my earlier equations between consonance/dissonance and frequency (see Chapter 3), Harrison's (2016) harmonic fluctuation could be analogized with fluctuations in a chord's probability. Tymoczko's (2011) requirements for harmonic consistency could be found in the chord vocabulary used in a harmonic reduction algorithm, while his understanding of macro-harmony could be analogized with the disposition of pitches within a key profile. Hynes-Tawa (2020) points to myriad historical commentary that links the notion of "tonic" to a relationship between pitches separated by fifth, and my corpus models demonstrate the situations in which these relationships arise. The YCAC's key profile – and especially its bass profile – shows the tonic and dominant being the two most frequent scale degrees: these two degrees are clearly foundational to tonal expression in this repertory.[7] However, the substantive rise in the sub-dominant degree in the rock/pop corpus's profiles illustrates how style dependent such pronouncements about key and tonality can be: the tonic/dominant fifth is less foundational to key expression in this corpus.

Finally, several theoretical understandings of key posit that listeners can impose a central tonic scale degree at the center of a passage even if that note is acousti-cally absent – that listeners can use other cues besides the apparent emphasis of a tonic scale degree to cognitively organize a passage around that note (Rings, 2020). The behavior of the 3-gram cursor analyses within the *Tristan* passage formalizes this idea – the reading snap toward an A tonal center not when it observes an A harmony but rather when it identifies the half-cadence that ends the phrase: A becomes tonic when the scale degrees of its dominant are assigned, computationally operationalizing how key can be assessed even in the absence of a tonic.

While much more could be said about the resonance between this chapter's corpus data and broader understandings of tonality, my point is less about the specific debates surrounding tonality's definitions and criteria and more about the role a corpus-based key-finding model can play in constructing those criteria. Corpus-based key-finding requires an analyst to formalize each step within some process; by painstakingly operationalizing this procedure, each assumption, argument, and theoretical claim can be located, tested, observed, and debated. In this way, corpus-derived models provide an invaluable tool for theoretical and cognitive studies of key and tonality.[8]

Contention #5: Corpus-Based Key-Finding Suggests That There Are Several Pathways Toward a Passage's Key

To this point, I have avoided claiming that one particular key-finding method is *better* than any other. Far from being the symptom of some sort of tonal agnosticism, this avoidance betrays my underlying heterodoxy and ecumenicism: in my estimation, a full and rich definition of musical key involves multiple overdetermined explanations of how scale degrees are garnered from a musical surface. This chapter's models – their results, their behaviors, and their connections to music theory and cognition – support this liberal approach to key. For instance, while it is true that key-profile methods perform with the highest degree of accuracy in the earlier analyses, this approach also neglects some of the most salient aspects of the passages I've analyzed. Recall from my discussion of the "Eroica" analysis that the example's C-sharp (enharmonically D-flat) triggered a momentary shift toward the key of A-flat in the classical sub-corpus's 3-gram model and that Beethoven thematizes this tonal suggestion in the movement's recapitulation. This tonal ambiguity hinges on the identity of the chord; the drama of interpreting (and reinterpreting!) a set class within different contexts is crucial to this passage yet is absent from the key-profile analysis.

But the fact that certain musical phenomena are unavailable to key-profile analysis does not make that approach *wrong*, no more than its higher precision makes it *right*. Key profiles and scale-degree *n*-grams each show something different about the tonal orientation of a passage; furthermore, they also explicitly model what exact characteristics of a passage are connected with which particular tonal centers. The pitch distribution of the "Eroica" passage might solidly point toward E-flat major, while the chord progressions contain an evocation of A-flat. Both claims are true, both derive from corpus-based connections between scale degrees and surface events, and both highlight different tonal relationships in the passage. From this perspective, *key* is not the result of a set slate of musical attributes but arises from some array of possible attributes, variously and concomitantly activated in different situations.

My contention – that key is not some immutable musical event but rather a mutable property – is admittedly bold. However, it is also eminently reasonable: my approach simply suggests that connections between a passage's observable

276 What Is Key?

events and its scale degrees can be made in several ways, and the variations between those options can highlight different aspects of the passage.

Contention #6: Tonal Corpus Statistics and Key Are Interlocked in a Chicken-and-Egg Relationship

To this point, I have argued (1) that a key-finding model can learn connections between musical events and scale degrees from a corpus, (2) that these connections are historically and stylistically situated, (3) that they may represent a relationship between the listener and composers, and (4) that the engineering of a corpus-based model operationalizes and formalizes aspects of these relationships and connections. My previous contention then suggested (5) that there are multiple potential parameters that may be useful in key-finding and (6) that different musical situations may suggest different and even multiple key-finding approaches.

The current contention returns to the relationship between corpus and key. By systematically deriving key-finding models from musical corpora, my approaches have located the statistics that create tonal concepts like key and scale-degree hierarchy within a corpus. Evoking the noisy channel and the Meaningful Corpus Model, I've argued that listeners use those connections to both learn about and undertake the key-finding task. From this perspective, the norms listeners use to hear key are created when a listener is exposed to a corpus: in this sense, *corpus statistics create tonal hierarchies*. But, on the other hand, we can just as easily argue the opposite. After all, reversing the noisy channel or the MCM would show composers relying on inherited stylistic norms and conforming to the prevailing tonal tendencies of a repertoire to make choices that are tonally legible to their listeners.[9] Here, a composer's understanding of tonality and key provides the events of a corpus. From this perspective, *tonal hierarchies create corpus statistics*.

Such intractable chicken-and-egg dynamics come part and parcel with the MCM/noisy channel. Composers take listeners' constraints into consideration when writing corpora, listeners learn from these corpora, and composers use inherited corpora to create their own styles. This tangle, however, has one common central nexus: the corpus. Corpus-based key-finding, then, finds itself at the center of listening, learning, and compositional processes, a dynamic I summarize in Figure 6.11. Again demonstrating the power of corpus analysis, such an approach to the study of musical key can make both compositional and perceptual claims, insomuch as a corpus sits at the center of the swirling tautology between musical learners and producers.[10]

However, as Figure 6.11 indicates, for a corpus to act as a tonal mediator between listeners and composer, the corpus must have accessible characteristics. Tonal listening does not come with a user's manual, and composers and performers cannot rely on their listeners receiving explicit tutelage on how to hear key: instead, key is something listeners implicitly learn simply by hearing music

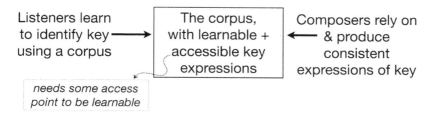

FIGURE 6.11 Dynamics of learning key from and embedding key in a corpus

and by being exposed to corpora. Because of this, the mechanics behind tonal orientations can't be *hard* to learn – the entire key-finding process must be an implicit, not conscious act, accessible and noticeable by listeners who are passively and casually consuming the music. We must be able to learn about key by going to concerts, listening to music in the car, or singing in a choir – *not* by explicitly learning about the inner mechanics of musical key in a classroom or by reading textbooks. Because it models both the kinds of events composers and listeners use when engaging with the concept of musical key, corpus-derived computational analysis provides a particularly useful tool when investigating how listeners might learn to associate perceived surface events with cognized scale degrees. My next contention argues for a specific location of this access point: the recurrent power-law distributions of the pitch contents of tonal music.

Contention #7: Key Is the Result of Power-Law Distributions, Distributions That Could Manifest in Any Number of Pitch-Based Parameters

In Chapter 4, I argued that exponential distributions were crucial to the definitions of the tonic and antitonic functions, with the former being a category of chord that occurs exponentially more frequently than any other chord category and the latter being the second-most-frequent category. Computationally, such distributions allow for these harmonies to serve as the pillars around which a categorization algorithm can organize a dataset: being exponentially more frequent than other events, these types of harmonies provide an initial access point for the algorithm by helping it organize and group less frequent chords by relating them to the corpus's most frequent events. I also argued that these types of distributions are important to human cognition, citing two foundational laws from psychology. Fechner's Law, on the one hand, describes the well-documented fact that humans notice differences in natural phenomena not when they increase or decrease linearly, but rather by some exponential factor. As I noted in the earlier chapter, we would certainly notice a difference in loudness if two violinists were playing in unison and then another two players joined in. However, if 20 were playing and another 2 joined in – even though the ensemble has again increased by the same number of violinists – we may not even notice. Instead, to make a similarly noticeable change in loudness, we would instead need to exponentially augment (perhaps again doubling) the ensemble.

The second law, Zipf's Law, describes human tendencies to reuse gestures, patterns, and words. According to the law, once someone speaks or writes a word in a conversation, speech, or essay, they are likely to use that word again; each time they subsequently use the word, it becomes more and more likely that they will yet again reuse the word. This compounding dynamic creates an exponential distribution – what I described in Chapter 4's appendix as a power-law curve. In that appendix, I graphed the word usage of Chapter 3, and Figure 6.12 reproduces the first 10 ranks of this distribution, with the most used word "the" occupying rank #1, and the 10th-most-used word "chord" occupying rank #10. Notice that less frequent ranks do not decrease their constituent frequencies by some constant amount (they don't, for instance, each consistently decreases by 2%). Rather, their relationships are best described by a curve with an immediate drop-off and a subsequent gently sloping plateau. Again, the appendix to Chapter 4 explains this curve in more detail, but in short: as ranks decrease, they become exponentially less frequent. These types of distributions have been shown to be ubiquitous in musical corpora across a variety of musical domains (Zanette, 2006).

This research suggests that power-law curves not only describe the kinds of distributions that are noticeable to human perception but also are endemic to how we produce language and music. Figure 6.13 provides examples of each musical domain used in my various key-finding models in each of the corpora: key profiles, bass profiles, salami slices, and set classes in both the YCAC and McGill-Billboard corpora. The lowest two graphs show the scale-degree

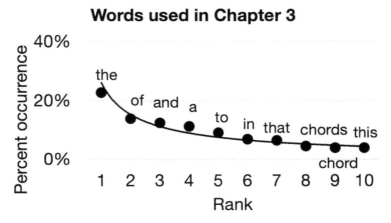

FIGURE 6.12 The frequency distribution of the 10 most used words used in Chapter 3, with the accompanying power-law curve

What Is Key? **279**

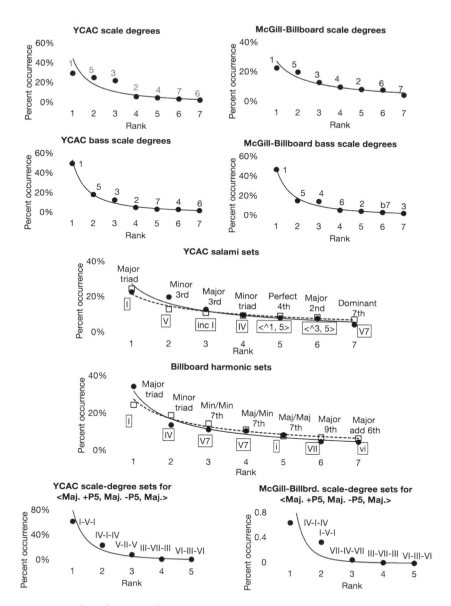

FIGURE 6.13 Distributions of parameters used in key-finding within the YCAC and McGill–Billboard corpora

3-grams associated with the set-class 3-gram used in Figure 6.8c within both the YCAC and the McGill-Billboard corpora. All follow power-law curves.[11]

In Figure 6.11, I noted that the corpus-centered feedback loop between listeners and composers needed some access point: because key orientation needs to be easily and implicitly learnable, tonal organization needs to be easily and casually accessible. I would argue that – because of their cognitive accessibility and recurrent presence in musical corpora – power-law distributions have the potential to teach listeners about musical key. Because of these distributions, it is plausible – and even potentially easy – for a listener to implicitly notice the overwhelming frequency of a I triad and its constituent scale degree when listening to such Western Common Practice music as constitutes the YCAC. Having internalized which events are most frequent in a style, the expected structure and relationship of the most frequent events within a piece in this style, a listener might then observe a distribution like that of Figure 6.14 – the distribution of chords and pitch classes in the Schumann excerpt – and align the pitch classes of the B-flat major triad with those they had heard most frequently in the larger corpus. In this sense, key-finding involves matching a passages' individual power-law distributions with the distributions of an entire corpus. In sum: by recognizing an analogy between the most frequent events of a corpus and a passage's most frequent events, a listener is engaging in key-finding, and this recognition is made possible by the power-law distribution of both the larger corpus and the individual piece.

In Chapter 4, I argued that such distributions sidestep the potential tautology within the tonic function's definition – i.e., tonic is the most stable harmony, and the most stable harmony is tonic – by linking what it means to be a tonic harmony with its location in a frequency distribution. Power-law curves may also help overcome the insufficient definitions of scale degrees that have haunted my discussions of key in this chapter. In each model's training data, key-oriented scale degrees were derived from a corpus's preexistent key labels, and those

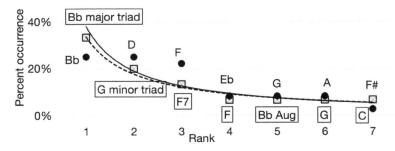

FIGURE 6.14 The Schumann excerpt's pitch-class and scale-degree set distribution

degrees' statistical properties were used to derive scale degrees from other testing data. Here, scale degrees in the training data equaled scale degrees in the testing data, without any larger definition of what it meant to be, for instance, a tonic or dominant scale degree. Additionally, my prior contention outlined a tautology between listeners' and composers' definitions of key: a listener's definition of key was how composers expressed key, and a composer's definition of key was how they expected listeners to hear key.

However, if scale degrees are defined by their position in a power-law curve, then the key-finding process has an initial access point to begin its organization of tonal space without relying on endless tautologies and self-reference. The *tonic key center* could mean the pitch and chord that sit at the peak of an exponential distribution, and the remainder of scale degrees can then be identified with different positions in this distribution. Harmonic relationships can be built from these scale-degree sets, and ultimately, chord progressions with scale-degree associations can be drawn from these sets. From this perspective, pieces, corpora, and styles that reliably express key – that are *tonal* – organize into easily accessible, learnable, and producible power-law distributions. To put it succinctly: *key is the distribution of musical parameters along a power-law curve in such a way that allows a hierarchy of chords and pitch classes to arise.*

Contention #8: If Key-Finding Is Defined by Particular Distributions, Then Aspects of a Corpus That Do Not Exhibit Such Distributions Are Not Useful for Key-Finding

Not *all* musical parameters in all corpora follow power-law distributions. The first two graphs of Figure 6.15 show the distribution of pitch classes throughout the YCAC and McGill-Billboard corpora. While pitch classes without accidentals are used relatively more than their chromatic counterparts, the decline in usage is far more gradual than across other domains. In contrast to scale degrees, pitch classes – at least in and of themselves – are not distributed along a power law in the corpora.

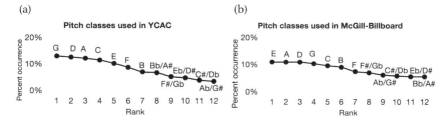

FIGURE 6.15 Pitch-class distributions in the (a) YCAC and (b) McGill-Billboard corpus

282 What Is Key?

I would argue that this more gradual distribution shows that absolute pitch identity is less useful to key-finding. If Figure 6.14's power-law distribution suggests that B-flat expresses the tonic of the Schumann excerpt, it was not due to the identity of the pitch class: a listener does not expect the note *B-flat* to be the most frequent. But a listener *does* expect the tonic scale degree to be most frequent. The former parameter does not use a power-law distribution; the latter does.

Earlier, I argued that different corpora – and even different musical situations – can express key differently using different kinds of musical statistics. In light of my current contention, that argument can be honed: key can be expressed differently by varying the order in which events appear within a power-law distribution or even which musical domains express that distribution. Comparing the YCAC and McGill-Billboard corpus's scale-degree and chord distributions provides an example of the former: while both corpora distribute scale degrees and scale-degree sets along power-law curves, the ordering within those distributions varies.

Figure 6.16 shows an example of corpus distributing a different combination of musical parameters along a power-law curve. Figure 6.16a shows the distribution of chords in HookTheory.com's "Popular Chord Progressions." Contrasting with the McGill-Billboard corpus's survey of mid-20th-century American popular music, the HookTheory corpus favors recent millennial and postmillennial pop. (To extract the distribution from the website's data, I scrape each progression listed on the webpage hooktheory.com/theorytab/common-chord-progressions along with the number of songs that use that progression; multiplying each chord by the number of songs that use that progression provides a basic distribution of each chord's relative usage.[12]) The first four chords, V, I, IV, and vi, are consistently used in the corpus's most frequent progressions (like I-V-vi-IV, vi-V-IV-V, and I-vi-IV-V); this consistency results in a distribution in which these four chords appear within 3 percentage points of one another, after which the remaining chords occur much less frequently.

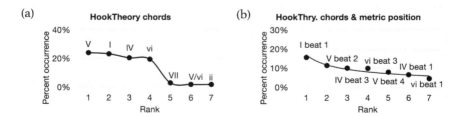

FIGURE 6.16 The distributions (a) of chords in HookTheory.com's "Popular Chord Progressions" and (b) of the same chords associated with their metric position

In contrast to all other distributions of scale-degree sets we've observed thus far, this distribution does *not* follow a power law. Crucially, as many analysts of this style have noted (de Clercq, 2021; Duinker, 2019; Nobile, 2020; Richards, 2017; Temperley, 2018), music that loops through these four most frequent chords – using progressions like the corpus's most frequent I-V-vi-IV – can be tonally ambiguous (i.e., that progression could just as easily be III-VII-i-VI in the relative minor). From a corpus-based key-finding vantage point, this ambiguity makes sense: because each set occurs with a similar frequency in this corpus, a progression like <C-major triad → G-major triad → A-minor triad → F-major triad> will not obviously point to any of those chords as necessarily the tonic. The lack of a power-law curve within the corpus's chord distribution therefore aligns with scholars' assessments that harmonic progressions – especially those that feature these top four chords – can lack tonal determinacy in this style.

Figure 6.16b, on the other hand, applies the website's ordering and metric information to show the distribution of chords combined with their metric weight.[13] This distribution now solidly follows the contour of a power law: the exponentially most frequent event is to align the tonic on beat 1. Again, this distribution aligns with the intuitions of analysts, as several commentators note (Duinker, 2019; Nobile, 2020) that the metrical orientation of a harmonic loop can determine which chord acts as tonic within that song. Now, my <C-G-a-F> progression will solidly point to C-major, if the C-triad occurs on the downbeat, aligning with the I-on-beat-1 that sits at the top of the power-law distribution.

Importantly, I am not suggesting that contemporary pop is not tonal but simply suggesting that its harmonic content reflects key in a different way than does harmony in classical music or even in 20th-century popular music. The contours of Figure 6.16b suggest that this repertoire communicates key with a combination of meter and harmony, indicating that meter may play a stronger role in key expression in this style than in other repertoires.

However, such diversity is to be expected. Many recent commentators (e.g., Harrison, 2016; Hynes-Tawa, 2020; Long, 2020) argue that notions of key and tonality may be best defined using a suite of overlapping and overdetermined musical parameters – from pitch to texture to meter to phrasing – that may be manifested and prioritized differently in different repertoires. My corpus models support this viewpoint: the connections between scale degrees and surface events varies between styles; as the current contention demonstrates, even the parameters used to express these connections can change between corpora. However, these different manifestations and prioritizations can often be located in the frequency distributions of various musical parameters. The following section continues to investigate this diversity, observing how power-law distributions can show key and key-like organization within pieces and corpora that are not traditionally considered *tonal*.

Contention #9: If Key-Finding Is Defined by Particular Distributions, Then Music With a Flexible Relationship Should Demonstrate This Flexibility Within Its Musical Distributions

As Harrison (2016) argues, there are many ways for music to eschew the trappings of Western European tonal norms while still retaining some fraction of that vestment. In what follows, I show several brief analyses of music that exists outside of traditional key/tonal expression but whose similarities with tonal music can be observed in their distributions. First, I show some examples of early-20th-century pieces creating hierarchies of chords and pitches using much the same techniques as do earlier tonal pieces: by treating each piece as an individual "corpus" – a dataset unto itself – I can illustrate how these pieces prioritize and emphasize certain events over others. I end by analyzing a corpus of Malian jembe performances and suggest that the power-law distributions essential to key expression might extend outside of Western European practices and even outside of the pitch domain.

Charles Ives: Sonata No. 2, iii, "The Alcotts" (1915)

Figure 6.17a shows the distribution of harmonies within the third movement of Charles Ives's Sonata No. 2. Aligning with the prevailing academic practices used to analyze 20th-century posttonal composition, my orthography now uses modulo-12 set-class and pitch-class set annotations. (However, those unfamiliar with this system can simply treat these as arbitrary designations with little harm to the overall argument behind these analyses.) The set-class distribution shows that major and minor triads ([0, 4, 7] and [0, 3, 7]) perch on top of a power-law curve, while the B-flat major, E-flat major, and C-minor triads (<10, 2, 5>, <3, 7, 10>, <0, 3, 7>) top the pitch-class sets' distribution. To my ear, the piece audibly features these harmonies – while the movement includes no shortage of complex and adventurous Ives-ian dissonances (Burkholder, 1990), the movement primarily oscillates between hymn-like developments of the sonata's overall theme and ostentatious quotations of Ludwig Beethoven's 5th Symphony (Gann, 2015). The hymn-like sections generally feature a B-flat/E-flat pairing (a pairing that treads ambiguously between a plagal and authentic relationship), while the Beethovenian passages often center around the pitch C, the quotation's original key. Indeed, these are the pitch classes and pitch-class sets that play a prominent role in Figure 6.17a's distributions. These distributions show aspects of the piece that share characteristics with the tendencies of tonal corpora – the movement's chords and chord types follow a power-law curve. In my estimation, by following a key-like distribution, the piece encourages its listeners to hear certain pitch-class sets, set classes, and intervallic relationships as central to the piece, and even tonic-like. In "The Alcotts," this distribution

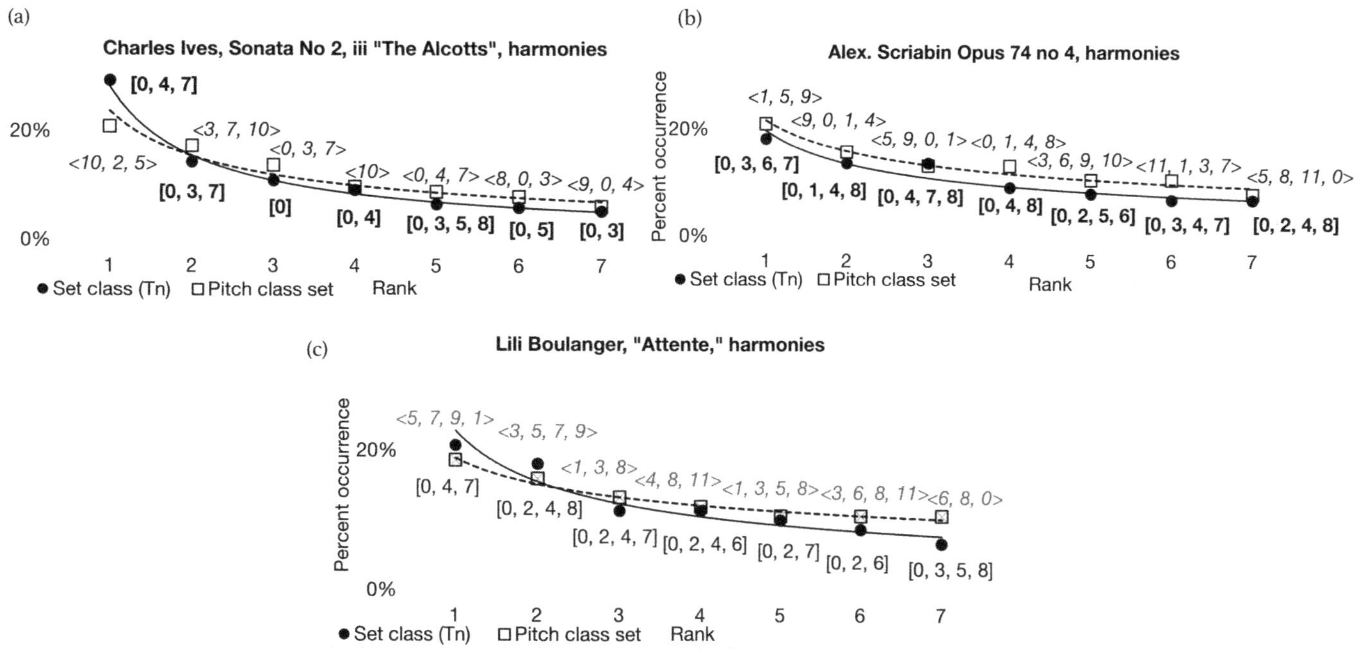

FIGURE 6.17 Power-law distributions in (a) Charles Ives's Sonata No. 2, iii, "The Alcotts," (b) Alexander Scriabin's Prelude Op. 74, no. 4, and (c) Lili Boulanger's "Attente," ILB 1

286 What Is Key?

lends a centricity and stability to B-flat, and affords E-flat a secondary priority, while drawing a listener's ears to moments that use major and minor triads.

Alexander Scriabin, Prelude Op. 74, No. 4 (1914)

Figure 6.17b shows the distribution of the most frequent harmonies in Alexander Scriabin's Prelude Opus 74 No. 4, one of his last published pieces. The two most frequent pitch-class sets are a D-flat augmented triad (<1, 5, 9>) and an A triad with both major and minor thirds (<9, 0, 1, 4>). The two most frequent set classes are [0, 3, 6, 7] and [0, 1, 4, 8]; the former can be imagined as a minor triad with a tritone added above the root, while the second could be alternately described as an augmented triad with a half step added above its root or a major triad with a half step added below its root. In tonal corpora in general – and in my earlier analyses of the Ives example – the most frequent pitch-class sets were always members of the most frequent set classes. However, in this piece, set classes and pitch-class sets are decoupled in the distribution: the set classes of the most frequent pitch-class sets (the augmented triad [0, 4, 8] and the double-third triad [0, 3, 4, 7]) are not highest ranked in the set-class distribution and are instead ranked fourth and sixth most frequent in Figure 6.17b.

Still, each of these most frequent structures plays an important role in the unfolding of the piece. Example 6.2a shows the first phrase of the prelude, annotating the piece's most frequent pitch-class sets and set classes. Scriabin adopts a sentential phrase structure, with measures 1 and 2 and their respective upbeats constituting the sentence's first basic-idea presentation and then its repetition, while bars 3 and 4 move into continuation rhetoric (Caplin, 1998). Each of the piece's most frequent structures plays a distinctive role in the phrase's construction: the A double-third triad begins both presentations of the basic idea, and these presentations also feature manifestations of the [0, 3, 6, 7] set class, the most frequent set class. The continuation then features the second-most-frequent [0, 1, 4, 8] set class and touches on what will become the piece's most frequent pitch-class set, the D-flat augmented triad. The excerpt "cadences" on the A double-third triad, the same sonority with which it began. Even in this short phrase, Scriabin associates two of the most frequent sets with a sense of beginning – the A double-third triad and the [0, 3, 6, 7] set class – and two with continuation – the D-flat augmented triad and the [0, 1, 4, 8] set class.

Examples 6.2b and 6.2c show some large-scale ramifications of these associations. Globally, the piece follows a rough ternary structure: the A double-third triad that ends the first sentence elides into the beginning of what initially appears to be a second sentence (the upbeat to m. 5) but dissolves into a developmental passage that yields to a truncated recapitulation of the opening material (the upbeat to m. 18). Example 6.2b shows measures 10 through 14, part of the developmental middle section. The passage fixates on the [0, 1, 4, 8] set, continually returning to the piece's first- and third-most-frequent pitch-class

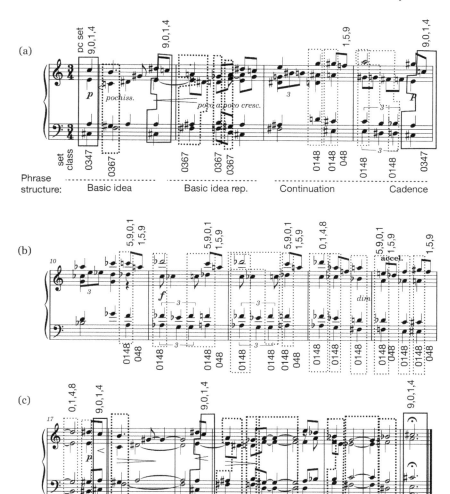

EXAMPLE 6.2 A. Scriabin's Op. 74 no. 4, (a) mm. 1–4, (b) mm. 10–14, and (c) 17–20, annotating the piece's most frequent pitch-class sets and set classes

sets, <1, 5, 9> and <5, 9, 0, 1>. Example 6.2c, on the other hand, shows the piece's return to the opening motive in its last measures. This recapitulation begins and ends with the A double-third triad (<9, 0, 1, 4>), and the texture is saturated with set class [0, 3, 6, 7]. In both these passages, sets that were associated with the initial phrase's continuation are employed in the prelude's developmental section – the entire form's "continuation" – while the sets involved in the initial presentation and cadence are used to signal the recapitulation and to close the piece.

288 What Is Key?

Surely, the distribution and usage of harmonic material in this piece departs from those I used in my key-finding models. For instance, while the A double-third triad seems to function as a point of departure and return and the [0, 1, 4, 8] set acts as a point of furthest remove, the difference between the piece's most frequent pitch-class sets and its most frequent set classes makes it difficult to argue for a crisp analogy between these chords and a traditional tonic/anti-tonic relationship. However, it is also evident that the moments emphasized by the form correspond to some of the piece's most frequent sets and that the function of these sets add to the drama of this piece. Scriabin's prioritization of certain structures produces distributions that follow power-law curves, ensuring a prominence – and cognitive salience – of these posttonal structures that mimics the prominence of tonal structures.[14]

Lili Boulanger, "Attente," ILB 1 (1910)

Figure 6.17c shows the relative frequencies of set classes and pitch-class sets within Lili Boulanger's song "Attente." As in the Scriabin example, the distribution features a slight mismatch between the two domains. In the set-class domain, the major triad is the most frequent set, followed by two whole-tone subsets ([0, 2, 4, 8] and [0, 2, 4, 6]) and a major triad with an added ninth ([0, 2, 4, 7]). The first two pitch-class sets, however, are members of the two whole-tone subsets, <5, 7, 9, 1> and <3, 5, 7, 9>; <0, 3, 8> is then the third-most-frequent pitch-class set and is a member of the fifth-most-frequent set class [0, 2, 7].[15] Example 6.3a shows how the song's vocal entry immediately highlights these sets; the dotted box shows the chords using the [0, 2, 4, 6] set class, and the solid boxes show the [0, 2, 4, 8] set classes. While both measures begin differently, they return to the same chords in their second halves, a return that features the song's two most frequent pitch-class sets. This dynamic continues through the initial section of the song, and the consistent return to this motive at the same pitch level ensures these chords' strong showing in the overall frequency distributions. (Note that the melody contributes an added detail not captured by a computational analysis: it outlines both of these most frequent pitch-class sets in its entry.) Examples 6.3b and 6.3c show two moments later in the piece in which set classes [0, 2, 4, 6] and [0, 2, 4, 8] prominently return. After several measures of harmonic exploration and motivic development, the piece enters a whole-tone collection in measure 12, allowing these whole-tone subsets to return. Measure 19, then, ushers in a quasi-recapitulation, returning to the opening's oscillating texture. While many aspects of this passage vary and are transposed from the opening passage, the measures return to set-class [0, 2, 4, 8] in their second halves, preserving the opening's near-obsessive usage of this harmony.

While Ives's and Scriabin's most frequent sets featured their respective pieces' moments of centricity and stability, Boulanger's most frequent sets behave markedly differently in this piece. The song begins and ends with C-sharp major

What Is Key? **289**

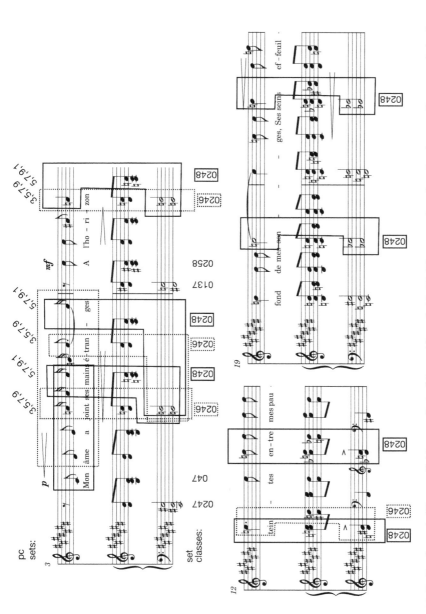

EXAMPLE 6.3 L. Boulanger's "Attente," (a) mm. 3–4, (b) m. 12, and (c) 19–20, annotating the piece's most frequent pitch-class sets and set classes

harmonies – insomuch as the harmony provides an initial point of a departure and the piece's point of final repose, C-sharp serves as something of a rhetorical tonic. However, the piece's frequency distributions do not necessarily lend commensurate emphasis to this harmony: several other pitch classes and pitch-class sets are more prominent, and while the major triad is the most frequent set class in this piece, the C-sharp major triad is less frequent than, for instance, the E-major triad. Furthermore, instead of emphasizing harmonies related to the C-sharp major triad, the piece consistently draws its listeners' attention toward such harmonies as the [0, 2, 4, 8] set class and the <5, 7, 9, 1> pitch-class set. To my ear, this lack of emphasis creates an unnerving sense that the piece's final arrival on C-sharp major is arbitrary at best and unwarranted at worst. However, in my own hearing, this unease resonates with the song's poetic content. The lyrics by Maurice Maeterlinck describe an expressionist mixture of dread and satisfaction behind unfulfilled expectation (*"Attente"*); the final C-sharp resolution even falls on the denouement of the poem's final word: "lies" (*"mensonges"*).

Some Contrasting Posttonal Examples From the Early 20th Century

In each of these analyses, I showed posttonal composers distributing set classes and pitch-class sets in ways that mimicked tonal corpora, with these pieces drawing attention to certain structures in the same way that a tonal piece might draw attention to its tonic, dominant, and further diatonic harmonies. I then commented on how the statistical emphasis on certain harmonies resonated with the formal, motivic, and even poetic content of these pieces. None of these pieces are *tonal*; however, if musical key is based in the distribution of pitch events along a power-law, then these posttonal pieces use aspects important to key-finding to either mimic tonal forces or draw listeners' attention to particular harmonic events.

Importantly, such distributions are not *necessary* in posttonal music. Figure 6.18 outlines three pieces whose distributions do not reliably follow power-law curves. First, Anton Webern's Op. 27, no. 1, (1935) distributes its pitch classes more or less uniformly (as would be expected in a piece of traditional serialism). However, illustrating Webern's prioritization of prime form [0,1,6] throughout this piece, the set-class distribution follows a power-law, with the most frequent sets either instantiating, inverting, or being a subset of that prime form. Again exemplifying a rigorous serial approach, Pierre Boulez's "Notation No. 6" (from *Douze Notations*, 1945) also uniformly distributes his pitch-class sets, while set classes descend somewhat linearly. Finally, reflecting the octatonic experimentation underpinning Béla Bartók's "Diminished Fifth" (*Mikrokosmos, 101, Vol. IV*; Burkhart and Rothstein, 2022), the song nearly uniformly distributes sets composed of the intervals available in that collection.

What Is Key? **291**

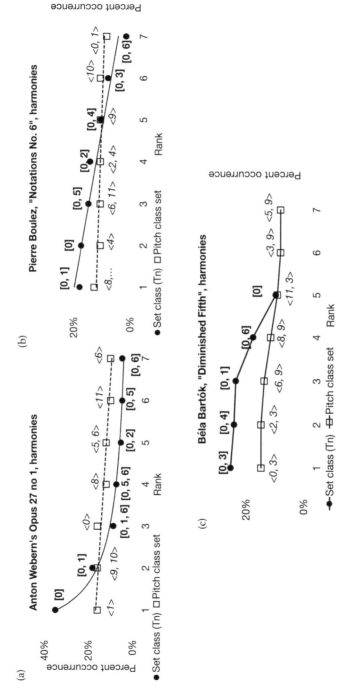

FIGURE 6.18 Set class and pitch–class set distributions in three further 20th-century posttonal pieces

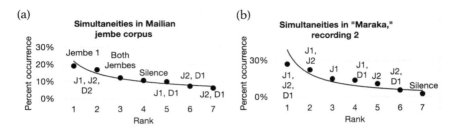

FIGURE 6.19 Power-law distributions of simultaneities in (a) a corpus of Malian jembe ensemble performances and (b) a single performance

Distributions of Instrumental Simultaneities in a Malian Jembe Corpus

Finally, it is possible that such tonal/key hierarchies expressed by power-law curves might manifest in non-pitch domains in other repertoires. Figure 6.19 shows the power-law distribution of drum simultaneities present in both the overall Malian jembe corpus used in Chapter 5's analyses and the distribution for a single performance of the tune "Maraka" (marked "Maraka 2" in the corpus; Polak et al., 2018). While more ethnographic and culturally based cognitive research would need to be done on this front, the similarities are suggestive that power-law distributions might play significant organizing roles across different domains in different musical traditions in ways that may resonate with key and tonal organization.

Summary

In this chapter, I have advocated for a flexible approach to musical key that does not rely on any specific musical parameter or particular set of rules but rather leverages any musical parameter that maps a hierarchy of scale degrees onto pitch classes. After outlining several approaches to key-finding, I suggested that each approach has its individual strengths. I also demonstrated how these key-finding processes were tethered to musical corpora, drawing connections between scale degrees and surface events from observations of musical datasets. I also showed that these connections are style dependent and that the same passage can be analyzed differently depending on which corpus/style is being used to train a key-finding algorithm's expectations.

More broadly, I argued that within a noisy-channel/MCM conception of key, a passage's tonal orientation should be accessible to musical learners, discernable by learners, and communicable by composers. This constant feedback between music's listeners and its producers creates a tautology when it comes to key: composers produce key-oriented music by relying on the connections between pitch events and scale degrees harbored by their listeners, while listeners rely on composers to consistently produce learnable pitch/scale-degree connections. However, I also suggested that such pitch/scale-degree connections must be *obvious* to be implicitly learned by exposure to the music. In other words, given that tonal pieces do not come with a user's manual and most listeners are never explicitly taught how to hear key, tonal music must contain some slate of generally accessible features to allow listeners to learn how to hear key simply by listening to key-oriented music.

Power-law distributions provide this access. Cognitive research has shown this sort of exponential distribution to help observers discern differences in the world around them and to also be the product of natural language production. My analyses showed that these distributions are ubiquitous in the data my models used for key-finding. Drawing on Chapter 4's argument that *tonic* is a corpus's most frequent category of event, I suggested that scale-degree hierarchies may initially arise from the ordering of a corpus's pitch-class and set-class distributions and that this hierarchy provides a point of entry as a listener learns to associate key with musical passages. Conversely, composers can rely on tonal centers being reliably communicated when their music expresses power-law distributions. Key-finding, from this standpoint, involves aligning an individual passage's power-law distribution of some pitch parameter (i.e., pitch classes, pitch–class sets, etc.) with that of a larger corpus's scale degrees. I showed that this type of distribution is not unique to tonal music but can also create a hierarchy of harmonic events in posttonal music and may even contribute to the organization of musical events in non–pitch-based repertoires.

There is much that my approach omits. For instance, this chapter did not use sets with designated bass notes, so the role of chord inversion within key-finding was left unaddressed in this chapter. Nor did I undertake a complete overview and investigation of computational key-finding or even ways to organize a surface for that task (see White, 2013; Yust, 2017; Shanahan et al., 2022; for broader overviews of these topics).

However, my approach to key does – I hope – contribute to a broader understanding of this concept. While established definitions of key and tonal orientation often rely on specific musical characteristics, my concept of key relies on how often events appear within a corpus: my methods focus on the statistics that describe a corpus's pitch events rather than on the pitch events themselves. Instead of pointing to some specific suite of musical characteristics, I am advocating that key can be instantiated using any number of musical parameters, as long as those parameters express a scale-degree hierarchy using a power-law distribution.

In my conception, then, musical key shifts from a property of musical events – of cadences, melodic emphases, and bass patterns – to a property of a corpus. I began this book by arguing that corpus analysis treats the tonal tradition as a text to be read, and in the ensuing chapters, I have used that stance to read

294 What Is Key?

stylistic groupings, chord vocabularies, meter, and harmonic and functional categories. In this chapter, I have turned that focus onto a foundational tenet of the tonal tradition: the transformation of pitches into scale degrees. This chapter has suggested that – similar to the topics of previous chapters – not only is key-finding tethered to individual corpus statistics, but the underlying tenets and mechanics of the concept itself are best located in the properties of musical corpora.

Postscript: Interpreting Tonality with Musical Statistics

In a lot of ways, this chapter is not a work of empiricism or music science but one of interpretation. I began this chapter by outlining models of key-finding; however, we have little conclusive evidence about how listeners engage in the act of hearing a key. The models I outlined are constructed around indirect observations, using evidence such as behavioral responses, composers' key labels, and my own intuitions to justify their usage. None of this evidence is *direct* observations – I am not directly observing the cognitive engineering that occurs in the head of a listener as they turn pitch perceptions into cognitive scale degrees. In Chapter 1, I argued that humanities-oriented corpus analysis is particularly suited to such situations, bridging the gap between the empirically observable and the intuitively speculative using evidence-based persuasion and argument. Key modeling – at least in its current form – involves such speculation and interpretation, negotiating available cognitive research and molding observable corpus statistics into reasonable, plausible, and convincing accounts of musical key.

In Chapter 1, I also suggested that a humanities-oriented approach to corpus analysis might treat corpora as texts to be read, digested, and creatively analyzed. My speculations surrounding power-law distributions do precisely this type of analysis. My arguments identified a recurrent and observable statistical property of tonal corpora, and I link that property with behavioral data, cognitive theory, and music analysis. In the end, I have not *proven* anything, but instead, I've shown my *reading* of these corpus properties – a plausible and convincing analysis of the existing data informed by behavioral, psychological, and theoretical research.

Outside of any specific claims about key, tonality, listeners, and corpora, I would argue that this type of inquiry shows the potential of music-theory-oriented corpus analysis. In other words, this chapter models how to analyze corpus data creatively and playfully in the service of a larger interpretive project. Furthermore, in my brief readings of three posttonal pieces, this chapter also demonstrated how corpus-informed theories can then be used to inform and inspire music analysis. In both these specific and general instances, I hope to have demonstrated the power of corpus analysis to provide a useful and

Notes

1. Huron (2006) lays out this basic formulation explicitly, and *countless* other theorists do so implicitly. There are certainly many ways to complicate this statement, from the ways that keys were potentially formulated more fluidly in earlier 16th- and 17th-century repertoires (Long, 2020) to the comfortable ambiguity of tonal centers within much contemporary American popular music (Nobile, 2020). Additionally, it should be noted that other definitions of the word "key" have been historically present at certain periods in music history; this terminological inheritance does not undermine my use of that term.

2. Importantly, key profiles did not initially arise from corpus studies but rather from behavioral "probe-tone" studies. In such work (pioneered by Carol Krumhansl), listeners are presented with a tonal context followed by a single pitch randomly selected from the chromatic aggregate. The listeners are asked to rate how well that single pitch fits into the previously heard tonal context. These studies found that tonic pitches were rated highest, followed by other notes of the tonic triad, followed by the remaining diatonic pitches, and with chromatic pitches rated lowest. Krumhansl (1990) then notes that these ratings align with the frequency with which scale degrees tend to occur within tonal corpora, thus giving rise to the corpus-derived key-profile concept.

3. His process reserves 35 chorales from the dataset to serve as the test set and uses the remaining chorales to train the model to make associations between set-class progressions and scale-degree progressions. In contrast to Figure 6.5, Quinn uses 2-grams instead of 3-grams, and his set classes note which member occurs in the bass. Quinn's model also includes a notion of "tonal inertia," or the preference of a previous moment's key to exert some preference on the current moment. If an F^7-to-B-flat progression was preceded by a passage clearly in B-flat, the program would solidly assess that 2-gram in the key of B-flat. However, if that progression was preceded by a series in the key of E-flat, the *inertia* of E-flat would exert pressure on the program to read that 2-gram as V^7/V-V in that key. This pressure is similarly accounted for in my *cursor voting* method, described in what follows.

4. More specifically, my programming calculates the intervallic distance between the first pitch classes in two adjacent normal-form orderings of set classes, essentially tracking the distance between the zero-th position within sequential set classes.

5. The counts reported here might seem low given the size of the YCAC. However, as I describe in Chapter 3, most events on the surface of the YCAC are not tertian sonorities but instead reflect an immense diversity of chord structures. A harmonic reduction of this corpus's music would have a very different number of events; however, given that the current example is examining the musical surface, it seems appropriate to use the YCAC's surface events.

6. In instances in which a set-class 3-gram in the test set did not occur in the training set – instances in which no scale-degree 3-grams could be associated with a piece's successions of set classes – no observations were recorded (and no key votes were cast) at that moment.

296 What Is Key?

7. The models also provide an opportunity to test a proposition like Hynes's. The frequency of the tonic/dominant pairing is exaggerated in the YCAC bass profile, almost to the exclusion of other scale degrees. This profile can therefore test the extent to which the tonic/dominant pair is sufficient for key-finding. However, while the bass-profile method performed relatively well, it underperformed relative to the key-profile method, suggesting that – while the frequency of the tonic/dominant degrees provides much tonal information – the more nuanced contours and hierarchies of a key profile offer important information. Along these lines, I also reproduced the key-profile's assessment of the test-set's key annotations, but with key, swapping in the YCAC's bass profile for the YCAC's key profile. The bass profile again underperformed the key profile. I conversely swapped the key profile for the bass profile and analyzed the key of only bass lines. Now the key profile overperformed compared to the bass profile. These comparisons confirm that the more nuanced contours of the key profile add value to a key-finding process.

8. One aspect of key-finding that I have not discussed is the role played by meter. Heuristically, my chord-reduction procedure partly models this role by using metric boundaries to create its chords, something I discuss in my appendix. However, other key-finding models explicitly operationalize the role of meter. For instance, Symons (2017) uses melody/bass pairings schemata to do key- and meter-finding. Additionally, metric emphasis has been shown to affect both corpus properties and listeners' assessment of key and tonal stability (Prince, 2014; Prince and Schmuckler, 2014; Prince et al., 2009).

9. Temperley (2004) argues for the concept of *communicative pressure* in which listeners have some limit as to the amount of information they can process when making sense of music. He suggests that this accounts both for the pace of developments in musical styles and for the trading off of complexities between musical domains (e.g., when pitch content becomes complex, rhythm complexity decreases, and vice versa), although preliminary studies from Josh Albrecht and Peter Martins have recently questioned this supposition.

10. However, for a key-finding model to participate in this chicken-and-egg tangle, the musical events and statistics must be available to a listener. Regardless of how effective a model might be, if it uses a characteristic of a corpus that is unhearable or unlearnable to make its key assessment, it cannot be connected to human experience. A model that, for instance, assigns key by only using a piece's closing harmonies might be very effective, but it would not have a clear connection to a listener's experience – listeners don't reserve all key judgments until the end of a piece or passage. Another more subtle example might involve *skip-grams*, a type of *n*-gram that use non-adjacencies: for instance, a skip-gram might use – say – every other event or every 5th event to create gapped 2-grams. This technology can be used to investigate an event's broader context, for instance, observing the kinds of harmonies that tend to appear in the general proximity of some chord (Jones, 2017; Sears et al., 2017a; Sears and Widmer, 2020). However, research has shown listeners to have a difficult time learning grammars based on non-adjacent events (Creel et al., 2004) and even to have trouble remembering musical events that occurred more than several seconds in the past (Cook, 1989). A key-finding model using skip-grams would have a potentially tenuous connection to a listening and learning experience. (Such connections are certainly not impossible! The work of Sears et al., 2017b, goes some distance on this front.) Additionally, deep learning algorithms like recurrent neural networks present a similar situation to skip-grams. Such machine-learning techniques are *very* useful and offer high degrees of precision (Ju et al., 2017); however, they often rely on

non-adjacencies and involve a complex engineering that may not mimic human thought processes.

11. Importantly, I do not mean to imply that power-law distributions function the identical way in spoken language as they do in music. In language, the highest-frequency words tend to be articles and prepositions, while in music, the most frequent chords are tonics and dominants: the former are considered the least structural parts of a sentence, and the latter are considered the most structural aspects of a musical phrase. This discussion merely identifies similarities in how different domains of human production and cognition are distributed within their respective corpora.

12. Website accessed February 10, 2022. Using the website's API (a process of interacting with the website's dataset using a remote interface) produces a very similar distribution. I chose this approach because it not only demonstrates the kind of corpus research that anyone with an internet browser can undertake but also implies metric/hypermetric information, which the API does not provide.

13. For this analysis, I assumed the reported progressions to be in a quadruple metric pattern, the prevailing meter for popular music (see Chapter 5). The first chord was assumed to be on a downbeat, the second on beat 2, and so on. This process is imprecise, as some songs within each progression's category will feature rotated progressions: some I-V-vi-IV progressions would become vi-IV-V-V progressions. To address this issue, I took 20 random songs from each chord-progression category and weighted the rotations based on that distribution. In my 20 random songs from the I-V-vi-IV category, I found that 10 began with I, 8 began with vi, 1 began with V, and 1 began with IV. I modified the distribution to reflect rotations of this progression proportional to the rotations I observed (i.e., half began with I, 40% began with vi, and so on). Again, my methods are just meant to approximate the role meter plays in this corpus; a more thorough study of this repertoire would entail more precise methods.

14. In this piece, Scriabin's adherence to traditional phrase structure and cadential rhetoric results in the piece's chord distribution sharing features with tonal distributions. This observation resonates with the argument in Long (2020) that the regularity of early-modern European popular poetry contributed to musical settings of those texts returning to the same chords at predictable intervals. Long suggests that this regularity gave rise to a predictable phrase and cadential rhetoric, which may have played an influential role in the development of European Common Practice tonality in the following centuries. In many ways, this Scriabin piece exhibits the same dynamics as Long's early-modern vocal composers, creating a harmonic regularity by adhering to an expected phrase structure.

15. It should also be noted that many of these most frequent sets (in both the Boulanger and the Scriabin) are either sub- or super-sets from one another or are related by minimal voice leading transformations. A fascinating follow-up study would apply Chapter 3's reduction tactics to a posttonal repertoire.

References

Aarden, B. J. 2003. *Dynamic Melodic Expectancy*. Ph.D. Dissertation, The Ohio State University, Columbus, OH.

Albrecht, J. D., and D. Huron. 2014. "A Statistical Approach to Tracing the Historical Development of Major and Minor Pitch Distributions, 1400–1750." *Music Perception*, 31/3, 223–243.

298 What Is Key?

Albrecht, J. D., and D. Shanahan. 2013. "The Use of Large Corpora to Train a New Type of Key-Finding Algorithm: An Improved Treatment of the Minor Mode." *Music Perception*, 1 September, 31/1, 59–67.

Arend, M. 1901. "Harmonische Analyse des Tristanvorspiels." *Bayreuther Blätter*, 24, 160–169.

Bellman, H. 2005. "About the Determination of Key of a Musical Excerpt." *Proceedings of Computer Music Modeling and Retrieval*. R. Kronland-Martinet, T. Voinier, and S. Ystad, eds. Pisa, Italy: Computer Music Modeling and Retrieval, pp. 187–203.

Brown, H. 1988. "The Interplay of Set Content and Temporal Context in a Functional Theory of Tonality Perception." *Music Perception*, 5, 219–250.

Brown, H., and D. Butler. 1981. "Diatonic Trichords as Minimal Tonal Cue Cells." *In Theory Only*, 5/6–7, 37–55.

Brown, H., D. Butler, and M. R. Jones. 1994. "Musical and Temporal Influences on Key Discovery." *Music Perception*, 11/4, 371–407.

Browne, Richmond. 1981. "Tonal Implications of the Diatonic Set." *In Theory Only*, 5/6, 3–21.

Budge, H. 1943. *A Study of Chord Frequencies Based on the Music of Representative Composers of the Eighteenth and Nineteenth Centuries*. Doctoral dissertation, Columbia University Teacher's College, New York.

Burkhart, C., and W. N. Rothstein. 2022. *Anthology for Music Analysis*, 7th edition. Boston: Cengage Learning.

Burkholder, J. P. 1990. "The Critique of Tonality in the Early Experimental Music of Charles Ives." *Music Theory Spectrum*, 12/2, 203–223.

Butler, D. 1989. "Describing the Perception of Tonality in Music: A Critique of the Tonal Hierarchy Theory and a Proposal for a Theory of Intervallic Rivalry." *Music Perception*, 6/3, 219–242.

Byros, V. 2009. *Foundations of Tonality as Situated Cognition, 1730–1830*. Dissertation, Yale University, New Haven, CT.

Byros, V. 2012. "Meyer's Anvil: Revisiting the Schema Concept." *Music Analysis*, 31/3, 273–346.

Caplin, W. E. 1998. *Classical Form: A Theory of Formal Functions for the Music of Haydn, Mozart, and Beethoven*. Oxford: Oxford University Press.

Cook, N. 1989. *Musical Analysis and the Listener*. New York: Garland.

Creel, S. C., E. L. Newport, and R. N. Aslin. 2004. "Distant Melodies: Statistical Learning of Nonadjacent Dependencies in Tone Sequences." *Journal of Experimental Psychology: Learning, Memory, and Cognition*, 30, 1119–1130.

de Clercq, T. 2021. "How Should Corpus Studies of Harmony in Popular Music Handle the Minor Tonic?" *Proceedings of Future Directions in Music Cognition*. J. Albrecht, L. Warrenburg, L. Reymore, and D. Shanahan, eds., Columbus, OH, 43–48. https://doi.org/10.18061/FDMC.2021

D'Indy, V. 1903. *Cours de composition musicale*. Paris: Durand.

Duinker, B. 2019. "Plateau Loops and Hybrid Tonics in Recent Pop Music." *Music Theory Online*, 25/4. www.mtosmt.org/issues/mto.19.25.4/mto.19.25.4.duinker.html

Fétis, F. J. 1958. *Traité complet de la théorie et de la pratique de l'harmonie*. Paris: Schlesinger.

Gann, K. 2015. "A Pre-Concert Talk for the Concord Sonata." Delivered at the Kansas City Central Library and at Western Missouri State University. kylegann.com/Concord-Preconcert.html

Harrison, D. 2016. *Pieces of Tradition: An Analysis of Contemporary Tonality*. New York: Oxford University Press.

Huron, D. 2006. *Sweet Anticipation: Music and the Psychology of Expectation.* Cambridge: The MIT Press.

Huron, D., and R. Parncutt. 1993. "An Improved Model of Tonality Perception Incorporating Pitch Salience and Echoic Memory." *Psychomusicology*, 12, 154–171.

Hyer, B. 2002. "Tonality." *The Cambridge History of Western Music Theory.* T. Christensen, ed. Cambridge: Cambridge University Press, pp. 726–752.

Hynes-Tawa, L. P. 2020. *How the Phrygian Lost Its Finality.* Ph.D. Dissertation, Yale University, New Haven, CT.

Jones, A. 2017. *Harmony and Statistical Temporality: Toward Jazz Syntax from Corpus Analytics.* Ph.D. Dissertation, Yale University, New Haven, CT.

Ju, Y., N. Condit-Schultz, C. Arthur, and I. Fujinaga. 2017. "Non-Chord Tone Identification Using Deep Neural Networks." *Proceedings of the 4th International Digital Libraries for Musicology Workshop (DLfM 2017),* Shanghai, China: Shanghai Conservatory of Music, 13–16.

Kane, B. 2011. "Excavating Lewin's 'Phenomenology'." *Music Theory Spectrum*, 33/1, 27–36.

Krumhansl, C. L. 1988. "Tonal and Harmonic Hierarchies." *Harmony and Tonality.* J. Sundberg, ed. Stockholm: Royal Swedish Academy of Music.

Krumhansl, C. L. 1990. *The Cognitive Foundations of Musical Pitch.* Oxford: Oxford University Press.

Krumhansl, C. L., and E. J. Kessler. 1982. "Tracing the Dynamic Changes in Perceived Tonal Organization in a Spatial Representation of Musical Keys." *Psychological Review*, 89, 334–368.

Krumhansl, C. L., and R. N. Shepard. 1979. "Quantification of the Hierarchy of Tonal Functions Within a Diatonic Context." *Journal of Experimental Psychology: Human Perception and Performance*, S/4, 579–594.

Kurth, E. 1920. *Romantische Harmonik und ihre Krise in Wagners "Tristan".* (reprint 1985) Zurich: Georg Olms Verlag.

Lewin, D. 1986. "Music Theory, Phenomenology, and Modes of Perception." *Music Perception*, 3/4, 327–392.

Long, M. K. 2020. *Hearing Homophony: Tonal Expectation at the Turn of the Seventeenth Century.* New York: Oxford University Press.

Longuet-Higgins, H. C., and M. J. Steedman. 1971. "On Interpreting Bach." *Machine Intelligence 6.* B. Meitzer and D. Michie, eds. Edinburgh: Edinburgh University Press.

Matsunaga, R., and J.-I. Abe. 2005. "Cues for Key Perception of a Melody: Pitch Set Alone." *Music Perception*, 23/2, 153–164.

Matsunaga, R., and J.-I. Abe. 2009. "Do Local Properties Function as Cues for Musical Key Identification?" *Japanese Psychological Research*, 55, 86–97.

Matsunaga, R., K. Yokosawa, and J. I. Abe. 2012. "Magnetoencephalography Evidence for Different Brain Subregions Serving Two Musical Cultures." *Neuropsychologia*, 50/14, 3218–3227.

Napolés, N., and C. Arthur. 2019. "Key-Finding Based on a Hidden Markov Model and Key Profiles." *6th International Digital Libraries for Musicology Workshop (DLfM 2019),* Delft, Netherlands.

Nobile, D. 2020. "Double Tonic Complexes in Rock Music." *Music Theory Spectrum*, 42/2, 207–226.

Polak, R., S. Tarsitani, and M. Clayton. 2018. "IEMP Malian Jembe: A Collection of Audiovisual Recordings of Malian Jembe Ensemble Performances, with Detailed Annotations." *Open Science Framework (OSF).* DOI: 10.17605/OSF.IO/M652X

Prince, J. 2014. "Pitch Structure, But Not Selective Attention, Affects Accent Weightings in Metrical Grouping." *Journal of Experimental Psychology: Human Perception and Performance*, 40, 2073–2090.

Prince, J. B., and M. A. Schmuckler. 2014. "The Tonal-Metric Hierarchy: A Corpus Analysis." *Music Perception*, 31/3, 254–270.

Prince, J. B., W. F. Thompson, and M. A. Schmuckler. 2009. "Pitch and Time, Tonality and Meter: How Do Musical Dimensions Combine?" *Journal of Experimental Psychology*, 35/5, 1598–1617.

Quinn, I. 2010. "What's 'Key for Key': A Theoretically Naive Key: Finding Model for Bach Chorales." *Zeitschrift der Gesellschaft für Musiktheorie*, 7/ii, 151–163.

Quinn, I. 2020. "Tonal Harmony." *The Oxford Handbook of Critical Concepts in Music Theory*. A. Rehding and S. Rings, eds. New York: Oxford.

Richards, M. 2017. "Tonal Ambiguity in Popular Music's Axis Progressions." *Music Theory Online*, 23/3. https://mtosmt.org/issues/mto.17.23.3/mto.17.23.3.richards.html

Riemann, H. 1893. *Vereinfachte Harmonielehre, oder die Lehre von den tonalen Funktionen der Akkorde*. London: Augener.

Rings, S. 2020. "Tonic." *The Oxford Handbook of Critical Concepts in Music Theory*. A. Rehding and S. Rings, eds. New York: Oxford.

Rothgeb, J. 1995. "The Tristan Chord: Identity and Origin." *Music Theory Online*, 1/1.

Schenker, H. 1935. *Der freie Satz*. Wien: Universal Edition. Tr. as *Free Composition* by E. Oster, New York, Longman, 1979; Pendragon Press, 2001.

Schwitzgebel, E., and C. W. White. 2021. "Effects of Chord Inversion and Bass Patterns on Harmonic Expectancy in Musicians." *Music Perception*, 39/1, 41–62.

Sears, D. R. W. 2015. "The Perception of Cadential Closure." *What Is a Cadence? Theoretical and Analytical Perspectives on Cadences in the Classical*. M. Neuwirth and P. Bergé, eds. Leuven: Leuven University Press, pp. 253–286.

Sears, D. R. W., A. Arzt, H. Frostel, R. Sonnleitner, and G. Widmer. 2017a. "Modeling Harmony with Skip-Grams." *Proceedings of the 18th International Society for Music Information Retrieval Conference (ISMIR)*, Suzhou, China, 332–338.

Sears, D. R. W., M. T. Pearce, W. E. Caplin, and S. McAdams. 2017b. "Simulating Melodic and Harmonic Expectations for Tonal Cadences Using Probabilistic Models." *Journal of New Music Research*, 47/1, 1–66.

Sears, D. R. W., and G. Widmer. 2020. "Beneath (or beyond) the Surface: Discovering Voice-Leading Patterns with Skip-Grams." *Journal of Mathematics and Music*, 13/3, 209–234.

Shanahan, D., J. A. Burgoyne, and I. Quinn (eds.). 2022. *The Oxford Handbook of Musical Corpus Studies*. New York: Oxford University Press.

Straus, J. N. 2005. *Introduction to Post-Tonal Theory*, 3rd edition. Upper Saddle River, NJ: Prentice Hall.

Symons, J. A. 2017. *Cognitively Inspired Method for the Statistical Analysis of Eighteenth-Century Music, as Applied in Two Corpus Studies*. Ph.D. Dissertation, Northwestern University, Evanston, IL.

Temperley, D. 1999. "What's Key for Key? The Krumhansl-Schmuckler Key-Finding Algorithm Reconsidered." *Music Perception*, 17/1, 65–100.

Temperley, D. 2004. "Communicative Pressure and the Evolution of Musical Styles." *Music Perception*, 21/3, 313–337.

Temperley, D. 2007. *Music and Probability*. Cambridge: The MIT Press.

Temperley, D. 2018. *The Musical Language of Rock*. New York: Oxford University Press.

Temperley, D., and E. W. Marvin. 2008. "Pitch: Class Distribution and the Identification of Key." *Music Perception*, 25/3, 193–212.

Tymoczko, D. 2011. *A Geometry of Music: Harmony and Counterpoint in the Extended Common Practice*. New York: Oxford University Press.

Vuvan, D. T., and B. Hughes. 2019. "Musical Style Affects the Strength of Harmonic Expectancy." *Music & Science*, 2, 1–9.

White, C. W. 2013. "An Alphabet-Reduction Algorithm for Chordal N-Grams." *Proceedings of the 4th International Conference on Mathematics and Computation in Music*. Heidelberg: Springer, 201–212.

White, C. W. 2014. "Changing Styles, Changing Corpora, Changing Tonal Models." *Music Perception*, 31/2, 244–253.

White, C. W. 2018. "Feedback and Feedforward Models of Musical Key." *Music Theory Online*, 24/2.

White, C. W., and I. Quinn. 2018. "Chord Content and Harmonic Function in Tonal Music." *Music Theory Spectrum*, 314–350.

Yust, J. 2017. "Probing Questions about Keys: Tonal Distributions through the DFT." *International Conference on Mathematics and Computation in Music*, Springer, Cham, 167–179.

Zanette, D. H. 2006. "Zipf's Law and the Creation of Musical Context." *Musicae Scientiae*, 10, 3–18.

APPENDIX TO CHAPTER 6

The Minor Mode

Throughout this chapter, I discussed major-mode key-finding models in the most depth but periodically referenced minor-mode analyses and corpus statistics. For instance, my analyses of both the "Eroica" and Schumann passages involved some possibilities of a G-minor tonal center.

I sidestepped the minor mode for one simple reason: the minor mode is more complicated than the major mode. As Albrecht and Shanahan (2013) outline, both behavioral and corpus data are more variable when they concern the minor mode versus major-mode music. In other words, it is not only difficult to construct reliable models of minor-mode key profiles, but it is also difficult to construct robust ground truth assessments of minor-mode keys that multiple listeners will consistently agree with.

Figure A6.1 shows the minor-mode profile in the YCAC. The profile illustrates one primary difficulty of minor-mode key-finding: the role of the subtonic, or the lowered seventh scale degree. While its frequency is lower than any other degree in the traditional harmonic minor scale, it is markedly higher than the profile's chromatic degrees, creating something of an in-between category for this not-quite-diatonic-not-quite-chromatic degree. Furthermore, because of the structural relationship between the relative major and minor keys, there are overlaps between the most frequent degrees in both profiles (i.e., the minor mode's $\hat{3}$ and $\hat{5}$ will map on the major mode's $\hat{1}$ and $\hat{3}$, all of which are among the profiles' three most frequent degrees). This confluence often makes for an ambiguity between a minor-mode passage and its relative major.

Additionally, while a key-profile approach must distinguish between the two modes in its analyses, a chord progression approach can bundle all information

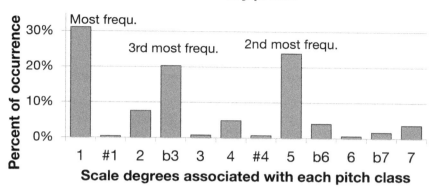

FIGURE A6.1 The minor-mode key profile in the YCAC

in the same dataset together. From a chord-progression perspective, such bundling makes sense. In contrast to a key-profile approach that matches pitch-class content to an idealized scale-degree distribution, an *n*-gram model tonally interprets set-class progressions according to their most probable (most frequent) scale-degree instantiations. The process is unencumbered by considering both major and minor versions of scale degrees and – if anything – benefits from including both modes in its training set. Consider a key-finding analysis of a C-minor triad progressing to an A-flat major triad. A key-profile analysis would first compare the pitch-class distribution of this chord progression to all 12 possible rotations of the major-mode profile and then all 12 rotations of the minor-mode profile: two steps are required, one for each mode, and the best match out of all 24 options is chosen. An *n*-gram approach, however, produces only 12 options. The process would align the C-minor-to-A-flat progression to the 12 possible tonics and identify the most probable scale-degree set. For instance, matching that progression to E-flat's scale degrees would produce a vi-IV progression, while matching that progression to C's scale degrees would produce a i-VI progression. Here, the scale-degree alignments (and eventual key assessments) are based simply on the tonic degree and not on mode. There is no distinction between a C-major versus C-minor interpretation of that 2-gram: if the broader passage is in C-major or C-minor, the same i-VI progression results (i.e., in the former key, the progression would use modal mixture). However, this interpretation is only possible if minor-mode data are included in its training data: the model needs to have seen a minor tonic in its training data in order to assess this possible scale-degree interpretation.

In sum, while the minor mode can be incorporated into (and accounted for by) various key-finding procedures, there is more variation in the data, less

304 What Is Key?

reliability in the ground truth, and different solutions provided by different models. There are interesting points to be discussed surrounding these modal differences; however, these insights are regrettably outside the purview of the current project.

A Closer Look at Key-Finding With Harmonic Reduction

Figure A6.2 shows two examples of the key-finding algorithm using Chapter 3's harmonic reduction process, with two similar passages being assessed in two different keys. The example uses Chapter's 3's adding/subtracting reduction method (i.e., it does *not* alter pitches by step in this application), and both illustrate the process's engineering along with some of the simplifying heuristics that I use. First, the most fundamental aspect of Chapter 3's reduction process was its "editing," in which consecutive slices are grouped together and notes are added/subtracted from the texture to create more probable chord structures. In a key-finding process, this editing conforms a surface event to a member of a corpus's harmonic vocabulary. As I showed in Chapter 3, in the case of the YCAC, this process generally transforms a surface event into a scale-degree set that can be described by a recognizable Roman numeral. In other words, the reduction process can more or less be thought of as conforming a surface to a typical Roman-numeral analysis by adding/deleting pitches and grouping together adjacent pitch–class sets.

Figure A6.2 isolates two passages within the opening measures of Wolfgang Mozart's K. 284, iii, with the passages' pitch-classes bundled into each quarter-note duration. (Aspects of this analysis appear in White, 2018.) The dotted boxes show instances where notes must be removed in order to create a more probable vocabulary item: the deleted pitch-classes are shown in grey in the figure's top row, and the resulting pitch-class sets and subsequent scale-degree sets are indicated in the following rows. The reduction process is undertaken for each possible scale-degree orientation (i.e., 12 times, once for each possible key). Four such reductions are shown in the figure. The 3-gram probabilities are calculated for each possible tonal orientation, and the most probable – the succession that has been observed most frequently in the corpus – is chosen. In the current example, the first passage is best analyzed in D, while the second is analyzed in A, as these orientations produce the most probable successions of scale-degree sets.

Two heuristics are also evident in this example. An important aspect of the reduction method involves bundling together adjacent salami slices when they are in a subset/superset relationship or when their combination produces a chord structure that increases the probability of the sequence. For instance, after finding that the final quarter-note duration can be reduced to a diminished triad, the process would notice that combining that set with the previous notes would produce the even more probable dominant seventh sonority. However, these combinations need starting points and boundaries. For instance, how does the

What Is Key? **305**

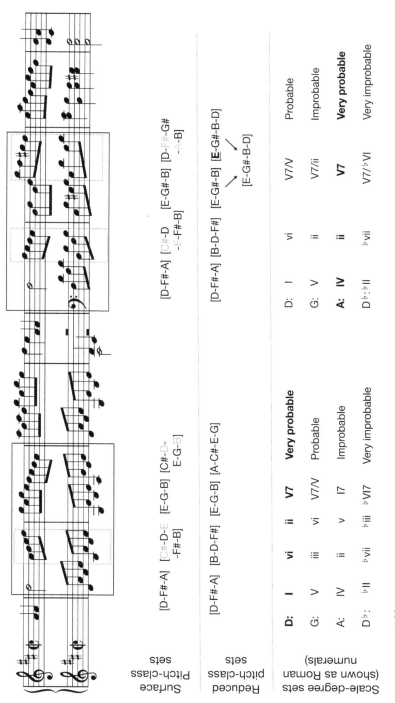

FIGURE A6.2 Wolfgang Mozart's Sonata in D-major, K. 284, iii, mm. 1–8 with key-finding process annotated

D/F-sharp salami slice that begins the second half of bar 5 (the second harmony in the second window) know to group with the following pitches to create a B-minor triad rather that with the previous pitches' D-major triad? Heuristically, I rely on metric boundaries in the initial bundling of pitch-classes: I program the chord-finder to prefer groupings within notated measures and beats.

Secondly, I also program a heuristic preference to minimize the number of edits being made and particularly to stop editing when one of the vocabulary's most frequent set-classes results (in the YCAC, these would be triads and sevenths). For instance, the second chord in measure 1 is analyzed as a vi chord in D; however, removing the B from the pitch-class set would make the set a subset of the previous I chord, and – when combined with its superset – would produce the even more frequent I-ii-V^7 succession. Then, removing the B from the ii chord's E-minor set would make that moment a subset of the subsequent set; and the recombination of sets would produce the yet more probable I-V^7. Finally, the seventh could be removed from the final chord, reducing the whole passage to a I-V succession. Indeed, running the key-finding algorithm with no boundaries or stopgaps reduces every passage to some combination of I, IV, and V chords, which – while potentially compelling for Riemannian and Schenkerian theories – confounds the key-finding process.

Figures A6.3a and A6.3b step through two of the reductions undertaken in the *Tristan und Isolde* excerpt discussed in this chapter, now using the stepwise

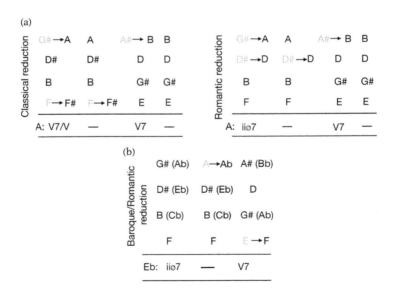

FIGURE A6.3 The reduction process behind the (a) Romantic and Classical sub-corpus models' assessments of the *Tristan* prelude's initial cadence and (b) the Baroque/Romantic E-flat/D-sharp reduction of the progression into m. 3's downbeat

edits outlined in Chapter 3 (that is, the reduction process can now create more probable successions by altering the contents of surface chords by step). The first figure shows the two divergent reductions made by the method when trained on the Classical and Romantic subsets of the YCAC, with modified or deleted notes shown in gray and stepwise edits shown with arrows. In the former, the edits produce an applied-dominant-to-dominant half cadence, while the latter produces a supertonic half-diminished chord moving to a dominant seventh. The differences, of course, result from the different proportional chord usage in each style. Figure A6.4b shows the edits underlying the momentary D-sharp/E-flat tonal center: the A-sharp edited away by the earlier figure becomes the root of a dominant seventh through only minimal surface changes.

Again, some heuristics were employed for these analyses. First, I did not allow the singletons to be deleted or moved by half step, meaning that the monophonic introductory pitch-classes would stay fixed throughout the analyses. I again added a preference for fewer edits and capped the possible number of voice leading transformations at two. Similar to the issues I outlined in the earlier example, greater modifications to the chords runs the risk of producing reductions that are too abstract and removed from the observed musical events to be useful in key and chord-finding.

X^2 Tests

The X^2 ("chi square") test is an often-used and straightforward procedure that determines whether categories contain significantly different numbers of events – i.e., whether categories contain significantly more or fewer events than one another. The test's two main parameters are the observed values and the expected values. The former is simply the number of events in each category, and the latter is the number of values that one would expect if events were spread evenly over the tested categories. In Equation A6.1, I show the X^2 value as the sum of all squares of observed values minus expected values, divided by the expected value. The value will be higher when the observed events in each tested category are not evenly distributed, and some categories have more or less values than the (evenly distributed) expected values. Conversely, the value will be lower when the categorical differences are smaller and events are more evenly distributed throughout. An analyst can then locate the resulting X^2 value on a p-value chart to determine whether the differences are large enough to be statistically significant: such X^2 significance charts are eminently available online.

Figure A6.4 shows the number of tonic and dominant scale degrees observed in the first 10 salami slices of the YCAC's major-mode pieces written in the 1700s and the 1800s, along with all the calculations to determine whether the chronological categories differ significantly. If both centuries behaved similarly, then their counts should be roughly the same. The figure's "Ratio of sums:total" shows the proportion of each scale degree in the two centuries: 54% of the

308 What Is Key?

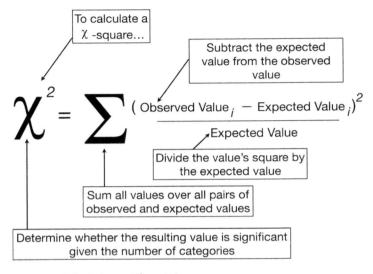

EQUATION A6.1 Calculating a X^2 statistic

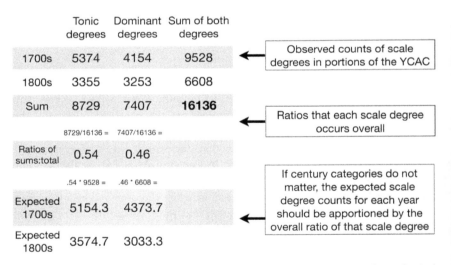

FIGURE A6.4 Calculating the observed and expected values in two chronological subsets of the YCAC

total degrees in the table are tonic degrees, and 46% are dominant. If these overall ratios predicted the distribution of scale degrees in both centuries (that is, if there was no difference between the two century's categories and only the chords' identities determined the proportion of events in each category), then 54% of the scale degrees in both centuries should be tonic: for instance, 0.54

of the 9528 total degrees observed in the 1700s should be tonic. Therefore, the expected number of tonic scale degrees in the 1700s category is 5154.3 (0.54 × 9528 = 5154.3). This process produces all the expected values for each category, which provides all values needed for Equation A6.1. The online spreadsheet applies these calculations and results in a total X^2 value of 49.8. A X^2 significance chart (again, eminently accessible through your favorite search engine) will be indexed by *degrees of freedom*, or the number of independent factors within a statistical test. In the case of a X^2 test, the degrees of freedom are the number of rows minus 1 multiplied by the number of columns minus 1 (or, $[r - 1] \times [c - 1]$). In other words, the more columns and rows, the more factors, and the more degrees of freedom (and the greater variation will be expected in the data). As our data has two rows for chronological categories and two columns for the tonic and dominant degrees, there is 1 degree of freedom ($[2 - 1] \times [2 - 1]$). Indexing our X^2 statistic with 1 degree of freedom on a significance chart finds these differences to be very significant ($p < 0.001$): the 18th- and 19th-century datasets use significantly different amounts of tonic and dominant scale degrees.

INDEX

Note: Page numbers in *italics* indicates figures and page numbers in **bold** indicates tables on the corresponding page.

2-gram 5–7, *5*, **7**, 14–15, 49, 104–105, 109–114, *114*, 134, 162, 167, 303; *see also* *n*-gram conditional probabilities
3-gram 59–65, **60**, *61*, *62*, *65*, 79, 84, 94, 257, *257*, 267, 270, 304; pitch-class 257, *257*; scale-degree 60, 257–258, *257*, 263, 265, 275, 280; set-class 257–258, *257*, 263–264, *265*, 268, 280, 303; *see also* *n*-gram conditional probabilities

accent 36, 190, 196, 199, 212, 214–215, 234–235, 235n3; durational 213, 235n1; metric 190–191, 194–195, 197, 199, 202–204, 208, 213–214, 216, 227, 229–234; phenomenal 190–192, 194, 197, 208, 213, 232–233
Agmon, E. 117, 138–140
analysis: computational 20, 22, 34, 234, 277, 288; corpus 2–3, 8, 12, 16, 21–22, 25, 30, 32–38, 43n31, 53, 66, 84, 101, 106, 114, 137, 144, 155–156, 172, 175–176, 189–190, 192, 196–197, 214–215, 229, 234, 247, 276, 293–294; music 3, 8, 20–21, 25, 31–35, 37, 42n28, 43n31, 101, 175–176, 196–197, 231, 260, 294–295; statistical 15, 20, 32, 37–38, 53, 92; style 66, 81–84
antitonic 152–156, 159–160, **161**, 164–167, 169–172, 174, 277, 288

applied chords 108, 125–126, 138, 169, 271, 307
argmax 132
Auskomponieren see prolongation
autocorrelation 199–203, 205–211, 213, 215, 219–220, 224, 227, 233–236
autonomous music 24, 28–29

Bach, J. S.: BWV 846, *Well-Tempered Clavier*, Book 1, Prelude 1 in C major 210–211, *210*, 233
Bach-Chorale corpus 109, 141–142, *142*, *146*, 156, 162, 165, 167, 171, 208, 258
backbeat 223–224
Bagnell, E.: "Pink Lemonade" 38n2
Baroque *see* music
Bartók, B.: *Mikrokosmos* IV, no. 101, "Diminished Fifth" 290, *291*
base 2 logarithm 23, 50–51
basic idea *see* sentence phrase structure
bass profile 253, *254*, 256, 258, 260, 264, *265*, 273–274, 278, *279*, 296n7; *see also* key-finding
Bayesian probability 252
Beethoven, L. 60–61, *61*, 76–79; Piano Sonatas, Op. 2 76; Piano Sonata Op. 31, no. 3, in E-flat major 270; Symphony 3, Op. 55, in E-flat major, *Eroica 266*,

266–268, 271, 275; Symphony 5, Op. 67, in C minor 284

behavioral analysis 53, 141, 156, 160, 167, 171–174, 199, 213, 216, 229, 248, 274, 294, 302

bell-curve distribution 18, 93

Bell Labs 9

Bellman, H. 253

bias 20–22, 37, 273

Billboard magazine 2

binary logarithm *see* base 2 logarithm

bits 23, 51, 87n14; *see also* base 2 logarithm

blank positions *see* *n*-gram conditional probabilities

Boone, G. 199

Boulanger, L.: "Attente," ILB 1 *285*, 288–290, *289*

Boulez, P.: *Douze Notations*, "Notation No. 6" 290, *291*

Brahms, J. 60, **60**, *62*, 63–64, **64**, 71, *74*, 74, 81

Brown, J. C. 201, 235n1

Browne, R. 248

Budge, H. 253

Byrd, W. 60, **60**, *62*, 63–64, **64**, 72

Byros, V. 40n11, 267–268, 272

cadence 140, 152, 270–271, 286, 293, *306*; authentic 13–14, 140, 142, 165, 245–247, *246*, *251*, 257, *257*, 261; deceptive 13–14, *168*, 169; evaded 54 [evade]; half 274, 307; *see also* sentence phrase structure

Cambouropoulos, E. 180n11

Caplan, L. 186n11

Chédeville, N. 79, *80*

Chen, P. 150–151

chi-square test 129n20, 264, 307–309, *308*

Chopin, F. *62*, 63, **64**, 71, *71*, 74, *74*, 81; 24 Preludes, Op. 28, no. 20, Prelude in C minor 102, *103*

chord 23–25, *24*, 35–36, 49–50, 59, 65, 96–98, 100–106, *106*, 110, 113–114, 117–121, 123, 126, 127n10, 128n11, 128n17, 132–133, 135–136, 140, 153–155, *154*, 157, 159, 176n2, 178n14, 179n17, 185, 257–258, *257*, 261, 270, 273, 275, 296n8, 304, 307; *see also* chord progression; functional prototype; harmonic function; harmonic syntax

chord-finding 261, *269*, 270, 307

chord-frequency model 151

chord profile 253, *255*, 256; *see also* key-finding

chord progression 6, 18, 22, 41n16, 49–50, 59–60, 100, *100*, 102, 104–106, *107*, 109–110, *115*, 122, 127n8, 180n12, 204, 256–257, 260–261, 268, 273, 281, 283, 295n3, 302–307; *see also* 2-gram; 3-gram

chord-progression model 109–112, 151–152

chord syntax *see* harmonic syntax

close reading 28, 32, 34, 41n21

cluster analysis 35, 61–62, 91, 114–115, *115*, 145, *145*; agglomerative 87n9, 89n27, 91; dimensions in 62–64, 91, *92*, 115, 252; divisive 87, 91; *see also* *k*-means clustering

code breaking 8–9

coherence 65–67, *65*, *68*, 69–70, 75–76, 81, 83, 86; *see also* coherence/ uniqueness rate; cross entropy; sub-corpus; uniqueness

coherence/uniqueness rate 69–71, 76, 81, 84

Common Practice 10, 96, 109–110, 120, 123–124, 126, 152, 163, 165–168, 171, 218, 220, 248, 253, 280

communicative pressure 304n9

compound meter *see* meter

computational algorithm 103

computational model 21, 106, 144, 146, 150, 155–156, 162, 171, 189, 199, 212, 274

conditional *n*-gram probability 4–5, 48–49

Cone, E. T. 17–19, 20, 31

confidence interval 69, 92–93

connective claims 30–32

consonance 28, 103–104, 121–122, 204–205, 218, 220, 231–232, 248, 271–272, 274

content/context dichotomy 101–103, *103*, 104–105, 108, 132–133, 137, 139–141, 144–149, *145*, 151–155, 173, 257

content-to-context generative model 144–146, *145*

contextual probability 132–133

continuation *see* sentence phrase structure

corpus: properties of 1, 11–14, 21, 26–27, 30, 32–38, 83, 121, 123, 176, 215, 225, 229, 232, 234, 247, 260, 267, 276–277, *277*, 297

corpus analysis *see* analysis

corpus data division *see* divisions, corpus data

312 Index

correlation *see* linear regression
correlational studies 28–31, 37
cross entropy 52, 66–67, *68*, 69–73,
   71–74, 75–77, *77–78*, 79, 84, 86,
   93–94, *95*, 110–112, *111*
cursor time 260–261
cursor voting method *see* key-finding

Dahlhaus, C. 24, 56
dance: and meter 231–232, 235
data 3, 13, 22, 32, 61, 83, 92, 127n5, 149,
   153, 172, 176, 180n14
Debussy, C. *62*, 63–64, *64*, 73–74, *74*
de Clercq–Temperley corpus 109–110, 112
deep learning algorithms 296
deformation 12
degrees of freedom 309
diatonic system 59, 106, 108, 114,
   117–118, 126, 138, 248, 262, 302
displacement dissonance *see* metric
   dissonance
dissonance 63, 98, 102, 110, 121–122,
   142, 204–205, 218, 220, 256, 261–262,
   271–272, 274
distant reading 22, 35
divisions, corpus data: beat method 58–59,
   58, 84, 206; division method 58–59,
   58, 84, 113, 207; salami-slice method
   57–59, *58*, 84, 98, 101–102, 112, 139,
   203, 205, 250, 253, 257–258, 260, 262,
   262, 273, 304–306
dominant function 114, *114*, *115*, 116–117,
   119, 123–124, 138–142, *138*, *142–143*,
   145–146, *146*, 151–152, 165–169, 173–
   174, 290; *see also* function prototype
Drum-Groove corpus **219**, 221–223, *222*,
   226, 231, *231*, 234
dundun 225–226
dyad 63, 102, 104–106

EM *see* expectation maximization
emergent creativity 83
empty start token *see* *n*-gram analysis
emulation 76–79
encoding/decoding 9, 11–13, 25–26, 28,
   33, 37, 85–86, 163–165, 247
entity functions *see* entity/relational
   dichotomy
entity/relational dichotomy 150–151,
   155, **161**, 166, 171; attributes in 150,
   153, 177n9, 178n12, 178n13; entities
   in 150–152, 156, 159, 161–162, **161**,
   164–165, 170–17; entity functions 152,

156, 159–160, **161**, 163, 165–168, 170,
   174; entity sets 150–155, 159–160,
   167, 171, 174; relationship functions
   152, 155–156, 159, 161–162, 164–165,
   170–174; relationship sets 150, 155,
   160, 165, 170; relationships in 150–151,
   153–154, 156, 160–162, **161**, 164–167,
   170–174, 176
entrainment 190–191, 196–197, 229
entropy 23–25, 27, 29, 50–52, *51*, 66–67,
   93, 134; *see also* bits; cross entropy;
   Shannon entropy
equivalency network *see* reduction
   network
E/R theory *see* entity/relational
   dichotomy
exclusion rate 111–112
expectation 10–12, 13, 17–18, 23, 37, 50,
   54, 56, 66–67, 85–86, 94, 100, 104,
   110, 125–126, 141, 147, 158, 174, 186,
   190–191, 213, 232, 234, 245–246, 250,
   252–253, 257, 266, 271–272, 280–282,
   292, 307–309, *308*
expectation maximization 177n8, 199
extramusical meaning *see* meaning

Fechner, G. 158
Fechner's Law *see* Weber-Fechner law
forgery *see* emulation
frequency-based modeling 59, 62, 99, 103,
   105, 108–109, 114–117, 119, 121–124,
   125, 134, 139–141, 148–149, 151–152,
   155–161, *157*, **161**, 163–165, 174,
   186–187, *186*, *187*, 229, 268, 274, *278*,
   280, 283, 302
F-score 207, **207**, 211, 214, 219–220,
   219, 222–225, 237, 243, *244*; precision
   in 243, *244*; recall in 243, *244*
functional paradigm *see* functional
   prototype
functional prototype 109, 114, *116*,
   117–123, *124*, 126, 168
functional zones 138–139, *138*

GCAMM *see* Generic Corpus Analysis of
   Meter Model
Generic Corpus Analysis of Meter Model
   195–196, *195*, 199, 212, 215, 231–232
genre 55–57
Google *see* Magenta database
groove 232
ground truth 212, 219, 222, 225, 227,
   252–253, 261, 263, 302, 304

grouping *see* metric dissonance
grouping dissonance *see* metric dissonance

Handel, G. F. 60, **60**, 63–64, **64**, 70–71, *71*, 77, 79; Water Music Suite No. 2, HWV 349, Alla Hornpipe *135*; Water Music Suite No. 2, HWV 349, Bouree *135*
harmonically reduced 3-grams *see* 3-gram, harmonically reduced
harmonic function 114, 121, 126, 137, 140–142, 144, 146, *146*, 148, 150–153, 155–156, 158, 160, 165, 167, 170–174, 176, 212; in popular music 124, 142–143, *143*, *146*, 166
harmonic grammar 2, 10–11, 17, 35, 38–39, 54, 97–98, 100, 104, 107–108, 110, 112, 114–117, *114*, *116*, *119*, 120–121, 124, 126, 138, 140–141, 162, 168, 173–174
harmonic minor scale *see* minor mode
harmonic rhythm 203, 220
harmonic syntax *see* harmonic grammar
harmonic vocabulary 28, 35, 96–101, *99*, *100*, 108–112, 125, 139, 261; reduced 98, 101, 103–104, 106, *106*, *107*, 108–110, 112–113, 118–119, *118*, 121–123, 125–126, **125**, 262–263, 274, 304, 306
Harrison, D. 248, 274, 284
Hartley, A. H. 15–17
Hatten, R. 84–85
Haydn, F. J. **64**, 73, 77–78, *77*, *78*; Cello Concerto in C major, Hob. VIIb:1 *136*
hemiola 206
Hensel, F.: *Sechs Lieder*, Op. 9, no. 6, "Die Mainacht" 197, *198*, 200–206, *201*, 208–209, *209*, 214, 216, *217*
hermeneutics 31, 42n28
heuristic listening 125
Hidden Markov Model 141–142, *142*, *143*, 149, 212
hierarchy 11, 122, 276; harmonic 98, 121–122, 276, 281, 284, 292–293; metric 190–191, 195–196, 203–204, 209, 212–213, 215–218, 231–234; scale-degree 121, 248, 273–274, 276, 284, 292–293
historically situated cognition 267, 272
HMM *see* Hidden Markov Model
HookTheory corpus 282–283, *282*
Hosken, F. 229
humanities, the 8–10, 12–13, 15–16, 20, 22, 31–33, 35, 172, 294

Huron, D. 28–29, 33, 125, 194–195, 245
hypermeter 206–207

Imbruglia, N.: "Torn" 220, *221*
influence 14–15, 75; *see also* emulation
informatics 9–12, 16, 20, 32, 37–38, 39n6, 110; *see also* music informatics
information theory 9–11, 25, 39n6, 94, 134
interdisciplinarity 15–17, 30, 175
intermediate chords 116–117, 120, 154, 167
interpretation 14–16, 20, 26–28, 30–35, 38, 56, 104, 172, 190, *193*, 194–195, 214, 230, 245–247, 249–250, 256–258, 263–265, 267–268, 270–271, 275, 294, 303; *see also* meaning
intersection *see* overlap
intuition *see* musical intuition
inversion 17, 23, 49, 58, 99, 126, 165, 257, 290, 293
inversional equivalence/nonequivalence 17, 23, 49, 58
inversionally non-equivalent prime form 49
isochrony 190–191, 199, 208–209, 211, 215–216, 220, 223, 227, 229, 232–234; *see also* pulse
Ives, C.: Piano Sonata No. 2 284–286, *285*

Jackendoff, R. 195–196, 231, 233
jembe 225–227

key 245–249, 252, 258, 261, 263–264, 267–268, 270–277, 280–281, 283–284, 290, 292–294, 302–303; foreign 108; global/home/tonic 99, 274, 281, 284; local 58, 98–99; opening 57, 98, 261; secondary 261, 274
key-finding 57, 218, 245, 248–249, 252–253, 256, 258, 260–261, *262*, 264, 270, 272, 274, 275–280, *279*, 282–283, 288, 290, 292–294, 302–304, 306–307; 3-gram reduction method 262–263, *262*, *265*, 269, 270, 273, *305*; with counts table 259, *259*; cursor voting method *259*, 260, *266*, 267–268, *269*, 270; distributional 256; melodic 2-gram method 273; simple voting method *259*, 260, 265–266, *266*; structural 256–257
key profile 249–256, *251*, 258, 260–261, 263, *265*, *266*, 267–268, 272–275, 278, 302–303, *303*; windowed 98; *see also* key-finding
key profile cursor correlation 261

314 Index

k-means clustering 63–64, **64**, 70, 73–74, 77, 91–92, 264; silhouette width in 91–92
Kozak, M. 197
Kramer, L. 31
Krumhansl, C. 197

Lakh MIDI popular-music corpus 218–219, *218*, **219**, 222, *230*, 234
language 8, 10–12, 25–26, 31, 104, 108, 151, 156, **161**, 165, 167, 170, 173, 186, 213, 278, 293; acquisition of 10, 12, 37, 161, **161**
Laplace smoothing method *see* smoothing
Lerdahl, F. 195–196, 231, 233
Le–Sol–Fi–Sol schema 267–268, 271
Lewin, D. 260
likelihood *see* occurrence probability
linear regression 24–25, 35, 52–53; correlation (*r*) in 52–53
linguistics 32, 36–37, 161, 174
listener 10, 12–14, *13*, 18, 21, 25–28, 37, 56, 85–86, 97, 107, 125–126, 151–152, 155, 157–158, 160, 162, 171–172, 174, 190–192, 194, 197, 204, 209–210, 214, 218, 229–231, 233–234, 246–249, 252, 257, 260, 263, 267–268, 272–274, 276–277, 280–282, 284, 286, 290, 292–294, 302
Liszt, F. 63, **64**, 74, *74*, 81
log *see* logarithm
log 2 *see* base 2 logarithm
logarithm 23, 50–52, 94, 105, 110, 134
logarithmic distribution 158, 187; *see also* Weber-Fechner law
London, J. 194, 197
long tail 18, 156–157, 159

machine learning 98, 133, 141, 149, 212–213, 215
macroanalysis 22, 35
macroharmony 274
Magenta database of drum-set grooves 235, *235*
magician's paradox 26–27, 37
Malian Drum corpus **219**, 225, *226*, *230*, 234, 292, *292*
"Maraka" 227–228, *228*
Martian effect 20, 22–23, 37, 98, 273
Marxism 24–25
McGill–Billboard corpus *123, 124*, 143, *146*, 156, 159, 166, 171, 264–265, *265*, *266*, 268, *269*, 270, 272, 274, 278, *279*, 280–282, *281*

MCM *see* Meaningful Corpus Model
mean 76, 92, 243; arithmetic 243; harmonic 243
meaning 8, 13–16, *13*, 24, 31–35, 38, 83–86, **161**, 172–173, 247, 311; extramusical 15, 17, 31, 38, 74, 82–86, 174
Meaningful Corpus Model 13–17, *13*, 20, 25, 30–33, 38, 84–85, 172, 247, 249, 276, 292
mediant 5, 6, 62, *105*, 115–116, **125**, 138, 141, 143, 145, 169, 250, 256, 264, 283
melodic repetition 4–7, 7; *see also* motive
Mendelssohn, F. **64**, 70–71, *71*, 78, *78*
mere exposure effect 11, 21; *see also* statistical learning hypothesis
message *see* noisy channel
metadata 57, 59, 205, 218
meter 57, 59, 190–197, *192*, *193*, *195*, 203–204, 206, 208, 211–219, *218*, 223, 229, 232–235; compound 216, 219, 225; grouping and 58–59, *58*, 196, 206, 211, 233, 306; and harmonic stability 208–209, 216, 230; and key expression 283; rhythm and 196, 206, 213, 224–225, 227, 229, 234; simple 219, 222; surface patterns and 190, 192, 195–196, *195*, 198, 210–217, 219, 223, 227, 229–234, *230*; *see also* isochrony; meter-finding; periodicity; pulse
meter-finding 197, 199, 202–204, 208, 213, 220, 229
metric pattern *see* meter
Metric Preference Rules 231
metric template 194, 197, 212, 213, 215
Meyer, L. B. 9–10, 28
MIDI 59, 219
Million Song database 217–218
minor dominant 54, *55*, 84, 109, 124, **125**
minor mode 54, 108, 115, *116*, 119, 252, 261, 265, 267, 270–271, 283, 302–304, *303*
modal mixture 303
modulation 18, *19*, 21, 261, 265
modulo 12 99, 284
Monteverdi, C.: Madrigals, Book 3, "O Primavera" *208*, 210–211, *210*
motive 4, 7, 196, 208, 210, 227, 229, 287–288, 290; *see also* melodic repetition
Mozart, W. A. 61, **64**, 73, 77–78, *77*, *78*, **207**, 208; Piano Sonata No. 1, K. 279, in C major 101–102, *102*; Piano Sonata

No. 6, K. 284, in D major 113, *113*, 120–121, *120*, 304–306, *305*

music: Baroque 54, 79, 268, 270–271, *306*; and the bourgeoisie 24, 28–29, 55; EDM 1–2, 4–6, 8, 15; German 23–25, *24*, 27–30, 49, 52–53, 64; historical and correlational studies of 28–29; of Mali **219**, 225, *226*, 236, 292, *292*; modeling 26–30, *27*; nineteenth-century 17, *19*, 22, 36, 54, 82, 267, 309; popular 55, 82, 112, 123–124, 140, 143, *143*, 147, 149, 152, 165–167, 187, 217–218, 220, 222–224, 231–232, 264, *266*, 268, 270–272, 274, 282–283; posttonal 284, 288, 290, *291*, 293; Romantic 64, 81, 268, 270–271, *306*, 307; Viennese Classical 54, 63, 77, 79, 272

music21 Western Art Music corpus 202, *202*, 205, *205*, 207, **207**, 219, *230*

musical gesture 31, 56, 174, 269–270

musical grammar 10–11, 26, 213; *see also* harmonic grammar

musical intuition 22, 54, 60–61, 63–64, 83, 97–98, 101, 105–106, 108, 110, 113, 115, 121, 140, 143, 147, 162, 194, 204, 209, 216, 218, 223 –4, 233, 256, 260, 272, 283

musical style 1, 10, 12, 14–15, 37, 55–56, 59, 65–66, 70, 73–76, 79, 80–86, 112, 142, 166, 170–172, 199, 207–208, 211, 232, 264, 272, 274, 276, 280–281, 283, 307

musical texture 17, 23, 28, 57, 59, 63, 70, 75, 98, 139, 151, 205, 208, 222, 257, 271, 283, 287–288, 304

music aesthetics 24–25, 29

music analysis *see* analysis

music cognition 16–17, 20, 37, 56, 85, 109, 126, 137, 150–151, 153, 162, 167, 172 –6, 190, 192, 194, 196, 204, 209–210, 213–215, 229, 232, 234, 248, 257–258, 272–273, 275, 292–294; *see also* historically situated cognition

music informatics 9–12; *see also* informatics

musicology 2–3, 31–32, 48, 55, 76, 199, 231

music psychology 98, 248; *see also* psychology

music theory 8, 10, 12–14, 16–17, 31–32, 34–35, 37–38, 54–55, 84, 93, 103, 107–109, 121–122, 137, 158, 160, 167–168, 172, 174–176, 199, 216, 234, 247, 275, 294–295

National Socialist German Workers' Party 8–9, 25

negative logarithm *see* likelihood

neurohumanities 15–16; *see also* humanities, the

n-gram conditional probabilities 4–6, 14, 48–49, *49*, 59, 134, 258, 273, 303; blank positions in 258; chained 5; empty start token in 46n3; pitch-class 257, *257*; *see also* 2-gram; 3-gram

Nieuwenhuizen, C. 76–78, 84

nineteenth-century music *see* music

Nobile, D. 140

noise 9, *9*, 28, 30, 59, 92, 119; *see also* noisy channel model

noisy channel model 8, *9*, 12–13, 25–28, 33, 85, 246–247, 276, 282

non-chord tones 28, 271; *see also* dissonance

normal distribution 83

occurrence probability 18, 102–103, 134, *134*; *see also* frequency-based modeling

ornament 23, 59, 119, 135; *see also* dissonance

overlap 104–105, 111–112, 117–118, 120, 134, *135*, 138–140, 144, *146*, 147, 185–186, 302; *see also* reduction

Palmer, C. 197

periodicity 191, 194, 196–197, 200, 202, 206–208, 211, 220, 229, 233–234; *see also* meter; metric template

phrase structure 6–8, *7*, 14, 296; *see also* melodic repetition; motive; sentence phrase structure

pitch class 17, 58, 211, 220, 245, 248, 250, 255–257; change *198*, 203–204, 208, 220, 222, 234; profile 220, 224, 250–252, *251*, 261; set 58, 99, 141, 211, 256–258

pitch-class 3-gram *see* 3-gram

pitch-class change vector *see* vector

plagal function 116–117, 141–143, 154, 165–166, 284

Poeppel, D. 15–17

popular music *see* music

posttonal music *see* music

power-law distribution 156, 158–160, 162, 171, 173–174, 186–188, *187*, *188*, 277–278, *278*, 280–286, *285*, 290, 292–294, *292*

precision *see* F-score

316 Index

predominant function 106, 108, 115–117, 119, 140–141, 145, 153–154, 165–166, 168–170, 173–174
presentation *see* sentence phrase structure
pretonic function 152–154, 173
prime note-onset vector *see* vector
probability 4, 23–24, 48–49, *48*; *see also* *n*-gram conditional probability
probability mass 106, 112, 116, 156
prolongation 103–104, 122, 135, 204, 261; *see also* reduction; replacement
psychology 10, 12, 20, 25, 32, 38, 277; *see also* music psychology
pulse 113, 190–191, 194–195, 197, 199–207, 209–212, 216, 219–220, 222–228, 231, 233–234; *see also* isochrony
pulse cycle 225–227, *226*

quantitative claims 30
Quinn, I. 141, 152, 258, 273
Quinn/YCAC model 109, 112

rare interval hypothesis 248
recall *see* *F*-score
recapitulation 268, 275, 286–288
receiver *see* noisy channel model
recurrent neural networks 212, 296
reduced vocabulary *see* harmonic vocabulary
Reduced YCAC model *107*, 110–112, 114–115, *114*
reduction: similarity of content or context in 102–103; subset/superset 101–106, *102*, *103*, *105*, 108, 117–120, 136, 139–140, 154, *154*, 156, 262–263, 304, 306; voice-leading *119*, 122–123, 154, *154*; *see also* overlap
reduction network *105*, 119, 121, 132, 136, *139*, 148, 153–154, 170
regression line *see* linear regression
relationship functions *see* entity/relational dichotomy
Renaissance music *see* music
replacement 103–104; *see also* prolongation; reduction
rhythm *see* meter
Riemann, H. 103, 117, 138
Roman numerals 60, 96, 99, 101, 108–109, 113, 117, 121, 167–169, *168*, 261–262, 304
Romantic music *see* music
Rothgeb, J. 270–271

Saint-Saëns, C. 63, *64*, 74, *74*, 77, *77*, 81
salami slice *see* corpus data division

scale degree 121–123, 145–149, 173, 194, 245–247, *246*, 249, 257–258, 263, 272, 280–281, 283–284; set 60, 101, 132–133, 205, 261, 281–283, 304
scale-degree *n*-gram *see* *n*-gram
scale-degree set probability vector *see* vector
Scarlatti, D. 63–64, *64*
Scheinkonsonanz 103–104
Schenker, H. 104, 116
Schubert, F. 17, 20, 29, **64**, 71, *71*; *Moment Musical*, Op. 94, no. 6, in A-flat 17–21, *19*
Schumann, C.: *3 Romances*, Op. 11, no. 2, in G minor 245–247, *246*, 249–259, *251*, *254*, *255*, *257*, *259*, 261 –3, *262*, 280, *280*, 282, 302
Schumann, R. 63, **64**, *74*, 77, 81, 196
Schwitzgebel, E. 158, 162
Scriabin, A.: Prelude, Op. 74, no. 4 285–288, *287*
secondary note-onset vector *see* vector
sentence phrase structure 286–287, *287*
set class 17, 24, 58, 211, 275; probability 203, 207, **207**, 219, **219**, 220, 223, 226, *226*, 227–229, *228*; transpositionally equivalent/inversionally nonequivalent 17, 23, 257; *see also* 3-gram; autocorrelation; chord progression; vector
set-class 3-gram *see* 3-gram
set-class probability vector *see* vector
set-class progression *see* chord progression
Shannon, C. 9
signal *see* noisy channel model
significant difference *see* *p* value
silhouette width 91–92; *see also* *k*-means clustering
simple meter *see* meter
simultaneity *see* chord
Sinclair, J. 9, 33–34
slice *see* corpus data division
slope 24, 52–53, 186–187
smoothing 109, 111–112; Laplace method 128n12
standard deviation 93, 185–186, *186*
statistical learning hypothesis 10–11
statistical significance *see* *p* value
stepwise equivalence *see* voice leading proximity
Stufen 116; *see also* intermediate chords
style *see* musical style

sub-corpus 59, 65–67, 69–70, 86; *see also* coherence; coherence/uniqueness rate; cross entropy; *k*-means clustering; uniqueness

subdominant 117, 119–120, *119*, 123, 138–140, *138*, 142–143, *143*, 145–146, 160, 165–166, 169

submediant 13, 109, 116, 147, 174

subset *see* reduction

subtonic 123

superset *see* reduction

supertonic 5–6, 60, 271, 307

support vector machines 212

syntactic pillar *see* functional paradigm

Tchaikovsky, P. I. 63, **64**, 74, *74*, 81

Telemann, G. P. 63, **64**, 73, 75, 79

telephonics 9, 25, 50

Temperley, D. 258, 272–273

Temperley/Kostka–Payne corpus 109–112

temporal convolutional networks 212

ternary form 286

test set 252–253, 258, 260, 281

texture *see* musical texture

time signature 58–59, 199, 206–207, 209, 214–216, 222, 233, 234

tonal center *see* key

tonal harmony 128, 170, 249

tonal inertia *259*, 260, 268; *see also* key-finding

tonality 248–249, 273–275, 283

tonic function 115–121, *116*, *118*, *119*, 138–141, *138*, 143, *143*, 145–149, *145*, 152–156, *154*, 159–161, **161**, 164–174, 277, 280, 288, 293; *see also* function prototype

tonic key center 281; *see also* key

Top-EDM corpus 1–8, *7*, 14

topic theory 174

T–P–D syntactical model 140–141

training set 252–253, 258–259, 263, 267, 270, 280–281, 303

transition *see* chord progression

transitional probability 134, *134*

trend line *see* regression line

transmitter *see* noisy channel model

Tristan chord *269*, 270–272, 306–307, *306*

Turing, A. 8–9

Tymoczko, D. 26; *see also* magician's paradox

Tymoczko/Bach model 109, 112

uniqueness 65 –76, *65*, *68*, 81, 83–84, 86; *see also* coherence; coherence/uniqueness rate; cross entropy; sub-corpus

vector 206–207, 220, 229–231: pitch-class change 203, 207, 218; prime note-onset 200–201, 207, 218, 227–230, *228*; scale-degree set probability 205, 207; secondary note-onset 200, 207; set-class probability205, 207, 222, *222*

Viennese Classicism *see* music

Viterbi algorithm 133

Vivaldi, A. 63, **64**, 71, 79, *80*, 86

voice leading proximity 114, 117–121, *119*, 126; *see also* reduction

Wagner, R. 64, *64*; Prelude to *Tristan und Isolde* 269–272, *269*, 306, *306*; *see also* Tristan chord

Weaver, W. 9

Weber, E. 158; *see also* Weber-Fechner law

Weber-Fechner law 155, 277

Webern, A. von: Variations for Piano, Op. 27, no. 1 290, *291*

West-Marvin, E. 256

"Woloso" 227, *228*

word book 32

X^2 test *see* chi-square test

Yale–Classical Archives corpus 11, 17–21, *19*, 23–25, 29–30, 49, *51*, 57–60, *58*, 62–63, 70, 73, 77, 92, 97–103, *97*, *99*, *100*, 105–107, *106*, *107*, 109, 112–113, 117, 119, *119*, 123–125, **125**, 136, 139, *139*, 153, 156–157, *157*, 159, 170, 250–258, *251*, *254*, *255*, 260–274, *265*, *266*, 278–282, *279*, *281*, 302–304, *303*, 306–308, *308*

YCAC *see* Yale–Classical Archives corpus

zero-probability event 110; *see also* smoothing

Zipf's law 156–157, *157*

z-score *146*, 147, 167, 185–186, *186*

Milton Keynes UK
Ingram Content Group UK Ltd.
UKHW031502071224
451979UK00020B/232